The United States Labor Force

The United States Labor Force

A Descriptive Analysis

Ruth W. Prywes

QUORUM BOOKS
Westport, Connecticut • London

Library of Congress Cataloging-in-Publication Data

Prywes, Ruth W.
　　The United States labor force : a descriptive analysis / Ruth W.
　Prywes.
　　　　p.　　cm.
　　Includes bibliographical references and index.
　　ISBN 1–56720–266–7 (alk. paper)
　　　1. Labor supply—United States—History.　I. Title.
　HD5724.P785　2000
　331.11′0973—dc21　　　99–13717

British Library Cataloguing in Publication Data is available.

Library of Congress Catalog Card Number: 99–13717
ISBN: 1–56720–266–7

First published in 2000

Quorum Books, 88 Post Road West, Westport, CT 06881
An imprint of Greenwood Publishing Group, Inc.
www.quorumbooks.com

Printed in the United States of America

The paper used in this book complies with the
Permanent Paper Standard issued by the National
Information Standards Organization (Z39.48–1984).

10　9　8　7　6　5　4　3　2　1

Copyright Acknowledgments

The author and publisher gratefully acknowledge permission for use of the following materials:

The Holland Hexagon was adapted and reproduced by special permission of the Publisher, Psychological Assessment Resources, Inc., 16102 North Florida Avenue, Lutz, Florida 33549, from the *Dictionary of Holland Occupational Codes* by Gary D. Gottfredson, Ph.D., and John L. Holland, Ph.D., Copyright 1982, 1989, 1996.

"The Union Member and the Relationship to the Various Union Bodies" is reprinted with the permission of the United Food and Commercial Workers Union, Local 1776.

This book is dedicated to my husband—
Noah S. Prywes, a pillar of strength

Contents

Illustrations

TABLES

FIGURES

Acknowledgments

This book evolved from material developed for courses which I taught at the undergraduate and graduate levels in the Management Department of the Drexel University School of Business and Administration over a period of years. I am indebted to the School for access to its many facilities which made my research possible, and, particularly, to Milton Silver who was Department Head during most of this period. I am also grateful to the many dedicated librarians of the Hagerty Library and to the staff of the University Computing Services for help in accessing material. I also greatly appreciate the secretarial support given me, in the person of Sandra Narinesingh. I further wish to thank the dedicated staff of the Philadelphia Regional Office of the U.S. Department of Labor who have so ably supplied requested material.

I wish to thank Professors Jeffrey Greenspan, Yoram HaLevi, Donald Jarrell, Christopher Jelepis, William Vosburgh, and Wayne Wormsley, as well as Charles Gentile, Vice President for Education, of the Food and Commercial Workers of America, Local 1776, and Selma Cohen, a social welfare administrator, for reading and critiquing material in their areas of expertise. Thanks also go to Michael Halvorsen who helped organize presentation of the material.

I am deeply appreciative of the efforts of Bobbie Goettler, of Greenwood's editorial staff, and Helen Subbio, an independent editor, both of whom provided invaluable assistance in preparation of this manuscript. I am also appreciative of the computer skills of Steven Karamitopoulos who produced the final document.

Introduction

During the twentieth century recognition of the contributions of the labor force of a society to its economic well-being became widely recognized. This understanding has led to interest in developing knowledge concerning the portion of the population that is involved and the factors which affect the numbers and the quality of participants. Recognition of the importance of human factors in productivity of the society has also led to greater willingness to invest in education and to protect the health and economic stability of workers through various pieces of legislation.

Labor force studies (known as *manpower* studies before feminism made this term unacceptable) tend to be descriptive as opposed to theoretical in nature, and designed to tell us the present state of affairs in relation to such topics as level and nature of union organization, types of work arrangements, levels and types of wages and salary modes, the nature and levels of current unemployment, and the role played by the country's income transfer system (social insurances and social welfare programs) in affecting both employment and unemployment.

Labor force studies are prone to show how each of the aspects of employment traditionally discussed tends to impact other aspects. Thus, the level of wages in a given community are believed to affect the size of the labor force, but so also do the social insurance and social welfare arrangements, as well as the current levels of immigration. The density of labor union organization is believed to affect both the level of wages of members, but also the wage and salary levels of non-members in the same establishment and in other establishments in the same and other industries. And the new work arrangements, (such as the rise of the *contingent workforce*) are shown to have been influenced by the costs of benefits, both voluntary and mandated.

This book describes the U.S. labor force according to the series of commonly utilized dimensions alluded to above, utilizing accessible English, and reference to theory where helpful. Because various topics discussed, for example, current educational needs, from high technology PhDs down to vocational education, are far more controversial than commonly perceived, contrarion views on such issues are frequently presented for the reader's consideration. The objective is to inform, rather than persuade or influence to any particular point of view. The author has attempted to cover a very large number of topics in limited space. Inevitably a series of topics which have legitimate claim for inclusion are not discussed.

Essentially, this book offers practical information on topics of interest to executives and managers in the business world, as well as students in areas in which labor force issues are an important aspect. The focus is on giving the background knowledge which. one needs to know to deal effectively with labor force issues which arise. This book should be useful to anyone who is interested in the general subject and who feels a need to be informed concerning current developments involving the subjects discussed.

Part I

Background

The basic facts about the American labor force that are provided here are necessary for an understanding of the more focused discussions that follow. Chapter 1 offers an overview. Chapter 2 describes a series of changes in the circumstances of employment in the United States, including the rise of nontraditional work arrangements and the so-called underground economy. Chapter 3 deals with factors affecting the current labor supply: hours of work; nonstandard work-week arrangements; and population mobility.

1

Origins and Characteristics of the U.S. Labor Force

The overview provided here includes the origins of the American labor force, a look at the ways in which people are thought to enter it, and notable trends such as distribution of the labor force by industry or occupation. By examining these elements and identifying members of the labor force in terms of demographic characteristics, one may begin to understand the state of the labor force and speculate as to its evolution.

HISTORY

The history of the American workforce is inextricably linked to the history of immigration to America and how this nation has responded to each wave of newcomers. The small number of original immigrants made for a condition of scarcity of labor both skilled and unskilled. This condition is believed by some to account for the greater independence and well-being of American workers as opposed to their counterparts in the societies left behind. The freedom to move about enjoyed by some early colonists, which, for example, English workers at the time did not share, gave rise to the concept of wage competition. To attract and maintain their workforces, employers found it necessary to offer their recruits more remuneration and better working conditions than they would have offered in Old World society.

Most early immigrants did not initially enjoy freedom of movement. Many had indentured themselves to pay for their passage costs. In addition, the infamous slave trade that began in 1610—almost from the onset of settlement in America—and lasted to 1808 denied all freedom to the individuals involved. Africans, whose enslavement was not abolished until the late nineteenth century, were the primary victims of this infamous practice.

Indentured workers constituted most of the labor force up into the 1750s. The majority worked in agriculture, but some also served as teachers and skilled technicians. While indentured workers were to be found throughout the colonies, they were employed most heavily in New England. In the South planters preferred to use African labor for agricultural work. At the time of the American Revolution, there were 500,000 persons of African origin in the colonies, 75,000 of whom resided in the North.

A major problem in colonial America was the scarcity of skilled workers. Even when workers had skills, they often abandoned them to achieve independence through land ownership. Many historians believe that this preference for farm ownership delayed the industrialization of the colonies.

Throughout the 1800s and early 1900s, large numbers of immigrants seeking a better standard of living and freedom from persecution or political strife poured into the land where the streets were supposedly paved with gold. By the 1820s about 14,000 persons were arriving annually; by the 1840s about 170,000. From the 1850s to the 1880s, immigration rose from 250,000 per year to more than 500,000 per year, the majority from Great Britain and Ireland (Cohen 1979).

During the second half of the 1800s, immigrants from Asia, spurred by the discovery of gold in California, arrived in increasing numbers. Canadians and Mexicans followed suit after World War I. But from the 1890s up into the post-WWI era, which saw a change in immigration laws, the majority still came from Europe. Most were single young men from Eastern and Southern European countries who came alone to establish a foothold in the "new country." They often settled in cities and, once established, sent home for other family members and young women to marry. Initially they were welcomed; their strong backs were needed in factories and on construction projects during the peak periods of the U.S. industrial age. Meanwhile, an internal, African-American migration from the South to the North began, despite this racial group's exclusion from most industrial jobs.

By 1914, the onset of World War I, immigration climbed to about 1 million persons annually. Between World War I and the onset of the Great Depression of the 1930s, it rose and fell between the parameters of 100,000 to 500,000 per year. From the Great Depression through World War II (1930 to the mid-1940s), immigration fell, but it resurged in the postwar period. Between 1950 and 1964 immigration was in the neighborhood of 200,000 per year. Since 1970 documented immigration has varied from about 300,000 to 850,000 per year; a large proportion has been Asian or Hispanic in origin.

As the population of the United States has grown, from just under 4 million in 1790 to over 250 million in 1990, the importance of immigration to the economy has shrunk. The issue of immigration as an economic factor remains controversial, however, primarily because of concerns about economic competition and adverse perceptions of the impact of foreigners on the social fabric of the nation. U. S. immigration policies, regulated through a series of Federal statutes, have varied over the years. For sociocultural or political reasons, they have often limited the inflow of persons. In 1921 a quota system that favored persons of northwestern European origin was established. In 1965 a policy was adopted that offered preference to three groups: (1) family members of persons already residing in the United States, (2) skilled workers, and (3) political refugees. One unanticipated consequence of this policy was a "brain drain" of highly educated persons from the third world.

During the 1970s and early 1980s, public concerns regarding immigration shifted to the problem of illegal immigration. Congress came to place responsibility for dealing with this problem on the employers of immigrants. This legislation of responsibility is generally recognized to have failed, in large part because of employer demand for cheap labor, particularly agricultural labor (Bipartisan Committee on Agricultural Workers 1992). Two real outcomes of the legislation are believed to be (1) increasing pressures on immigrants to enter the so-called informal economy—that portion of the overall economy that is populated by persons who are protected, by means of obscurity, from the knowledge and constraints of government; and (2) a decrease in real wages.

In 1996 Congressional hearings on immigration policy revealed the multiplicity of interests at play in the situation. Early in that year, both the *New York Times* (March 6; April 15) and the *Washington Post* (April 14) reported that employers were allegedly abusing various programs to facilitate the import of both high-level and low-level foreign workers for the purpose of lowering wages and salaries. Business leaders rallied to support and expand the professionally oriented H1B program, allowing a foreign national in possession of a needed skill to work in the United States. Meanwhile, agricultural interests in Texas, California, and Florida lobbied against new restrictions. They pressed for 250,000 temporary visas for farm workers—documents that are generally thought to be sure lures for illegal immigrants—although some of the same interests had been calling earlier for restrictions on illegal immigration, citing immigration's hidden costs, such as "welfare" and the education of children. The situation provides a good example of conflicting and competing interests in regard to immigration policy, even among the same groups within the electorate.

The general public's response to contemporary immigration waves has varied. Positivists see a need for the overwhelmingly youthful immigrants to compensate for the aging population in the United States, and they note that such young people tend to rehabilitate decaying areas of the inner cities. During the mid-1990s, however, anti-immigration sentiment flourished, with emphasis on the expense involved in educating immigrant children. Borjas, an economist who posits that low-skill immigration is depressing U.S. wages, has been influential in legitimizing the position of those who believe that the immigration of all workers, skill levels notwithstanding, should be curtailed or eliminated.[1] Hostility to immigration is particularly strong in states of heaviest immigrant settlement, New York, California, Texas, Illinois, and Florida, the states that must provide services for immigrants and their families without Federal help.

DESCRIPTION OF THE LABOR FORCE

The phrase "labor force," as used by the U.S. Bureau of Labor Statistics (BLS), refers to "all persons, age sixteen and over, who are in the civilian, non-institutional part of the economy." Unemployed persons are included, provided they meet certain criteria, but military personnel and inmates of jails and mental institutions, even if employed, are not. Also excluded are unemployed persons who are not actively seeking work. Each element in the definition is significant, affecting counts of the size of the labor force, assessments of employment and unemployment levels, and other related matters.

Proportion of Population Employed

In 1997 a larger proportion of the American population was employed than ever before: 67.1 percent (about two out of every three persons), up from 58.75 in 1964 (BLS 1998). Labor economists have isolated four factors that determine who in the population works and who does not, as follows: (1) the size and composition of the population, (2) the percentage of those in each group within the population who choose to work, (3) the hours of work, and (4) the quality of the workforce.

Theories Concerning the Decision to Work. Economists offer two alternative theories as to what makes people decide to be part of the labor force. The first, which involves wage levels, states that people accept jobs only when the amount of salary or wage they have in mind, their *reservation wage*, is guaranteed by prospective employers. If a person does not receive such a guarantee, she or he is likely to refrain from working. The concept of reservation wage is particularly critical for women workers with young families. It is believed that when potential workers are members of a household, they decide to accept employment if doing so would be advantageous to the household. This is known as the *work-leisure choice*, where "leisure" signifies involvement in unpaid activities. As economists explain the dynamics of household decision-making, they consider the income and work-leisure tradeoff preferences of all household members of working age. Where the income of one member, usually the male head of the household, is high, other family members feel less pressure to work. At the same time, the high-wage earner may choose to sacrifice leisure. Typically, young husbands with mortgages and small children have done so more often than older men with paid-off mortgages and children out of college. Such young men were once disproportionately prominent among the moonlighting population, but they have been joined by hordes of women.

A different scenario is evidenced among low-income families. When the father's income is low, the mother may feel a great deal of pressure to supplement her husband's earnings. However, she often remains at home because her potential earning power is so low that she cannot afford to work.

The second theory involves levels of demand for labor. When more opportunities for employment open up, the labor force somehow expands: people who never worked before may take jobs. The women who went out to work during the World Wars provide a historical example. In more recent times increased opportunities following a deep recession have attracted dropouts or "discouraged workers," adolescents, and retirees into the workforce.

Demographics

The easiest way to describe a labor force is by way of its demographics, that is, characteristics such as gender, race, age, and distribution across industries, occupations, and areas of the country. The most utilized statistics are those generated by the Bureau of Labor Statistics (BLS), often in cooperation with the Bureau of the Census; they are heavily cited throughout this volume.

Projections. Basically, the BLS expects continuing expansion of work-age groups (consisting of persons age 16 and over), from about 200 million in 1996 to around 221 million by 2006. These figures represent a lower growth rate than the one experienced during the previous decade, and a continuation of a long-slowing trend. Table 1.1 illustrates trends in the distribution of the work-age population by age, sex, and race, and Hispanic origin (any race); it represents pools of potential—not necessarily actual—workers.

According to BLS analysis the actual number of persons predicted to enter the labor force by 2006 will be 15 million above the 1996 level, with a large increase among members of the baby-boomer generation, persons age forty-two to sixty. There will also be a disproportionate increase in working youths (age 16–24) than has been seen for twenty-five years. Overall growth can be attributed to both increased population (89%) and increased participation (11%) rates. The age twenty-five-to forty-four group will shrink proportionately, while the age fifty-five to sixty-four group will expand, creating in the very early part of the twenty-first century a workforce that will be considerably older than in the mid-1990s. These demographic developments have serious implications for employers in terms of relative availability of labor and pay rates. The labor force will also be slightly more female and generally less white. Among minority groups Hispanics will surge ahead of African Americans to become the largest in the United States.

Increasing Involvement of Women. One of two more interesting demographic-developments of recent years is the heightened participation of women, especially those ages twenty-five to forty-five (generally regarded as the child-bearing and child-rearing years), in the workplace. The roughly 60:40 male : female ratio of 1995 fell to 54:46 in 1997 and is expected to be in the 53:47 range by 2006. While men's overall workforce presence has been steadily falling (from about

---

Table 1.1
Civilian Labor Force, Age 16 and Over, by Age, Sex, Race, and Ethnic Origins, 1976, 1986, 1996; and Moderate Growth Projection to 2006

	1976	1986	1996	2006
Total civilian labor force, age 16 and over	96,158	117,834	133,943	148,847
(Numbers in thousands)				
Distribution by Percent				
16 to 24	24.3	19.8	15.8	16.4
25 to 54	60.8	67.6	72.3	68.2
55 and over	14.9	12.6	11.9	15.4
Men	59.5	55.5	53.8	52.6
Women	40.5	44.5	46.2	47.4
White	88.2	86.4	84.4	83.0
Black	9.9	10.7	11.3	11.6
Asian, Native Americans, and other	1.9	2.9	4.3	5.4
Hispanic origins	N.A.	6.9	9.5	11.7

*Hispanics may be any race, racial totals exceeding 100.
Source: Howard Fullerton, Jr. "Labor Force 2006: Slowing Down and Changing Composition," *Monthly Labor Review* 120 (November 1997): 25-26.

85% in 1955 to 75% in 1997) 1975 fell to 54: 46 in 1997 and is expected to be in the 53: 47 range by 2006. 85% in 1955 to 75% in 1997), women's has been rising, from about one-third in 1955 to almost two-thirds (about 60%) in 1997 (Fullerton 1997).[2] The issue of greatest interest concerning women's participation has become how high the participation rate for mothers of young children will rise. In 1975 over half (55%) of all women age twenty-five to forty-four were employed; by 1997 slightly over three-quarters (77%) were working.

In recent years issues regarding women's employment have shifted from whether married women should be "permitted" to work to whether there is a preferred stage of child-rearing at which mothers "should" reenter the labor force. The employment of mothers at all stages is accepted to some degree; in fact, in the case of "welfare mothers," it is expected. American society's collective failure to provide an adequate support system can be attributed in part to ambivalence about this issue. It is commonly theorized that mothers are working not because the activity is more socially accepted, but because available jobs pay wages attractive enough to persuade them to make a work-leisure choice in favor of a paid position. Many mothers strike a compromise by accepting part-time employment.

Withdrawal of Older Males. A second interesting development is the accelerated withdrawal of men from the labor force during their preretirement years (age 55–64). Despite much research, economists still lack a satisfactory explanation as to why in 1975, for example, over three-quarters of this group were employed; but between 1990 and 1997, only about two-thirds. Examination of figures from 1997 reveals that the most extensive withdrawal begins around age sixty; only about 55 percent of all men age sixty to sixty-four remain in the labor force (BLS 1998).

Why are older men withdrawing so far ahead of the traditional age of retirement (65 years) in an era in which the desirability of a longer work-life is widely recognized, forced retirement is illegal, health is generally better, and age discrimination has been officially forbidden? Is it due to personal preferences, to years of disguised push-outs, to buyouts or downsizing? Are these men to be found in the informal economy? If so, is their withdrawal a result of recent trends or is it an independent phenomenon? No one can say with certainty. Curiously, although exodus from the workplace by men age fifty-five to sixty-four is at an all-time high, employment of men of traditional retirement age (65) or older has fallen only modestly. In 1975, 20 percent of men age and older were still working; in 1997, 17 percent (BLS 1998).

One speculation is that workers age fifty-five and over often simply drop out of the labor force when they lose their jobs; they then rely on pensions and other resources unavailable to younger persons. Analysis of a study of older workers with at least three years' tenure who lost their jobs between December 1993 and December 1995 reinforces this hypothesis, according to Gary Burtless of the Brookings Foundation. Of more than 577,000 older workers who lost their jobs during this period, nearly one-third left the labor force, up from the 24 percent who left during 1991 and 1992 (quoted in the *AARP Bulletin* 1996).

An alternative suggestion concerning the upsurge in the early withdrawal of workers is that a large increase in real Social Security benefits between 1970 and 1980 created for workers an unexpected source of wealth, and it triggered their desire to retire and enjoy it. This suggestion is reinforced by changes in Social Security rules that had formerly discouraged workers from retiring prior to age sixty-two, and by private pension rules that have been changed to encourage early retirement. R. Ippolito speculates that at least one-half of the drift into early retirement by workers after 1970 stems from Social Security and pension-fund changes (1990). He suggests that, in time, the incentives provided by Social Security regulations will taper off. And since private employers are encouraging early retirement and are often discontinuing defined pension plans, the effects of these factors in future trends in withdrawal from the workforce are unclear.

Ethnic Composition.. Highly noticeable changes in the racial and ethnic composition of the labor force abound in major U.S. cities. The rising proportion of nonwhite members of the workforce and of so-called new ethnics, non-European immigrants, is expected to continue, increasing the most among Asians and Hispanics, a reflection of recent immigration trends. The African-American portion of the workforce is also rising, but this upsurge is due more to population increases associated with births, and fair employment practices embedded in law. However, the vast majority of the labor force remains white, with African Americans and Hispanics each holding around 10 percent of available jobs. While reportage on Asians, Pacific Islanders, and Native Americans is limited, it appears that these small groups are expanding. They represented 4.3 percent of the workforce in 1996, and are predicted to represent 5 percent by 2006. Figures on these groups are often misleading. However, these groups are often quite important labor factors in the geographic areas or specific industries in which they are seen to cluster.

DISTRIBUTION OF EMPLOYMENT BY INDUSTRY

Many of the painful changes in employment opportunities since the 1970s lie essentially in the quality of available work, which is often discussed in terms of the *industrial distribution* of employment. Employment by industry is customarily described in terms of the inclusion of major groups in either the goods-producing sector or the services-producing sector. Employment offered in the former is considered more desirable than employment offered in the latter. A common belief is that employment erosion in the goods-producing sector of the economy, especially in manufacturing, is primarily responsible for the fall in quality jobs for workers with less than college educations over the past twenty years. Historically, manufacturing establishments, with their large number of relatively high-paying jobs and relatively low-skill demands, were seen as the typical blue-collar worker's ticket to the middle class. With the collapse of manufacturing (and the decline of mining), there is little that the unskilled worker can do to make a middle-class living. The services-producing sector, on the other hand, has been seen as the source of large numbers of relatively low-paying, low-skill jobs that offer neither job security nor much hope of betterment.

What are the facts? By 1996 only one job out of every seven (13.9%) was in a manufacturing establishment, and, as shown in Table 1.2, decline is expected to continue. Filling the void are service-sector jobs, which now provide over 70 percent (71.2%) of all U.S. employment. This share is projected to expand as manufacturing declines further.

Three huge industry groups are responsible for about two-thirds of all employment in the service sector: government (14.7%), wholesale and retail trade (21.3%), and the *services* (25.4%), a diverse group of industries that include hospitality (hotels and other lodging places), recreation, law, health, and other social services; cosmetics; home, auto, and office maintenance; advertising; and computing, particularly data processing The services industry is often wrongly blamed for the deterioration in the quality of employment and wages in the United States; the problem is not the industries but the occupations within them. As for employment in the government, a hot topic in recent years, under the strain of political pressures to shrink Federal payrolls, aggregate Federal employment has decreased, though only modestly, since the 1970s. At the same time, state and local payrolls have increased considerably, by close to 1 million workers in the decade from 1986 to 1996 alone.

Through the late 1970s the demise of manufacturing was often discussed in terms of the implications for the U.S. military and industrial position as a world power. Alarms were raised as to whether the nation could defend itself in the event of war without a basic steel industry, and whether it could compete industrially without a basic microchip industry. More recently, concerns have focused on the fall in the standard of living for the nonprofessional portion of the American labor force.

Causes of employment declines in manufacturing are a matter of continuing debate. One unresolved issue is whether the problem stems mainly from export of jobs to lower labor-cost countries or from greater efficiency on the part of domestic production, which would preclude mass employment. Policy responses depend on one's position on this issue. It may be argued, although such discussion is beyond the scope of this book, that the BLS has failed to accurately "capture" productivity increases thought to result from investments in technology. If that failure is real, it becomes impossible to either gauge the true productivity of American industry or to assess how efficiency affects the elimination of jobs. A relatively recent development in the workplace, the use of the team approach, has also been implicated in the elimination of many jobs. One observation is clear: mass-production factories that used to employ thousands now have payrolls of several hundred at most.

The service industries are not widely viewed as highly productive in economic terms; as such they are not considered to contribute substantially to the nation's well-being. Such views are obvious fallacies to individuals living, for example, in developing countries where industry cannot grow because credit, reliable sources of electricity, and communications facilities are nonexistent. Business people have cited the lack of legal codes and functioning court systems as a major impediment to dealing with third-world countries, the former Soviet Union, and China. And efficiency is undermined when employees of the goods-producing industries must struggle to maintain (or substitute for) water and electricity supplies for their personal residences. It is also obvious that in advanced societies, such service industries as the computer industry have revolutionized the world of work, creating vast, lucrative areas of employment. Intellectual property, for example, is produced by the service sector, and is now a major U.S. export. The services industries are expected to absorb vast numbers of workers in the near future.

Table 1.2
Employment by Major Industry Division: 1986, 1996; and Moderate Level Projections to 2006

(Total jobs in thousands)*	1986 111,374	1996 132,352	2006 150,927
	(*Distribution by Percent*)		
Industry	100.0	100.0	100.0
Goods-producing	22.0	18.5	16.2
Mining	0.7	0.4	0.3
Contract construction	4.3	4.1	3.9
Manufacturing	17.0	13.9	12.0
Durable	10.1	8.1	7.0
Nondurable	7.0	5.8	5.0
Services-producing	66.6	71.2	74.1
Transport, communications and utilities	4.7	4.7	4.7
Wholesale trade	5.2	4.9	4.8
Retail trade	16.1	16.3	15.8
Finance, insurance, and real estate	5.6	5.2	5.1
Services	20.0	25.5	29.7
Federal government	2.6	2.1	1.8
State and local government	12.4	12.6	12.2
Agriculture, forestry, and fisheries	3.0	2.8	2.4
Private household wage and salary	1.1	0.7	0.5
Non-agricultural self-employed and unpaid family workers	7.3	6.8	6.8

*Some data is not directly comparable to data appearing in *Employment and Earnings*.
Source: James C. Franklin, "Industry Output and Employment Projections to 2006," *Monthly Labor Review* 120 (November 1997): 40; using BLS Current Employment Statistics (a payroll survey), which counts jobs, and Current Population Survey (household survey), which counts workers.

DISTRIBUTION OF EMPLOYMENT BY OCCUPATION

The work force is also analyzed by the distribution of participants by occupation. Such data tends to attract public attention because some occupations carry more prestige and promise more earning power than others. The most frequently utilized scheme for distinguishing among occupations is the classification system appearing in Table 1.3 which is organized by prestige rather than function; the first occupation listed affords more status to incumbents than the next one listed, and so on. Usually, but not always, greater prestige and status bring greater financial rewards. It should be noted that "prestige" refers to authority or importance due to past achievements or reputation—ascendancy based on recognition of power—while "status" refers to relative position or rank.

Occupations Most in Demand

According to BLS forecasts, by 2006 the outlook for members of the occupational categories most associated with the principle of prior investment in education and training tends to be favorable. Relatively fewer opportunities will be available in the occupational groups requiring less preparation, with one important exception: the *services* occupations. These occupations, widely viewed with contempt as low-paying, unstable, dead-end work situations, now claim approximately 16.1 percent of all employment. The occupations predicted to be least in demand in the early 2000s are those most closely associated with manufacturing and agriculture. In fact, the latter has long represented a diminishing source of employment, as efficiency has pushed the need for "hands" downward to less than 3 percent of the workforce. The minute size of the agricultural workforce has often been obscured by the considerable political clout of its advocates, partly because farming is concentrated in a relatively few states and because deep-pocketed, corporate agriculture is on the rise.

Growth of jobs in the services *occupations* (as opposed to the services *industries*) tends to be viewed with disdain because of the unfavorable secondary labor-market characteristics (low pay, much part-time work, absence of benefits, and high turnover) associated with them. In contrast, desirable employment is, and will continue to be, largely defined by educational credentials, but the identification of optimal credentials is at issue. Expansion of the services occupations offers some perspective on job outlook. Most of those occupations, such as human services worker or corrections officer, involve some education or training. Few intrinsically require college, even though it may be demanded of employees. Many of the occupations with the largest projected growth are in the technician category; they include paralegals, radiology technologists, respiratory therapists, and the like. These occupations often require more-than-high-school but less-than-college education or training, which suggests that educational planners should focus their efforts on establishing and funding institutions that provide postsecondary degrees or certification in less than four years.

Table 1.3
Employment by Major Occupational Group: 1986, 1996; and Moderate Level Projections to 2006

	1986	1996	2006
Total, all occupations (numbers in thousands)	111,375	132,353	150,927
(Distribution by Percent)			
	100.0	100.0	100.0
Executive, administrative, and managerial occupations	9.5	10.2	10.5
Professional specialties occupations	12.2	13.7	15.2
Technicians and related support occupations	3.3	3.5	3.7
Marketing and sales occupations	10.3	11.1	11.2
Administrative support occupations, including clerical	18.8	18.1	17.2
Service occupations	15.6	16.1	16.7
Agriculture, forestry, fishing and related occupations	3.3	2.9	2.5
Precision production, craft, and repair occupations	12.4	10.9	10.2
Operators, fabricators, and laborers	14.6	13.5	12.8

Source: George Silvestri, "Occupational Employment Projections to 2006," *Monthly Labor Review* 120 (November 1997).

Effect of Shifts on Income

It is commonly believed that U.S. incomes have been depressed by shifts in employment from the goods-producing-sector to service-sector industries and by shifts from blue-collar (manual) occupations to services occupations. Aggregate statistics demonstrate that on the average, full-time nonsupervisory services workers earned $400.33 per week versus $553.14 for manufacturing workers (both without overtime) in 1997. The actual wage gap tends to be much greater because a disproportionately large number of part-time workers (1–34 hrs./wk.) are employed in the services as opposed to manufacturing—for example, 29 percent versus 11.8 percent in 1997.

Some analysts question these beliefs, noting that conclusions based on aggregate statistics can be misleading. Lost in discussions of low pay is the fact that not *all* manufacturing jobs are, or ever were, high-paying; similarly, not all service-sector or service industry jobs are low-paid. For example, in 1997, according to the BLS, production or nonsupervisory workers in manufacturing earned an average of $13.17 per hour, while service-industry workers took in $12.28, and service-sector workers made $11.25 per hour. The last wage cited is depressed primarily by jobs in retail that pay an average of $8.34 hourly, as of 1997; otherwise, there is not much difference among the three figures. Clearly, it is necessary to look at pay by occupational group, determining what mix of occupation and pay exists within both manufacturing and service-industry employers, before generalizing about relative pay levels.

To see that earnings levels span a wide range in the manufacturing industries, one might examine median weekly earnings in 1997 for several occupations closely associated with manufacturing, the largest employer in the goods-producing sector: (1) mechanical engineer, $974; (2) precision metal worker, $584; (3) machine operator, assembler, or inspector, $390; (4) textile, apparel, and furnishings machine operators, $277. A considerable variation in pay is evident. What is more, it exists in the service-sector industries as well. Examples of 1997 median weekly earnings in the service sector include: (1) mathematical and computer scientists, $908; (2) librarians, $638; (3) dental technicians, $366; (4) food-preparation and service occupations, $273 (BLS 1998). Broad generalizations serve as rough indicators, but they describe no one in particular. Specific industries and occupations must be scrutinized before drawing conclusions about pay-rate superiority in either sector of the economy.

A controversy over the location of so-called good versus bad jobs was specifically addressed in a BLS analysis (Meissenheimer 1998). It corroborates statements made above, concluding that as to *job quality*, in terms of pay, benefits, job security, occupational structure, and job safety, the services industries rated variously per criterion. Still, an impressive number of specific industries within the services-industry group matched or exceeded the quality of jobs in manufacturing and other industries. So, even though some services-industry groups do fit into the "less desirable" jobs category, it is not valid to say that job quality is deteriorating along with a shift from manufacturing to the services industries. Nor is it valid, based on the BLS analysis, to assess job quality strictly in terms of pay.

NOTES

1. Borjas's 1995 article, "Know the flow: economics of immigration" is exemplary of his position.
2. These statistics represent the percentage of those in the civilian noninstitutional population who are members of the workforce, that is, are either employed or unemployed but seeking work.

REFERENCES

AARP Bulletin. 1996. "Dropouts" may help explain decline in midlife jobless rate. October.

Bipartisan Committee on Agricultural Workers. 1992. Reported in *New York Times,* Law is said to fail to stop abuse of agricultural workers. 22 October.

Borjas, George. 1995. Know the flow: economics of immigration. *National Review* 47, no. 7: 44–52.

Cohen, Sanford. 1979. *Labor in the United States.* 5th edition. Columbus: Charles E. Merrill Publishing Co.

Franklin, J. C. 1997. Industry output and employment projections to 2006. *Monthly Labor Review* 120 (November): 39–57.

Fullerton, Jr., Howard N. 1997. Labor force 2006: slowing down and changing composition. *Monthly Labor Review* 120 (November): 23–38.

Ippolito, R. 1990. Toward explaining earlier retirement after 1970. *Industrial and Labor Relations Review* 43 (July): 556–69.

Meissenheimer II, J. 1998. The services industry in the "good" jobs versus "bad" jobs debate: a deeper look reveals a range of quality jobs in the industry. *Monthly Labor Review* 121 (February): 22–47.

Silvestri, G. 1997. Occupational employment projections to 2006. *Monthly Labor Review* 120 (November): 58–82.

U.S. Department of Labor. Bureau of Labor Statistics. 1998. *Employment and Earnings* 45 (January).

2

New Work Statuses
and the Rise of the
Underground Economy

This chapter surveys two important areas of change in those circumstances of U.S. employment which are associated with a weakening of employee security and earning power. Since the mid-1980s, anxiety concerning job security has pervaded American society, in good times as well as bad. As extensive job cutbacks by prosperous companies spread and many persons, young and old alike, lost jobs that had been considered secure, the traditional assumptions of lifetime employment for the competent came crashing down. The *social contract*, the concept that the well-being of employees and community was the obligation of the employer which had long been a component of doing business, was breached. The *implicit contract*, the unwritten understanding that employers offered permanent employment in return for life-long loyalty, evaporated. Instead, all personnel fell into the category of commodities to be used to maximize shareholders' profits in the global economy; at least that is a popular view of the situation. Whether that view is valid, that is, whether previous standards for employment have eroded substantially, is addressed here.

The second area of change discussed is the rise and expansion of the informal or underground economy, to which the usual safeguards and benefits associated with employment do not apply because the workers involved are uncounted and beyond the control of labor law.

MANIFESTATIONS OF INCREASING JOB INSECURITY

The expansion of alternative work arrangements, such as part-time employment, businesses' use of third parties to hire and sometimes even supervise workers, and the establishment of a new category of worker, the contingent, reportedly have made for a pervasive sense of job insecurity. Little firm evidence existed, however, until BLS conducted a special study in 1995, producing a series of analyses that appeared in 1996. Study of these topics is difficult, since it is necessary to untangle and differentiate between a series of now widespread alternative work arrangements. For example, when reporting on findings concerning part-time employment, one must be careful to observe that not all part-time workers are also contingent workers, although many are. The same is true for workers in other nontraditional statuses, such as on-call workers and those working for contract agencies. Since the increased presence of a part-time work force and the emergence of contingent workers are two of the most common, nonstandard work statuses evidenced in recent U.S. history, their development is worthy of considerable attention.

The Part-Time Workforce

Recent decades have seen the expansion of part-time employment into a significant portion of total employment. Employers tend to claim that short hours are advantageous to both parties, while unions, among others, often hold that the trend is associated more with lowering payroll costs by reducing wage levels and eligibility for benefits (Nardone 1986). It has been widely reported that 30 percent of the "new jobs" created between 1991 and 1994 were either part-time or *temporary*, another nonstandard work status. The part-time work force consists of three categories of members: (1) employed persons working less than thirty-five hours a week, on a voluntary basis; (2) part-time employees who would prefer to work full-time; and (3) unemployed persons seeking work, who either want part-time work or will "settle for" same. If members of the workforce largely go against preference when they accept part-time work, then much part-time employment may be said to represent *disguised unemployment*, or underemployment. Although the Department of Labor reports that most part-time workers accept this status as one of preference as opposed to one of economic necessity, the matter remains controversial. With 29.7 million persons, or 24 percent of all employed in the U.S. workforce as part-timers as of December 1997, the matter of whether this status is one of choice assumes importance (BLS 1998).

According to the BLS (1998), part-time workers may be characterized as follows:

1. Age—disproportionately below age.
2. Gender—disproportionately female.
3. Marital status—disproportionately single.
4. Race—proportionately more whites than African Americans, but this is a modest actor.
5. Industry—primarily (52%) in retail and wholesale trade, and in the services.
6. Choice of status—estimates range from overwhelmingly voluntary to largely involuntary.

Some independent researchers, using BLS data, contest the conclusion that part-time work is the preference of the workers involved. For example, Christopher Tilly (1992) concluded that about three-quarters of a great increase in part-time employment between 1969 and 1988 was involuntary in nature. He also noted the increasing presence of men (as opposed to women and all youths) within the ranks of part-timers, which fuels skepticism concerning the voluntary acceptance of part-time employment. Tilly explained that the increasing demand for part-time workers prior to the 1970s was driven by demographic shifts; afterward it was driven by employer preferences. Partly, this had to do with the expansion of employment in the areas of the services and retail trade, industries that are large-scale users of part-time employment, as opposed to manufacturing, which traditionally has been less prone to use part-timers, due in part to union objections.

The findings of case studies conducted by Tilly of insurance and retail industries in the late 1980s clearly show why some people are likely to opt for part-time work while others may accept the status involuntarily. Using dual labor market theory, Tilly shows that a portion of available part-time employment consists of desirable high-wage jobs that provide stability and benefits, but another portion involves low-wage employers who offer only intermittent, dead-end work with few, if any, benefits. He suspects that much of the latter part-time employment is undertaken involuntarily. Other researchers have also concluded that more part-time employees are characterized by involuntary work status than is reported by BLS (Appelbaum and Batt 1994).

Multiple Jobholders. Increasing numbers of persons work for more than one employer. Such persons are often referred to as *moonlighters*, a term that the BLS applies to the following types of workers: (1) persons who hold jobs with two or more employers, (2) persons who are mainly self-employed but also hold a paid job, (3) persons who are primarily unpaid family workers but also hold a paid job. About 7.9 million Americans or approximately 6.3 percent of the workforce now hold more than one job. Most of these workers hold a full-time job that they supplement with secondary, part-time employment. Some workers have no full-time employment; instead, they hold several part-time jobs. All of these multiple jobholders, with the exception of a few who work two full-time jobs, may be counted as part-time because their second or third job is a part-time position.

Multiple jobholders may be characterized as follows (Stinson 1986, Amirault 1997):

1. Age—Ages twenty to fifty-four reflect the highest participation rates.
2. Gender—Slightly more women than men, especially among the younger categories, are involved.
3. Race and ethnic origin—Whites are involved at the highest rates, followed by blacks, then Hispanics.
4. Education—The incidence increases as education level rises.
5. Primary occupations—Professional specialties, technician and service occupations are most prominent.
6. Primary industries—Public administration and services industries predominate.
7. Marital status—A slightly lower rate prevails among women, spouse present; a slightly higher rate prevails among men with this status.
8. Full-time vs. part-time status—Men are more likely to hold a primary full-time job and secondary part-time job.
9. Motivation—Workers do not appear to be driven primarily by economic need.

The phenomenon of multiple jobholding is of particular interest; it has risen from about 4.5 percent of the workforce in the mid-1970s to 6.2 percent in 1996, and it has seen the increasing involvement of women workers. What drives this trend? And what does it say about work-leisure choices? Multiple jobholders used to offer economic reasons to explain their lifestyle. They were trying to meet regular expenses, pay off debts, or save for the future; a minority said that their main objective was to gain experience or build up a business. Most tended to be modest earners. It was observed in some circles that moonlighting might well be a phenomenon of young married men still in the early stages of their careers who are burdened by big mortgages and the expenses of young families. More recent data refutes this view: nowadays, moonlighting occurs at remarkably similar rates across all income levels. It increases with educational level, which would not be the case if the main objective of the individuals involved were to satisfy basic economic needs, however defined. Fully 10 percent of the holders of doctorates but only 3 percent of high-school drop-outs hold more than one job. Other factors must be at play.

Sociologist Muhammad Jamal proffered an alternative mode of studying the motivations of moonlighters (1986). Using the *small group* approach, he examined the differences between male moonlighters (male blue-collar workers and firefighters) and nonmoonlighters on a number of dimensions: economic need, psychological and personal characteristics, indicators of participation in voluntary organizations, and, among the blue-collar workers and firefighters, behavior in organizations. Jamal found no differences between moonlighters and nonmoonlighters along the dimensions of physical health, job stress, social support, absenteeism, job performance, and job turnover; but the moonlighters were found to be more active in voluntary organizations than nonmoonlighters. He concluded that moonlighting was more a phenomenon of greater aggressiveness, higher levels of energy, and social and economic expectations, than the outcome of social constraints as often thought.

Thomas Amirault, a BLS analyst, speculates that people take more than one job because their schedules permit it and their skills are in great demand, or because they have financial desires that do not involve basic needs (1997). Heavily represented among multiple jobholders are certain professional occupations and workers in protective services, such as police and firefighters. Multiple jobholding, in this view, is driven mainly by the opportunities open to highly trained, educated people, not by need. The majority tend not to confine themselves to their same occupational group; instead they disperse across the occupational spectrum. Their secondary jobs derive primarily from professional specialties, sales, and such service work as protective workers, food-service workers, and cleaners.

Interest in the number of multiple jobholders is high among professional analysts; with better knowledge of the nature and extent of secondary jobholding, it becomes possible to identify how many jobs actually exist in the economy versus number of workers. One finding of the first BLS survey of multiple jobholders, in 1995, is that the total number of jobs in the economy is higher than was previously thought, 125.0 million people with primary jobs and 7.9 million persons with secondary jobs, making the total number of jobs, 132.9 million, about 6.3 percent higher than regularly published figures, according to Amirault.

More secondary jobs exist in the professional specialty occupations than any other occupational group: 1.5 million, or 20.3 percent of all secondary employment. Retail sales, however, is the single occupation that attracts the most secondary workers because people in many other occupations supplement earnings by working in local stores. The industry groups with the largest amount of secondary employment (as a percent of the number in the occupation who are employed in secondary employment) are educational services, justice, and public order and safety administration, industries that include the large numbers of teachers and protective workers holding more than one job. It is suspected that multiple jobholding is frequently underreported among employers in these three groups.

The Contingent Workforce

A second employer technique for acquiring greater flexibility and cutting payroll costs, believed to have come into widespread usage during the 1980s, is the establishment of *contingent jobs,* defined by the BLS as "jobs structured to last for only a limited period of time." This practice on the part of large corporations was viewed as a breaching of the social contract by employers who were heretofore identified with stable employment. However, empirical evidence of the extent of this practice, the employers involved, and the main industries and occupations affected, was lacking until BLS experts released a series of analyses of data collected to supplement the 1995 Civilian Population Survey, and National Longitudinal Youth Studies data. These articles contain the largest body of knowledge yet produced on this group of workers, so defined. The material reported here depends mainly on these analyses. What is perceived as new is the reputed breadth of the practice and its reach into areas of the workforce formerly considered safe and secure by incumbents. In other words, employers have been unabashedly achieving flexibility in staffing through several alternative work arrangements they formerly eschewed. BLS estimates that anywhere from 2.7 million to 6.0 million workers (2.2% to 4.9% of all employment), depending on the definition used, are in contingent jobs (Polivka 1996a).

Originally, BLS defined contingent work as "any job in which an individual does not have an explicit or implicit contract for long-term employment." Because so broad a range of employment situations is covered, BLS was obliged to develop three different sets of specifications by which it measures contingent employment. The first and narrowest includes wage and salary workers who expect to work for their current employer for a year or less and who have worked for their current employer one year or less; the second estimate includes the self-employed and independent contractors who have worked and expect to work for their employer less than a year; while the third and broadest estimate includes all wage and salary workers who do not expect their jobs to last, removing the one-year requirement. It may be readily seen that some alternative work arrangements, such as on-call work, independent contracting, and part-time employment, may not be contingent in nature. The varying concepts of contingent work status permit no choice but to refer to the BLS definition of contingent worker when making statements about this work status. Tables 2.1 and 2.2 summarize the characteristics of contingent workers and several other work statuses, contingent and noncontingent, discussed in this section.

Table 2.1
Characteristics of Contingent Workers, Temporary-Help Workers, and On-Call Workers

	Contingent Workers	Temporary-Help Workers	On-call Workers
Numbers (in millions)	2.7 to 6.0	1.2	2.0
Percent of the work force	2.2 to 4.9	1.0	1.7
Gender	Over 50% female	53% female	Females over-rep'd.
Race	Blacks over-represented	Highly black or Hispanic	
Age	Under 25 over-represented	Under 25 over-represented	Under 25/over 64 over-represented
Education	Younger: more than older Older: fewer high school	Less educated than average	Less than average, but 31% females are college grads
Occupations of concentration	Professional services, administrative support	Males: machine operators Females: clerical workers	Males: 60% blue-collar, professional specialities include substitute teachers, farm workers. Females: service; white-collar.
		Low	
Industries of concentration	Services and Construction	Males: manufacturing Females: the services	——

	Contingent workers	Temporary help workers	On-call workers
Occupational skill-level	—	Low	Varies: frequently low
Hours of work	40% part-time	Mostly full-time	65% part-time
Earnings	Lower pay, full and pt time	60.4% median pay	80.4% average wage
Health insurance benefits	Rarely given	5.7%	17.2%
Pension coverage	Rarely given	2.5%	18.6%
Duration of employment	Expectation: temporary	Short	Short, on job; 2.1 years with agency
			35%, more men
Contingent status*	—	Yes	
Work status preference	Traditional arrangements	Traditional arrangements exception: students	Part-timers : mainly traditional arrangements

*under broadest definition
Source: A February 1995 BLS survey reported in a series of articles in the Monthly Labor Review (October 1996).

Table 2.2
Characteristics of Independent Contractors and Contract Agency Workers

	Independent Contractors	Contract Agency Workers
Numbers (in millions)	8.3	0.65
Percent of work force	6.7	0.5
Gender	51.6% female	71.5% male
Race	92% white	————
Age	Older: 76% 35 years or above	54.2% under 35
Education	Better educated: 34% college graduates	Very high; very low
Level of occupational skill	Relatively high	Varies greatly
Hours of work	Fewer or more than standard	Mostly full-time
Occupations of concentration	Males: management, administration, teaching; Females: service and professional occupations	Cleaning, construction, building security, computer programming
Industries of concentration	Construction, finance, insurance, real estate; the services	Public sector industries
Earnings	108% median pay alternative work forces	Second highest, among
Health insurance benefits	3% by employer; 73% other coverage	42.5%
Pension coverage	2.5% by employer; 35% other coverage	28.5%
Duration of employment	High; 6.9 years	40% over one year with customer
Contingent status	4.0% (under broadest definition)	Low: 8% to 20%, depending on definition
Preference for work status	Alternative arrangement: yes, 82.5%	Males: 60% no; Females: 60% yes-personal reasons

Source: BLS; a February 1995 survey reported in a series of articles in *Monthly Labor Review* (October 1996).

The following distinct work statuses are identified by BLS as constituting the contingent workforce: (1) employment obtained through temporary help agencies, (2) self-employment as independent contractors, and (3) work performed at the work site of a customer of a contract agency. According to the Upjohn Institute (Houseman 1997), while the use of alternative hiring practices is widespread, the amount of employment added at any one point in time is small. For example, the 1995 survey data under discussion shows that agency temps added 1.5 percent and short-term hires, 2.3 percent. But episodes of hiring multiply the number of short-term jobs created during the period of a year, making it difficult to report meaningful data. Five to six times as many short-term hires occur over a year as can be captured at one point in time.

Early Findings on the Contingent Workforce. The major preliminary findings of BLS's first survey of contingent workers (1995) are the following:

1. Contingent status is linked to youth. Twice as many contingent workers are likely to be age sixteen to twenty-four, as noncontingent workers.
2. Women and African Americans are disproportionately represented. Over one-half of contingent workers are women, versus 46 percent in the noncontingent work force; about 14 percent of blacks are in the contingent workforce, versus about 10 percent in the noncontingent workforce. It is interesting that a disproportionate number of women in the contingent workforce are youths (age 16–19), while a disproportionate number of the men are over fifty-five.
3. More youths (age 16–24) in the contingent arrangements are likely to be enrolled in school than in the noncontingent workforce, but a larger proportion of adult workers (age 25–64) are less likely to have a high-school diploma than those working in standard arrangements.
4. A disproportionate share of part-time workers have contingent status, but the great majority of part-time workers are employed under traditional arrangements. Over 40 percent of contingent workers are part-time (42.9 to 47%, depending upon estimate), but only 18.2 percent of the noncontingent workers are part-time.
5. Occupational concentration is to be found in professional services, administrative support and semiskilled blue-collar workers, and laborers occupations.
6. Contingent workers are disproportionately represented in services and construction.
7. Health insurance benefits are rarely given to contingent workers. Some obtain benefits on their own, but they do so considerably less often than their noncontingent counterparts.
8. Excluding students, the overwhelming majority of contingents prefer traditional work arrangements. Only the independent contractors, a relatively small group, express a preference for their nontraditional employment status.

Whether contingent workers are able to obtain their desired amount of work in terms of hours is a matter of interest (Polivka 1996c). According to survey responses, though a disproportionately large number of contingent workers are part-timers, the vast majority (80%) reported this to be their choice, especially those who worked the fewest hours. Most part-timers who prefer to work full-time report stable employment; that they are *not* contingent workers. A significant minority reportedly desire full-time employment but say that they cannot obtain it. And most temps prefer permanent jobs.

To summarize, most part-time work is voluntary in nature and *not* contingent, but most temporary workers desire permanent jobs. BLS also concludes that most contingent workers who are members of families tend to have at least one member of the family with a secure income. In terms of earnings, contingent workers earn much less than noncontingent workers, according to the first available earnings data on this group (Hipple and Stewart 1996a). Low pay appears to be partner to the job insecurity associated with contingent status. For example, full-time contingent job earnings for males in 1995 were 82 percent of noncontingent full-time male workers.[1]

Explanations for the Rise in Contingent Employment. In an attempt to explain the rise in use of contingent workers, Anne Polivka (1996a) examined two factors often proposed as explanatory: (1) the fall in the rate of unionism and (2) variations in employment among industries. Unable to establish a linkage between unionization level and contingent worker use, she conjectured that variations in demand over time might explain the latter, although the industry with the largest percentage of contingent workers, the services, experiences only moderate variation in demand. She concludes that both explanations fall short, so more research appears to be warranted.

Other Nonstandard Work Statuses

Several nonstandard work statuses that have become more prominent in recent years, and that may or may not involve contingent status, are *temporary employee*, *on-call worker*, and *self-employed worker*. The latter may include the independent contractor and the employee of a contract company.

Temporary Employees. Manpower agencies recruit these workers, screen and refer them to employers, prepare payrolls, and take responsibility for withholding payroll taxes and deductions for Social Security and unemployment insurance from the workers' pay. In some cases, manpower agencies pay benefits; employers seldom do so.

Some employers, especially those with highly seasonal products or services, have always used temporary workers. Now, however, large, wealthy, *primary labor force* employers are using staffing practices associated with *secondary labor force* establishments.[2] While hiring of temporary workers covers a broad spectrum of jobs, the majority of them are clerical.

For years some companies have used manpower agencies, officially or de facto, as their recruiting organizations. During an earlier period the popular perception was that such employment would become permanent if the temp proved satisfactory. It is now believed that for a major portion of temp recruiting, this is no longer a valid expectation. Relatively few employers reported in a 1997 survey by the Upjohn Institute that they "often" promote such workers, and a majority reported "seldom" or "never" absorbing them into their regular workforces (Houseman 1997).[3]

Temporary hiring has the potential for serving the needs of both employers and the workforce, fulfilling such obvious functions for the employer as helping meet sudden demand for skilled workers, addressing seasonal upsurges in business, bringing in special skills needed only occasionally, and trying out workers for permanent assignments. Workers may accept temp-agency assignments while seeking permanent employment, use temporary employment as a means of obtaining work experience, or even land a permanent job with the temp agency. Since temp-agency employment is not the employment of choice for most participants, however, and since only a small minority achieve permanent employment, the arrangement does not appear to be mutually advantageous. Not without reason, it attracts the most marginal of workers.

A July 7, 1993, *New York Times* article described a typical scenario involving temporary workers, and the wages associated with the practice. The following is a paraphrased segment of this report:

According to the National Association of Temporary Services, temporary workers earn at least as much as similar workers in other countries. By this reasoning, their presence in the work force is advantageous to both workers and the country, as their jobs remain in the United States. NIKE, in Atlanta, Georgia, for example, employs 345 repackaging workers: 120 "permanents" at $13 per hour and 225 "temporaries" at $8.50 per hour. The temporary service collects $2.00 of the $8.50 per hour as its fee. The leasing employer pays for the temps' Social Security and Worker's Compensation, but no health benefits. The employer also avoids Unemployment Insurance premiums. Regular employees of NIKE are described as serving as supervisors or "team leaders" of the temps.

On-call Worker. Although these workers number about 2 million, the second largest group involved in alternative work arrangements, almost nothing was known about them until the 1995 BLS survey. Their unique characteristic is the sporadic nature of their employment. The majority, especially males, report preference for traditional work arrangements.

The BLS posits that on-call workers and temp-agency workers constitute different populations and experience real differences in their conditions of work, particularly in regard to duration of employment. Many on-call workers are well educated, perform professional services, and are at least twenty-five years of age and college graduates.

Independent Contractors. Speculation abounded during the mid-1990s about the identity of this newly prominent group of workers, which may be described as self-employed persons who work for an employer on contract. Are they well-paid professionals on their own? Are they former employees of large companies fired-to-be-hired under less advantageous conditions? And are they all high-level professionals and managerials?

According to the first hard evidence (BLS 1995), about 8.3 million workers, 6.7 percent of all employment, fit into this category as either independent contractors, independent consultants, or freelance workers; they were all termed "independent contractors" for purposes of the BLS analysis. BLS differentiates this group from the self-employed, such as shop owners, although some independent contractors fall into the self-employed category. Basically, independent contractors work for themselves, taking full responsibility for their own activities or for those of a company. They may incorporate or not, have employees or work alone. Typical among this group are freelance writers, computer consultants, real estate agents, and home remodelers.

Independent contractors, about half of all reported self-employed workers, differ markedly from other workers in alternative arrangements and in the work force at large. As shown on Table 2.2, they include a considerable number of well-educated individuals who are also well paid, as seen by their high comparative earnings. BLS analyst Cohany (1996) speculates that the proclivity toward part-time employment may stem from the older age of many of the males; and from the desire of many women in the group to work short hours, which stems primarily from such noneconomic reasons as home responsibilities.

Perhaps the issue of greatest interest concerning independent contractors is whether this employment status tends to be voluntary or involuntary. During 1996, a year of considerable downsizing, the news media carried a series of stories suggesting that large employers were reshuffling their workforces through the device of creating a fictional category of workers for the purpose of lowering pay and benefits costs, including pension outlays. Reports alleged that employers fired employees on their payrolls and almost immediately filled the positions with the same persons as independent contractors.

What are the facts? When BLS asked questions concerning job loss in the February 1995 survey, it failed to find evidence, as of that time period, of such practices as "firing and rehiring" on contingent status. On the contrary, the BLS reported a high overall level of satisfaction of incumbents with independent contractor status; 83 percent claimed that the status represented their preference. Contrary to expectations, most independent contractors do not see themselves as contingent workers; instead, they expressed a feeling of security. BLS interpreted these sentiments as indicative of greater employment stability on the part of independent contractors versus average traditional workers, and speculated that perhaps the contractors should not be considered contingent workers.

Contract Companies. Recruits of such companies are dispersed to other organizations' premises to perform services for an organization that prefers to have its work done by outside persons. These workers are differentiated from others in that they work for one employer, performing services for a customer of the company on the customer's premises. Specified tasks are performed by employees of the contract company for client companies, though the client company supervises the day-to-day functioning of the workers. At least 40 percent of all contract workers tend to have more than a year of tenure, but few have worked for long periods for one employer, largely because most are relatively young (Cohany 1996).

The most typical services performed by contract-company workers are cleaning, building security, computer programming, and construction work. Unsurprisingly, they include highly marginal groups among the workforce—the young, the old, and the less educated; but a sizable group of them, substitute teachers and many computer programmers, possess college degrees. About 650,000 workers fall into this category. A majority (60%) of the men are working in this status involuntarily, according to the survey, but only about 40 percent of the women. A sizable minority feel insecure in their jobs, that is, they see themselves as contingent workers. Pay for full-time workers in this category is relatively high; median weekly pay for this group was $512, the second highest among all alternative work arrangements (as of February 1995).

MOTIVATIONS FOR ALTERNATIVE WORK ARRANGEMENTS

Employer Motivations

Despite the reluctance of the great majority of employers included in the Up-john survey to associate financial gain with the use of alternative hiring practices, the data they report on wages and benefits indicate that costs are indeed lower and that the major savings lie in the benefits area. The greatest savings occur in industries that offer benefits to regular employees. That is, employers who are generous to their regular, full-timers tend to withhold benefits from their alternatively hired employees, including contingent workers. And analysis reveals that the generous payers are the ones most likely to engage in alternative hiring practices. The most common reasons cited by employers for use of alternative arrangements are workload fluctuations and staff absences. Some also stated that they use agency temps and part-timers as part of their recruitment practices, screening for possible "regular" employment.

Worker Motivations

Until recently little has been known about why workers enter into alternative work arrangements, since most appear to be nonadvantageous. While researchers could speculate about the reasons by looking at the demographics of the groups of workers involved, no direct evidence concerning individuals was available. To rectify this gap, BLS researcher Donna Rothstein (1996) plumbed data collected by the National Longitudinal Survey of Youth (NLSY), a Labor Department project that interviewed a nationwide sample of youths who were fourteen through twenty-one in 1979 and has done so every year since that date. Her findings about the individual behaviors of twenty-nine- to thirty-seven-year-olds with job tenures of three years or less include the following:

1. The birth of a child or a change in marital status affects work behavior more than any other life event. These particular life changes strongly influence men to take full-time jobs, leave part-time employment, and commence self-employment. Changes in marital status also prompt women to take full-time jobs, but at a lower rate than men. Childbirth appears to spur women into self-employment more than any other life event.
2. Time investments in employment two years prior to the acceptance of an alternative work arrangement were found to be predictive of subsequent choices. Full-timers in standard jobs, especially women, worked more weeks than those in alternative arrangements, except for self-employed men and contractors.
3. Regarding overall wage growth, men in nonstandard employment situations do not appear to be progressing significantly less well than their counterparts in standard employment; but women in regular part-time employment, in regular self-employment, and in employment by temporary agencies did less well than their counterparts in standard full-time jobs. This suggests that the alternative work arrangements are less advantageous to women than standard full-time employment arrangements.

FUTURE EXPECTATIONS

The great expansion of the part-time work force during the 1980s began as a response to intense labor scarcity in many parts of the the United States, caused mainly by demographic factors, but exacerbated by the inability of the public-education system to prepare candidates for the lower end of the job market. But as the decade progressed, a more competitive business environment drove employers to achieve greater flexibility by developing part-time and so-called disposable work forces. This trend may be expected to continue, according to the Upjohn Institute, which found that since 1990 more employers have increased hiring according to alternative work arrangements than have decreased these practices. And many more employers increased their relative use of part-time workers than decreased their use. Outsourcing is also increasing, with more employers in their sample reporting that since 1990 they have been contracting out work that was previously done in-house, than those reporting that they have been bringing contracted work "back in" to their plants.

Long-term Earnings Impact

An analysis of the effect of nontraditional work status on long-term earnings (Ferber and Waldfogle 1998)[4] found that strong differences in earnings of those in nontraditional work statuses persisted over time, with men and women being affected differently. Men who had worked on a temporary job in the past reported slightly below average earnings and benefits than those who had not. Past part-time work appears to make little difference in either wages or benefits over time, while past self-employment makes for slightly higher than average wages, but less than average benefits. Among women, the picture is quite different. Those who have had past experience in temporary or part-time work were earning more than the average female wage and enjoyed benefits only slightly below average. But unlike men, women with a history of self-employment were earning less than the average female wage. And the small group of men and women who had never experienced any sort of nontraditional work arrangement were found to have, on average, lower wages, but a much higher than average benefits coverage than those who had. The self-employed men had higher earnings but fewer benefits than traditional male workers in the sample, while the part-time male workers had lower wages and lower benefits. The same pattern held for women, but with narrower wage differentials.

Some efforts have been made to discourage involuntary part-time employment by making it more costly for employers by such means as mandating health-care coverage for all workers and equal benefits for part-time employees. With little support, such proposals have foundered. It could be speculated that the public displays minimal interest in the issue because this work status is not seen as exploitative—a view shared by most of the part-timers themselves, as reported by the BLS.

THE UNDERGROUND ECONOMY

To fully understand the current composition of the labor force, the population of the "underground" economy must be taken into account. In a sense, "underground worker" is another alternative work status, but it is not customarily described as such. Since the 1970s economists have become aware that an increasing number of people are earning their living in ways obscured from the knowledge and constraints of government. This realm of economic activity is variously known as the underground economy, the unofficial economy, the informal economy, or simply as "off the books." These terms are used because the participants—employers, employees, and suppliers—violate tax laws, licensing requirements, labor standards, and other governmental regulations that exist to protect both workers and law-abiding employers.

The expansion of the underground economy in the United States and other developed countries is explained mainly in terms of the increasing difficulty people are having in establishing a full-time, secure relationship with an employer and by the enhanced opportunities for businessmen to avoid government regulation and control. Some observers blame the rise of the underground economy on excesses in regulation and taxation, while others stress the increasing problem of competing with cheap third-world labor. While the majority of the members of this sector of the labor force may be women, minorities, and immigrants, including children, some undergrounders are highly paid professionals and business entrepreneurs whose skills are in demand.

Since no one has yet devised satisfactory means by which to enumerate underground workers, estimates vary greatly and must be regarded as "educated guesses" at best. Two fairly recent studies put the participation rate at about 10 percent and 17 percent of the official workforce, respectively. Philip Mattera (1985), using evidence that includes a report of the Joint Economic Committee (U. S. Congress 1983), concluded that about 10 percent of the official workforce (26.1 million workers) are in the unreported sector. The most likely participants, by this calculation, are moonlighters, part-timers, the self-employed, persons not officially in the labor force, the unemployed, and illegal immigrants. Table 2.3 shows numerical estimates of involvement, by group.

The discrepancies in numerical and percentage estimates between the two studies are noteworthy. Harry Greenfield produced the higher estimate—17 percent of the civilian labor force (22.5 million)—from an analysis of 1990 Census data. His conclusion, shown on Table 2.3, is that while the majority of the informal labor force figures in official counts of the nation's civilian labor force, including about 2 million self-employed workers, another sizable group of underground workers is not included in official counts. Some are engaged in clearly illegal activities; others, by their statuses (retired, illegal alien), are suspect, and may be engaged in either legal or illegal work.

Employment in the underground economy results in workers losing the protections of government in such areas as minimum wage, safety standards, and hours limits. It also puts legitimate employers at a disadvantage because they must compete with the underground employers whose expenses are lower and

Table 2.3
Estimates of the Composition and Size of the Underground Workforce

	Mattera, 1983		Greenfield, 1990
Constituents	Numbers (*in millions*)	Constituents	Numbers (*in millions*)
Moonlighters	0.8	In civilian labor force, including 2 million self-employed	14.0
Self-employed	2.1	Not in civilian labor force: workers in illicit industries (drugs, gambling, etc.)	4.0
Part-timers	4.2	Illegal aliens	2.0
Nonparticipants	8.4	Retired workers	2.5
Unemployed	6.6		
Illegal immigrants	4.0		
Totals	26.1		22.5

Sources: Philip Mattera, *Off the books: the rise of the underground economy* (New York: St. Martin's Press, 1985) and Harry Greenfield, *Invisible, outlawed, and untaxed: America's underground economy* (Westport, Conn.: Praeger, 1993).

who probably do not pay full taxes, if any. *Off-the-books* workers may be people piecing a living together through combinations of full-time and part-time work, the latter unreported; through combinations of legal and illegal activities; and through combinations of work and income-transfer payments. Underground workers often supplement what amounts to inadequate unemployment insurance, disability payments, and "welfare" through *off the-books* employment, both legal and illegal.

The Internal Revenue Service calculates that it is losing $114 billion dollars annually in taxes on legal but unreported economic activities. Legal unreported activities are estimated to account for $600 billion, approximately 10 percent of GDP. How much more revenue loss can be attributed to illegal economic activities is unknown, but could be sizable. Greenfield, using IRS data for 1987, calculated that over $52 billion was lost that year in tax evasion, and that additional tax revenues were lost due to $197.2 billion in underreported income. But the losses cannot be stated in purely dollar terms since tax evasion breeds a climate of disrespect for law in the community.

Several researchers (Portes, Castells, and Benton 1989 and Feige 1989) who have surveyed the international scene present a grim picture of rapidly burgeoning informal economies that are altering established businesses organizational structures and practices throughout the world. They picture a situation in which large companies are abandoning their traditional pyramidal-type organization for flat, horizontal structures, ridding themselves of some or all of their production staffs and engaging in ever-expanding outsourcing. Neither Mattera nor Greenfield support the above thesis with reference to the United States. Neither found reason to conclude that the unreported portion of the U.S. economy is increasing markedly. Both contend that the majority of unreported activity is probably legal and that many of the participants are also, concurrently, members of the official labor force. They also believe that workers today are probably behaving no differently than people did in the past, working at unreported work on a full-time or part-time basis when it serves their purposes. They clearly reject the "scare" theses and conspiracy theories of the above mentioned, European-based researchers who have focused on non-American economic systems.

Individuals who conduct research on the informal economy tend to be economists who approach the subject by reviewing various types of statistics. The small-scale studies of sociologists and anthropologists, on the other hand, tend to illuminate the human face of the phenomena under study. An insight into the motivations that lead to employment in the informal economy is provided by sociologist Bruce Wiegand (1992) who found, for example, that Nashville, Tennessee workers who are capable of only low-wage earnings prefer to work *off the books*, demanding a premium at least double the minimum wage to work in reported employment. Wiegand's mid-1980s studies led him to conclude that the underground economy has moved up into the working and middle classes—a significant conclusion, since many researchers maintain that, historically, the informal economy was (and is) peopled by the poorest, least skilled, most marginal individuals. This assumption is also rejected by Mattera and Greenfield as an unwarranted stereotype.

As shown in Table 2.3, Mattera posits that six groups of potential workers are responsible for populating the underground economy. Included are the following groups whose characteristics suggest the difficulties in identifying them:

1. Moonlighters—Most are believed to be low-wage men with families who are not reporting second jobs.
2. Part-time workers desiring full-time work—Some would-be full-time workers may take more than one part-time job but only report the first one.
3. Self-employed workers—For these full-time workers in the informal economy, the term "self-employed" is believed by some to be a respectable cover for *off-the-books* employment.
4. Nonparticipants—Many older, male workforce drop-outs and retirees are believed to actually be working; their numbers include many who are collecting disability payments.
5. Unemployed persons—Many recipients of Unemployment Insurance are allegedly failing to report various types of employment they undertake while waiting to re-enter former positions or find desirable replacements.
6. Illegal immigrants—The size of the underground workforce populated by illegal immigrants is highly controversial. Educated estimates have ranged from 2 to 10 million. Most (as many as 88%), however, work for legitimate employers.

Small studies of groups often provide insights impossible to garner from BLS-type statistics. Such is Barry Chiswick's 1988 survey of the Chicago labor market. Regarding illegal aliens, he found the following:

1. The great majority are employed in secondary labor markets.
2. Their inadequate wages are above the official minimum wage.[5]
3. Their low wages are explained by their low levels of education and skills, a situation that is exacerbated by their limited ability to speak English.

The Immigration Control Act of 1986, discussed earlier, is believed to have abetted the growth of the underground economy by fueling the reluctance of many employers to hire anyone who might be an illegal. Consequently, illegal immigrants tunnel deeper underground; as such they constitute a seemingly unlimited supply of labor, which contributes toward the depression of wages (Bipartisan Commission on Agricultural Workers 1992).

NOTES

1. In 1995 median weekly earnings for full-time contingent male workers were $443 versus $541 for noncontingent male workers; for female workers, $322 versus $409.
2. The *primary labor force* includes workers who have full-time, stable employment , and a spectrum of employer-paid benefits. Some skill-attainment tends to be associated with this level of employment. The *secondary labor force* is usually described as including workers with low-level skills that require little education or preparation, who receive poor pay and minimal benefits, and who change jobs frequently.
3. This survey was taken from a random, stratified national sample of 550 establishments with five or more employees, undertaken to learn more of employer motivations for hiring by alternative arrangements.
4. The analysis used the same National Longitudinal Survey of Youth database,

but limited the analysis to part-time and temporary workers and the self-employed, voluntary and involuntary.

5. As of the time of the survey this meant $4.52 per hour versus the $3.35 per hour legal minimum.

REFERENCES

Amirault, Thomas. 1997. Characteristics of multiple jobholders, 1995. *Monthly Labor Review* 120 (March): 9–14.

Appelbaum, Eileen, and Rosemary Batt. 1994. *The new American workplace: transforming work systems in the United States.* Ithaca, N.Y.: ILR Press.

Bipartisan Committee on Agricultural Workers. 1992. Reported in *New York Times*, the law is said to fail to stop abuse of agricultural workers. 22 October.

Chiswick, Barry. 1988. *Illegal aliens: their employment and employers.* Kalamazoo, Mich.: W.E. Upjohn Institute for Employment Research.

Cohany, Sharon. 1996. Workers in alternative employment arrangements. *Monthly Labor Review* 119 (October): 3–45.

Feige, Edgar, ed. 1989. *Underground economies: tax evasion and information distortion.* New York: Cambridge University Press.

Ferber, Marianne, and Jane Waldfogel. 1998. The long-term consequences of nontraditional employment. *Monthly Labor Review* 121 (May): 3–12.

Greenfield, Harry. 1993. *Invisible, outlawed, and untaxed: America's underground economy.* Westport, Conn.: Praeger.

Hipple, Steven, and Jay Stewart. 1996a. Earnings and benefits of contingent and noncontingent workers. *Monthly Labor Review* 119 (October): 22–30.

———. 1996b. Earnings and benefits of workers in alternative work arrangements. *Monthly Labor Review* 119 (October): 46–54.

Houseman, Susan. 1997. New Institute survey on flexible staffing arrangements. *Upjohn Institute Employment Research* 4 (Spring): 1, 2–3.

Jamal, Muhammad. 1986. Moonlighting: personal, social and organizational consequences. *Human Relations* 39 (November): 977–87.

Mattera, Philip. 1985. *Off the books: the rise of the underground economy.* New York: St. Martin's Press.

Nardone, Thomas. 1986. Part-time workers: who are they? *Monthly Labor Review* 109 (February): 13–19.

Polivka, Anne. 1996a. Contingent and alternative work arrangements defined. *Monthly Labor Review* 119 (October): 3–9.

———. 1996b. In contingent and alternative employment: by choice? *Monthly Labor Review* 119 (October): 55–74.

———. 1996c. A profile of contingent workers. *Monthly Labor Review* 119 (October): 10–21.

Portes, Alejandro, Manuel Castells, and Laura Benton. 1989. *The informal economy: studies in advanced and less developed countries.* Baltimore: John Hopkins Press.

Rothstein, Donna S. 1996. Entry into and consequences of nonstandard work arrangements. *Monthly Labor Review* 119 (October): 75–82.

Stinson, John F. 1986. Moonlighting by women jumped to record highs. *Monthly Labor Review* 109 (November): 22–25.

———. 1997. New data on multiple job holding available from the CPS. *Monthly Labor Review* 120 (March): 3–8.

Tilly, Christopher. 1992. Short hours, short shrift: the causes and consequences of part-time employment, 15–44. In du Rivage, Virginia L., ed. *New policies for the part-time and contingent work force.* Armonk, New York: M. E. Sharpe.

U.S. Congress. Joint Economic Committee. 1983. *Growth of the underground economy, 1950–1981*. Washington, D.C.: Government Printing Office.

U.S. Department of Labor. Bureau of Labor Statistics. 1995. *Employment and Earnings* 40 (January).

————. 1998. *Employment and Earnings* 45 (January).

Wiegand, Bruce. 1992. *Off the books: a theory and critique of the underground economy*. New York: Gen. Hall.

3

Work Hours, Work Weeks, and Population Mobility

A description of the workforce is incomplete without a look at two supply considerations: the hours of work supplied by employed workers, including changes in work-week arrangements, and population mobility.

HOUR OF WORK

One "supply consideration" with reference to the U.S. labor force is the number of hours of work supplied by employed workers. According to Gary Becker (1965), these numbers are based on household decision-making, which implies that they are left to the discretion of the worker. An alternative view holds that workers do not control their hours of work, and existing data tends to lend credence to this position. According to a study based on Canadian data (Kahn and Lang 1991), over two-thirds of the workers sampled stated preference for more hours than their employers offered, a finding differing only in strength from the U.S. worker preferences reported in a 1985 BLS survey using CPS data. This study found that one-quarter of the workers wanted more hours, and that fewer than one-tenth (8%) desired fewer hours (Shank 1986). Those desiring more hours (and more money) were mainly youths; those desiring fewer hours were mainly married women. The overall findings of satisfaction with hours of work, stemming from an analysis of trends between 1976 and 1993 (Rones, Ilg, and Gardner 1997; BLS 1998) are surprising, since articles in the popular press have frequently claimed that people desire more leisure time. Perhaps these writers are describing themselves: two-earner families overwhelmed by competing career and child-care demands.

On the average, the number of hours supplied by employed persons in private employment has been falling over the past third of a century, from 38.7 hours in 1964 to 34.6 hours in 1997 (BLS 1998). This evidence of downward movement is a deceptive, statistical artifact that can be explained by several, mainly demographic factors. People who normally work full time now average 43.6 hours weekly, the overall count in recent years being affected by the explosion of part-time employment (BLS 1998).

MAJOR TRENDS

The major trends since the mid-1940s have been the rise in the employment of women and the increasingly early retirement of men (Rones, Ilg, and Gardner 1997). These factors affect the average numbers of hours worked: women's are rising because more women are working and because the female work week has been getting longer; men's are falling because they are working fewer hours and are withdrawing altogether at an earlier age. But another demographic change, the changing age distribution of the workforce, is more important. Baby-boomers are now in the prime age years (25–54); at the same time, not only in the population but in the workforce, there are fewer youths—which is partially explained by increasing school enrollment—and elderly. Since these two groups work typically fewer hours than the mid-age group, the current age distribution contributes to the overall rise in hours of work, for those who customarily work full time.

Long Work Weeks

In view of general concern about increased work-weeks, the BLS found that, when adjusted for age differences, the length of the average work-week between 1976 and 1993 differed very slightly: a two-hour per week increase for men and a one-hour increase for women. In 1993, however, a much larger proportion of persons were found to be working forty-nine hours a week than in 1976. Persons reporting long work weeks tend to be professionals and managers, commissioned sales workers, and transport workers. Each of these occupational groups was found to be expanding in the workforce, which contributed to higher overall averages.[1]

Hours of Full-time Workers Only. In this category hours vary from 46.2 hours worked by transport workers and material movers, to the 40.5 hours reported by administrative support, including clerical workers, and the 40.9 hours worked on the lowest blue-collar levels—the handlers, equipment cleaners, helpers, and laborers. Interestingly enough in this status-oriented society, the top occupational levels (executives, managers, and administrators) followed the transport workers, reporting only 45.8 hours weekly; and those in professional specialties claimed 43.8 hours, not far separated from some other, less-educated occupational groups.

Gender Differences

Hours of work (age-adjusted) over a year have been rising for both sexes. Women's hours rose until the late 1980s, but then slowed modestly, according to BLS. Men's annual hours (as of 1993) are up more than 3 percent (52 hours) since 1976; women's, up about 15 percent, nearly 200 hours. Men's average, overall weekly work time exceeds women's by 6.4 hours for full-time workers (BLS 1997). In addition, men not only work more hours per week than women, but more weeks per year, which also increases the total number of hours worked by males.

Differences by Industry

As of December 1997 average hours worked weekly by nonagricultural industry, in descending order, are: mining, 47.7; transportation and public utilities, 42.8; manufacturing, 42.7; public administration, 41.3; construction, 40.3; finance, insurance, and real estate, 40.2; the services, 38.0; and wholesale and retail trade, 37.4. Were the data for trade disaggregated, the figure for retail trade would most likely be much lower.

Differences by Occupation

Numbers of hours worked by occupation as of 1997 vary from the 44 hours reported by executives, administrators, and managers, and the 43.5 hours worked by transport workers and material handlers, to the 34.4 hours worked by service workers and the 36.3 hours worked by the handlers, equipment cleaners, helpers, and laborers who are at the very bottom of the occupational hierarchy. Administrative-support workers, including clerical workers, spent an average of 36.3 hours per week on the job; salespersons, wholesale and retail, 38.7 hours.

Geographic Differences

Finally, differences across the country are noteworthy. BLS's reports on overall hours worked per state show considerable variation. For example, in November 1997 Louisiana reported the most hours worked weekly: 44.7. Michigan and Ohio followed, reporting 44.4 and 43.3 hours, respectively. New Mexico reported the fewest hours: 39.2.

For a decision-maker, the existence of such figures as those listed above points to the need for even more detailed data as to the actual state of affairs concerning the labor supply. For example, where the involved labor force is unionized overtime hours worked may be of great interest.

CHANGES IN WORK-WEEK ARRANGEMENTS

For more than two decades, news media and popular literature have referred to new work-week arrangements so as to suggest that they are, if not standard, at least widespread and widely accepted. Unfortunately, there is no body of evidence substantiating such views. Extant literature, mainly small surveys by consulting firms, suggests that some changes, such as nonstandard work-weeks, have been driven by employers' needs, even though most discussions attribute such changes to adjustments made on behalf of working parents. The major changes are described below.

Flextime

Flextime is the practice of permitting employees, after working a specified number of core hours per week, to schedule the remaining hours of work according to their needs. For example, an employer may require all employees to be at their posts between 10 AM and 2 PM, but starting and ending times might be somewhere between 6-10 AM and 2-7 PM, respectively. According to Mellor (1986), flextime is more talked about than existent. Only about 12.3 percent of all workers in his CPS data reported being able to vary their hours. However, it is more prevalent in some industries than others.

Short-Time

Also referred to as the *short work-week*, an arrangement providing abbreviated hours has been discussed during periods of massive layoffs and pervasive pessimism concerning the possibilities of replacement employment. It involves the idea of "spreading work" by having incumbents each work fewer total hours per week. Prompted mainly by a few unions and state governments, several state legislatures have revised their unemployment insurance programs to permit the use of this option, that is, they have authorized the payment of benefits for paid time lost due to the use of short time.

Alternative Work-Weeks

A development seldom reported in the press is the increasing use of alternative or compressed *work-weeks* (CWW) by industrialists who wish to utilize their capital equipment more intensively. Employers in the textile and garment industries, especially in the South, are keeping their machinery running twenty-four hours daily, seven days weekly through use of such arrangements. In practical terms, then, employees might work three twelve-hour shifts one week, followed by four twelve-hour shifts the following week. On the average, the workers receive some overtime every two weeks, since more than 40 hours of work per week is performed during the second week. Employees are reportedly amenable to this practice, which reduces their total number of episodes of work in a highly adverse environment.

According to Shirley Smith (1986), CWW employment has grown about 4.5 times as fast as total employment during the twelve years preceding May 1985, the date of data collection. However, whereas the BLS defines CWW as "40 hours' work completed in 4 to 4 1/2 days," Smith notes that there is some evidence of other forms of work-week compression. Overall, her BLS data indicates that the overwhelming majority of the U.S. workforce conforms to what she says has become a social norm: about forty hours of paid employment over a five-day period.

THE MIGRATION ISSUE: GEOGRAPHIC MOVEMENTS

Another important factor in labor supply is population mobility. Both employers and workers are better able to respond to market opportunities when the workforce is geographically mobile, for two reasons: (1) in good times labor shortages tend to occur because younger workers leave their homes for geographic areas with better job opportunities; and (2) conversely, in bad times unemployed workers often leave the worst-hit areas to search for work elsewhere. In recent years workers have been attracted principally to the U.S. South and West. The willingness of workers to move for job-related reasons makes for workforce flexibility. Traditionally, however, employees have tended to prefer staying with a firm that offers stable employment, even when alternative employment offering marginally higher wages is available.

The major factors believed to inhibit employment mobility (meaning job change) are: (1) job seniority, including associated benefits packages; (2) lack of geographic mobility; and (3) inadequate information. Job seniority is greatly valued, especially by less skilled and older workers and is a principal factor in their job immobility. For less skilled workers or those with skills of value only to their current employer, detachment from a long-term employer equates to the loss of pay associated with seniority. Traditionally, seniority as opposed to productivity plays a large role in paycheck size. Older workers are aware that they are unlikely to be hired where alternatives exist for potential employers. Therefore, change of employment is viewed as dangerous for both the relatively unskilled and older portions of the work force.

Factors Impeding Geographic Mobility

Four major factors are thought to inhibit the geographic mobility of the labor force, that is, readiness to physically move one's residence in order to change jobs: home ownership; the two-earner household; reluctance to move children, especially teens, from their schools; and inadequate information about the availability of opportunities. Particularly because of the fourth factor, extensive resources have been invested in improving the quality of the U.S. Employment Service, a free employment exchange that has been run on the basis of federal-state partnership over the years.

However, better information is unlikely to significantly overcome the reluctance of home owners, two-income households, and parents of school-age children to move. A look at the proportion of movers in a given year, by age, immediately impresses the importance of this factor on the decision to move. The statistics on mobility of the population by age show that young adults ages twenty to twenty-nine are far more likely to move in any year than adults of other ages. About one-third of all twenty-something adults moved in 1995–96, some only to another house, about one-fifth no farther than another house in the same county. Only one-twentieth of the twenty to twenty-nine-year-olds who moved between 1995 and 1996 relocated in another state (*Statistical Abstract of the United States, 1998*. 118th ed. Table 32, p. 32.). So most members of the labor force are unlikely to move very far if they decide to move at all. A February 28, 1997, *New York Times* report, paraphrased below, demonstrates how one company takes these factors into account.

In early 1997 Fujitsu Ltd, one of the world's greatest telecommunications and computer firms, announced that it was locating a research and development plant in central New Jersey, home to some of the U.S.'s most prestigious high-tech firms. Fujitsu has a policy of locating R&D plants in areas with high concentrations of highly trained scientists and engineers, which they then poach from established employers in the area.

Fujitsu has learned that, for successful recruitment of highly trained, much-in-demand personnel, such as in telecommunications and the computer industries during "good times," it is necessary to move the jobs to the people. Fujitsu decentralized its research efforts in the U.S. after finding marked regional differences in the willingness of U.S. scientists and engineers to relocate. Scarce personnel is reported more willing to move from coast to coast and mid-America, within their region, but not outside it.

Patterns of Mobility

About 16 to 18 percent of the total population one year and over moves each year. Irrespective of age, few move far, the majority moving to a residence within the same county, about 10 million of the 16 to 18 million persons who moved within 1980 and 1996. During the same period, of those who moved to another county, about half of the new residences were within the same state. In other words, during the years between 1980 and 1994, the percent of migrants who moved to another state remained between 16.6 and 18.8 percent, about one in six. An additional group, equivalent to one percent of the resident population, enters the United States from other countries each year. Although Americans tend to be more mobile than Europeans, available statistics say little about how much other geographic mobility is associated with employment and job search [2] (*Statistical Abstract of the United States, 1998*, 118th ed., Table 32).

Within-Region Changes

Population change varies considerably within regions of the country and between them. Some experience net gains and others net losses, both represented by the differences between natural increase and movements in and out of the regions, including the attraction of immigrants from outside the country. The South and the West experienced the most net population gain in the decade prior to 1990, while the Northeast and Midwest lost population. But since the mid-1980s, the Midwest began to gain and has continued to do so, while the long-ailing Northeast, a net loser most years throughout the 1980s and early 1990s, experienced a small gain in 1995–96 (51,000). Whether this is the beginning of a new trend for the Northeast remains to be seen. What is most impressive is the large amount of immigration that all sections of the country have been receiving, which greatly affects their total migration figures. In 1995–96, for example, the Northeast received 285,000 immigrants from abroad; the Midwest, 130,000; the South, 470,000; and the West, 476,000. [3] The immigration from abroad is of particular significance in that, since immigrants tend to be disproportionately composed of young people, they will make a greater contribution to labor supply than the general population (*Statistical Abstract of the United States, 1998*. 118th ed. Table 31).

NOTES

1. This conclusion is based on comparisons between 1985 and 1993 data.
2. The Bureau of the Census found this to be 0.7 percent of the population during the year studied.
3. These figures report legal immigration; the illegal supply would greatly inflate these figures, especially in areas close to borders and port cities.

REFERENCES

Becker, Gary. 1965. A theory on the allocation of time. *Economic Journal* 75 (September): 494–517.

Kahn, Shulamit, and Lang, Kevin. 1991. The effect of hours constraints on labor supply estimates. *Review of Economics and Statistics* 73 (November): 605–11.

Mellor, Karl F. 1986. Shift work and flextime: how prevalent are they? *Monthly Labor Review* 109 (November): 14–26.

Rones, Philip, Ilg, Randy, and Gardner, Jennifer. 1997. Trends in hours of work since the mid-1970s. *Monthly Labor Review* 120 (April): 3–14.

Shank, Susan. 1986. Preferred hours of work and corresponding earnings. *Monthly Labor Review* 109 (November): 40–44.

Smith, Shirley. 1986. The growing diversity of work schedules. *Monthly Labor Review* 109 (November): 7–13.

U.S. Department of Commerce. Bureau of the Census. *1998 Statistical Abstract of the United States*, 118th ed. Washington, D.C.: Government Printing Office, Tables 31 and 32.

U.S. Department of Labor. Bureau of Labor Statistics. 1997. Workers are on the job more hours over the course of the year. *Issues in Labor Statistics* (February): Summary 97–3. Washington, D.C.: Government Printing Office.

———. 1998. *Employment and Earnings* 45 (January) Washington, D.C.: Government Printing Office.

Part II

Education for Employment

In recent years, and with relatively little public discussion, community colleges have proliferated, partly for economic reasons and partly to perform new tasks about which relatively little is known. The public generally accepts the view, warranted or not, that everyone should go to college if they want to get ahead. Public opinion is divided over the needs of those who are less ambitious or less able. The two prevalent, antithetical views are (1) that the "new workplace" requires more highly trained, *thinking* workers; and (2) the American workplace is being systematically *deskilled*, as employers determine to be part of a low-skill, low-pay economy.

The discussion of education in the following chapters deals primarily with economics and the effects of educational investment on employment. While many Americans might think that education —and particularly higher education—contributes to the well-being of both the economy and to the futures of the individuals who pursue higher education, serious questions have arisen about the economics of education. These questions are addressed, but not resolved.

Chapter 4 presents mainstream views on the values of education, followed by reevaluations of the payoffs associated with college education. Programs directed toward the disadvantaged are noted. Chapter 5 presents the major theories on the relationship of education to workforce productivity (the *demand* side of the labor market) as well as current findings on the costs and benefits of education to the student-consumer (the *supply* side). It also covers the differential payoffs of human-capital investment in education for women and minorities. Chapter 6 deals with vocational education and training, describing their various forms and the controversies that surround them. It also reports on the outcomes of employer-provided education to both employers and employees. Government programs for disadvantaged adults are noted, as well as possible directions for future efforts.

4

Differing Views Concerning Investment in Education

In the United States access to higher education is widely viewed as the individual's ticket to upward mobility, which in turn offers payoffs to society as a whole. In the early years of the republic, the belief in the power of education to promote both public and private well-being provided the rationale for a publicly supported system of free education for everyone (Squires 1979). Widespread literacy and educational achievement were seen as means of establishing and extending democratic society and of establishing greater equality throughout the citizenry. The existence of state-supported universities has been cited as additional evidence of an American commitment to egalitarianism (Bendix and Lipset 1959). And when the failure of the public-school system to educate large numbers of disadvantaged children is discussed, the schools are often faulted for making equal opportunity impossible. Civil-rights leaders and other reformers look to education to reduce poverty, another confirmation of the belief that education is the optimal vehicle for social progress. So the expectations of Americans concerning education cover a broad territory, and about one-third of U.S. residents now hold some academic degree. Formal education has helped democratize U.S. society because of its tendency to reward people on the basis of *achieved* rather than *ascribed* characteristics. When rewards go to those who are able to produce, rather than to those who were born into money or privilege, the resulting society tends to be both more open and more productive. Upward mobility becomes more possible. Peter Blau and Otis D. Duncan (1960), in a book that is the cornerstone of American thinking on the subject, point out that the main considerations influencing employment recruitment, that is, the determination of who will people the various occupational layers, are increasingly such criteria as educational achievement and performance. [1] The increasing recognition of these "achieved" characteristics by prospective employers makes it possible for the United States to avoid the rigid class systems of other societies.

American ideals notwithstanding, however, educational opportunity has been uneven in this society, in terms of both quantity and quality. For example, in

Table 4.1

Educational Attainment, by Race and Hispanic Origin: 1960 to 1996; and High-School Dropouts, by Race and Hispanic Origin: 1975 to 1995

	1960	1975	1995	1996
		(*Percentages*)		
Completed four years of high school or more				
Total	41.1	62.5	81.7	81.7
White	43.2	64.5	83.0	82.8
Black	20.1	42.5	73.8	74.3
Hispanic origin	(NA)	37.9	53.4	53.1
Completed four years of college or more				
Total	7.7	13.9	23.0	23.6
White	8.1	14.5	24.0	24.3
Black	3.1	6.4	13.2	13.6
Hispanic origin	(NA)	(NA)	9.3	9.3
High-school dropout rates*				
Total	(NA)	15.6	13.9	—
White	(NA)	13.9	13.6	—
Black	(NA)	27.3	14.4	—
Hispanic origin	(NA)	34.9	34.7	—

*Percentage of persons, age 18 to 24, who have not completed high school and are not enrolled in school.
Source: U.S. Department of Commerce, Bureau of the Census, *1997 Statistical Abstract of the United States*, 117th edition (Washington, D.C.: Government Printing Office, 1998), Tables 243 and 272.

1996, 74 percent of African Americans and 53 percent of Hispanics, as opposed to 83 percent of whites, had completed high school; and while almost one-quarter (24%) of all whites had completed four years of college, only 14 percent of African Americans and 9 percent of persons of Hispanics did so. Depending upon one's point of view, these figures may be interpreted as indicating steady movement forward toward the ideal of universal educational opportunity or as a disappointment at the pace of progress. Consider that between 1960 and 1996 the percentage of blacks securing high-school degrees advanced from 20 percent to 74 percent, and baccalaureate-degree attainment more than quadrupled, from 3 percent to 13.6 percent. And between 1970 and 1996, Hispanic high-school graduation rates rose from 32 percent to 53 percent, while baccalaureate-degree attainment rose from 4.5 percent in 1970 to 9.3 percent in 1996. Table 4.1 and the case study below provide differing pictures of educational opportunity in the United States.

A small, but intensive study of Hispanic students in the state of Minnesota revealed Hispanic students to be doing poorly academically by all standards despite a high valuation of education by parents and youths themselves. Education is seen as the key to upward mobility. Interviews also showed that Hispanic youths' academic performance is influenced by the socioeconomic background of parents, in line with mainstream findings. Further, educational goals of Hispanic youths in all income brackets are being influenced by the kinds of opportunities they foresee for themselves in the work world ahead. However, most want to become professionals though the same youths also believe that they are unlikely to be able to achieve their goal. Despite the high evaluation of education, Hispanic youths are dropping out of high school at about triple the rate of the larger community, with only a little more than 70 percent graduating, as opposed to over 90 percent of non-Hispanics. (Menanteau-Horta 1995)

PERCEPTIONS OF PROBLEMS IN AMERICAN EDUCATION

An extensive body of literature, largely sociological, holds that the socioeconomic status of the family—family background, including parents' educational attainment and occupations, and family income—primarily determines the educational performance of the children. Since the 1960s a widespread perception has also persisted that public-school systems are failing to educate disadvantaged children, who are often members of minority groups. Increased immigration, with the attendant entrance of large numbers of students who cannot speak English into many big-city school systems, has exacerbated the problems. And there is a commonly held belief, noted, for example, in the April 17, 1995, issue of *Business Week*, that American students are less well prepared for employment than their international counterparts, especially in the areas of mathematics and science. Educational inadequacy, or at least mediocrity, is now seen as systemic; it does not just affect the indigenous poor or immigrants who are suffering from language disadvantages as well as poverty.

Inadequate educational preparation has been increasingly identified as one of the primary causes of both the inability of a large portion of the non–college-educated workforce to (1) gain entry into lower-level, secondary labor-market jobs; and (2) take advantage of new opportunities afforded by the increasingly service-oriented and high-tech U.S. economy. The standard defense of educators and their supporters to the charge that *they* are responsible for youth unemployability has been that the schools are expected to solve social problems originating outside the classroom that are beyond their control or ability to even influence. Although this issue remains open, the events of the late 1980s and 1990s have raised questions that go beyond the matter of the educational system's ability to educate the less advantaged. During this period, in prosperity and recession, people at all points along the spectrum of educational achievement lost jobs and experienced difficulty in replacing them with positions of equal quality. Yet statistics show that the pain of unemployment and, increasingly, lower earnings, are being borne disproportionately by persons with less-than-college education.

DOUBTS ABOUT THE NEED FOR MORE EDUCATION

Surprisingly, perhaps, considerable skepticism exists among academics about the correctness of popular concepts concerning the educational preparation of the workforce. Not only do many critics question the accuracy of the claim that higher levels of education and training are required by the current economy, but there is even controversy over whether the present level is needed. A major criticism of the educational system in general is that much money has been spent since 1965—funding per student has doubled—without apparent result. According to one recent analysis, most added funding has been absorbed by "nonacademic goals," such as administrative costs, education of the handicapped, nutrition programs, and school busing for integration (Rothstein 1993). But some success has been achieved, such as reduced dropout rates, higher test scores for all, but especially for minority students, and increasing numbers of science and engineering students.

Despite the widespread belief that overall educational performance has fallen in the United States, the 1990 survey of more than 400 U.S. employers, performed by the Commission on Skills of the American Work Force, funded mainly by the Carnegie Foundation, drew the conclusions that, while the skill levels of the noncollege workforce are very low compared to other industrial nations, there is no evidence that shortages of skilled labor presently exist. The only shortages reported by the employers surveyed were in the skilled-worker category, mainly in low-paying female-dominated occupations now being abandoned by women for better opportunities, and in some skilled craft areas. As for reports of "shortages," the Skills Commission found that employers were referring to lack of reliability, poor work ethic, and lack of social communications skills as opposed to educational shortfalls. The problem of communications skills was emphasized.

The Skills Commission emphasized that the employers felt confident that their workforce needs would be met in the future; only 15 percent reported difficulties in locating workers with appropriate occupational skills. Nevertheless, the Commission called for *more* education and training, the kind that would prepare workers for high wages as opposed to the low returns for current non–college-level work. Where the jobs are to come from is another matter.

Another group of scholars has long approached the matter of so-called "shortages" as stemming from the fact that employers' demands for a more educated workforce is based on considerations that transcend the demands of the work itself. Since the 1970s a series of reviews of the evidence (Berg 1971, Squires 1979, Cattan 1987) has repeatedly concluded that existent studies fail to establish a convincing connection between contemporary job needs and rising employer demands. To the contrary, *de-skilling*, a lessening of required skills due to the simplification of jobs through the breakdown of tasks or through automation, has occurred in many cases. The Cattan study concluded that blue-collar workers have increased their educational levels outside of any relationship to the needs of their jobs. A compelling reason is believed to be the increasing gap in earnings between college and non–college-educated workers, one that encourages blue-collar and white-collar workers to go to college. Nor has evidence forthcoming from these investigations succeeded in justifying—in terms of actual job requirements—increased demands by employers that personnel on the professional/managerial/administrative levels pursue higher education.

EXPLANATIONS FOR THE PARADOX

What about the blizzard of newspaper and magazine articles blaming the problem of alleged noncompetitiveness on the lack of adequately educated workers? One recent critic, claiming that an adequate labor supply exists despite low educational achievement, offered the following example: the chairman of Pacific Telesis, in a 1991 press conference, complained that over half of 8,400 applicants for the job of "operator" failed a seventh-grade reading test. However, he neglected to note that only 700 jobs, which paid less than $7.00 per hour, were available for the 2,700 who did pass (Rothstein 1993). Two alternative conclusions are possible from the above example: first, that the educational system is failing or that second, the system supplied this firm with four times as many qualified candidates for low-paying jobs as it needed. A counter argument is that the U.S. labor force is adequate for present modes of production, but it would not be if the high-wage jobs of the future, envisioned by the Skills Commission, were developed. Such jobs are likely to emerge in the United States; they reportedly exist now in Germany and Japan.

Another argument used to explain widespread job *overqualification*, despite the relatively poor training of the non–college-educated, is that the level of education needed in the "new economy" may be overestimated. The *New York Times*, September 27, 1994, cited the case of the Ford Motor Company's plant in Chihuahua, Mexico, reportedly the most productive in the world, which employs workers with nine years of education. Ford has given school dropouts four- to twelve-week courses in a technology institute, where they study gasoline engines, mechanical drawing, mathematics, and the processes of tearing down and reassembling engines. Ford started with higher level workers; they later began to hire workers with less education and they trained these workers themselves. Production workers are promoted into skilled technician positions. Could plants in the United States not do the same?

The boom years of the 1980s saw a proliferation of employer complaints about worker shortages and undereducation on the part of available workers. Their complaints have been attributed to two separate phenomena: (1) the unavailability of workers who were willing to accept low-level wages in the suburbs and small-town areas to which many formerly urban employers moved; and (2) the unemployability of many residents of center-city areas of big cities where large, potential low-wage populations live. Those reported shortages that occurred during the late 1980s were mainly limited to untrained workers who appeared to be either uninterested in accepting minimum-wage employment or unable to do so because they lacked basic education and social skills. Since the mid-1990s, a period of economic prosperity, one hears of shortages of jobs—not workers—and of a "jobless recovery". Even so, the idea prevails that employers suffer from a lack of adequately educated workers.

Sources of Challenges

Challenges to the traditional belief that an unending flow of educated people is required for the well-being of society have been launched at least twice during the past two decades. The first arose in the mid-1970s, in Harvard economist Richard Freeman's influential book, *The Over-Educated American*. The second emerged in the pessimistic conclusions of BLS economist Daniel Hecker (1992, 1995), which inspired many books and articles in the popular press. After studying the years 1970 to 1990, Hecker reinforced Freeman's earlier negative view of college education as an investment by reporting that 20 percent of all college graduates were underemployed in 1990 versus 11 percent in 1970. Hecker concluded that urging large numbers of young people to go to college in a situation of excess prior graduates is poor public policy. He and other readers of Freeman, however, neglected to note that Freeman attributed the oversupply to demographics, specifically, the disproportionately large number of youths entering the labor market during the 1970s; and Freeman forecast that demand would rise and the earnings advantage of the college-educated would be restored after the baby-boomer generation passed through.

Freeman's views and his optimistic forecast were upheld by a team of researchers (Tyler, Murname, and Levy 1995) who agreed with his allocation of the problem to demographics. They maintain that the great rise in the proportion of underemployed college graduates in the labor market between 1970 and 1990 was a reaction to the 7 percent annual increase in supply generated by the baby-boomers, one that dropped to 4.5 percent, a level that could be absorbed, during the 1980s. To reiterate, according to this school of thought, although some college graduates are employed less advantageously than in the past, even those who work in high-school level jobs earn more, on the average, than the high-school graduates who represent the traditional occupants of these jobs. In other words, the increasing earnings inequality that exists in the United States is attributable to educational differences, and extends even to those at the bottom rungs of the labor ladder. This statement is quite significant in that the supply of college graduates grew 60 percent during the 1980s.

The view that college education continues to be a solid investment is upheld by economic developments. During the 1980s the wage premiums of the college-educated stabilized, while those of the non–college-educated plummeted. As of 1996 the overall wage premium for college graduates was 74%.[2] And on average, a master's degree brought almost twice the earnings of a high-school graduate ($39,980 to $21,431), while a professional degree generated quadruple the high-schooler's earnings, on average ($85,322 to $21,431). The doctorate, so prized by academics, brings less, about triple the earnings of a high-school diploma holder ($64,550 in 1996).

The college premium holds for all groups, by gender, race, and Hispanic origin, but unevenly. Men of all groups earn more, per educational credential, than women of their group, while whites, at all educational levels, earn more than blacks and persons of Hispanic origin. For example, whites holding a bachelor's degree averaged $37,711 in 1996; blacks, $29,666; and Hispanics, $30,602 (Bureau of the Census 1997). These must be read as broad social- indicator figures only, since the degrees held by each group tend to differ. For example, women take far fewer engineering degrees (a relatively high paying undergraduate degree) than men, and more education degrees and other female-associated courses of study that pay less than predominantly male-inhabited occupations. A parallel situation exists for blacks and Hispanics, compared to whites.

OTHER EDUCATIONAL ISSUES

It is beyond the scope of this book to discuss the educational issues and proposed remedies that have come to the forefront over the last quarter-century. Nonetheless, some are mentioned, since all such programs tend to be influenced by considerations involving the employability of the present as well as the potential labor force.

In the 1960s and 1970s, concern for the disadvantaged gave rise to Operation Head Start and Get Set, both early-intervention efforts; financial aid based on need for aspiring college students; and school busing, to promote equal access to quality education for all races. In the 1980s there emerged the fight for school vouchers, a device designed to allow parents more flexibility in their choice of schools for their children. Perhaps the most important development of the 1990s has been the increasing pressure, in the form of lawsuits, exerted on states, to abandon the personal property tax as the main source of public-school funding, the goal being to bring more equal resources to poor school districts through access to state, as opposed to local, funds.

Another highly significant development of the past quarter-century has been the fall in school dropout rates, true for all groups—even though they rose for most groups in 1994 and 1995 (*Statistical Abstract* 1997). Whether this rise is an aberration or the beginning of a new trend remains to be seen. One thing is certain: those who fail to complete high school are often treated as unemployable. The experiences as members of the labor force of the 604,000 school dropouts of 1994–95 (October to October) illustrate this point. Only 68 percent of the school dropouts of 1994–95 entered the labor force, as opposed to 80 percent of their high-school-graduate counterparts; and of those who consider themselves to be part of the labor force, the unemployment rate was almost 30 percent, as opposed to 9.6 percent for high-school graduates (National Center for Education Statistics 1995).

Misperceptions Concerning the Costs of Higher Education

According to a recent survey, the majority of the American public identifies "costs of higher education" as one of their greatest worries concerning their children. The reality is that the high tuitions commonly cited ($20,000 and above per year) by anxious parents are associated largely with prestigious universities, not the ones most students will be attending. For example, according to the College Board, as reported in the *New York Times* (September 26, 1996), tuition and fees in the 1996–97 academic year averaged $2,966 for public four-year colleges and $12,823 for private ones. Two-year public institutions were charging considerably less, $1,394; private ones, $6,673.[3]

The College Board survey found few parents to be adequately knowledgeable of financial-aid availability, even at the prestigious schools. Over half of all full-time undergraduate students at four-year schools were paying less than $4,000; three-quarters were paying under $8,000. Less than one in twenty were paying $20,000 or more. Where board is involved, the average cost at four-year private colleges in 1996–97 was $5,361; $4,152 in public four-year institutions.

The September 9, 1996, *New York Times* reported that according to the National Association of Independent Colleges and Universities, the 1996–97 school year represented the eighth consecutive year during which tuition at private schools had not risen beyond the rate of inflation. Some tuition increases were actually less than the inflation rate, which reversed a trend toward accelerating rises that began during the 1980s. Tuitions at state schools began to rise sharply in the next decade as state legislatures cut appropriations during the 1990s, but public pressures are forcing more support to state schools, resulting in a slowdown in their cost increases. Increases in student aid are said to be more in the form of loans than direct grants.

NOTES

1. Writing prior to the enactment of major civil-rights legislation, Blau and Duncan noted the exception of race.
2. The ratio of mean average earnings of a bachelor's degree holder to a high-school diploma holder in 1996 was $36,980 to $21,431.
3. This College Board survey included 1,601 public and private four-year colleges with total full-time enrollment of over 5 million undergraduate students. Tuition for some prestigious four-year public universities may be as high as the average for private ones.

REFERENCES

Bendix, Reinhard, and Seymour Lipset. 1959. *Social mobility in industrial society.* Berkeley: University of California Press.

Berg., Ivan. 1971. *Education and jobs: the great training robbery.* Boston: Beacon Press.

Blau, Peter, and Otis Dudley Duncan. 1960. *The American occupational structure.* New York: John Wiley & Sons.

Cattan, Peter. 1987. Underutilization in the U.S. manufacturing sector, 1960 to 1970. *International Journal of Sociology and Social Policy* 7, no. 4: 99–115.

Commission on the Skills of the American Work Force. 1990. *America's choice:*

high skills or low wages. Rochester, N.Y.: National Center on Education and the Economy.

Freeman, Richard. 1976. *The Over-educated American.* New York: Academic Press.

Hecker, Daniel. 1992. Reconciling conflicting data on jobs for college students. *Monthly Labor Review* 115 (July): 3–12.

———. 1995. College graduates in "high school" jobs: a commentary. *Monthly Labor Review* 118 (December): 28.

Marshall, Ray, and Tucker, Marc. 1992. *Thinking for a living.* New York: Basic Books.

Menanteau-Horta, Dario. 1995. Hispanic students: adjusting dreams to reality. *CURA Reporter* 25, no. 1: 7–10.

Rothstein, Richard. 1993. The myth of public school failure. *American Prospect* 3 (Spring): 20–34.

Squires, Gregory. 1979. *Education and jobs: the imbalancing of the social machinery.* New Brunswick, N.J.: Transaction Books.

Tyler, John, Richard Murname, and Frank Levy. 1995. Are more college graduates really taking "high school" jobs? *Monthly Labor Review* 118 (December): 18–27.

U.S. Department of Commerce. Bureau of the Census. *1997 Statistical Abstract of the United States,* 117th edition. Washington, D.C.: Government Printing Office.

U.S. Department of Education. Office of Education Research and Improvement. National Center for Education Statistics. 1995. *Digest of education statistics.* Washington, D.C.: Government Printing Office.

5

The Relationship Between Education and Employment

This chapter looks further at education for employment, particularly with reference to the varying payoffs provided by education to different population groups.

HUMAN-CAPITAL THEORY

The idea that education represents investment in "human capital" became popular around 1960 (Cohen 1979; Becker 1975; Schultz 1961). According to human-capital theory, all workers produce at an enhanced level once they have acquired education, both general and specialized. Gary Becker, in his classic discussion of human capital, enumerates the contributions of on-the-job training to worker productivity, focusing on such issues as the costs of training to both employer and employee, and the effects upon each. Becker claims, for example, that employers who invest in on-the-job training are inhibited from laying off such workers during downturns in the economy. Conversely, employees who have learned employer-specific skills are inhibited from leaving the firm for other jobs during economic upturns, reasoning that their skills are unlikely to be of value to other employers.

Becker was the first to systematically analyze the economic implications of education for the individual and for society as a whole, that is, the *private rate* and the *social rate* of returns. He was interested in such matters as the money rates of return on education for white male college students, looking at costs[1] and returns on lifetime earnings as compared to those of high-school graduates. While analysts can estimate the return on education for the individual, using the concept of *present value*, it is much more difficult to quantify the *social return*, despite general agreement that society benefits from aggregate personal investments in education. In his education-earnings productivity analysis, Becker allowed for the role of ability. He took the position that people of ability tend to undertake higher education more often than others.

Table 5.1

Mean Annual Earnings, 1996, Persons 18 and Over; and Ratio of Earnings, by Degree, to Earnings of Persons with High-School Diploma Only

	Annual (dollars)	Ratio to high-school graduates
Professional	85,322	4.0
Doctorate	64,550	3.0
Master's	47,609	2.2
Bachelor's	36,980	1.73
Associate's	27,780	1.30
Some College, no degree	22,392	1.04
High-School graduate only	21,431	—
Not a High-School graduate	14,013	0.65

Source: 1996 Statistical Abstract of the United States. 117th edition. Washington, D.C.: Government Printing Office, Table 246 and calculations by the author.

Payoffs to Individuals

Statistics are increasingly being churned out to prove the existence of educational payoff to individuals. Exemplary figures are shown on Table 5.1.

Earnings Advantage of Higher-Education Degree Holders. The current ratio of mean average yearly earnings of college graduates (bachelor's only) to high-school graduates, the traditional measuring stick, was 1.73 in 1996, historically a very high figure. One can even consider the figure to be understated in the sense that it includes only *employed* persons, persons with lesser education having higher unemployment rates. But it may be interpreted as somewhat overstated in the sense that it represents the mean earning rather than the median, which is a better measure. As shown on the table, professionals are the best paid occupational group, quadrupling the earnings of high-school graduates; while high-school dropouts, on the average, earn only about two-thirds (65%) of the wages of high-school graduates.

Lifetime Advantage. Economists believe that educational advantage is maintained over a lifetime. According to Census Bureau analysts, the lifetime advantages of education are anticipated to increase, based on past experience. For example, between 1975 and 1992 average earnings (in nominal dollars) for high-school dropouts doubled; rose 2.5 times for those with high-school diplomas only, almost tripled for those whose highest degree was the Bachelor's, and tripled for those with advanced degrees. This actually underestimates the loss of income for those at the bottom since it is not expressed in real dollars. As one Census Bureau report (1994) points out, the consumer price index was 2.5 time higher in 1992 than in 1975, meaning that dropouts lost to inflation and high-school graduates tended to just about keep up with it. Only those with some education beyond the high-school diploma experienced any rise in real wages.

The relative advantage of educated persons not only sustains itself throughout the earner's lifetime, but exhibits a different pattern from those without college education. For this reason, statistics on earnings are often presented in terms of age cohorts (groups). Although the college-educated may start their earning years later than the non-college group (the *opportunity costs* of education) and very likely begin their career work lives with debts incurred while in the educational processes, they both begin and end at higher rates. It is often stated in economic literature that more educated persons *peak* (reach their highest lifetime level of earnings) later than other groups, but this has not seemed to be the case in recent years (Census Bureau 1991). According to the Census Bureau data, among males working full-time and year-round with all levels of educational background, those with postgraduate education reach their highest mean earnings levels early, around ages forty-five to forty-six. While the high-schoolers experience an ongoing drop thereafter, however, the postgraduate males' earnings drop only somewhat; and as a group, they recoup most of their losses and improve their earnings after age fifty-five, continuing to do so until at least age sixty-two (the last year reported upon).

Payoffs for Bachelor's Degrees

Since for most people the bachelor's is the first and last higher degree earned, economic payoffs for the bachelor's should be of interest. According to a first-of-its-kind study earnings returns for the bachelor's degree vary mainly according to two factors: course of study; and occupation entered. In other words, there is no one single market for college graduates, but a series of markets, according to specific occupation. These factors are hardly news to college graduates, but they were never verified before through statistical analysis (Hecker 1995, from National Science Foundation data; the Census Bureau). Illustrative of findings, in 1993 male engineers, including computer personnel, had median annual earnings of $51,483, while male public-school history teachers received $33,261 and male social workers, $26,600. Persons with majors specific to high-paying occupations, such as engineering, were found to have higher median incomes than bachelor's degree-holders without any clear occupational association, for example, history, French literature, or sociology. At the same time, persons without a clear postbaccalaureate destination tend to have higher-than-average incomes for their major when they enter occupations that are traditionally high-paying, such as the nonengineering major employed as an engineer or the education major whose occupation involves real estate, insurance, and securities.

Application of Theory to Poverty Issues

Human-capital theory had a heavy influence on the War on Poverty launched by President Lyndon Johnson in the 1960s. If the poor, the *structurally unemployed*—those workers whose skills are different from those demanded by employers in a given area or throughout areas—fail to secure work because they lack skills, the solution was defined as some form of job training or remedial, vocationally oriented, basic education. Thus developed the Manpower Development and Training Act (MDTA) of 1962, the Comprehensive Employment and Training Act (CETA) of 1973, and the Job Training and Partnership Act (JTPA) of 1982.

Alas, a few billion dollars later, it became clear that the problem of the United States' "disadvantaged," as the unemployed, marginal, and submarginal work forces came to be labeled, was not to be resolved by quickie programs in typing or "maintenance engineering," augmented by remedial English and math, with a dash of "socialization to work" thrown in. Some critics claimed that human-capital theory was misdirected; they argued that the real problem was that the economy no longer provided high-paying, manufacturing jobs; in essence, then, it no longer offered uneducated persons a stepping-stone out of poverty. The problem, in other words, lay in the demand side, not in the supply side, of the labor equation.

Challenges to reliance on education as the cure for inadequate earnings has arisen on an additional basis. Striking correlations between education and earnings levels exist for white, college-educated males, but this relationship does not hold for all groups. The payoffs for women and minorities of both sexes are less. As shown on Table 5.2 African-American males with bachelor's degrees earn little more, on the average, than white, associate's degree holders and those with professional degrees, close to what a white bachelor's makes. Hispanic females' earnings follow similar patterns. Women of all groups tend to receive lower returns per degree than males. White female professional degrees tend to earn less than white male master's degrees, and so on. However, while women and minorities with degrees do earn less than white males, they earn more than less educated members of their respective groups. Education does pay, but unequally.

The impact of unemployment upon earnings can also be differentiated by education. The unemployment experiences of high-school dropouts are far greater than for persons with high-school diplomas, and greater still than for persons with four or more years of college. This impact is particularly acute in so-called bad years for the economy. In 1988, for example, the rate for dropouts was 9.4 percent; for high-school graduates, 5.4 percent; but only 1.7 percent for those with four or more years of college (Census Bureau 1993).

Credentialism

From the belief that individuals acquire much formal education in excess of job requirements, a new theory has emerged concerning the association between education and employment: *credentialism,* or the *screening hypothesis.* According to this theory, employers who are faced with large numbers of probably adequate job applicants tend to use degrees as a shortcut to hiring. The most common shortcut is to demand a high-school diploma (also an easy way for a racially biased employer to eliminate minority youths). Similarly, a college degree may be demanded regardless of whether there is any clear cut need for such to perform the tasks required in the job.

The theory of credentialism as an explanation of the education-employment relationship has not displaced the human-capital theory, partly because not only initial earnings, but lifetime earnings, are closely associated with educational attainment. Nonetheless, credentialist claims do raise important policy issues. Foremost issues are whether additional education is needed in terms of the demands of the present economy and whether students can expect to see continued economic payoffs to advanced education. If employers are raising edu-

Table 5.2
Earnings by Highest Degree Earned, Gender, Race, and Hispanic Origin, 1996

Level of Education:	White		Black		Hispanic	
	Men	Women	Men	Women	Men	Women
	Mean annual earnings (*dollars*)					
Not a high school graduate	17,032	9,582	14,877	10,739	14,774	9,809
High school graduate only	27,467	16,196	19,514	14,473	20,882	14,989
Associate's degree	34,286	22,547	33,674	22,113	24,021	22,883
Bachelor's degree	47,016	26,916	36,026	25,557	35,109	25,338
Master's degree	58,817	35,125	41,777	35,222	38,359	33,390
Professional degree	100,856	48,562	(B)	(B)	(B)	(B)
Doctorate	72,542	45,202	(B)	(B)	(B)	(B)

(B) Base figure is too small to meet statistical standards for reliability of a derived figure.
Source: 1996 *Statistical Abstract of the United States.* 117th edition. Washington, D.C.: Government Printing Office, Table 246.

cational demands because of an excess of highly educated personnel, what can the payoff for more education possibly be? For example, during the 1990–91 recession, a very bright and attractive college senior confided that she was obtaining a job with a prestigious consulting firm, the only bachelor-level candidate to be considered that year. All other persons being hired for the same position held master's degrees, even though the job officially called for a bachelor's degree. In other words, the employer was upping educational requirements because of a temporary excess of supply over demand. Not only was pay on the bachelor's level, but the employer also made it clear that the firm would not help with tuition toward a master's degree because the job was not seen as demanding it. Another good example is the demand by a prestigious Ivy League university for two master's degrees for librarian positions. This has resulted in situations in which librarians with second degrees in such fields as French literature or sociology may work in unrelated areas such as chemical engineering. Claims for a strong association between education, productivity, and financial pay-off weaken in such circumstances.

Not everyone is convinced that U.S. workforce members should be considered overeducated merely on the basis that job content often fails to match the levels of education now demanded by employers. Nor do all students of the subject believe that this constitutes a social problem. One explanation of the degree-demand level present in many establishments is that employers tend to believe that education has merits beyond the demands of the immediate job description. The following statement by Blaug (1973) articulates traditional employer sentiments concerning the "bonus" associated with formal education:

Employers pay highly educated people more, even when their education has taught them no special skill, because they are more achievement motivated, are more self-reliant, act with greater initiative in problem-solving situations, assume supervisory responsibilities more quickly, and benefit more quickly from work experience and in-plant training. They not only pay them more when they hire them, but they go on paying them more throughout their working life. In short, they expect them to be more productive than less-educated people, and the expectation is borne out: the economic value of education thus resides principally in certain social and communication skills imparted to students and only secondarily in the formation of those "technically required productive skills" advocated by manpower forecasters. If, therefore, education contributes to economic growth, it does so more by transforming the values and attitudes of students than by providing them with manual skills and cognitive knowledge; education is economically valuable not because of what students know, but because of how they approach the problem of knowing.

A further explanation of credentials oversupply is that the educational system has failed to retrench and limit its "production" when demand falls. Toward this end, a few brave souls occasionally suggest that it might be advisable for institutions of higher learning to curtail output. Such proposals draw deafening silence from income-hungry education establishments. Another explanation may be that the level of work demanded in certain nonprofessional occupations has risen. More skills may now be required in such occupations than in the past; and just because certain levels of education were considered adequate for certain jobs in the past does not mean that this judgment was necessarily correct. For example, why should a police officer (protective worker) be regarded as overqualified if he or she has a bachelor's? In fact, this is the current trend: the *New York Times* (March 20, 1988) reported that New York state troopers are required to have an associate's degree at minimum "to improve the judgment and training of members of the police force."

An insightful study of employment histories ending in 1993 revealed that underemployment of the credentialed is a transitory state, tending to last only a few years (Tyler, Murname, and Levy 1995). By the time such once underemployed individuals turn thirty, they often find their way to more education-appropriate work and to middle-class status. Serious underemployment appears to be a phenomenon limited to older male college graduates who, disproportionately, are victims of corporate restructuring and skill obsolescence. Median real earnings, among the group studied, increased during the 1980s for both sexes and all age groups except for mature men (45–54), whose earnings declined. The 13.7 percent drop in real earnings of young male high-school graduates during the same period can be taken as validation of the researchers' conclusions that educational investments tend to pay off, even when the work history is inferior. A further advantage accrues to the educated in terms of greater employment stability, which results in larger average yearly income.

Yet, as Hecker (1995) has pointed out, the market for degrees is highly market-specific. It has been documented that the rewards for advanced degrees are large; nevertheless, for persons in certain fields, the future may be bleak. Demand is greatly affected by patterns of government spending, particularly for occupations affected by military spending, itself a reflection of current perceptions of national security considerations. Consider the following study by the RAND Corporation and Stanford University, reported in the July 5, 1995, *New York Times*, regarding the overeducation of Americans:

A RAND Corporation-Stanford University survey of demand and potential support for young scientists in 13 scientific and engineering fields among 210 doctorate-granting institutions and 1,000 educational institutions which employ people with doctorates concluded that "universities in the United States are producing about 25 percent more doctorates in science and engineering fields than the United States economy can afford." The figures cited do not refer to actual current employment, but estimated future oversupply. Reduced demand is associated with decline in Defense Department and other governmental support of basic research.

The idea of investment in education is not limited to the United States, of course. According to a survey of the leading industrial nations by the Organization for Economic Cooperation and Development (O.E.C.D.), the United States appears to be about mid-range in its commitment to investment in education, with the exception of its proportionately low level of spending on preschool and kindergarten. Comparative educational-spending data, presented according to three different measures, is shown in Table 5.3.

Table 5.3
Comparative National Investment in Education of Various Types by Three Criteria, 1995, per Student

	Percent of GDP*			Constant 1991–92 U.S. $			Percent of GDP per capita		
	Pre-pri-mary	Primary-secondary	Higher	Pre-pri-mary	Primary-secondary	Higher	Pre-pri-mary	Primary-secondary	Higher
G-7 countries:									
Canada	—	4.4	2.6	—	4,752	10,715	—	23.9	53.8
France	0.6	3.4	0.8	2,302	3,636	4,701	12.4	19.6	25.4
Former West Germany	0.2	2.0	0.8	1,180	3,048	5,749	5.8	15.0	28.3
Italy	—	3.3	0.6	—	3,978	3,676	—	22.9	21.2
Japan	0.1	2.3	0.3	1,300	2,698	2,103	6.6	13.6	10.6
United Kingdom	—	3.9	1.0	—	3,473	9,154	—	21.3	56.2
United States	0.2	3.5	1.2	2,286	4,950	7,097	9.7	21.1	30.2

* GDP (Gross Domestic Product) equals GNP (Gross National Product) minus net property income from abroad.
Source: U.S. Department of Education, Office of Educational Research and Improvement, National Center for Education Statistics, *The Condition of Education.* Washington, D.C.: Government Printing Office, 1996, p.162.

NOTE

1. The term "costs" here implies tuition and living expenses, plus *opportunity costs*, the amount that would have been earned if the student had been working.

REFERENCES

Becker, Gary. 1975. *Human capital*. 2nd edition. New York: National Bureau of Economic Research.

Blaug, Marc. 1973. *Education, work, and employment: a summary review*. Report of the Education Research and Advisory Group, a project of the International Development Research Centre: Ottawa, Canada.

Cohen, Elchanon. 1979. *The economics of education*. Revised edition. Cambridge, Mass.: Ballinger Publishing Company (Harper & Row), 13–26.

Ehrenberg, Ronald, and Robert Smith. 1994. Investments in human capital: education and training: 279–325. In *Modern labor economics*. 5th edition. New York: HarperCollins College Publishers.

Hecker, Daniel. 1995. Earnings of college graduates, *Monthly Labor Review* 118, no. 9 (September): 3–17.

Schultz, T. W. 1961. Investment in human capital. *American Economic Review* 51, no. 4: 1–17.

Tyler, John, Richard Murname, and Frank Levy. 1995. Are more college graduates really taking "high school" jobs? *Monthly Labor Review* 118, no.12: 18–27.

U.S. Department of Commerce. Bureau of the Census. 1991. Money incomes of households, families, and persons, in the U.S. *Current population reports*. Washington, D.C.: Government Printing Office.

―――. 1993. Money incomes of households, families, and persons, in the U.S. *Current population reports*. Washington, D.C.: Government Printing Office.

―――. *1993 Statistical Abstract of the United States*. 114th edition. Washington, D.C.: Government Printing Office.

―――. 1994. More education means higher career earnings. Statistical brief, SB/94/17 (August).

―――. *1996 Statistical Abstract of the United States*. 117th edition. Washington, D.C.: Government Printing Office.

U.S. Department of Education. Office of Educational Research and Improvement. National Center for Education Statistics. 1996. *The Condition of Education*. Washington, D.C.: Government Printing Office.

6

The Outlook for Non-College Graduates

Work-related education attracts relatively little public attention. Perhaps this reflects the low status held by manual occupations in U.S. culture and a general lack of knowledge of the vastness of the activities involved in preparing youths for the world of work outside of institutions of higher learning. No discussion of American education could be complete, however, without consideration of these educational delivery systems and the efforts put forth to better serve non–college-bound youths. Vocational education and employer-provided training are the major vehicles through which the majority of the workforce improves its employability and value to employers, and, traditionally, improves its earning power. However, college graduates are the major beneficiaries of most employer-provided training. Employers who can afford to do so often pay for college courses for their professional and managerial employees, as well as for other types of education and training, on-site and off, for workers at lower levels in the occupational hierarchy, white-collar and blue-collar.

This chapter summarizes recent efforts, capsulizes the thinking underlying these activities, and discusses the issues surrounding *life-long learning*, a frequently discussed although loosely understood topic, and government-sponsored job training for the disadvantaged (aka "welfare" recipients).

COMPARATIVE SKILL LEVEL OF THE AMERICAN WORKFORCE

It is logical to begin by determining how well-prepared the blue-collar and white-collar workforces in the United States are to do the jobs that need to be done in U.S. workplaces. Determinations will depend upon point of view. In June 1990 the Commission on the Skills of the American Work Force, after conducting intensive studies of workplaces in the United States, (West) Germany, Sweden, Denmark, Ireland, Japan, and Singapore, reported that American workers rank among the lowest in terms of work preparedness in the industrialized world. Other than Ireland, all were found to offer better education to non–college-bound youths than the United States. In addition, all offered more help in the transition of youths from school to work.

Though the United States once possessed the world's most skilled workforce, its slide to near bottom in the industrialized world is largely attributed by the Commission to contemporary employer disinterest in making the necessary investments in education. Instead, more than 90 percent of 400 employers surveyed are attempting to deal with their staffing problems through other means. These include downgrading skills, which includes de-skilling through the use of automation, cutting wages, and moving low-wage jobs overseas. Some employers divulged their preference for considering a college degree to be an easy screening device in hiring, with the result that some successful applicants are underemployed.

More than 59 percent of all American youths now attend college. College graduates constitute 25 percent of the entire workforce, the highest in the industrialized world. The availability of an overqualified workforce sheds light on employer unwillingness to invest heavily in job training. The 1990 Skills survey found most employers able to meet current needs without setting up training programs. Fewer than 10 percent of the representative sample of American employers contacted indicated interest in trying to redesign the workplace and reeducate workers for high-skill jobs commanding superior pay.

There is a general consensus among students of the subject that the United States needs to improve the capabilities of non–college-directed youths in order to help them increase their earnings levels and income stability. This belief is rarely questioned, partly because of the commonly accepted assertion that the high-paying factory jobs of the recent past no longer exist. Whether employers do indeed need a better trained workforce is open to question. Numerous articles in the popular press and journals, such as those found in *Business Week*, regularly report on how current employers require a nimble, well-trained, self-supervised "thinking" worker for the high-tech workplace of today. Such was the thesis of Ray Marshall and Marc Tucker's *Thinking for a Living* (1992). Many articles have also been written, however, about how employer preferences for low-paid, disposable workers are leading them to systematically de-skill their workforces. Offering support to the first position were the pressures that a number of major technology employers placed on Congress in 1998 to increase the number of H1D temporary visas from 65,000 to 100,000 annually, because of their need for trained workers. Without trying to resolve this contradiction, it may be said that there is a general acceptance of the desirability of developing a better trained workforce.

Explanations of Low Skill Levels

Why have past efforts at work-related education in the United States been relatively unsuccessful, as compared to other advanced nations? One frequently offered explanation is the lack of any integrated delivery system. As put succinctly by Louis Ferman and colleagues (1990), U.S. training efforts are characterized by extreme fragmentation. Different sources serve different groups: employers offer these services mainly to professionals and managers; unions, mainly to skilled workers; and the Federal government offers training for the so-called disadvantaged. Little planning or coordination exists, and overall, relatively little train-ing is offered in comparison to the size of the U.S. workforce. On the other hand, this lack of integration is interpreted by another distinguished observer (Osterman 1990) as an indication of strength in that individuals may find many avenues by which to access a particular type of occupation or a new career, if they so wish. Each appraisal holds its truths.

The Institutions Involved. The fragmentation of education and training efforts is due, in large part, to the great number of institutions involved. To adequately cover the diversity of institutions offering *tech-prep* and job-associated training, it is necessary to mention the following:

1. Public high schools—general, vocational, and vocational-technical
2. Proprietary schools
3. Community colleges—associate-degree programs, customized programs for indi-vidual companies, and adult education or life-long learning programs
4. Colleges and universities—day and night programs, employer subsidized or oth-er- wise customized programs, on-site programs for professionals and managers
5. Correspondence schools, including programs on the Internet and distance learn-ing
6. Adult education or life-long-learning programs, under the auspices of a number of the institutions above
7. Professional organizations, including seminars and conferences for membership
8. Unions offering apprenticeships, sometimes in collaboration with public schools
9. Employer institutions, on-site and off, formal and informal, including skills centers and some degree-awarding colleges and graduate schools
10. The military
11. Vendors

Clearly, anarchy reigns in this extensive array of programs and institutions, each one operating autonomously. Available statistics on work-associated train-ing include activities so highly diverse that the data's applicability to any par-ticular type of institution or program is dubious. That is, any statistics that may be cited are unlikely to include all of the offerings of the institutions listed above, and one can seldom know just which ones are included.

PROVISIONS FOR VOCATIONAL EDUCATION

During President Johnson's War on Poverty in the 1960s, vocational educa-tion attracted considerable attention because it was seen as the most logical ve-hicle for helping disadvantaged persons, particularly youths, gain a foothold in the labor force and develop raised earnings potential. Attempts to mobilize this motley system to meet newly defined needs led to disillusionment with existent high-school vocational programs. Since then Congress has attempted to im-prove educational opportunities for the non–college-bound through several piec-es of legislation backed by considerable financial resources.

A History of Vocational Education

Government-offered vocational education in the United States has been avail-able since the passage of the Morrill Act in 1862, which established agricultural and mechanical colleges, contributed to the development of a strong manual-training program and the beginnings of trade education—but left out most youths. To remedy this situation, the Smith-Hughes Act of 1911 provided a revised model for offering vocational education; but by the 1960s it was deemed obsolete and of little value to participants or employers. Through the Vocational Education Act of 1963, stimulated by demands placed on the system by the War on Poverty programs, Congress directed that vocational education be made available to people of *all ages* in the country. The new legislation did little, however, to strengthen the reputation of vocational programs offered by public institutions.

The Perkins Act. In 1990 Congress tried again, passing the Carl Perkins Vocational and Applied Technology Education Act, which was designed to establish voc-ed as a major vehicle for resolving the education-employment problem. This legislation was intended to upgrade the vocational high-school curriculum as follows: (1) by raising the level of jobs for which students are being prepared; (2) by improving the integration of vocational and academic subjects, thereby providing a mix of broad and specific occupational skills needed by a wide range of students for various purposes; and (3) by prioritizing resources for counseling, guidance, and other supplementary services, in order that such special populations as the disadvantaged or the disabled might achieve success.

In writing the Perkins Act, Congress was particularly concerned about improving vocational-education opportunities in the most needful schools, those with students in the bottom 10 percent of average family income, the least well served by the existing system. The Senate expressed particular interest that four-year technical preparation programs be developed for the dual purpose of providing clear educational paths for students to rewarding careers in technical fields and stimulating local economies through significantly expanding the available supply of well-trained and educated people, while the House was more interested in improving traditional vocational education, directing the larger portion of the money toward the last two years of high school because that is where the students are. One compromise was that 5 percent of the appropriated funds are directed toward *tech-prep* programs, discussed next (*Congressional Quarterly Almanac* 1990). Among the usual struggles were whether the programs would be mandated or optional to the states (they are optional, but with mandates if a state chooses to participate) and how the monies would be funneled to their ultimate destinations, that is, how much state control and bureaucracy would be involved in the obtaining of funds by local groups.

In the process of legislative debate and conferencing, a certain ambivalence in program intent surfaced. Were these programs, for which Congress authorized $1.6 billion for the initial year, fiscal 1991, designed to lower the dropout rates among less privileged youths or were they designed to prepare the workforce for the complex workplace that many anticipate? Are the programs meant to develop better technicians or to prepare *technologists*, whom some hoped would be a different breed? To access Congressional thinking concerning this and other legislation, and obtain easily understandable, authoritative information concerning the contents of pieces of legislation, it is advisable to refer to the *Congressional Quarterly Weekly Digest* reports and the *CQ Almanac* for the year involved, once legislation is passed.

The Tech-Prep Movement. A few years prior to passage of the Perkins Act, the *tech-prep* associate-degree movement developed. The goals of the movement, which are largely parallel to the intents of the Perkins Act, include the development of a technical-education alternative to traditional college-preparatory education, beginning in public school and culminating in an associate's degree in college. Varying models exist, from general career-oriented education throughout the entire primary-secondary school experience to structured programs involving two years of high school, followed by two years in a two-year institution, such as a community college. Some versions of the movement include all of high school, plus two additional years; some are limited to persons who wish to obtain an associate degree, but lack adequate preparation; and some are work-based only (Bragg 1994). Some community colleges identify themselves as tech-prep institutions and state in their literature that they aim for students in the mid-range ability level. Some describe themselves as committed to the development of technicians for technical and services occupations and claim that their graduates have the advantage of being able to present work portfolios to prospective employers.

Extant documentation on the tech-prep movement leads to the conclusion that, while some changes in the orientation of public education may have been realized, *technology education* has not. This would be education designed to produce an individual who can approach work tasks on a theoretical level, albeit to a lesser extent than a college graduate, but it has not been included in most, if any, curricula (Anderson 1992). Moreover, enrollments in programs labeled tech prep remain very limited. Meanwhile, the entire movement is being obscured by (or melding into) *school-to-work* programs, which are described below. According to one report (Silverberg and Hershey 1995), only a small proportion of students in the school district consortia offering tech prep have participated; and only a small proportion of those students have been involved in any workplace activity (Silverberg 1996). In fact, an earlier report noted that most of the consortia involved focused on introducing applied approaches to the instruction of basic subjects, such as math and English. While almost half of the school districts in the United States have been involved, the average participating student has been identified as a white resident of a suburban community in a southern state (Imel 1996).

School-to-Work Act. In the 1994 School-to-Work Act, Congress moved further toward meeting two of the severest criticisms of the U.S. vocational-education (non)system: the first is the lack of national standards and a skills-certification program; the second is the absence of transitional help for the non-college-bound individual who is proceeding from school to work. In so doing, Congress appears to have adopted some of the concepts of tech prep, but having done so, has taken some of the steam out of the tech-prep movement (Bragg 1996). Using European-type apprenticeship programs as models, the strategy of the 1994 legislation is to give non–college-bound students "on-site, work-based career training" to enable them to move to skilled jobs (*Congressional Quarterly Almanac* 1994a). Other points emphasized in the Act include the following:

1. Specification of the work site as the preferred location of training, based on repeated findings by researchers that employer-based training is more effectual than that offered by the public vocational schools or other academic institutions.
2. Partnerships between schools and employers, with the goal of making it possible for high-school juniors and seniors to spend a portion of each school day at a work site.
3. Payment for work, lest students be used as a source of cheap labor.
4. Provision of career guidance.
5. Provision of encouragement to non–college-directed high-school graduates, to obtain one or two years of postsecondary education, most likely in a community college or technical institute. In many states, governance of School-to-Work activities (STW) is by councils or boards dominated by private employers.

The goals of the school-to-work model are for every non–college-bound student to receive a high-school diploma; a certificate or diploma from a postsecondary school (a community-college-type institution); and an occupational-skills certificate upon successful completion of the program's three phases, high school, apprenticeship, and postsecondary school. It is hoped that, as national competency and skills standards come into being, the credentials issued by the postsecondary institutions will help blue-collar and white-collar workers become more employable individuals with transferable, documented skills. At the time of this writing, it is expected that after an initial five-year period in which the program is Federally funded and administered jointly by the Departments of Education and Labor, individual states will assume responsibility for upholding or rejecting STW.

In an early evaluation of the School-to-Work program, the Upjohn Institute came to four conclusions (Hollenbeck 1997), as follows:

1. The approaches used by states in implementing the STW program vary greatly.
2. The activities most often undertaken on the local level pertain to career awareness, and include "job shadowing" sometimes expressed in terms of mentoring. Overall, STW-stimulated educational reform is described as "marginal at best."
3. Work-based training, to be effective, must be carefully cultivated from broad objectives to detailed implementation.
4. The STW program's success depends on leadership and investments in professional development. Concerns were reported in such areas as the program's future; the possibility, articulated by parents and students, that the latter are being directed into vocational education rather than postsecondary education; the possibility that students are being pushed into making premature career decisions; and the lack of solid evidence concerning the impact of STW on student achievement.

The Goals 2000: Educate America Act. Congress also established national education standards for the first time when it enacted the Goals 2000 program in early 1994. Adoption by states is optional, with participation encouraged by the lure of funding for programs designed to help implement the goals. Of most specific interest to this discussion are two of the eight specified goals: first, that at least 90 percent of students finish high school; and second, that every adult be literate and possess the skills to compete in a global economy (*Congressional Quarterly Almanac* 1994b).

Present Directions

The tech-prep and school-to-work literature is discomforting to pundits with a long view of efforts to improve or change educational directions and programs for non-college-bound youth. Nonetheless, the following assessment of the current state of U.S. educational policy, offered by a high U.S. policy maker who declined to be identified, clarifies the situation somewhat. It is believed that some progress has been made with children in grades one through four with the help of Federal initiatives and funding. The Federal government is now attempting to stimulate improvement of the public-education experience in grades five through eight.

Interest in work-associated education is focused on development of programs leading to output of technologists, as opposed to technicians. These persons may not be "conceptionalists," as is expected of college graduates, but they should be able to understand "snippets of technology." As such, they are what high-paying employers (who are now pushing for visas for trained immigrants) need in large numbers for the jobs that pay $17 per hour to non–college-graduates. Thus far, there is no evidence that tech-prep or STW programs are contributing to the development of such personnel. The community college is a good base upon which to build such programs, partly because many (perhaps 25%) current employees of these two-year institutions are people with hands-on experience; they are often retired persons, who "know how to get things done" (personal communication, 1998).

EMPLOYER-PROVIDED EDUCATION AND TRAINING

Explanations for Limited Employer Activities

American employers, historically, have offered relatively little job training and education to persons who are on their payrolls, as compared with other advanced nations. Some of the major reasons are summarized here.

1. Uncertainty of return on investment by employers. The argument commonly offered is that the American workforce is uniquely mobile, making return on investment to employers risky, especially when the training offered is portable, the employees lack traditions that discourage job change, and other employers lack inhibitions against poaching. Problems associated with employee mobility are exacerbated by a lack of tradition for employee sharing of training costs through the device of accepting lower wages, which is a necessity, according to standard economic theory.[1]
2. A tradition of local control of education. The lack of national standards and the nonexistence of a coordinating organization has inhibited employers from exerting strong, coordinated influence on current vocational-education programs; as a result, decisions are made mainly by individual employers and workers (Lynch 1994a). Only in 1989, under President Bush's leadership, did a movement for establishment of national standards commence.
3. Insufficient motivation on the part of employers to force the issue. Employers, in general, give no indication of serious lack of skilled personnel and apparently feel no need to become involved in extensive training activities. When a specific need arises, such as for trained computer personnel, as occurred during the late

1990s, employers have found it possible to raise the supply of desired personnel through lobbying for selective expansion of immigration quotas.

4. A correspondence between readiness to engage in training and size of the company or firm. Small firms, the great majority of employers, avoid becoming involved in skill development due to their relatively higher per capita costs and loss of productivity during training activities (Lynch and Black 1998).

5. Lack of commitment to community, combined with the view of labor as just another commodity.

Extent of Current Employer-Provided Education

In light of the negative picture presented above, the findings of two comprehensive surveys of employer-provided training are somewhat surprising. Of 4.5 million establishments surveyed by BLS in 1993, 70 percent reported offering some type of *formal training*, that which provides training planned in advance with a structured format and defined curriculum (as opposed to informal training, which has no structure nor plan and can be adapted to situations and individuals). This figure rises to over 98 percent if the very smallest employers (fewer than 50 employees) are excluded. And no less than 69 percent of the smallest (68.9%) offered some type of training. The types of training offered, by size of employer, are shown on Table 6.1. The so-called EQW-NES survey, made in 1994, using a different national database—employers with two or more employees, oversampled for establishments in manufacturing and for employers of 100 or more employees—found 81 percent of the employers offering some type of formal training, 57 percent reporting an increase since 1991. These employers are taken to be representative of employers of 75 percent of the U.S. workforce (Lynch and Black 1998). Before proceeding it is best to clarify that the large percentage of employers offering training does not obviate the fact that most workers are believed not to receive any formal employer-provided training. The 1991 Current Civilian Population Survey set the recipient figure at 17 percent; the 1994 EQW-NES survey, at over 40 percent. It is thought that the discrepancy occurs because of differences in the proportion of small employers in the two databases and the fact that employer usage is believed to have increased between 1991 and 1994. Employees are most likely to receive formal training in large firms that make large investments in physical capital and have adopted new forms of work organization.

Employer Motivations in Providing Education and Training

As for employer motivations in offering formal job training, three-quarters of the 1993 BLS survey respondents stated that they aim to develop skills specific to the needs of the firm; about one-half also reporting that employee skills required upgrading to cope with higher-level technology. Other motivations included retaining valuable employees (52.6%), while a quarter (24.6%) reported that they were responding to laws or regulations. This survey clearly confirms the view that employers prefer to offer *employer-specific* job skills training and other workplace-related training, such as apprenticeships, in order to make employees more productive; but sometimes they are also motivated by an interest in maintaining long-term relationships with valuable employees.

Table 6.1
Employer-Provided Training, by Type and Size of Private, Nonfarm Establishment, 1993

	Total employees	Fewer than 50 employees	50 to 249 employees	250 or more employees
All establishments (*thousands*)	4,501	4,198	257	46
All establishments that provide any formal training	3,192	2,895	251	46
Percent of all establishments with formal training	70.9	68.9	97.9	99.3
Orientation training	31.8	28.5	74.9	92.5
Safety and health training	32.4	29.5	70.2	88.3
Apprenticeship training	18.9	17.5	35.6	51.1
Basic skills training	2.0	1.7	7.2	19.3
Workplace-related training	36.1	33.0	77.3	89.6
Job skills training	48.6	45.8	85.8	95.9
Other	4.1	3.6	10.5	17.1

Source: Frazis, Harley, Diane Herz, and Michael Horrigan 1995. Employer-provided trainnng: results from a new survey. *Monthly Labor Review* 118 (May): 5.

Another survey by Hewitt Associates, reported in the *New York Times* on May 5, 1994, shows that employers may be more involved in encouraging the educational efforts of their workers than the preceding poll seems to indicate. In this survey of 851 medium-and large-sized employers, a large majority (85%) reimburse employees for any job-related course. A large majority (71 %) pays tuition for work toward a bachelor's degree, and about half (48%) will pay for graduate courses. As is often reported, the employers polled are far less likely to reimburse for basic education, such as GEDs, or for certificate programs. For example, only 29 percent will help with the GED and still fewer (17%) with certificate programs. These figures confirm the general impression that establishments' educational subsidies go mainly to upper-level employees, mainly professionals and managerials. As for the practices of smaller firms, at least one source notes that employers usually hire already-trained workers or, when necessary, send their workers outside the firm to obtain needed skills or knowledge (Carnevale and colleagues 1990).

More hard facts concerning employer investments in formal training emerged in a 1995 BLS survey of the training practices and programs of 1,800 organizations with fifty or more employees (BLS 1996; also see Frazis et al. 1995 and 1998). According to this survey the critical factors influencing employer investments in formal (as opposed to on-the-job training) are size of employer (as measured by number of employees) and type of industry. Financial investments by employers of all sizes is impressive. Annual average 1995 training expenditures, that is, trainer costs exclusive of employees' time, for small employers (50–99 employees) were found to be $159 per employee; for medium-sized ones (100–499), $248; and for large ones (500+), $456. But costs were actually considerably higher in that costs for lost work time per employee amounted to $647 each, $224 for formal training and $423 for informal training (Frazis, Gittleman, Horrigan, and Joyce, 1998).

By industry, fairly modest differences exist in terms of the proportion of employers offering formal training to employees. With 92.5 percent of all employers (of 50 or more) expending some funds for formal training, the proportions range from 98.4 percent by wholesale trade to 88.1 percent by durable manufacturers. Of greater significance are the proportions of employees in each industry who are the beneficiaries of this employer investment. With about 70 percent of all employees receiving some investment in formal training from their employers, the differences by industry range from 94.7 percent of all employees of mining companies to less than 50 percent of all retail tradespeople. This was taken by the BLS analysts to indicate that employers invest in their more valued workers whom they intend to retain long-term. It follows from the findings that the employers most likely to offer formal training are the larger ones (500+) with low turnover rates, larger numbers of benefits, and greater usage of contract workers and other alternative work arrangements. Time investments in training by employers were found to be considerable, about 4 percent of total standard work hours.

The industries prone to invest the most time were found to be transportation (18.3 hours per employee) and finance, insurance, and real estate (16.6 hours); the least, construction (5.0 hours) and retail trade (3.7 hours). Manufacturing and the services tend to offer eleven to twelve hours per year (BLS 1996).

Employer readiness to engage in formal training appears to be related to the presence of high-performance work systems (Frazis, Herz, and Horrigan 1995; Lynch and Black 1998). The type of training offered in firms with such systems appears to be of a more general type, for example, computer training, teamwork training, and basic education (Frazis, Herz, and Horrigan 1995). Lynch and Black (1998) note that such employers tend to train a higher proportion of their workers than others. These researchers interpret employers' propensity to engage heavily in formal training to mean that this training complements, rather than substitutes for, investments in physical capital and education. Another factor found to be closely associated with provision of formal training by the employer is company generosity in offering a broad span of employee benefits (Frazis, Herz, and Harridan, 1995).

Interest in training appears to be on the upsurge, with a majority of firms (70%) reporting an increase in training expenditures over the past three years and about two-thirds (65%) reporting the inclusion of a larger proportion of their employees during the same period. Most are focusing mainly on job-specific skills (two-thirds of all training hours financed, and about one-half of total training activities). In line with prior reports, the great majority of job-skills training (about 66%) is invested in management-level employees. Computer training is the single most popular type of training (about 20%) across all industries. Of the specific job skills taught, communications, quality, employee development, and occupational safety absorbed the largest number of hours of instruction.

Ninety-one percent of all firms found to provide formal training used in-house staff at least in part, while 80 percent reported that they financed some off-site training. The use of community colleges and other institutions of higher learning appears to be restricted to larger employers; nevertheless, they mainly use in-house trainers.

Sources of Training

How trainers are supplied depends upon company size. Companies with 500 or more employees sometimes utilize community colleges or other educational institutions; but most employers, including the larger ones, do the majority of their informal training in-house. Still, a large majority (80%) allocate some funds for outside training. Product education, training by manufacturers or producers in the use of their products to their customers' employees, is offered by about half of the companies.

Anthony Carnevale and Janet Johnson, authorities on the education-versus-training issue, believe that employers are impelled to develop their own programs, either because educators fail to accept employers' concepts of needs or because the programs offered by educational institutions are often obsolete technologically or delivered inefficiently (1989). According to this view, which challenges the common wisdom that abstract learning is more effectual in enabling workers than job-specific training, employers may be more realistic than traditional educators. As Carnevale and Johnson point out, current findings in learning theory—that teaching by specific application is no less effective than traditional methods of teaching general principles—affirm the validity of employer preferences; and they note that these preferences have had a substantial impact on long-term productivity and employees' earnings.

Institutionalized educational programs have always been slow to respond to workplace needs, particularly in technical fields, with lag time between employers' immediate needs and academia's readiness to absorb new material into curricula. An example is manufacturing engineering, for which employers developed a full curriculum long before schools of engineering were ready to include it as a legitimate area of study (Lillard and Tan 1986).

As stated previously, employers tend to be biased toward investment in higher level employees. Employer offerings tend to be departmentalized into three groups: one for managers and supervisory staff; a second for personnel requiring technical skills, including professional technicians and floor level workers; and a third for sales and marketing people. Most of the skills training currently realized occurs on-site. But when skills training aims beyond current needs, it often takes place off-site, perhaps at a company headquarters or at divisional levels. Programs to develop engineers, scientists, and executives are also likely to be given off-site. For them, employers tend to turn to traditional educational institutions, primary and secondary schools through colleges and universities, for over half of their educational/training undertakings.[2]

Level of Expenditures

Private employers' training expenditures for 1995 (according to the BLS and other data sources) have been estimated by the American Society for Training and Development to have been $25.2 billion dollars in direct costs, plus $27.1 billion in indirect, including wages and salaries of both trainees and trainers, a total of $52.3 billion. With annual government training costs of $3 billion, the country is expending $55.3 billion on formal training alone (Benson 1996). Informal training, believed to be far more prevalent than formal, may well incur considerably more expense, but valuation of it is more difficult. No comprehensive data exists on the extent of informal training in the United States.

Outcomes of Employer-Provided Training

Does vocational education contribute to a better work life for the non–college-bound? Past studies of value tended to focus on how the earnings of vocational high-school graduates compared with general high-school graduates over time. Most current studies of vocational-education effectiveness also include data from the newer institutions, the proprietary school and the community college. Findings of various researchers during the 1960s, 1970s, and early 1980s (Eininger 1964; Grasso and Shea 1979; Gustman and Steinmeirer 1982) were inconsistent, but mainly negative. Recent work by Lynch (1991a, 1992, and 1994a,b) exploring the payoffs to both employer and employee, tends to be more illuminating and more positive. But overall, knowledge remains fragmentary.

Recent research suggests that formal, employer-provided training is effective in terms of productivity gains, and tends to be more so than informal training. Major findings are as follows:

1. Formal training programs have a marked and lasting effect on productivity, while informal training for new hires brings only one-time, short-term productivity gains (Lynch 1991a). Productivity enhancement of 17 percent (measured by net sales per worker) was found in a before-and-after comparison of U.S. manufacturing plants between 1983 and 1986 (Bartel 1991). Subsequent study of a large manufacturing plant found higher supervisory ratings for workers receiving formal training (Bartel 1992).
2. Formal job-training is more portable than informal, on-the-job training (OJT). Job-switchers carry the effects of formal job-training (increased productivity, wage improvement, and employee innovation) with them to their new job more than those engaging in OJT. A subsequent study of newly hired employees in small- and medium-sized firms found that training by a previous employer boosted productivity by 9.5 percent, but had little effect on wages received. The employer gains by not having to offer initial training. However, without additional training by the new employer, productivity gains decline over time (Bishop 1994).

In addition, major findings tend to conclude that formal training programs and apprenticeships, generated either by unions or employers, bring gains to employees and that these are higher than gains from public school or other government-sponsored training programs. The effects of informal training appear not to be portable, being lost upon switch in employers.

Best estimates of employee returns from company programs are from 4.4 percent to 11 percent (Lynch 1994a). This range almost equals findings for the Netherlands, and exceeds those for Great Britain and Australia.The finding that formal, OJT programs do not bring wage increases despite productivity increases has been interpreted as an argument for a national certification program in the United States, so that high-achieving employees can transfer jobs more easily if their enhanced productivity is not rewarded. Returns on apprenticeships to employees were found to be high in the United States, while school-based and government training programs bring lower returns than employer-provided programs.

Some types of school-based job training bring gains to students. Business, vocational, and technical schools and institutes all can help youths make career changes (Lynch 1991b and 1992). Proprietary schools, together with the others mentioned, can have positive effects on productivity and earnings (Bishop 1994; Lynch 1992), their returns being very similar to those from U.S. community and junior colleges (Kane and Rouse 1993). This data can be interpreted as indicating that non–college-graduates can benefit financially from various other types of postsecondary education that are now available. The efforts, then, of the approximately one-half of all high-school graduates who do complete at least one year of some type of post–high-school education can be expected to pay off.

CONTINUING, LIFE-LONG, AND ADULT EDUCATION

Thus far, in this discussion of education and employment, education has been considered in terms of initial preparation for the world of work. Since the 1950s concern has been expressed that the education of youth and early adulthood would prove inadequate over individuals' work lives and that further education, sometimes termed retraining, would be necessary. Some go so far as to say that retraining will have to be continuous. The retraining concept is sometimes referred to as lifetime learning, continuing education, or adult education.[3] Does such a trend or movement exist? The best answer is that there is no such *system*, but rather a polyglot group of mainly classroom activities existing outside the traditional programs of standard institutions. Such educational activities may be of any length or duration; may or may not offer credit; may be directed toward job advancement or efforts to keep abreast of professional developments or other work-associated goals. Travel-study programs are sometimes included. Recertification and relicensing programs belong in this category, as do some basic-skills training programs

Several organizations and associations of continuing-education instructors and administrators exist. A review of their activities and publications show them striving for better status, funding, and recognition from traditional educational institutions, professional organizations, and the general public. Marginality could be said to be their major characteristic. But their strivings for greater professionalization are tempered by expressions of fear that the very process of conforming to traditional norms could adversely affect the unique qualities that distinguish *continuing education* from standard educational offerings (Pearce 1992; Collins and Carvero 1992; Dejardin and Kothernbeutel 1992). Persons interested in obtaining recent statistics on adult education should refer to the most recent *Digest of Education Statistics*, issued by the U.S. Center for Educational Statistics, Office of Education Research and Improvement, U.S. Department of Education.

Empirical Knowledge of Adult Education

Little specific knowledge exists about who offers adult-education programs and for what purposes; how effective the programs are; and who participates and toward what ends. Some general statistics about the vast and diverse area of current adult-education programs are the following:

1. About one-third (32%) of the noninstitutional population, seventeen and over, engages in some type of *adult education* during a year's time, with considerable participation among all age groups.
2. Participation is equal between the sexes, though the objectives are not always entirely parallel.
3. Modest differences in participation rates by race and ethnic origin exist. Minorities participate at modestly lower rates than whites.
4. The higher an individual's level of education; the more prestigious the occupation; the higher the income level, the greater the likelihood that the individual will be involved in some educational pursuit.
5. By far the most common reason for educational involvement by all status and income groups is the desire for job advancement (60%). Training for a new job or completion of a degree were mentioned by only a small minority, on average. A good majority (60%) of those involved undertake their educational effort for the purpose of "advancing on the job." The proportion of those reporting participation for this reason rises with age (25 to 65).

6. The small minority (9%) who report that they are "training for a new job" consists mainly of younger persons and declines with age, educational attainment, and income. Minorities are more likely to be so involved than whites.
7. Youths (under 24) are the most represented among the small proportion (13%) reporting involvement for reason of completing a diploma.

As shown on Table 6.2, desire for job advancement heavily motivates all occupational groups, and it rises along with income. Motivation to train to obtain a new job, on the other hand, is most important to the group at the bottom of the income and occupational hierarchy.

Effects on Employment and Earnings

As to the *effect* of this amorphous group of educational activities on employment and earnings, evidence is very limited. The general impression exists that the credentials offered by continuing-education/adult-education programs do not command the respect accorded those acquired from traditional programs. This belief may have motivated about one-third of recently polled deans of nontraditional higher education programs to urge that "nontraditional education be seen as a fundamental component of higher education, rather than as an alternative path" (Sparks 1994).

Status of the System

Finally, skepticism that the concept of continuing education has been institutionalized in the United States is enhanced by the recent report of the Carnegie Foundation (Eurich 1991), which concluded that, while a vast network of adult-education programs exist, they are poorly distributed and inadequate to meet the challenges posed by changing technology. More collaboration between business, labor, education, and government, and better use of technology in program delivery is urged. Industry is reported to be spending $60 billion a year on training covering about one-third of the workforce; the military, an additional $18 billion. Government, unions, and private institutions also run programs. These efforts have several limitations, among them, the failure to reach the most needful: *displaced workers* (age 20 years or older, who have lost jobs dues to plant closings, position or shift discontinuation, and company moves), unemployed youths, immigrants, refugees, and welfare recipients. In other words, serious problems exist in terms of both program content and whom the programs reach. Probably the most severe problem is inability to conceptualize what education for the future might be and how individuals can know how or what to prepare themselves for throughout their work lives if continuing education calls for more than merely "keeping up to date" in one's present occupation. Is the concept itself realistic?

GOVERNMENT PROGRAMS FOR DISADVANTAGED PERSONS

The 1996 welfare legislation, which mandates the movement of states' caseloads into work situations within two years, renewed public interest in the gov-

Table 6.2
Participation in Adult Education, by Occupation and Income

	Total labor force 189,543,000 / Number taking courses 76,261,000	Adult-education participant's reason for course			
		Personal or social	Advance on the job	Train for a new job	Complete degree or diploma
Percent of total	40	44	54	11	10
Occupation					
Professional	73	37	74	8	10
Executive, administrative, managerial	57	37	76	8	10
Technical, sales, and related support	69	32	73	9	11
Sales workers	46	41	53	12	11
Administrative support	52	43	62	11	6
Service	47	37	51	14	12
Agriculture, forestry, and fishing	26	40	49	6	12
Precision products, craft, and repair	43	30	62	8	11
Machine operators and assemblers	30	28	58	10	9
Transportation and machine moving	29	25	60	13	12
Handlers, equipment cleaners, helpers and laborers	26	33	43	24	5
Non-classifiable, undetermined	59	35	71	6	4

	Total labor force 189,543,000 Number taking courses 76,261,000	Adult-education participant's reason for course			
		Personal or social	Advance on the job	Train for a new job	Complete degree or diploma
Percent of total	40	44	54	11	10
Income					
Under $10,000	23	48	25	20	12
$10,001 to $15,000	27	51	32	17	10
$15,001 to $20,000	32	45	38	15	12
$20,000 to $25,000	31	47	44	13	11
$25,001 to $30,000	38	45	38	15	12
$30,001 to $40,000	43	45	55	11	9
$40,001 to $50,000	47	41	61	10	8
$50,001 to $75,000	52	39	67	7	8
$75,001 and above	58	43	64	7	8

Source: 1997 Statistical Abstract of the United States: Washington, D.C.: Government Printing Office, Table 312.

ernment-training programs for the poor, disadvantaged, or welfare population. Since the 1960s several programs have been launched for the purpose of transforming the most marginally employable persons into credible job candidates through a variety of "quick fixes."

Succession of Programs for the Disadvantaged

For the purpose of describing the extent of efforts made in the recent past on behalf of the target groups, the major Congressional endeavors are listed here. The intent is neither to blind the eyes nor to test the reader's memory for acronyms, but rather to convey some of the reasons for the frustration felt by some members of Congress, planners, and program administrators regarding employment efforts for the targeted groups. The Manpower Development and Training Act of 1962 (MDTA), a Great Society program, initiated the practice of offering job-training programs that specifically targeted the poor. The Comprehensive Employment and Training Act (CETA) programs of 1973 came next, followed by the Joint Training Partnership Act (JTPA) programs of 1983, which are still in operation. Additional programs, specific to welfare (AFDC) recipients, are: the Community Work and Training Program (CWEPs) of 1962, the Work Experience and Training Program, an offspring of the Economic Opportunity Act of 1964; and the Work Incentive Programs (WIN) of 1967 and 1971.

Currently existing programs, whether aimed at the poor, in general, or at welfare recipients, in particular, often represent meldings of the flow of mandates of successive programs throughout the years, which makes for inconsistencies, overlaps, obsolescence, and the general lack of any comprehensive set of approaches, population targets, or accountability. In short, they equate to a vast nonsystem that, in 1995, consumed $20.4 billion. Actually, the hodgepodge is worse than it seems: each state runs its own programs, which translates into even more chaos. One stated goal of the 1996 welfare-reform legislation is to encourage consolidation of this myriad of programs by giving to the states block grants for job training and the freedom to use them at their discretion. Some skeptics, however, fear that the ultimate goal is elimination of the programs by the states, now freed of mandates (Grubb 1996).

As of October 1996 Federal subsidies for state welfare programs are available to states that move at least 20 percent of adult welfare recipients into employment or some form of *work experience* within two years. A likely, resulting scenario is that a tremendous burden is placed upon states in which job markets cannot rapidly absorb so many marginal workers. In such cases, the states are expected to create "work experience" situations in which recipients "work off" their welfare checks. The financial burden borne by the states will affect the decisions they make concerning future job-training programs within their jurisdiction.

The Federal government's programs for the disadvantaged have been heavily criticized over the years for their emphasis on services for the target populations, as opposed to actual job-skills training. These programs have usually included such components as literacy education; "socialization for work"; short-term work experiences, perhaps in a government or charitable facility; help with job-hunting; and a few weeks of job training in a specific occupational area. Child daycare, health care, and help with transportation to work are often included in programs, as well.

Since their appearance in the 1960s, evaluation of these Federal job-training programs has become a minor industry. The approach has been to measure program "success" or "failure" in terms of whether the graduate finds employment; whether he or she earns more than similar persons who have not been through the training program under evaluation; and how much welfare payments have been decreased. The general consensus, according to Grubb (1996), is that many, but not all, programs lead to small but statistically significant increases in employment and earnings, and, for welfare recipients, to small decreases in payments. Since cost-per-benefit analyses usually show that the social benefits outweigh the costs, the programs are often considered to be worth doing at least in that regard. But the gains in employment and earnings are too small to move families out of poverty or off welfare, and they decrease over time. Upward mobility into middle-class occupations is unlikely for participants in these programs, which last only a few weeks.

Future Directions: Utilization of the School-to-Work Model

W. Norton Grubb, an outstanding authority on these programs, sees opportunity for improvement of the hodgepodge of programs, which he describes as too narrowly conceived, too short-term, and generally too limited to make much difference in the lives of participants. Grubb cites their lack of integration with basic education as the main reason for the ineffectuality of job-training programs, beginning with initial efforts in the 1960s. He notes that a model for achieving this integration exists in the 1994 School-to Work Opportunities Act (SWOA), which provides for the development of hierarchies of educational attainment.

Utilizing the SWOA model, Grubb would have student participants begin in the lowest-level, work-based programs, those that emphasize "work experience" (work created primarily to benefit the trainee). While their participation at this stage might meet their immediate needs, the students would not be cut off from mainstream education and the possibility of progressing upward as their capabilities increase. To illustrate this proposal Grubb suggests that program participants might first take short-term job-training courses (15–30 weeks) in such venues as community-based organizations, community colleges, area vocational schools, or private firms. Hopefully, such "work-based learning" experience would be sufficient to establish the trainees in the world of work. But past experience has taught that the rewards for attainable entry-level jobs are meager, so opportunities should not end here.

Individuals who adjust to employment should be able to move on to more advanced work-based learning, Grubb suggests. For such intermediate level job-training, he proposes making use of community colleges' certificate programs. These first two levels of training, Grubb believes, can lead to only relatively unskilled work and, at each level, would require remedial work and generous provision of services, such as career guidance, tutoring, and child care. To move higher into moderately skilled employment, Grubb still recommends work-based learning, but in the context of cooperative education experiences. Associate degree programs offered by a community college or technical institute are the most obvious vehicles for ascendance, at this point. To move into middle-skilled employment, a four-year baccalaureate-degree program is seen as necessary. In short, the two-year and four-year college degree programs, the technical institutes' programs, and the community colleges' certificate programs represent high schools' "first chance" programs. The short-term job-training programs for welfare populations and other depressed groups have been "second chance" programs that have failed to serve their populations satisfactorily.

Summary of Recommendations for Future Training Efforts

Given the number of questions raised about job-associated training, as opposed to initial, formal-educational investments, for present and would-be members of the workforce, it is appropriate to point to some directions for future efforts. They may be summarized as follows:

1. Greater employer participation in employment training is to be encouraged, because it will produce training that is most likely to be demand-based.
2. Improvements in vocational education and training must be considered in terms of the different needs and points of delivery (public or private) of the three different components: entry level, further, and remedial.
3. Employees should be represented in the design of programs to ensure that general, as well as firm-specific skills be taught. Without employee participation, programs would be too narrow.
4. Development of a national program to certify skill attainment, called for in the Perkins Act, should be pushed. This would encourage more general training and make certificate holders more employable and more mobile. Such effort needs to be coordinated with the work of the National Conference of Governors who have been engaged for several years in writing standards for skill attainment.
5. The goals of the School-to-Work Act, the development of a cohesive, comprehensive transitional program for all non–college-bound youths, which ultimately will arm them with respected credentials leading to a skilled job, should be supported.
6. Programs must be backed by adequate funding, a goal of the Perkins Act. This means convincing a belt-tightening public that vocational education and training are priority spending items.
7. New jobs must be constantly developed, and obsolete jobs discarded, if any educational program is to enjoy even the possibility of success.

In addition to the above recommendations, the present writer proposes that, in view of the consensus favoring employer-based training, Congress should attempt to create incentives for employers to continually invest in the education of their employees. Also, means must be found to encourage individuals to actively pursue additional training throughout their work lives. Before individuals can be expected to make informed choices as to directions of their efforts, however, we need to have much clearer ideas as to what types of curricula are likely to be useful for various groups of workers, including welfare recipients. At this point a large percentage of the prescriptions for the future lack much earthly substance. Yes, we should all continually prepare ourselves for the future, and reintegrate work and training for the most deprived among us. But how? And what might our expectations be if we retrain?

Readers interested in training programs abroad should refer to Lisa M. Lynch's *Training and the Private Sector: International Comparisons* (1994b). Readers interested in the subject of transitional school-to-work programs may refer to the work of Hollenbeck (1996 and 1997) and Stern and colleagues (1994). The most comprehensive book on job-training for welfare populations in the United States is Norton Grubb's *Learning to Work: the Case for Reintegrating Job Training and Education* (1996).

NOTES

1. Baran and Parsons (1986) and other recent researchers claim that no evidence exists to uphold this widespread belief. For example, many employers pay college tuition for their professionals and managerial employees without lowering salaries. Other researchers (Lilard and Tan 1986; Carnevale and Johnson 1989) point out that in the real world the differences between job-specific and general or portable training are blurred.

2. This refers to services directly purchased by private enterprise.

3. The Department of Labor favors the first two terms, while the Department of Education appears to favor the last.

REFERENCES

Anderson, Lowell D. 1992. Relationship of technology education to tech-prep. Paper presented at the Mississippi Industrial Teacher Educational Annual Conference, Chicago, Ill. November.

Baran, Barbara, and Carl Parsons. 1986. Technology and skill: a literature review. Prepared for the Carnegie Forum on Education and the Economy. January.

Bartel, Ann. 1991. Productivity gains from the implementation of employee training programs. NBER Working Paper 3026.

———. 1992. Training, wage growth and job performance: evidence from a company database. NBER Working Paper 4027.

Benson, George. 1996. How much do employers spend on training? *Training and Development* (October): 56–58.

Bishop, John. 1994. Formal training and its impact on productivity, wages, and innovation. In L. Lynch, ed. *Training and the private sector: international comparisons*. Chicago: University of Chicago Press.

Bragg, Debra. 1994. Emerging tech prep models: promising approaches to educational reform. *Centerfocus* 5 (June): 1–7.

———. 1996. The status of tech prep in the United States. Paper presented at the American Vocational Association Convention, Cincinnati, Ohio. 6 December.

Carnevale, Anthony, and Janet Johnson. 1989. *Job-related learning: private strategies and public policies*. Washington D.C.: Government Printing Office.

Carnevale, Anthony, and colleagues, eds. 1990. *New developments in worker training: a legacy for the 1990s*. Madison, Wisc.: Industrial Relations Research Association.

Collins, Michael, and Ronald Carvero. 1992. Part two: should adult and continuing education strive for professionalization? *New Directions for Adult and Continuing Education* 54 (Summer): 35–50.

Commission on the Skills of the American Work Force. 1990. *America's choice: high skills or low wages*. Washington, D.C.: National Center on Education and the Economy.

Congressional Quarterly Almanac. 1990. Vocational education act provisions, 620–23.

———. 1994a. National education goals set: 397–99.

———. 1994b. Clinton signs School-to-Work Act,: 400.

Dejardin, Conrad, and Nancy Kothernbeutel. 1992. The comprehensive community college: who took "comprehensive" and "community" away? *Community Services Catalyst* 22 (Summer): 19–21.

Eininger, Max U. 1964. *The process and product of T & I high school level vocational education in the United States.* Pittsburgh, Pa.: American Institutions for Research.

Eurich, Neil. 1991. *The learning industry.* Report of the Carnegie Foundation. New York: Carnegie Foundation.

Ferman, Louis, et al. 1990. *New developments in worker training: a legacy for the 1990s.* Madison, Wisc.: Industrial Relations and Research Association.

Frazis, Harley, Diane Herz, and Michael Horrigan. 1995. Employer-provided training: results from a new survey. *Monthly Labor Review* 118 (May): 3–17.

Frazis, Harley, and colleagues. 1998. Results from the 1995 survey of employer-provided training. *Monthly Labor Review* 121 (June): 3–13.

Grasso, John, and John Shea. 1979. *Vocational education and training: impact on youth.* Berkeley, Cal.: Carnegie Council on Policy Studies of Higher Education.

Grubb, W. Norton. 1996. *Learning to work: the case for reintegrating job training and education.* New York: Russell Sage Foundation.

Gustman, Alan L., and Thomas Steinmeirer. 1982. The relation between vocational training in high school and economic outcomes. *Industrial and Labor Relations Review* 36 (October): 73–82.

Hollenbeck, Kevin. 1996. An evaluation of the manufacturing technology partnership (MTP) program. Upjohn Institute Technical Report #96–007.

———. 1996. In their own words: student perspectives on school-to-work programs. Washington, D.C.: National Institute for Work and Learning.

———. 1997. School-to-work: promise and effectiveness. *Employment Research* (Fall): 5–7.

Imel, Susan. 1996. Tech prep: trends and issues alerts. ERIC Clearing House on Adult Career and Vocational Education, Columbus, Ohio.

Kane, Thomas, and Cecilia Rouse. 1993. Labor market returns to two and four-year colleges: is a credit a credit and do degrees matter? Mimeograph, Harvard University.

Lilard, Lee, and Hong W. Tan. 1986. Private sector training: who gets it and what are its effects? Santa Monica, Cal.: Rand Corporation. March.

Lynch, Lisa M. 1991a. Private sector training and skill formation in the United States. In G. Libecap, ed., *Advances in the Study of Entrepreneurship, Innovation, and Economic Growth.* 5: 117–45.

———. 1991b. The role of off-the-job vs on-the-job training for the mobility of women workers. *American Economic Review* (May): 151–56.

———. 1992. Different effects of post-school training on early career mobility. NBER Working Paper No. 4034.

———. 1994a. Payoffs to alternative training strategies at work. In R. Freeman, ed. *Working under different rules.* Washington, D.C.: National Bureau of Economic Research.

———, ed. 1994b. *Training and the private sector: international comparisons.* Chicago: University of Chicago Press.

———, and Sandra Black. 1998. Beyond the incidence of employer-provided training. *Industrial and Labor Relations Review* 52 (October): 64–79.

Marshall, Ray, and Marc Tucker. 1992. *Thinking for a living.* New York: Basic Books.

Osterman, Paul. 1990. Elements of a national training policy. In Louis Ferman et al. *New developments in worker training: a legacy for the 1990s.* Madison, Wisc.: Industrial Relations Research Association, 257–82.

Pearce, Sandra. 1992. Survival of continuing higher education: deans' perceptions of external threats. *Journal of Continuing Higher Education* 40 (Spring): 2–7.

Silverberg, Marsha. 1996. Building school-to-work systems on a tech-prep foundation: the status of school-to-work features in tech-prep initiatives. Mathematica Policy Research, Princeton, N.J.

———. and Alan M. Hershey. 1995. The emergence of tech-prep at the state and local levels. Mathematica Policy Research, Princeton, N. J.

Stern, David, and colleagues. 1994. *Research on school-to-work transition programs in the United States.* Berkeley, Cal.: National Center for Research in Vocational Education.

———. 1997. *Statistical Abstract of the United States, 1997.* Washington, D.C.: Government Printing Office, Table 312.

U.S. Department of Labor. Bureau of Labor Statistics. 1996. BLS reports the amount of employer-provided formal training. USDL 96-268, 10 July.

Part III

Initial Entry into the
Labor Force and Recruitment

How youths manage their entry into the labor force is a multiface-
ted subject. The next three chapters discuss three aspects of this
question. Chapter 7 takes up the subject in terms of the career concept, presenting the dominant views on how career choice is established. Chapter 8 describes how occupational entry is limited by
members (insiders) intent on preserving a monopoly on occupational membership and concurrent privileges. Chapter 9 focuses on
methods utilized by occupational aspirants to locate work situations of choice for themselves, as well as those used by recruiters of
new employees.

7

Career Choice and Initial Entry

This chapter discusses specific steps taken by people choosing a vocation. Although there is general agreement that most occupational decision-making is not a particularly informed process, considerable controversy exists as to the weights placed by youths on such competing factors as level of demand, likely financial returns, and personal qualifications and preferences.

THE CAREER CONCEPT

From the viewpoint of the individual, a career involves the whole of the individual's work life, encompassing past work history, present occupation, and plans for the future (Krause 1971). A person may work in one or more occupations, for one employer, or for a series of employers. The term career is sometimes used in a popular sense, to indicate seriousness or stability (she is a "career" housewife or mother; he is a "career" policeman). The career, seen as a person's work-life history, is experienced; it cannot be viewed as a whole until it is completed.

How much control the individual has over his/her career is always a question. As will be shown, analysts of different disciplines attribute dominant roles to different factors in the making of the "choice." The behavioral psychologists emphasize personality factors; the sociologists, preexisting socioeconomic conditions; the economists, broader environmental happenings that affect entry into certain occupations during a particular time span, especially anticipation of lifetime earnings. At the same time each discipline accepts the relevance of factors emphasized by the others.

One contemporary issue involving career choice is whether any choice, however carefully planned, will be viable over the work life of the individual. Whether or not lifetime employment in one occupation remains a viable option, the expectation of remaining with one particular employer has been abandoned over the past decade or so. This chapter does not delve into those complexities, but is confined to career choice and first entry into the workforce. It is impossible to say with any certainty how a youth can best position him/herself, at career onset, for a series of changes, in terms of employers and perhaps occupations as well, over a lifetime.

PSYCHOLOGISTS' VIEWS ON CAREER CHOICE

Psychologists' analyses of how youths make their initial decisions to enter an occupation have attracted more attention than those of other professions and so will be discussed first. The summary below of the major concepts of the two most influential psychologists of our period, Donald Super and John Holland, leans heavily on Samuel Osipow (1983), a major interpreter. Both Super and Holland have large numbers of disciples whose work is based on the concepts outlined below.

Super's Views

Super emphasizes the role of a person's *self-concept* or self-perception, an image that develops and becomes modified over time as the individual matures and reacts to new experiences and a changing sense of reality. Super (1957) views the self-concept and, concurrently, the direction of career interests as changing throughout the work life of the individual.

In Super's scheme of career choice, the most important element is the exploratory stage, which he divides into three periods: the tentative substage, the transition substage, and the advancement substage. The exploratory stage typically begins in early childhood, influencing education and sometimes leading directly to a first-time vocational decision. With continuing growth and enhanced experience, these first decisions tend to be altered, and they crystallize as the youth enters the mature stage of career exploration.

According to Super, individuals must master five vocational developmental tasks over the course of their careers, as follows:

1. Crystallization, usually occurring between ages fourteen and eighteen
2. Specification, eighteen to twenty-one
3. Implementation, twenty-one to twenty-four
4. Stabilization within the chosen occupation, twenty-five to thirty-five
5. Consolidation and advancement, late thirties and forties.

Crystallization involves coming to a clear self-understanding and conclusion as to an appropriate field of work for the person, still broadly defined. For example, the youth might decide to go into some aspect of health care or some field of construction. Specification requires the youth to move forward from the general to a more specific vocational category. For example, a would-be engineer surveys the various fields of engineering and decides to focus on electrical engineering as a career goal; an education-oriented youth might narrow his/her options to one of the various educational levels. Implementation of the vocational preference requires the youth to take preparatory study and obtain an entry-level position in the occupation of choice.[1]

Essentially, Super argues that people engage in age-related tasks involving aspects of vocational life, each of which prepares them for subsequent stages over their lifetimes. The better they prepare for and engage in each vocational development task, the more satisfactory the following stage is likely to be. Each life stage calls for a different type of vocational behavior. The theory assumes that people have the capability to enter many vocations, but that most are likely to perform better in some than others. Also, when people enter that kind of employment that affords them the opportunity to utilize their particular abilities and that engages their interests, they feel a sense of personal gratification. Ultimate choices evolve out of a series of successful life experiences, from the early years on.

Congruence. Super and his followers stress this concept, the fit between the individual's vocational choice and self concept. The quality of the fit depends on the degree of emotional maturity with which each individual performs the vocational development tasks. But environmental factors, such as family finances and educational level, are also seen as affecting the person's vocational decision-making and ultimate achievements. Success in academics and sports, participation in other types of extracurricular activities, and independent behavior factor in as well.

Self-efficacy. The concept of self-efficacy, the individual's confidence in his/her ability to successfully accomplish the basic vocational development tasks, has been used in recent years to flesh out Super's theory. Primary sources of *self-efficacy* have been identified as vicarious learning, performance accomplishments, psychological arousal, and verbal persuasion (Bandura 1986). Self-efficacy is believed to affect career choices, as well as later career behavior (Betz 1991). People tend to be attracted to career paths in which they feel their self-efficacy is high and to avoid those in which they feel it is low. Weak self-efficacy expectations are thought to explain the tendency of many women to avoid male-dominated occupations. Psychologists of the Super school believe that vocational counselors have a role in improving people's self-efficacy.

Career Education. Development of the Career Education movement, a series of organized efforts to expose youths to information about occupational possibilities from an early age, has been attributed to the influence of Super and associates, particularly Super and Overstreet (1960) who, on the basis of their studies of the vocational maturity of ninth-grade boys, recommended that schools, beginning in primary school, should encourage vocational thinking, without pressing for premature vocational decision-making. Before leaving Super and his school behind, it is important to note the time-relatedness of their formulations, their assumptions of life-long association with one occupation (and one or two employers) as the norm under attack today.

Holland's Views

John Holland's work in the area of career choice and career entry has perhaps been even more influential than Super's. According to Holland, whose seminal work has been widely tested by himself and many of his students, individuals differ in their interests and aptitudes for particular types of work due to inherited characteristics, interests, and environmental influences (especially the values of their parents). These factors meld to develop a particular type of person who requires a certain type of work to fulfill his/her interests and utilize his/her competence. Holland's theory deals with how types of people come to enter types of work appropriate to their needs and abilities (1959, 1985).

Holland proffers that a matching process occurs in which the person finds the occupational environment in which his/her needs and competence come into congruence with the demands of the occupation. The quality of the match can be measured by such variables as consistency, differentiation, and identity of the Holland code-type with the type of person. The ultimate test is whether a good person-environment fit is obtained. One complaint about Holland's topology of occupations is that it is male-oriented. However, subsequent work has shown the model to be relevant for women. Holland's topology, for which he is noted, is shown on Figure 7.1.

Most people undertake employment, according to this theory, in an occupation that includes their personal vocational orientation type or the type most closely associated with it. Research findings indicate that the relationship between the six orientations can be configured roughly in hexagonal form. The placement of the orientations on the hexagon indicate their relationships to each other. Those placed closest to each other have the most in common, while those furthest apart include occupations calling for personality traits that are the most dissimilar.

Holland has attempted to demonstrate that some people (and some occupations) are more similar or different than others. Thus, the occupations appearing next to each other on the hexagon, in Figure 7.1, are most similar to each other and those farthest away, most dissimilar. Holland points out that many persons who are one type actually work in an alternative, similar-type occupational group. For example, persons who would prefer to work in an unconventional occupation might accept a job in a realistic one; an artistic type might end up in a social occupation.

The uniqueness of Holland's work lies in the key concept that people identify their personal vocational preferences with stereotypes represented by occupational titles. Holland built on this identification with job titles to develop a system of vocational counseling based on *self-discovery* of the occupational titles that most closely correspond with the individual's interests, capabilities, and personality needs. Satisfactory choice, Holland and his followers believe, depends on both the adequacy of the person's self-knowledge and information about the occupation selected. Thus, both Super and Holland emphasize the importance of information. Readers may recall having been exposed to Holland's Vocational Preference Inventory or his Self-Directed Search exercise in high school or college, as part of career counseling activities.

Holland does not have much to say about how people acquire their personal orientation (type), but he and like-minded researchers have investigated events in the external circumstances that mold or reinforce membership once it has been established. They have identified family and school experiences as the major contributors. Self-evaluation and self-knowledge are also major influences on career choice. Underlying all of this is the notion that the more clearly an individual understands (has knowledge of) the nature of work associated with each personality orientation (realistic, investigative, social, conventional, enterprising,

Figure 7.1
The Holland Hexagon

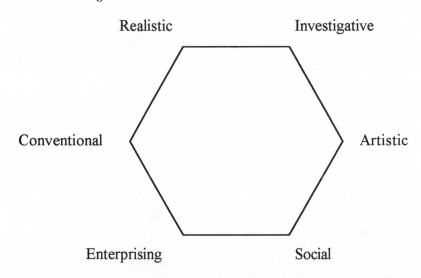

Realistic   Investigative

Conventional   Artistic

Enterprising   Social

Source: Adapted and reproduced by special permission of the Publisher, Psychological Assessment Resources, Inc., 16102 N. Florida Avenue, Lutz, Florida 33549, from the *Dictionary of Holland Occupational Codes* by Gary D. Gottfredson, Ph. D. and John L. Holland, Ph. D., Copyright, 1982, 1989, 1996.

and artistic), the more firmly established will be his/her personal hierarchy of preferences. Examples of occupations associated with each work-and-environment type are the following:

realistic type: farmer, professor of engineering, construction engineer;
investigative type: anthropologist; computer designer, medical researcher;
social type: minister, high school teacher, social worker;
conventional type: clerk, accountant, records supervisor;
enterprising type: salesperson, auctioneer, business executive;
artistic type: musician, furniture designer, writer.

Both Super and Holland have influenced several generations of psychologists who continue to use and further develop their concepts, without changing the basic insights that they advance.

Role of Social Class in Career Choice

In recent years psychologists have recognized a role for *social class* in career choice but have not yet done enough work in this area to offer a well-established body of explanations. In a 1995 book two leading theorists (Osipow and Fitzgerald) acknowledged that social class affects a whole range of issues involving career choice, including access to knowledge about occupational possibilities and the resources necessary for career preparation. An amalgam of economic, prestige, and power aspects of a person's circumstances, social class also affects the reactions of others to one's ambitions and efforts toward attainment (Rossides 1990). According to a review of recent literature (1990–96), the modest number of studies by sociologists on social class show little consistency, but they do indicate that prestige aspirations are highly correlated with social class and the self-confidence with which youths approach vocational choice, as well as their beliefs concerning ability to control and achieve. Occupational prestige was found to be more important to students from families of higher social class than lower (Brown et al. 1996).

Role of Gender in Career Choice

Two competing gender-related notions concerning women's career aspirations are the *socialization dominance* and the *opportunity dominance* hypotheses. The first holds that only fundamental changes in early socialization of females could change the direction of their interests, while the second posits that wider opportunities by mere fact of their existence could cause females to redirect their career goals (Harmon 1989). Unsurprisingly, psychologists have tended to investigate vocational behavior related to socialization factors.

The socialization dominance theorists, when confronted with the increasing entry of women into traditionally male-dominated fields, have attempted to explain the phenomenon away on the basis that the tradition-breakers have unique backgrounds. Examples of traits deemed to lead to breaking of the norms are attendance at a single-sex school, lack of math fear, and strong support from professors or parents (Murrel, Frieze, and Frost 1991). Meanwhile, the changing demographic profiles of entrants into some formerly male-dominated occupations suggest that women (and minorities) tend to enter formerly male bastions as men leave, which further contributes to the devaluation of the occupation. These movements of men "out" and women and minorities "in" point to the importance of greater attainability as the force behind such changes in the populations of occupations. The successful invasion of relatively large numbers of women into many formerly closed fields suggests that vocational researchers should shift their attention to other areas. But such directions would not be central to standard psychological theories, so the behaviorists tend to ignore them. Curiously, their own profession is one that has been drastically feminized.

The college-bound female has preempted the attention of researchers, with the result that little is known about the decision-making processes of blue-collar and other nonprofessional women (about 80% of the female workforce). According to one exceptional study (Mazen and Lemkau 1990), blue-collar and other nonprofessional women in nontraditional occupations are more active, assertive, dependable, and task-oriented than professional women, conclusions which do not differ from findings concerning nontraditional professional women.

Career Choice-Making by Minority Group Youths

Do youths from minority groups go about making career choices in ways that depart from the established norms? The little that is known about African-American, Hispanic, and Asian-American youths' career decision-making behaviors is summarized here.

African Americans. The few investigators of African-American choice-making processes criticize standard theorists for failing to account for the effects of discrimination and inadequacy of career information and guidance (Cheatham 1990; Miller et al. 1992). A major finding of the few active investigators of black students' career choice-making is that, while self-esteem and levels of aspiration tend to be high, belief in ability to achieve aspirations lags (Hughes and Demo 1989). But according to another small study (Evans and Herr 1994), the career aspirations of African-American students could not be predicted by their racial identity attitudes or perceptions of discrimination. So it may be, as in the case of women, that the most important career choice considerations among African Americans are the current state of the economy and perceptions concerning availability of opportunities in fields not heavily penetrated by persons of color.

Hispanics. Even less is known about career choice-making among Hispanics. A highly diverse group, about which generalizations are unwise, the majority are Mexicans (about 50%); the second largest group are Puerto Ricans (15%). A review of Hispanic vocational choices by Arbona (1990) emphasizes differences in vocational behaviors by national origin and social class, pointing out that the failure of most studies to take social class into account casts doubts as to the reliability of reports of differences in Hispanic vocational behavior from the Anglo norm. Noting that Hispanics lag behind other groups in terms of educational and occupational attainment, Arbona debunks earlier, culturally deterministic theories concerning the allegedly negative role of Hispanic culture in discouraging high career aspirations among youth, aligning herself with those who attribute lack of upward mobility to inferior opportunities (Kuvlesky and Patella 1971). In general, Arbona concluded that the small amount of literature available makes the case that Hispanic youths are desirous of climbing the occupational ladder and that parents' values do not inhibit them. Rather, the realities of life (economic status of parents, perceived discrimination, difficulties in obtaining necessary education, etc.) tend to reduce their ability to attain their goals.

In regard to vocational interests of Hispanic high-school and college students, a major finding is that their personality traits seem to fit the Holland model (Hansen 1987; Harrington and O'Shea 1980; Montoya and DeBlassie 1985). Arbona concluded that the vocational-interest literature suggests that Hispanic-American students' views concerning employment and vocations strongly parallel those of the dominant culture and that the Holland model is applicable in understanding and guiding them.

Asian Americans. Still less is known about the career decision-making and early-entry decisions of Asian Americans, also a diverse group. A rare review of ethnic-identity issues (Leong and Chou 1994) discusses career choice in terms of the *level* of *acculturation* of individuals. Acculturation refers to the adaptation of individuals and groups from one culture to another and the level of comfort they feel in the new environment, a factor in their functioning. Career choice for Asian Americans, several researchers speculate, may be affected more by cultural factors than by personal needs. In this light, priority may be given to the possibility of meeting financial obligations of self and family; success may be sought more for the honor it brings to the family than to satisfy the job-seeking individual (Leong and Serafica 1995). Since Asian cultures emphasize collectivism, not individualism, career choice may be regarded in the light of the possibility of making contributions to the group (Leong and Gim 1995). A comparative study of the influence of parental pressures on career choice found that, of African Americans, Chicanos and/or Latinos, Asian Americans, and European-American students, only Asian Americans reported parents' wishes to be among the top five reasons for determining their occupational choice (Gim 1992).

Despite the perception that employment discrimination persists, the reviewers proffer that Asian Americans suffer from the "success" stereotype that is attributed to them. Actually, Asian Americans are distributed bimodally, one group being highly educated and successful; the other, poorly educated and less successful (Brown and Brooks 1991). It is safest to merely say, in view of the limited data, that this group's career entry does not appear to be significantly different than for the majority group, and that, although career choice may be affected by cultural factors, career development is more of a problem than choice or entry.

SOCIOLOGISTS' VIEWS

When analyzing career choice and initial entry, sociologists focus on socioeconomic background and other factors outside individuals' control. The factors that most heavily influence personal decision-making in this view are family background, social attitudes of others, availability of resources, institutional factors, and impersonal labor markets. All these are believed to limit individual choice and ability to proceed toward implementation of personal preferences. Therefore, the work of sociologists does not attract much attention since it permits little room for personal inputs into career/occupational outcomes.

As outlined by Duane Brown, Linda Brooks, and Associates (1990), there are two basic, competing sociological views as to the nature of career attainment as an aspect of occupational mobility, a central issue of sociology. The possibilities for occupational mobility within a society are seen to greatly affect the career choices that youths will make and the types of organizations that they will attempt to penetrate. One sociological view is ensconced in the *status attainment* model; the competing view is the *structural* model.

The Status Attainment Model

According to the most sophisticated formulation of the status attainment model, the Wisconsin model, occupational attainment occurs as a result of "paths of influences," beginning with the influence of parental status on "significant others."[2] In the model individual ability and school achievement combine with parental status as the three initial factors interacting in the *social-psychological processes*—the most important variables that contribute to a youth's decision to undertake a particular vocational path. The outcome of this interaction is a determination of those educational opportunities that will be offered to an individual as a member of a group. Educational attainment, in turn, leads to ultimate occupational attainment.

It is the attitudes of "significant others," various resource allocators and school personnel, such as vocational counselors and teachers, parents, and peers, that make up the milieu of decision-making that starts the process of career determination, according to the Wisconsin model. These "influentials" make the decisions as to the level of education and occupation appropriate to the individual. Their attitudes, in turn, influence career plans, subsequent education, and the ultimate outcome, the occupational status achieved by the individual. A great deal of empirical research based on several versions of the status attainment model tends to uphold its basic premises, according to Brown and Brooks.

The Structuralist Approach

The *structuralists*, critics of the status attainment approach, downplay the role of individual preferences, ability, and levels of initiative in determining career choice and occupational entry. Rather, they see youths as being *allocated* into educational and employment tracks, that is, they espouse a labor-market-segmentation orientation in which entry into various fields is blocked to many youths irrespective of merit or demand (Kerckhoff 1976). In its most extreme form, the structuralist approach holds that the blockages are associated with race and gender.

Geographic location, rural versus urban, has traditionally been a variable used by the structuralists to explain differences in career choice and entry tendencies. As large-scale state-to-state migration of youths has become substantial, the explanatory power of geographic location has been eroding. Yet, since *most* youths do not migrate, location of residence remains a dimension of inequality of career opportunity built into youths' career perspective, in the structuralist view.

The structuralists reject not only those sociological interpretations that allow that individual initiative has a role in career choice and entry, but also the claims of mainstream economists as encapsulated in *human-capital theory*. They challenge the human-capital economists' basic premise that career choice is primarily, or at least heavily, influenced by youths' calculations of the economic returns of alternative career options.

Much empirical work has been done in an effort to provide validity to the structuralists' positions, but direct evidence of the influence of structural factors on career choice and entry is difficult to produce. Perhaps the most easily studied structural factors are race and gender, discussed in another part of this book. As noted above, there is not much that an individual youth contemplating his career possibilities can do about his/her immediate social milieu, so action-oriented persons tend not to turn to the sociologists for pathway directions.

ECONOMISTS' VIEWS

Economists' views on career choice and initial entry are less well known than those of psychologists and sociologists. Unsurprisingly, they think "money figures." While acknowledging the importance of individual appraisals of personal abilities and preferences, economists believe that the primary motivators of youthful occupational choices are (1) the relative financial returns from alternative occupational possibilities and (2) the availability of job (career) opportunities. Underlying economists' views is *competitive markets theory*, the theory that wages rise and fall according to the level of current demand for each occupation and the extent of available supply.

According to the economic version of career choice, youths calculate potential lifetime earnings of alternative career choices, taking into consideration *opportunity costs*, which are held to be earnings foregone during the period of education/training and expenses incurred in the process of career preparation, such as the cost of tuition, books, and board. To determine *present value* of alternative careers, students are said to *discount* the value of projected life-time earnings, measured in dollars as prospective earnings are worth less than money presently held in hand. Youths are said to weigh the utility of alternative careers, comparing the goods and services purchasable with income from each against the others. The career chosen is that which maximizes utility for the individual.

Richard Freeman (1971, 1976), long one of the most influential U.S. economists, believes that students also include in their calculations perquisites associated with their choices, such as attractive working conditions in the executive suite for managers, long vacations for schoolteachers, and so forth. Freeman posits that the weights assigned by youths from well-to-do families to the several versions of career choice differ from those assigned by youths from less affluent families. This is because income from unearned sources makes it possible for well-to-do youths to give greater consideration to the nonfinancial rewards of an occupation. Youths, he holds, calculate the utility of every prominent aspect of an occupation in determining their choice. Embroidered explanations of Freeman's ideas are to be found in any contemporary labor economics textbook.

The College Premium

Currently, higher education is seen as the key to enhancement of earning power. Little attention has been paid to the fact that the relative advantage of the more educated over the less varies over time. Freeman, in another influential work entitled *The Over-Educated American* (1976), predicted a fall in the rewards for education, the so-called *college premium* (which is expressed in terms of the ratio between the earnings of a four-year college graduate and those of a high school graduate). Writing initially in the 1970s, Freeman reasoned that a preexisting excess of educated persons would result in the lowering of wages/salaries. Fall in demand would occur, said Freeman, due to two factors: lessening in demand on the part of industries that have traditionally absorbed large numbers of college graduates during the same period in which an unusually large number of youths were ready to enter the labor force (a demographic aberration). Due to the presence of excess supply of the college-educated in the labor market, wages did fall during the 1970s, which caused much gloom among the public. Comments such as "It doesn't pay to go to college" became prevalent. Whether such assertions were accurate is beside the point; the fact was that public confidence in the education road to economic success had eroded. But this situation did not remain for long; as Freeman had also predicted, the returns on education began to rise again during the 1980s when the number of youths available to enter the labor force was much smaller than during the 1970s.

The college premium has continued to rise since Freeman made these observations. In 1969, for full-time, year-round male workers, age twenty-five and over, the premium was 1.39; by 1974–75 it had fallen to 1.16 (BLS and Census

Bureau, in Freeman 1977). But by 1989 the ratio rose to 1.45; and by 1993 and 1994 it was still higher, at 1.56 (*Digest of Education Statistics* 1996). The 1990–1991 recession did not appear to depress the college advantage, throughout these years, though the advantage fell very slightly in 1992 to 1.52. According to Freeman, the college premium of each period will represent a response to two factors: level of demand for the college-educated; and the size of available supply. The impact of new factors, such as globalization—in this case, the importation of needed personnel—upon compensation levels in relevant fields remains to be seen.

The Cobweb Feedback System

An analysis of the supply of graduates in the range of occupations requiring higher education has led to identification of a pattern of occupational supply known as the *cobweb feedback system* (Freeman 1976). According to the *cobweb* concept, high-school seniors, in the process of choosing the educational path they will enter, tend to look at the market experience of college and graduate students who are securing their degree that year or who graduated during the previous year. The currently graduating seniors tend to choose fields that are offering recent graduates entrance and superior salaries. Likewise, they are prone to avoid those fields that recent graduates are having difficulty penetrating and that are paying less attractive salaries (Freeman 1976).

The above suggests that the labor-market experiences of high-school graduates of four or five years earlier influence the present career decisions of the current crop of high-school graduates. It also suggests that in another four or five years, the currently glutted occupations will experience a shortage and, with jobs abundant and pay necessarily raised to compete for scarce personnel, they will attract many high-school graduates of those years. The "good jobs" situation for aspirants to particular occupations appears to be one of alternating periods of feast or famine.

Evidence of shifting interest in different fields is demonstrable, as in Table 7.1, which shows the academic degrees earned during a couple of two-year periods, twenty years apart. It can be inferred that interest in certain majors rose or fell markedly in the immediate periods prior to the two different sets of years.It is likely, according to human-capital theory, that the operation of the cobweb effect is being seen, and students are choosing fields of study according to their perceptions of the possibilities for good career chances and good earnings. As pointed out earlier, analysis of the economic aspects of career choice, such as these, are often ignored in favor of psychological ones.

FORTUITOUS CHOICE-MAKING

Before ending this description of alternative career choice theories it should be noted that some students of career behavior think that choices tend to be less deliberate and less rational than suggested by the above theories. These rejectionists see youths as tending to consider a number of possibilities, gradually eliminating some in favor of others until a final choice emerges. In the process youths

Table 7.1
Earned Degrees by Selected Fields of Study and Level of Degree, 1970–71 and 1990–91

(in thousands)

	1970–1971			1990–1991		
	Bachelor's	Master's	Doctorate	Bachelor's	Master's	Doctorate
Agriculture and natural resources	12,672	2,457	1,086	13,124	3,295	1,185
Architecture and env'tl. design	5,570	1,705	36	9,781	3,490	135
Business and management	114,865	26,481	807	249,960	78,681	1,243
Communications	10,802	1,856	145	52,799	4,336	274
Computer and information sciences	2,388	1,588	128	25,083	9,324	676
Education	176,614	88,952	6,403	111,010	88,904	6,697
Engineering and eng'g technologies	50,046	16,443	3,638	78,864	24,959	5,272
English and literature	57,026	8,935	1,441	41,712	6,326	1,068
Modern foreign languages	19,057	4,410	704	11,726	1,974	478
Health professions	25,190	5,445	459	59,268	21,228	1,614
Life sciences	35,743	5,728	3,645	39,530	4,765	4,093
Mathematics	24,801	5,191	1,199	14,661	3,615	978
Physical sciences	21,412	6,367	4,390	16,344	5,309	4,290
Psychology	37,880	4,431	1,782	58,451	9,731	3,422
Public affairs	6,252	8,215	185	16,976	18,534	430
Social sciences	155,236	16,476	3,659	124,893	12,069	3,012
Visual and performing arts	30,394	6,675	621	41,854	8,655	836

Source: United States Department of Education. *Digest of Education Statistics*. Washington, D.C.: Government Printing Office, 1993, Tables 267 through 288.

tend to flounder rather than choose: gradually they drift into an occupation, sometimes passing through a series of occupations until finding a niche in one.

The *fortuitous approach,* believed to best describe the behaviors of persons entering occupations that do not require educational preparation, is considered less likely to be adopted by those interested in occupations requiring degrees and formal credentials. However, many college graduates without specialties, those in the liberal arts and humanities, for example, probably find their niches through some process of occupational entry occurring on a nonrational basis (Caplow 1954; Katz and Martin 1962; Pavalko 1971). People are seen as being heavily influenced by random events and influences: a young woman goes to beauty school and brings a nondirected friend with her; a neighbor who works for a certain manufacturing plant recommends a young man for a job in his department. The rejectionist school fulfills no needs for theorists and has not been heard from for many years; nonetheless, some readers may recognize the behaviors it describes. It is quite possible that the fortuitous approach enjoys little popularity because it focuses on the non-college population and embodies no grand theory of happenstance.

NOTES

1. Stabilization and consolidation are tasks of the later career and are not discussed here.

2. Family status, for purposes of this model, is determined by a measure of a father's occupation and education, by means of a graded scale that determines place on a socioeconomic index developed by Duncan (1961).

REFERENCES

Arbona, Consuelo. 1990. Career counseling research: Hispanics: a review of the literature. *The Counseling Psychologist* 18 (April): 300–323.

Bandura, A. 1986. *Social foundations of thought and action: a social cognitive theory.* Englewood Cliffs, N.J.: Prentice Hall.

Betz, N. E. 1991. Twenty years of vocational research: looking back and ahead. *Journal of Vocational Behavior* 37 (November): 305–10.

Brown, Duane, and Linda Brooks. 1991. Ethnicity and race in career counseling, 149–83. In *Career counseling techniques.* Boston: Allyn and Bacon.

Brown, Duane, Linda Brooks, and associates. 1990. *Career choice and development: applying contemporary theories to practice.* 2nd edition. San Francisco: Jossey-Bass Publishers.

Brown, Michael T., and colleagues. 1996. Annual review, 1990–1996: social class, work, and retirement behavior. *Journal of Vocational Behavior* 42 (October): 159–89.

Caplow, Theodore. 1954. *The sociology of work.* New York: McGraw-Hill Book Co.

Cheatham, H. E. 1990. Africentricity and career development of African Americans. *Career Development Quarterly* 3: 333–56.

Duncan, Otis Dudley. 1961. A socioeconomic index for all occupations:115–24. In Reiss, A. .J. Jr., and colleagues, eds. *Occupations and social status.* Stratford, N.H.: Ayer, 1977 (Reprint).

Evans, K. M., and E. L. Herr. 1994. The influence of racial identity and the perception of discrimination on the career aspirations of African American men and women. *Journal of Vocational Behavior* 40 (April): 173–84.

Freeman, Richard. 1971. The economic theory of occupational choice. Chapter 1. *The market for college-trained manpower: a study in the economics of career choice*. Cambridge: Harvard University Press.

———. 1976. *The over-educated American*. New York: Academic Press: 60–62.

———. 1977. Economic rewards to college education. *The Review of Economics and Statistics* 59 (February): 18–29.

Gim, R. H. C. 1992. Cross cultural comparison of factors that influence career choice. Paper presented at the Association for Asian American Studies Conference, San Jose, Cal.

Hansen, J. C. 1987. Cross-cultural research on vocational interests. *Measurements and Evaluations in Counseling and Development* 18: 163–76.

Harmon, Lenore. 1989. Longitudinal changes in women's career aspirations: developmental or historical? *Journal of Vocational Behavior* 35: 46–63.

Harrington, T. F., and A. J. O'Shea. 1980. Applicability of the Holland model (1973) of vocational development with Spanish-speaking clients. *Journal of Counseling Psychology* 27: 246–51.

Holland, John. 1959. A theory of vocational choice. *Journal of Vocational Counseling* (no. 6): 35–45.

———. 1985. *Making vocational choices: a theory of careers*. 2nd ed. Englewood Cliffs, N.J.: Prentice Hall.

Hughes, M., and D. H. Demo. 1989. Self-perceptions of black Americans: self-esteem and personal efficacy. *American Journal of Sociology* 95, no. 1: 132–57.

Katz, Fred, and Harry W. Martin. 1962. Career choice processes. *Social Forces* 41 (December): 149–54.

Kerckhoff, A. C. 1976. The status attainment process: socialization or allocation? *Social Forces* 55, no. 2 : 368–81.

Krause, Elliott A. 1971. *Sociology of occupations*. Boston, Mass.: Little, Brown.

Kuvlesky, W. P., and V. M. Patella. 1971. Degree of ethnicity and aspirations for upward social mobility among Mexican American youth. *Journal of Vocational Behavior* 17, no. 1: 231–44.

Leong, F. T., and F. Serafica. 1995. Career development of Asian Americans: a research area in need of a good theory: 67–102. In F. T. Leong, ed., *Career development and vocational behavior of racial and ethnic minorities*. Mahwah, N.J.: L. Erlbaum.

Leong, Frederick, and E. Chou. 1994. The role of ethnic identity and acculturation in the vocational behavior of Asian Americans: an integrative review. *Journal of Vocational Behavior* 40: 173–84.

———, and R. H. C. Gim. 1995. Career assessment and intervention for Asian Americans, 193–226. In F. T. Leong, ed., *Career development and vocational behavior of racial and ethnic minorities*. Mahwah, N.J.: L. Erlbaum.

Mazen, A., and Jeanne Lemkau. 1990. Personality profiles of women in traditional and nontraditional occupations. *Journal of Vocational Behavior* 36: 4–59.

Miller, L. A., and colleagues. 1992. Perceived barriers to careers involving math and science: the perspectives of medical admissions officials. *Teaching and Learning in Medicine* 4: 9–14.

Montoya, H., and R. R. DeBlassie. 1985. Strong-Campbell interest inventory comparisons between Hispanic and Anglo college students: a research note. *Hispanic Journal of Behavioral Science* 3: 285–89.

Murrel, A. J., I. H. Frieze, and L. Frost. 1991. Aspiring to careers in male and female-dominated professions: a study of black and white college women. *Psychology of Women Quarterly* 15: 103–26.

Osipow, Samuel. 1983. *Theories of career development*. 3rd ed. Englewood Cliffs, N.J.: Prentice Hall.

————, and Louise Fitzgerald. 1995. *Theories of career development*. Needham Heights, Mass.: Allyn and Bacon.

8

Professionalization
of the Workforce

Most people who invest in higher education do so because they want to enter an occupation considered to be a profession. This desire is associated with the belief that establishment in a profession will produce a series of benefits, among them status, prestige, and enhanced earnings. But as college graduates too often discover, attaining a degree, even two degrees, does not necessarily signify attaining a profession. Many degrees are not occupation-specific; many occupations open to degree-holders are neither prestigious nor very remunerative. Just what makes an occupation unique enough to offer the many rewards and privileges of professional status is the subject of this chapter.

In addition, the discussion considers how members of many occupations not associated with "higher learning" work to expand the boundaries associated with and thus include themselves in the world of professionals. This so-called work professionalization seems to have a unique impact on the ability of an individual to enter a desired occupation and function within it. The literature on professionalization is heavy on theory, but very light on empirical evidence as to the consequences of the professionalization movement. Of interest here is the claim that the extent of professionalization of an occupation is what affects both a person's right to perform desired tasks and his/her chances of attaining the privileges associated with that occupation. The power relations involved in the acquisition and maintenance of professional privileges are indicated, as are the means—licensure, certification, and accreditation—through which professional privileges are entrenched. Descriptions are provided of the ongoing efforts of various occupational groups, professional and otherwise, to expand their boundaries and penetrate the territory (monopolies) of others; and the changes in occupational/professional tasks that result from these efforts.

WHAT IS AN OCCUPATION?

An understanding of people's unrelenting efforts to gain professional status for their occupations begins with an understanding of how the full range of employment is built around the concept of occupation. A good definition of occupation is hard to come by, but most available definitions including the following elements: one's employment, vocation, or "calling," with a grouping of various job titles that are closely related in terms of skills and duties, and mention of common roles (functions) and values.

The most commonly used occupational classification is the one utilized by the Census Bureau and is based on the work of Alba Edwards (1943). It consists of the following: managerial and professional specialty; technical, sales, and administrative support, including clerical (white-collar) service occupations; precision production, craft, and repair (skilled blue-collar) operators, fabricators, and laborers (semi- and unskilled blue-collar); and farming, forestry, and fishing. This delineation of the U.S. occupational structure has been criticized as being based on status, rather than function, but, despite some efforts to displace it, it remains the standard job classification system.

THE DRIVE FOR PROFESSIONAL STATUS

Much of the push for higher education today involves young people's desire to attain professional status, which according to the Census Bureau classification equates to becoming part of the first group of occupations listed above. In this chapter, however, the term *profession* is used in a different way. It will be shown that certain occupations, classified by the Census Bureau as professions, are more privileged and more prestigious than others; and that the drive for inclusion of one's occupation in a more prestigious group is fierce and intense, fueled by anticipated financial rewards, associated status, and the privileges gained through a monopoly of employment. Monopoly of employment, used in this context, refers to the exclusive right of a formally organized occupational group to limit the right to perform its occupational tasks to its members, who are given this permission through such means as licensure, certification, or some other form of accreditation, sometimes acquisition of a specified college degree or successful fulfillment of a series of courses.

WHAT IS A PROFESSION?

The professions, as discussed in this chapter, are occupations that involve extensive educational preparation, often followed by certification and/or licensure. With certain exceptions, such as the clergy, the most desired professions tend to bring the highest rewards in terms of money or status. Some professions are more "professionalized" than others. In an era in which a large number of occupations are claiming professional status (undertaking, automotive sales, real estate brokerage), a look at a classification of professions may be helpful.

A useful framework for analysis, provided by Reiss (1955), divides the occupations claiming professional status into five groups, based on level of professionalization: the old, established professions; the new professions; the semiprofessions; the would-be; and the marginal. The *old, established professions* include religion, law, medicine, higher education, the military, and esthetics. These occupations have existed in some form for hundreds, even thousands, of years. The importance of science and technology in modern life has forced the recognition of the *new professions*, which include the various fields of engineering and the physical, natural, and social sciences.

The *semiprofessions* include nursing, social work, teaching, librarianship, and pharmacy.They are denied full professional status on the grounds that their knowledge base is more technical than based on any unique body of knowledge, which is one of the prerequisites for full professional status. These fields are mainly female-dominated and emphasize supervision, which is in conflict with the expectation that a full professional plays an authoritative role based on expertise (Etzioni 1969). Both earnings and status tend to be lower than for more fully professional occupations. Sometimes certain occupations within semiprofessions pay better than full professions, but this is unusual.

The *would-be professions* include many occupational groups involved in dealing with business and government, such as tax collectors, police, personnel staff, funeral directors, and managers of businesses, social agencies, and hospitality centers. Members often possess college educations and may hold positions involving much responsibility. Some may have a high level of expertise, such as computer programmers and systems analysts. The *marginal professions* include occupational groups that perform technical functions, often for professionals. They include medical and dental technicians, laboratory technicians, interpreters, illustrators, and draftsmen. Educational preparation for these occupations is limited and not theory-oriented.

Members of the semiprofessions, the marginals, and the would-bes invest a great deal of effort in their attempts to elevate their status by increasing their level or degree of professionalization. Possible motivations include the desire to maintain a present monopoly on work tasks, or to obtain access to tasks not previously available, by gaining more power against a dominant or competing group (Reiss 1955).

Attributes of a Profession

The traditional standards for acceptance of an occupation as a full-fledged profession, in the United States, grew out of a study designed to reform medical education in the United States, commissioned by the Carnegie Foundation, which culminated in a series of recommendations concerning standards that all privileged occupations, including medicine, should meet in order to justify their special status. These recommendations (Flexner 1910) specified the so-called *attributes of a profession,* criteria that remain, over time, the most clearly delineated guidelines to identifying the occupations that have established themselves as full-fledged professions.They remain the clearest means of differentiating the competing claims of members of the many occupations fighting for official status as "professions." The term "profession" as used here differs from the BLS use of the word to indicate an occupation requiring a college education. The following seven items represent attributes of a profession.

1. Possession of a systematic body of knowledge
2. Professional authority
3. Obligation to uphold community as opposed to self-interest
4. Receipt of community sanction
5. Possession and adherence to a regulative code of ethics
6. A distinct professional culture
7. Recognition by the public as a professional

The demand that an occupation be based on a unique and systematic body of knowledge to be fully professional is perhaps the most stringent of all the conditions to be met. The knowledge must be theoretical in nature, with emphasis on rational, as opposed to traditional, behavior. The demand that professional authority prevail refers to the insistence that the expertise of the practitioner be accepted by the recipient—a client as opposed to a customer—without question. The professional is expected to act not out of self-interest, but to respond first and foremost to the responsibilities and obligations of his profession and community needs. Psychic rewards for service are valued and may be considered more important than monetary returns. Service without remuneration may be required.

The community bolsters the professional's authority by associating it with power. Among these powers are the sole right to conduct occupational training as well as entry, through demanding and authorizing licensure; the right to control practice by demanding adherence to professional norms and values; the right to confidentiality in client-practitioner relationships; and the right to be disciplined only by peers. To provide the means for this self-policing, every full-fledged profession must have a regulative code of ethics. The code also provides the framework for the individual practitioner's standards of behavior.

As for recognition and respect accorded by the public, the most extreme example is the status associated with the medical doctor, a member of perhaps the most prestigious of the old professions, as opposed to the nurse, a semiprofessional. The doctor, traditionally a male, is regarded as an authority; his opinion is requested and honored, and he is highly paid; while the nurse, traditionally a female, is regarded as a helper, is rarely asked for advice nor turned to for consultation either by doctors or patients, and is (usually) paid modestly.The last important characteristic of all professions is a distinctive occupational culture. Group identity, reinforced by long-term training and formal and informal groups, publications, and professional organizations, fosters a feeling of uniqueness and togetherness that causes members to associate with each other informally, professionally, and socially.

Certainly the characteristics of professions, as presented, represent an idealized version of what their originators (Flexner 1910) thought professions ought to be. The principles articulated, however, were effectively used to improve medical education and subsequent practice in the United States. Clearly many of these tenets have been eroded over the years, some by reason of professional self-interest and others by public rejection. And, as will be be shown, power relations play a big role in "which occupations make it" (which is another dimension of the professionalization issue). A reader who wishes to evaluate the degree or level of professionalization of a particular occupation in which he/she is interested might try to estimate *to what extent* the occupation possesses the above attributes.

As a case study, the stock broker occupation/profession is of interest. Stock brokers number about 450,000 in the United States, are licensed, and are identified to customers as "registered representatives." Their occupation is fraught with tension between the demands of professionalism versus real-world ambitions, accompanied by high-income expectations that are (or are not) met mainly through commissions. What exactly is their professional status? The spouse of a stock broker offers the following analysis.

The Stock Broker: Professional or Salesperson?

The following represents an attempt to analyze the status of stock brokerage in regard to its claim to professional status, using the norms developed by the Flexner Commission.

1. Systematic and unique body of knowledge: No specific educational requirements are demanded for occupational entry. Considerable on-job training is often offered. Brokers must be both licensed and registered. These credentials have little to do with "success" which is measured by sales. Only 25 percent of persons passing required exams are ultimately successful in the industry after five years.
2. Professional authority: The broker is essentially a salesman, his expert knowledge coming from the firm's market analyst. Brokers are discouraged from attempting their own research.
3. Community as opposed to self-interest: The broker lives from his commissions. This fact creates tension between his ethical obligations toward buyers and his own interests.
4. Community sanction: Access to the occupation is controlled through licensure and registration. The credentials required to become and maintain status as a stock broker are Series 7 General Securities License; Series 63; and a State License. Additional licenses required to become and maintain status as a "full-service" broker include the Commodities Trading License; and the Life/ Health, Variable Annuities, and Disabilities License(s).
5. Regulative code of ethics: Series 7 and Series 63 examinations are heavily focused on rules, regulations, and ethical behavior. "Sanctions are very severe for violation or nonadherence to the established requirements."
6. Recognition by the public as a profession: The public often looks to the broker for advice. This may create undue dependency upon the broker's personal judgment.
7. Distinct occupational structure: Professional journals, conferences, societies and other knowledge-enhancing activities are limited. *Registered Representative Magazine*, the industry journal, is available to all brokers. Trade journals for individual sectors are also published. (C. Pery 1995)

The fact that medicine is one of the old, established professions and that electrical engineering and economics qualify as new professions is not controversial. But what about computer science and MBAs? And does an under-graduate degree in biology or other life science suffice to meet the above criteria? And if so, what difference does it make? It is easy to become tangled in the issue of whether a particular occupation is truly a profession, but this issue is beside the point. What is significant, as already noted, is to what extent or degree a particular occupation may be described as professionalized. The relative power (and rewards) of an occupation are often associated with its level of professionalization.

Expectations of Professional Behavior

Many students of the professions have pointed out that the real-world performance of members of established professions often fails to measure up to established norms. Can physicians and lawyers be said to always fulfill their obligation to the public? Do physicians serve everyone in need? Are lawyers, who as officers of the court have an obligation to the public, always advising their clients with the public interest in mind? How can an accountant demand professional status, yet collude with a client to misrepresent? Such problems have fueled demands for modification of some of the privileges enjoyed by the more powerful professions, and these demands will likely increase as the population becomes more astute. Already demands for deregulation of some occupations surface from time to time, in the interests of both would-be entrants (easier access) and the public (lower costs, etc.), discussed later.

Despite all the attacks on professionalization in recent years, some claim that professional privileges are here to stay—that their existence reflects the way advanced societies organize expertise. Others continue to express the fear that control over work may be overwhelmed by organizations that find it more profitable and convenient to dilute the power of professions. Andrew Abbott (1988) refers to a trend toward treating knowledge as a commodity. He expresses the fear that alternative forms of structuring professional expertise are on the rise, pointing to competition from large organizations dealing with commodities "embodying expertise [that] require development, maintenance, and support that increasingly exceed the resources of individual professionals. The commercial organizations and governments that invest in commodified professional knowledge compete directly with professionals for client fees, whether the commodities provide services directly or are simply used by professionals in practice." Abbott fears that since nonprofessionals increasingly own and operate professional commodities, this competition promises to become "dangerous to the idea of professionalism itself."

Strategies Used to Attain Professional Status

A major issue of interest in this discussion of the professionalization of work is *how* the struggle for professional status takes place. One view is that as needs arise, an existing occupation (or perhaps more than one) expands its task roles to meet the new needs. Another view holds that several existent occupations compete with each other for the right to monopolize the new task roles. Sometimes two occupations battle for control of existent tasks, and the stronger of the two prevails. An important example in history is the struggle between doctors and nurses for the preeminent or dominant role in hospital-based health care in the nineteenth century. In such situations the losing occupation sometimes carves out a series of lower-status task roles for itself with the acquiescence of the dominant occupation. Nursing, now considered a semiprofession, has never recovered from its early defeat. In recent years nurses, chafing under the limitations of inferior status, have been pressing for higher professional status in both traditional and new roles. One result of this struggle, noted in the February 7, 1997, *Wall Street Journal*, is the emergence of the nurse-practitioner. The same is true for other health-care semiprofessionals (White 1987); in fact, many of the best documented studies of the struggles of semiprofessions and would-be professions to improve their status deal with a health-related occupation in conflict with medicine.

Optometrists vs. Ophthalmologists. Many of the best documented studies of the struggles of semiprofessions and would-be professions to improve their status deal with a health-related occupation's conflict with medicine. An interesting illustration of the struggle of a health-care semiprofession to encroach on the territory of a full-fledged medical specialty is the ongoing battle between optometrists and ophthalmologists for a piece of each other's work. The optometrists, particularly the younger ones, reportedly better educated and more self-confident than the older generation, not only want the right to write prescriptions for treatment, but aim ultimately to replace ophthalmologists as the gatekeepers to eye care. In other words, according to researchers (Begun and Lippincott 1987), the optometrist's ultimate goals are to become the first and foremost professional whom a patient would consult for eye care, and to refer only serious cases to an ophthalmologist. One might speculate that an HMO would find this proposition rather attractive.

According to two researchers who studied the aspirations of each eye-care group in Maryland and North Carolina, the optometrists were successful in persuading the state legislature in North Carolina to expand their rights in regard to prescription-writing, but unsuccessful in Maryland. The reasons given for success and failure related to two factors: differences in the level of confidence of the optometrists in the two different states; and differences in organizational pressures on the state legislatures by the respective groups in the two states. In other words, the outcome was due to a combination of factors involving both competency issues and power relations. Before leaving this illustration of boundary-moving by occupational groups, the researchers point out that the ophthalmologists, feeling the pinch of HMO-inspired income constraints, are honing in on the territory of the optometrists by setting themselves up in the business of fitting glasses, using low-wage, low-level health-care workers (Begun and Lippincott 1987).

NPs vs. MDs. An even bigger battle is being waged by medical doctors (MDs), particularly primary-care physicians, against the encroachment of nurse-practitioners (NPs) into gatekeeper positions, critical figures in HMO "systems." Nurse-practitioners, nurses with two-years advanced training, often leading to a master's degree, who have passed a state certification examination now number 70,000 nationally; but most still work under physicians' supervision. The nurse-practitioner's goal is to dispense with the necessity of a link to a physician. When this writer first reviewed the literature during the early 1990s, the physicians were winning the battle, forcing the nurse-practitioners into support roles, such as helping to regulate diabetics and offering guidance with obesity problems; but as of the late 1990s, pressures from HMOs are permitting them to play a more prominent role. For example, by 1997 about 6,000 NPs were functioning as midwives, with services paid for by the health plans of many states. More than 20,000 were certified as specialists in anesthesiology or other medical specialties and working in hospitals. Since NPs average about $60,000 per year and primary-care physicians $135,217, numbers-crunchers in the medical field will obviously find NPs more attractive than MDs. Strong medical backlash is underway and it includes, as indicated in the September 30, 1997, *New York Times*, efforts to push back these developments legislatively.

LICENSURE, CERTIFICATION, ACCREDITATION

Much of the professionalization process that has been discussed in this chapter is directed toward the establishment of eligibility for licensure, the acquisition of which makes a monopoly of employment possible. Sometimes professionalization issues turn around a struggle for dominant position among segments of a vaguely perceived profession or occupation. In such instances, one or more of the competing segments will attempt to demonstrate that they are "more professional" than their competitors. A variety of tactics may be used, as has occurred in the longtime campaign of Canada's chartered accountants (similar to CPAs in the United States) to achieve dominance in the accounting profession, a process that ultimately led to redefinition of the tasks performed by certified accountants (Richardson 1987).[1] Although they were only partially successful, in at least two provinces of Canada the chartered accountants CAs) succeeded in achieving their goal of obtaining professional licensure and the right to control professional entry, the ultimate prize.

The chartered accountants (CAs), in their struggle to dominate the various occupational groups vaguely covered by the term accounting, set up a lower-status organization for company accountants. Thus they limited company accountants to semiprofessional work, at the same time redefining the content of their own occupational tasks. More generally, Richardson notes that since the 1920s the CAs have pursued their goals by claiming to possess a unique body of knowledge, demanding both degrees and the completion of apprenticeship programs given through proprietary schools, and administering mandatory examinations. Aware of the value of symbols, the CAs purchased the right to use the designation of CPA, the U.S. equivalent of the CA, to prevent competing groups from using it.

Professional privileges rarely go uncontested by excluded groups. The appeals of a competing group, the Certified General Accountants, protested that the definition of public accounting, as designated in the mission statement of the Cost Accountants organization, was too narrow. It campaigned for a revised definition that would permit its membership access to the field that was becoming monopolized by CA membership. At last report the issue was before a Parliamentary Committee.

Many contemporary analysts, mainly economists, are uninterested in the "laundry list" of professional attributes presented above as justification for professional status. The economic analysts believe that many latter-day occupations can lay claim to professional status on the basis of the attributes listed above. Hair stylists, real-estate salespeople, and pest controllers, to cite a few examples, may claim a specialized body of knowledge, a code of ethics, and a professional organization. Furthermore, economic analysts consider self-interest, as opposed to a concern for the common good, to be an "acceptable" motivation for professionalization. The ultimate goal of most professional/occupational groups is to obtain the right to licensure. If that goal does not appear attainable, the group may settle for certification, often a way station on the road to the prized licensure status that is embedded in law.

Licensure affects occupational entry and labor mobility, the latter referring to workers' ability to move about geographically from jurisdiction to jurisdiction (usually state to state). The heated controversy over whether the monopolies of employment obtained through licensure are used for the public good (the public-interest model) or to further private gain (the economic or capture or acquired model) will be mentioned, but it is not of primary relevance to this discussion.

Definitions

Differences exist among the various ranks afforded to the occupations claiming professional status. Through *licensure* an agency of government (usually a state) grants permission to an individual to engage in a given occupation, once the agency finds that the applicant has attained the minimal degree of competency required to insure that the public health, safety, and welfare will be reasonably protected. It therefore becomes illegal for the nonlicensed to perform services reserved for a particular occupation. The avowed purpose of licensing laws is to ensure the protection of the public. *Certification* does not restrict anyone from working in a particular occupation, but it offers titles that may be used only by those certified. It is a voluntary process that usually implies expansion of formal training under the auspices of an occupational or professional association. The association measures its members' competency, and recognizes the merits of individuals in order to help them gain a return on their investment (Friedman 1976). Certification as a public accountant (CPA) is probably the best-known and most-valued occupational certification. *Accreditation*, also a voluntary process, measures the content and quality of the educational and training programs of occupational groups. The present discussion is limited to the process of licensure because only licensure has the force of law behind it. This is the tool ultimately sought by all who aspire to full professional status.

History

The practice of restricting the right to enter an occupation goes back to the Middle Ages, when guilds restricted entry into many craft occupations. In the United States the first known state regulation occurred in Virginia, in 1639, when the state legislature regulated medical practice; but it did not become widespread until the nineteenth century, a great expansion occurring after 1950. While only seventy occupations were subject to state licensing at that time, the number grew to more than 500 by the late 1970s, including about 18 percent of the U.S. workforce. A continued expansion is projected, due to the continuing growth of the service sector (Kleiner and Gordon 1996).

Example of Expansion of Licensure. A situation in the state of Minnesota, one that is described by Kleiner and Gordon, offers a view of the growing spread of occupational licensure, despite the skepticism of an unusually aware state legislature that has unsuccessfully attempted to stem the tide. Following Federal guidelines, Minnesota's licensing boards are autonomous, though they fall nominally under a central administrative agency. Boards perform such tasks as setting standards for licensing and practice, preparing examinations, and determining applicants' eligibility for licensure. In 1975 the legislature specified that further occupational licensure should not occur unless it could be proven essential to the protection of the citizens of the state. Pressures from members of aspiring occupations intensified, and in 1978 the state legislature acted again. This time it set out to establish that less rather than more occupational regulation be required, and that citizenship, moral character, age, and health requirements be eliminated. Despite such efforts, the number of occupations acquiring licensure increased dramatically in Minnesota, with the proportion of the state's workforce in licensed occupations rising from 5 percent in 1950 and 11.9 percent in 1970, to 13.5 percent by 1990.

Rationales of Occupational Groups for Licensing

The licensure referred to here is mandatory licensure by state regulation. The researchers quoted here utilize the economic model of analysis. The following represents a sampling of occupations requiring licenses in some or all states: medicine, dentistry, nursing (including practical nursing), physical therapy, dental hygiene, biomedical hygiene, ophthalmic dispensing, plumbing, electrical work, refrigeration contracting, swimming-pool contracting, well-drilling, roofing contracting, stationary engineering, portable steam engineering, electrician supervision, barbering, cosmetology, mobile-home servicing, aircraft mechanics, deck and engineering offices, Merchant Marine, over-the-road driving, funeral directorship, real-estate brokerage and sales, watchmaking, and welding (Young 1987).

The major arguments that the proponents of licensure usually offer is that consumers are necessarily less well informed about the quality of services than producers. Therefore, licensure offers consumers some protection against malpractice and fraud. Another outcome is that limitation of occupational entry probably encourages would-be entrants to undertake more educational preparation than otherwise would occur (Kleiner and Gordon 1996).

Factors that Influence Success in Obtaining Licensure

According to Young (1987), the following factors influence the success of occupational groups and their associations in persuading state legislatures to meet their demands for licensure:

1. Group size. Small groups appear more able to mobilize their members on behalf of self-interest lobbying than large groups. Each member of a small group, it is hypothesized, can better see benefits arising from his/her personal lobbying efforts than members of large groups can.
2. Homogeneity of interests. Where group members have a clearly understood objective, it is easier to mobilize them than where interests are highly diverse.
3. Self-interest. Licensure protects members of an occupation from market competition. Members of other occupations cannot perform tasks reserved for the licensed occupation's members, nor can members of the same occupation cross state boundaries (unless reciprocity agreements exist). This insures human-capital and career investments against risk.

Customary Requirements for State Licensure

Aspirants for a state licensure must usually fulfill four types of criteria: (1) satisfactory completion of a formal course of study; (2) some form of supervised experience, internship, or apprenticeship; (3) personal qualifications, often including residency, citizenship, and moral rectitude; and (4) passing an examination given by the state licensing board for that occupation. Those researchers who use the economic model tend to dismiss claims that such requirements are for public protection. They maintain that many of the courses of study are unnecessary for performance of the reserved tasks; that the experience requirements often are unnecessary or excessive; that citizen and residency requirements are unjustified; and that examinations often have little relevance to the tasks to be performed. They claim further that licensure of an occupation offers no protection to the public: unscrupulous practitioners are rarely disciplined by their professional associations despite the self-policing powers granted by the license. One example of an effort to protect the public is given below, as reported in the *New York Times,* July 10, 1996.

The Case of Errant Stock Brokers in New York State

The National Association of Securities Dealers (NASD) was established to assure that the stock-buying public would be advised and serviced by qualified persons. With the booming stock market, record numbers of persons have entered the field, being hired with the understanding that they would pass the standard brokers' examinations. To the embarrassment of the NASD, a number of nonlicensed brokers who failed the exam more than once have attempted to secure their credentials through fraud.

Most of the cheating has involved the Series 7 exam which the NASD administers for the entire industry (although cheating has also occurred in regard to the Series 63 exam which covers state laws). Any broker wishing to sell the full range of securities products must pass the Series 7 exams. The peak in applicant number was in 1994 when 58,629 persons took the exam. While the pass rate has been rising since 1991 (63% to 71% by mid 1996), a number of brokers who failed the exam apparently sought the services of others to take the exam for them, often in other cities to lessen the possibility of detection.

The industry association plans to ban these brokers permanently from employment in the industry. Persons who refuse to accept the ban have the right of appeal to a NASD panel and, ultimately, all the way up to the Securities and Exchange Commission.

Criticisms of Licensure

Need for Required Credentials. Theory and practice are two different things, as evidenced in the implementation of licensing activities. Young found that the requirements set forth in state licensure regulations are rarely subjected to objective analysis (1986, 1987). Concerning educational requirements, no rationale nor empirical evidence is ordinarily produced to justify a particular set of demands. For example, why is each occupation's period of formal education the length specified? Is it necessary that a lawyer go to graduate school for three years? Why not two? In some countries a law degree is an undergraduate degree. Why must the law degree be preceded by a full baccalaureate? Why must a hairdresser be a high-school graduate, as is the case in some states? The fact that educational requirements for the same occupation vary considerably throughout the states suggests that educational demands are often set arbitrarily.

Time Requirements. Experience requirements are also often arbitrarily set, with little relevance to the time necessary to learn the occupation. An example is that the time required to become a master plumber in Illinois was longer than that needed to produce a physician eligible for the American College of Surgeons (Gellhorn 1976), a practice struck down by the courts during the civil-rights struggle.[2] According to another study (Shimberg, Esser, and Kruger 1982), cosmetologists in Oregon are forced to train for 2,000 hours, up from 1,500, before they can receive a license to work. The pressure here came from schools of beauty culture who could charge more tuition and use students longer for "practice" customers. In Illinois a rise in hours of experience drove would-be barbers away, reducing the competition for already licensed ones.

Experience Requirements. In the most comprehensive study of experience requirements (Cathcart and Graff 1978), the researchers examined fifty-eight licensed occupations in California that required passage of an examination, twenty-nine of which also required experience. To assess the relative importance of experience, the researchers ranked the occupations in terms of their impact on the public. They found no rational basis for some occupations to require experience and others to require none. Nor did they find any rational basis for the amount of experience demanded. One example they cited was a comparison of pest-control representatives and construction inspectors. Both occupations' impact on the public was equal; but pest-control representatives were required to have half a year of experience; construction inspectors, four to six years.

Citizenship and Residency Requirements. Many states pass laws requiring members of licensed occupations to be U. S. citizens and even residents of the particular state for a long period of time. According to Young (1987) the citizenship requirement spread during the early 1930s as an effort to bar European refugees from taking employment in a wide variety of occupations during a period of job scarcity. For example, the large number of physicians fleeing Nazi Germany led to the tightening of these requirements in medicine. In some occupations, plumbing, for example, the right to work may be limited to a county or municipality.

In recent years courts have tended to strike down restrictions on geographic mobility when challenges arise. However, since most aspirants do not challenge licensing requirements, such restrictions continue to be commonplace. Interstate reciprocity is the means by which some state licensing boards voluntarily permit limited interstate mobility. For example, psychologists licensed in certain states may practice in others with whom their state has an agreement. However, such agreements are spotty. Some states tend generally to be shut tighter to outsiders than others (Maurezi 1981).

Relevance of Examinations. Passing an examination offered by the state licensing board is a requirement for obtaining a license. Such examinations, whether prepared by the state board, national professional association, or other group, should determine the ability of the candidate to satisfactorily perform the required tasks. In fact, many examinations are not job-related. One reason is that it is often technically difficult to make a determination of fitness, that is, of what abilities and competences are necessary for safe and responsible practice of the occupation. In addition, state boards who often prepare such examinations seldom have adequate training. And state examinations are given in great secrecy, with few outsiders ever seeing them. This "lack of sunlight" obscures from the public the serious deficiencies of most tests.

The following are illustrations of the problematic nature of many licensing examinations, cited by Young. Consultants to the California Board of Landscape Architects in 1983 found that fewer than half the questions in the Uniform National Examination given to landscape architects had any relationship to the public health or to the safety of consumers of their services. Much of the examination involved memorization of facts irrelevant to practice, such as details concerning an Egyptian temple and a historic Greek edifice. A 1984 study found that Washington, D.C., cosmetologists must be able to produce hairdos of a previous generation, but are required to display very little of their knowledge of procedures, such as bleaching or permanent waving, which are potentially dangerous to their clientele. A 1998 study of outcomes of dentists' licensing requirements concluded that the dental health of group of new Air Force recruits was about the same, regardless of whether the recruits' home states had tighter or looser restrictions on the practice of dentistry (Kleiner and Kudrie 1998).

Cost to Consumers. Most studies show that licensing increases costs of the service produced. States with more rigorous occupational licensing requirements tend to produce higher charges than those with less regulation (Kleiner and Gordon 1996). One example is the Federal Trade Commission's estimate that states limiting optometrists more severely than others raise the cost of eyeglasses at least by 25 percent. Practitioners in states with rigorous regulations, depending upon occupation and level of regulation, earn about 10 to 20 percent more than in states offering less protection. Findings concerning dentists are similar: dental fees are 14 to 16 percent higher in strongly regulated states; overall dental income is 10 percent higher. A related issue, often overlooked, is that when the quality of a service is demonstrably improved through regulation, the cost of the service increases; as a result, fewer members of the public can afford to use the service (or product).

The charge has been made that the overall movement toward professionalization of work has had an adverse effect on the poor and on minorities. The accusation is often leveled that licensure is a way to limit the number of occupation entrants during periods of low demand. One study supporting this view found that in ten out of twelve license-requiring occupations studied, a statistically significant relationship existed between failure rates and unemployment rates (Rayack 1976). While licensing was deliberately used to exclude African Americans and women in the past, it continues to have the inadvertent effect of discouraging would-be aspirants to occupations who can neither afford the required schooling nor testing. It also encourages the illegal practice of many occupations by the poor. For example, unlicensed barbers and cosmetologists in poor neighborhoods sometimes practice at home. Where the poor do attempt to obtain licenses, written examinations often pose a formidable challenge. For example, one study (Dorsey 1980) investigating applicants for beautician's licenses in

Missouri and Illinois found the chances of passing to be increased 2.9 percent in Missouri and 2.1 percent in Illinois by each additional year of general education.

The problem of relevancy of licensure requirements is due in large part to a passive public who is largely unaware of the issues, as well as to occupational aggressiveness. With the help of modern technology, this may be changing. Early in 1997, for example, the New York Board of Regents launched an effort, via the Web site of the State Education Department, to advise the public as to the backgrounds and standing of 610,000 professionals in thirty-eight categories in the state. Data includes information on license expiration dates and pending disciplinary actions. The *New York Times,* February 2, 1997, noted that other states were contemplating similar utilization of the Internet. Such interest suggests that licensure will retain its credibility as a means of protection for the public.

An example of an effort, purportedly to make the practice of law more accessible to less affluent persons by whittling away at the privileges of the legal profession—in this case, an attack on the gatekeeping function, the right to determine who offers the obligatory professional education and the standards which must be met—is given below. It was gleaned from the February 2, 1994, and June 7, 1995, issues of the *New York Times.*

In February 1994, a small Massachusetts law school was denied accreditation by the American Bar Association (ABA) on grounds that (1) the school did not meet standards set by ABA and (2) that the "special mission" claimed by the school as reason for exemption was not unique. The school thereupon filed an antitrust suit against the ABA, charging that current standards are unnecessarily inflated, interfering with the efforts of innovative schools with shallow pockets to establish themselves.

The ABA was given the authority to accredit law schools 73 years ago by the United States Department of Education. In forty-two states the right to practice law is contingent upon passing an examination given by the State Bar. The claim has been made that expensive standards reduce the opportunity for lower income persons, minorities, and older persons to attend law school; that innovation is stifled. One such effort was the effort of the Massachusetts school to substitute electronically obtained legal information for an expensive law library. Standard law school tuitions, at the time of the suit, were in the range of $15,000 to $20,000 per year. The challenging school's projected tuition, $9,000.

In June 1995, the Justice Department moved to limit the power of the American Bar Association in the accreditation of law schools. This is the first time the government has moved against a professional organization to see if it was being used as a subterfuge for anticompetitive practices. Hints were made by the Justice Department that other professional organizations would also be watched for indications of anticompetitive practices.

The antitrust division of the Justice Department settled the suit under terms that will prevent the organization from manipulating its right of accreditation of law schools "for the purpose of jacking up faculty salaries and improving working conditions." The rules "have nothing to do with guaranteeing students that they are gaining professional training, but everything to do with guaranteeing faculty that they would be paid top dollar." The ABA was required to review their practices and refrain from those which were seen as imposing anti-competitive standards, an order seen by the *New York Times* as putting every professional society on notice that "it may not use professional standards as a backhanded tactic to insulate itself from competitive pressures."

A review of the literature on licensure, certification, and other forms of accreditation reveals that the subject is much neglected. The focus of individuals and occupational groups lies in efforts to "become professional," particularly, in relation to medicine's battles with encroaching occupations. Little contemporary, empirically based work is to be found on the promised protections of existent licensure and licensure's other impacts on the public.

NOTES

1. The case of the battle in Canada between different segments of the accounting profession contains every aspect of the professionalization struggle that is discussed here, and therefore serves as a good, although foreign, example.
2. This practice ended through challenge by would-be African-American plumbers to union apprenticeship practices, seen as exclusionary in intent.

REFERENCES

Abbott, Andrew. 1988. *The system of professions: an essay on the division of expert labor.* Chicago: University of Chicago Press.
Begun, James W., and Ronald Lippincott. 1987. The origins and resolution of interoccupational conflict. *Work and Occupation* 14 (August): 368–86.
Cathcart, James A., and Gil Graff. 1978. Occupational licensing: factoring it out. *Pacific Law Review* 9 (January): 147–63.
Dorsey, S. 1980. The occupational licensing queue. *Journal of Human Resources* (Summer): 424–34.
Edwards, Alba. 1943. *Population: comparative occupational statistics for the United States, 1870 to 1940.* Washington, D.C.: Government Printing Service.
Etzioni, Amitai. 1969. *The semi-professions and their organization.* New York: The Free Press.
Flexner, Abraham. 1910. *Medical education in the United States and Canada.* New York: Carnegie Foundation, Bulletin No. 4.
Friedman, Marcia. 1976. *Labor markets: segments and shelters.* Montclair, N.J.: Allanheld, Osmun, and Co.
Gellhorn, Walter. 1976. The abuse of occupational licensing. *University of Chicago Law Review* (Fall): 6–27.
Kleiner, Morris, and Mitchell Gordon. 1996. The growth of occupational licensing: are we protecting consumers? *CURA Reporter* (December): 8–12.
———, and Robert Kudrie. 1998. Giving dentists a check-up. *Business Week* (12 January).
Maurezi, Alex. 1981. Occupational licensing and the public interest. *Journal of Political Economy* (March/April): 399–413.
Pery, Cynthia. 1995. The stock broker. Class paper. Drexel University.
Rayack, Elton. 1976. *An economic analysis of occupational licensure.* A report prepared for the U.S. Department of Labor.
Reiss, Albert J. 1955. Occupational mobility of professional workers. *American Sociological Review* 2 (December): 693–701.

Richardson, Alan. 1987. Professionalization and intraprofessional competition in the Canadian accounting profession. *Work and Occupations* 14 (November): 591–615.

Shimberg, Benjamin, Barbara Esser, and Daniel Kruger. 1982. *Occupational licensing: practices and policies.* Washington, D.C.: Public Affairs Press.

White, William D. 1987. The introduction of professional regulation and labor market conditions: occupational licensure of registered nurses. *Policy Sciences* (April): 27–51.

Young, S. David. 1986. Accounting, licensure, quality, and the "Cadillac effect." *Journal of Accounting and Public Policy* 5 (Spring): 5–19.

———. 1987. *The role of experts: occupational licensing in America.* Washington D.C.: Cato Institute.

9

Organizational Recruitment
and Job Search

This chapter focuses on how employers hire and individuals locate employment. Interest in job search has intensified in recent years, partly due to employer concerns about the increasing costs of job turnover, which in turn are fueled partially by the rising costs of unemployment insurance since the 1960s. In response, many mainstream economists have suggested that reducing the duration of job search following job loss may be the best way to lessen the burden on employers. This in turn has pointed to a need for greater understanding of the search process for purposes of encouraging efficiency on the part of job seekers.

ECONOMISTS' VIEWS ON RECRUITMENT AND JOB SEARCH

Recruitment and job search take place in highly imperfect employment markets, meaning that supply and demand factors do not interact optimally. Lack of information, skill limitations, and inaccessibility to jobs outside local labor markets greatly limit the ability of employers to hire and job seekers to locate maximally desirable employment. Labor-market segmentation is another factor limiting both hirers and job seekers. Labor-market segmentation is the practice of allocating workers with certain characteristics, such as race and gender, to certain types of jobs. Both employers and job seekers identify potential workers with their previous employment and each are reluctant to cross boundaries, such as the one that separates blue-collar and white-collar work.

Economists interested in job-matching and hiring issues have consistently emphasized the role of information. From the onset of job-search research, investigators have agreed that the limited information available to individuals in the process of job-searching makes it impossible for them to maximize earnings potential. There is also continuing consensus that information gathered by *informal method*, that is, from currently employed friends and relatives, is both cheaper and more accurate than information gathered through other means. From the employer point of view, referrals by current employees have consistently been found to produce a pool of new hires offering more productivity and producing less turnover than employees otherwise recruited. Graduating college students who have access to college job lists and employer recruitment teams may find these generalizations do not apply to themselves at the time of their initial job-entry.

Economists who emphasize labor-market segmentation see employment possibilities for job seekers limited by the job-allocation practices of employers within the internal labor market, often exacerbated by policies of conducting job training within the firm and promoting from within. Such practices make access to the internal labor market the most critical economic determinant of job search, in the view of segmentalists (see Doeringer and Piore 1971).

CONSTRAINTS ON RECRUITMENT AND PLACEMENT

The Industrial and Salary Models

Employers' hiring practices are embedded in some fundamental decisions about how the employer desires to organize work. They follow from the model the employer chooses to utilize (Osterman 1987). If the employee is constrained by the presence of a union (the industrial model), freedom to move employees about, both vertically and laterally, is limited. Internal recruitment must take seniority into account, a practice also followed by some nonunion plants. Employers have traditionally chosen to limit use of the salaried model, which involves recruitment and promotion according to merit principles, to professional, managerial, and other white-collar employees. Recently, however, some employers have begun to apply this model to their blue-collar workers, especially in situations where they are introducing "participative management."

The Craft Model

In the craft model employers often hire for the short term, as needed. Craft workers, only a small segment of all U.S. labor, have not been attached to any one workplace. Usually obtained through a union hiring hall, their advantage to the employer is that they come pretrained, require minimal supervision, and have very limited expectations concerning the period of employment. The employers pays a higher daily rate, but they have no continuing responsibility to accommodate such workers.

The Secondary Labor Market Model

Employers do not attach career ladders to most of the jobs that fall within the secondary labor market model. The entry job is the only job that the new hire can expect to obtain within the organization. There is no intention to promote; in fact, high turnover may be desired to maintain entry-level wage rates and minimize benefits eligibility. Included in this group are many clerical and sales situations, factory assembly jobs, and jobs in the service occupations. The jobs exist in large firms as well as in small businesses.

The Choice of a Model

The basic rules, regulations, and procedures that employers use to develop their employment models fall into four categories:

1. Job classification and job definition, including how broad or narrow a job is, and whether job occupants may perform a few or many tasks.
2. Deployment, the freedom of the employer to move the worker from task to task or job to job.
3. Security, the commitment made by employers for maintaining the worker's employment, ranging from lifetime employ-ment to temporary or contingent worker status.
4. Wages, whether there are set wages or salaries by job category and seniority or whether remuneration is based on individual factors, such as education, experience, and effectiveness.

In choosing models for recruitment (and promotion) policies, employers focus on three goals: cost-effectiveness, predictability, and flexibility.

Cost Effectiveness. Employer strategies regarding cost effectiveness have often been described as being a choice between use of large numbers of low-wage workers who work with low-level technology, on the one hand, and heavy investment in equipment and technology requiring fewer, but more highly trained and more expensive workers, on the other. While the latter mode costs more in direct wages and benefits, considerable savings may be gleaned in recruitment, training, and placement costs, lower experience ratings, and fewer accidents (Baron, Black, and Lowenstein 1987). Although many writers continue to suggest that the latter mode is more cost effective in the long run, employers are widely believed to have been systematically de-skilling jobs over the past several decades and, accordingly, decreasing opportunities for the non–college-educated workforce.[1] Such workers have few alternatives but to accept whatever jobs are available. The quality option is now seen as only one of a series of employment possibilities open to employers, not as something that is uniquely beneficial to them.

Predictability. To ensure the availability of a predictable labor supply, employers traditionally have been willing to develop their labor supply internally so that the workers will be there when they need them, perhaps five to ten years hence. For this purpose larger employers have maintained manpower inventories and engaged in intensive in-house training. They seek to hold their workers not only by high-level wages, but also by establishing paths for advancement within the internal labor market. This staffing mode, and its antithesis, are exemplified below:

A cemetery owner in the Philadelphia suburbs runs two facilities, one large and famous for the beauty of its grounds; the second, small and dingy-looking. The unionized workers in the larger cemetery are well trained and relatively well paid. They know their jobs and can be depended upon to perform their work assignments diligently and without supervision. Absenteeism and turnover are low. The opposite situation prevails in the small, nonunionized facility. The company recruits from the most marginal labor pools, pays the minimum wage, and invests in a large amount of supervision, experiencing a high level of absenteeism and turnover. Benefits are few and rarely does anyone stay long enough to be eligible. The owner reportedly prefers the second situation, finding it more profitable. (Student contribution 1994)

Flexibility. Employers are enormously interested in being able to move their workers about the firm, as needed, which means they may be more interested in an employee's adaptability than his/her cost-effectiveness. To secure workers who are capable of meeting organizational goals as they develop, employers may be willing to hire a worker with more education or skill than that which is needed for the immediate entry position. Toward the same end, employers have often refrained from laying off such workers during economic down-turns, preferring to hoard them in anticipation of future demand. It is too early to know how much these traditional goals/practices are being affected by employers' widespread of temporary agencies to secure staff.

HUMAN-RESOURCES MANAGEMENT VIEWS

When human-resources management researchers discuss specific recruitment and selection procedures, they concentrate on the outcomes in terms of the actual performance of workers, once hired, often focusing on the effects of different recruitment sources on the productivity of "hires." The common wisdom generated from these studies is that current employees are the best source of high-performance, low-turnover workers. Researchers have also studied such issues as the costs and benefits associated with various recruiting and selection practices (Boudreau and Rynes 1985); the validity of various selection techniques; and testing and validity issues concerning minority groups. Since the passage of civil-rights legislation and the establishment of equal employment opportunity requirements, employers have been paying more attention to the predictability of their selection practices, especially of testing for women, minorities, and varying age groups.

The following passage from a January 5, 1997, *New York Times* report illustrates employers' faith in the current workforce as a source of new workers.

According to a two-year study of hiring practices of 80 Western branches of one bank, it was found that preference was systematically given to those referred by present employees. Although less than 8 percent of the 5,568 applicants were referred by present employees over a 26-month period beginning January 1993, 80 percent were interviewed and they received 115 (35%) of the 326 entry-level jobs.

The key difference between those who were referred and other applicants was that the referees had more information about the bank and what was required of employees. Also, the referees were coached by their friends as to how to present themselves and how to respond to questions.

Early findings from the study suggest that the referred applicants made better employees, which could be advantageous in terms of superior performance and reduced turnover.

One of the most impressive studies of recruiting methods is by Harry J. Holzer (1987), who hypothesized that employers make decisions concerning hiring policies on the basis of the minimum expected level of productivity for each job slot filled. The objective is to maximize profits through each job-hiring decision. The amount of profit realized if the job slot is promptly filled is weighed against the profits lost if a time period elapses before hiring occurs. This may involve tension between time gained and quality of hires. A longer recruiting period may produce a more productive employee, but involve temporary losses in interim, "might-have-been" productivity. According to the Holzer hypothesis, the likelihood of hiring depends on the number and quality of applicants and the probabilities of an offer being made and one being accepted. Basically, Holzer sees a trade-off between the costs of using alternative recruiting methods and the benefits that accrue when a new hire meets the productivity expectations of the recruiters. Holzer's findings, derived from data produced by a phone survey of 3500 employers, reaffirm the conventional wisdom that current employees are both the most used and most effective sources of worker recruitment.

All studies of recruiting agree that employers differentiate their use of recruitment methods according to the type of position being filled or occupational group being sought. For example, recruiting from within the organization is more popular among those seeking managers and supervisors than among those recruiting commissioned sales persons. While the great majority of proffesional/technical workers are solicited from outside referral sources, very few production workers are. A study by the American Management Association (1986) of recruitment practices for twelve managerial/professional occupations shows that practices vary even within given groups.

Effectiveness Versus Usage of Various Recruitment Methods

Employers' experiences with the effectiveness of the recruitment methods they use are not closely correlated with their level of usage. The effectiveness of each method differs by major occupational group. For example, the most prevalent method of recruiting office/clerical workers is promotion from within, but this fills only about one-third of available positions. Newspaper advertising, while utilized less often, appears to result in a far greater proportion of recruiting successes.

Impact of Recruitment Methods on Job Choice

Little attention has been paid to how recruitment methods affect the decisions of job seekers. One small study of forty-one graduating students of various disciplines in a northwestern university found varying impacts. For example, interviewees drew parallels between their recruitment experiences and actual working conditions within the firm. When long delays in response by the firm to the application occurred, the more competitive applicants, especially males, reacted negatively. Women tended to react negatively to comments about personal appearance during their interview experience; to being told they would not advance as rapidly as men; and to inappropriate places for interviewing (Rynes, Bretz, and Gerhard 1991).

JOB SEARCH BY INDIVIDUALS

Surprisingly little research has been done in recent years on the methods utilized by job seekers to locate employment, the subject not generating much interest. A number of recent analyses are based on data that are quite old. The yearly BLS report, summarized on Table 9.1, represents the most up-to-date data available, but is very limited in terms of the subjects reported on. The matter of job search commands greater interest during periods when public policy is geared toward moving people off welfare, unemployment compensation, or other transfer payments. With the legislated (as of 1996) movement of welfare recipients into the workforce, it is not unlikely that job-search issues will generate more interest in the foreseeable future.

Major Factors Influencing Job Search

Search Methods Most Used. According to the 1997 BLS survey of job-seeking methods by unemployed workers, the major means used are direct approaches to prospective employers (65%) and submission of resumes or applications to employers (48.4%). Only about one in every five or six job seekers places or answers ads, consults with friends or relatives, or uses the public employment service; and only one in fourteen unemployed persons uses a private employment service. Most unemployed job seekers use only one or two methods of job search.

Demographic Factors. Age appears to influence job search practices more than any other factor. For example, job seekers are less likely to send out applications as they advance in years, but more often consult friends or relatives and use private employment agencies. Very little variation exists by race or gender, although blacks are slightly more prone to use the public employment service than whites. Table 9.1 reflects the interplay of these factors. For reasons unknown, women, irrespective of age, are less likely than men to seek employment while still employed , according to BLS data (1997).

These job-search findings are noteworthy in terms of how individuals' practices diverge from the methods deemed most effective by employers. For example, job seekers typically do not strive to locate openings through contacts with current employees (their "friends or relatives"). Also of interest is the small number of job-seeking methods used. Was unemployment so low during the period surveyed that little effort was required? So-called good times notwithstanding, the average duration of employment during 1997 was around sixteen weeks; the median duration, about eight weeks (BLS 1998). In view of these facts, it would seem that efforts to reduce the duration of unemployment spells should focus on encouraging greater use of the more effective methods and a larger number of them.

Some additional insights into job-search methods by unemployed workers have been provided by small studies, utilizing alternative databases. According

Table 9.1
Active Job Search Methods Used by Unemployed Workers by Gender, Race, and Age, 1997

	Employer directly	Resumes or applications	Ads	Friends or relatives	Public agency	Private agency	Other	Average number methods used
				Methods used as a percent of total job seekers N=5,808,000				
Total, 16 and over	65.0	48.4	16.9	16.1	18.7	6.9	8.1	1.8
Age:								
16 to 19	62.6	52.8	10.7	11.6	8.7	2.6	5.1	1.5
20 to 24	66.1	50.1	14.8	13.0	18.4	6.1	7.3	1.8
25 to 34	65.2	48.2	18.4	16.7	22.4	7.4	8.2	1.9
35 to 44	67.0	47.1	19.9	18.5	23.8	9.0	9.6	1.9
45 to 54	64.7	46.1	21.7	21.2	22.7	10.8	11.1	2.0
55 to 64	64.1	41.7	20.7	19.6	18.6	8.4	10.7	1.8
65 and over	58.1	30.4	13.0	21.5	8.2	4.6	7.9	1.4
Gender:								
Men	66.1	46.7	17.2	17.8	19.5	7.0	8.7	1.8
Women	63.7	50.2	16.6	14.2	17.9	6.8	7.5	1.8
Race:								
Whites	65.1	49.2	17.4	16.3	17.5	6.8	8.8	1.8
Blacks	64.7	46.5	15.2	14.7	23.0	7.2	6.2	1.8

Source: U.S. Department of Labor. Bureau of Labor Statistics. Unemployed Job Seekers by Sex, Age, Race, and Active Job Search Methods Used. *Employment and Earnings* (January 1998): Table 33.

to one such investigation (Blau and Robins 1990), four components of the job-search process determine the job-finding rate:

1. the choice of search methods.
2. the choice of how many prospective employers to approach.
3. the rate at which offers are received.
4. the rates at which acceptance or rejection of offers are made.

Many people commence their job search while still employed (about one-third of the male job changers; one-fifth of the women; and one-tenth of the teenagers). In reporting on this aspect of job seeking, Holzer finds most search behaviors similar to those of the unemployed. While Holzer posits some advantage in searching while unemployed, especially for youths, David Blau (1992) disagrees. Using data from the Employment Opportunity Pilot Projects baseline household survey (data collected from a sample of 29,620 families in 20 sites in the United States from April through October 1980), Blau's findings confirm the popular impression that the employed have a much better possibility of receiving a job offer than the unemployed. Employed men receive about 6 percent more offers than unemployed males, while unemployed women receive about 7 percent fewer offers than the employed women, despite the fact that both employed and unemployed job seekers make about the same number of contacts weekly. Blau concludes that the employment status of the job seeker appears to make a difference in job search results: despite essentially similar search behavior, outcomes differ. This was true for every method of search used. While no explanation is apparent, the researcher speculates that a stigma is attached to unemployment, one that affects job offers.

Disposition of Offers

It is quite commonplace for searchers, employed and unemployed, to reject at least one job offer (Blau 1992). This is true whether the job seekers eventually accept an offer or not. Around 40 percent of both employed and unemployed job seekers who ultimately accept a job reject at least two offers. And of those who ended up without a new job, almost half of the employed and about a fifth of the unemployed reported declining at least one offer. Unsurprisingly, the unemployed seem far more likely to accept an offer than the employed. The average number of job offers rejected is close to one. Blau speculated that job seekers run out of employer possibilities after a certain point. Such decline in possibilities is shown by a rapid drop in the daily offer rate, which dips severely after the first quarter (3 months) of job seeking. This observation contradicts the findings of an earlier, large-scale survey that most unemployed searchers tend to accept the first offer received (Rosenfeld 1975). Blau also found that experience and education have a strong positive effect on search outcome; age, a negative effect.

Relationship of Offers to Reservation Wage. A surprising finding in the Blau study is that most job seekers ultimately accept a job offer below their wage goals. Contrary to theory, 67 to 70 percent of all unemployed searchers and 95 percent of the employed searchers who accepted a job and ceased searching took less pay (in real money) than their estimated reservation wage. And once a given job seeker accepted an offer, he/she ceased to look further. One speculation is that the acceptance of less-than-reservation wages may have been due to the inflation rampant during the years covered by Blau's survey. Nonetheless, researchers remain perplexed as to why people stop searching for a job that fulfills their reservation-wage requirements when they accept jobs offering lesser pay. Such job seeking behavior seems to run counter to what mainstream economists consider the major goal of the job search: finding a job that promises one's reservation wage.

Job Search by Employed Youths

Job search behavior of youths, considered a problem group by employers, is of particular interest because of young people's high-level propensity for job-hopping, leaving employers wary of hiring them. It is low pay that sets off the impulse for frequent job search by employed youths, according to an analysis of the National Longitudinal Survey of Youth, an ongoing study of a large sample of U.S. young people, financed by the Labor Department for use by researchers. Many youths have been found to begin their job search while employed; but as their current wage decreases in relation to possible alternative wages, they quit their jobs in order to search more effectively (Parsons 1991).

Youths' job-hunting modes may change over time as desirable employment remains elusive, a small study of almost 200 vocational school and college graduates revealed (Barber, Giannantonio, and Phillips 1994). In the beginning, youthful job aspirants search broadly to develop a pool of possibilities. Then they investigate the pool and, if they exhaust it without success, move on to develop a new pool. In the process, a three-month period between the onset of the job search and graduation, these job seekers were found to decrease their search intensity, to rely more on informal sources of information, and to reduce their dependence on information. If still unemployed upon graduation they repeat the process, beginning with intensive search. The behavior is interpreted as indicating a sequential mode of change in search behavior as opposed to learned change or emotional response.

Gender Differences in Job Search

Other group differences to be found in job search are those between men and women. True in all types of environments, big city to small town, women tend to spend about 15 percent less time traveling then men (Wyly 1996). This implies that women look for employment closer to home. However, Wyly's analysis of travel within various areas of Minneapolis indicated such great differences in travel time for both men and women, depending on the district of the city, that overall averages are not very enlightening. Also, the study included only those women using automobiles. Women limited to public transportation would more likely experience limited work possibilities due to geographic constraints. Larger studies are needed to establish the facts in this area. If Wyly's conclusions were to be substantiated on a broader scale, it might be advisable to encourage women to job seek over a larger geographic area for the purpose of identifying better work opportunities.

It is generally believed that job search within a narrower radius of home reflects women's self-image as homemakers and their desire to be closer to home and children than men deem necessary for themselves. It has also been widely speculated that many employers have migrated to the suburbs to take advantage of the relatively large supply of well-educated women with a propensity to work close to home, whom employers believe would therefore be available at low wages. The topic requires further investigation.

USE OF THE INTERNET

According to an on-line newsletter, *Electronic Recruiting News,* more than a million jobs across the occupational spectrum are listed on 5,000 Web sites, with the number expanding daily. The driving force for both employers and job seekers is reportedly lower costs and speed in filling jobs. One advantage for job seekers is the Net's round-the-clock accessibility, which allows people to more easily pursue new positions while they are still employed.

The largest job site is offered by the U.S. Department of Labor (DOL) and its state affiliates. Known as "America's Job Bank," this service is said by DOL to offer listings from both large and small employers throughout the country. Its address is: www.ajb.dni.us. DOL offers three other Internet-based services: a resume-posting service for job seekers called "America's Talent Bank" whose address is the same as that of the Job Bank. Potential users are instructed to sign on to the Job Bank address, click on Job Seekers and the "New Users Register Here List" to register themselves, by home state, and post their resumes. DOL's two other Internet services supplement these: America's Career InfoNet (www.acinet.org) service provides job-related information of potential interest to both employers and job seekers, while America's Learning Exchange (www.alx.org) offers information concerning training opportunities. DOL envisions the Internet opening up possibilities for the development of an on-line national job market, with the potential for relieving regional fluctuations in employment.

The private sector is also testing the Internet's recruitment potential. One of the largest groups, the On-Line Career Center, founded in the early 1990s by six major corporations, claims participation by 2,500 employers. Reports are that Internet hiring is faster and cheaper than traditional newspaper advertising; in fact, recruitment appeals on company Web sites are a part of the landscape. Perhaps the best indication of widespread usage is the proliferation of "how-to" books on Internet usage on publishers' lists.

If the Internet were to become a primary factor in job search and recruitment, the present conclusion that personal referrals represent the method of choice for both recruitment and job search would be in question. Such Internet utilization might also make job search more difficult for less-educated and older workers who are unfamiliar with its technology. And it remains to be seen whether a country-wide jobs bank could create a national labor market to the extent that regional downturns might be ameliorated by increased information about opportunities elsewhere; worker mobility, after all, is strongly associated with the age of job seeker.

CRITICISM OF CURRENT EVALUATION METHODOLOGY

Some critics, such as Holzer (1987), believe that labor economists at the end of the twentieth century have paid insufficient attention to the specific activities that are part of the hiring process, focusing instead on the costs of recruitment, and minimally acceptable productivity requirements. As such, they are held to have failed to adequately examine recruiting procedures from the viewpoint of simple effectiveness. They concentrate, instead, on how frequently certain recruiting procedures are used, and the circumstances under which hiring practices reflect profit-maximizing principles as opposed to distribution of jobs based on equity. Equity considerations are reflected by the inclusion of new groups, be they women, minorities, or the disabled, into a firm, or by aspects of the internal labor market, such as who is involved in job rotations and promotions, or the role of seniority versus marginal productivity. Equity considerations will be discussed in Chapter 16, which deals in part with the different labor-market experiences of women and minorities.

NOTE

1. This belief is periodically challenged and remains controversial.

REFERENCES

American Management Association. 1986. *Hiring costs and strategies: the AMA report.* New York: AMA.

Barber, Allison, Christina Giannantonio, and Jean Phillips. 1994. Job search activities: an examination of changes over time. *Personal Psychology* 47 (Winter); 739–64.

Baron, John, Dan Black, and Mark Lowenstein. 1987. Employer size: the implications for search, training, capital investment, starting wages, and wage growth. *Journal of Labor Economics* 5: 76–89.

Blau, David. 1992. An empirical analysis of employed and unemployed job search behavior. *Industrial and Labor Relations Review* 45 (July): 738–52.

———, and Philip Robins. 1990. Job search outcomes for the employed and unemployed. *Journal of Political Economy* 98, no. 3.: 637–55.

Boudreau, John, and Sara L. Rynes. 1985. Role of recruitment in staffing utility analysis. *Journal of Applied Psychology* 70 (May): 354–66.

Doeringer, Peter, and Michael Piore. 1971. *Internal labor markets and manpower analysis.* Lexington, Mass.: D.C. Heath.

Holzer, Harry J. 1987. Hiring procedures in the firm: their economic determinants and outcomes, 243–74. In Morris Kleiner, Richard Block, Myron Roomkin, and Sidney Salsburg, eds., *Human resources and the performance of the firm.* Madison, Wisc.: Industrial Relations Research Association.

Lewis, Robert. 1997. Looking for work in all the right places: cyberspace offers job opportunities. *AARP Bulletin* 38 (May): 1, 11.

Osterman, Paul. 1987. Choice of employment systems in internal labor markets. *Industrial Relations* 26 (Winter): 46–67.

Parsons, Donald. 1991. The job search behavior of employed youth. *The Review of Economics and Statistics* 73, no. 1: 597–603.

Rosenfeld, C. 1975. Job-seeking methods used by American workers. *Monthly Labor Review* (August): 39–42.

Rynes, Sara, Robert Bretz, Jr., and Barry Gerhard. 1991. The importance of recruitment in job choice: a different way of looking. *Personnel Psychology* 44, no. 3: 487–518.

United States Department of Labor. Bureau of Labor Statistics. 1997. Looking for a job while employed. *Issues in Labor Statistics.* Summary 97–14 (November). Washington, D.C.: Government Printing Office.

————. 1998. Unemployed job seekers by sex, age, race, and active job search methods used. *Employment and Earnings* 45 (January). Washington, D.C.: Government Printing Office, Table 33, 204.

Wyly, Elvin. 1996. Women, work, and the city. *CURA Reporter* 26 (December): 12–18.

Part IV

Union Organization
and Its Future

The two chapters in this unit discuss the unionization of the labor force, as it exists in the United States, including unions' new directions and some speculation as to what could or should be their future. Chapter 10 gives a brief description of current union membership, structure, and functioning. Chapter 11 offers explanations for the decline of unionism, reports on some contemporary initiatives, and presents views concerning possible new union initiatives.

10

Union Organization:
Its Structure and Functioning

This chapter focuses on the organization and functioning of unions. Emphasis is placed on the operations of local unions, the level at which most readers—and members—come into contact with unionism.

CURRENT UNION STATUS

Total union membership in the United States as of 1997 stood at 16.1 million, 14.1 percent of total U.S. employment (BLS 1998). However, the proportion of the workforce represented by unions is slightly higher: 17.9 million workers, 15.6 percent of the employed.[1] The highest union density levels were experienced between 1946 and 1960, when unionized employees averaged 23.6 percent each year; the highest yearly level, 25.2 percent, occurred in 1956. Since then the density rate has been falling; the 1997 rate was just 14.1 percent. During the glory years the unions did better in the nonagricultural sector of the economy than the overall figures suggest; about one-third of the nonagricultural workforce was organized. By 1997 this divergence no longer existed.[2] For figures on historical trends in union membership and demographic characteristics, see Tables 10.1 and 10.2.

The U.S. union movement has three levels of organization: the umbrella organization, the American Federation of Labor-Congress of Industrial Organizations (AFL-CIO); national unions; and locals. Some additional organizational structures exist and will also be described. Because union structure and constitutions are highly varied at both the national and local levels, the descriptions are highly generalized and cautious. The following leans heavily on Estey (1981), Sloane and Witney (1988), Rees (1989), Dunlop (1989), Katz and Kochan (1992), Ehrenberg and Smith (1994), Filer, Hamermesh and Rees (1996), and Masters (1997). The author is deeply indebted to Charles Gentile, long-time V.P. for Education, Local 1776, Food and Commercial Workers, Nor-

Table 10.1
Union Affiliation of Employed Wage and Salary Workers, 1930–97

	Labor force employment* (1,000s)*	Union members (1,000s)**	Union Members in labor force(%)***
1930	29,424	3,401	11.6
1935	27,053	3,584	13.2
1940	32,376	8,717	26.9
1945	40,394	14,322	35.5
1950	45,222	14,267	31.5
1955	50,675	16,802	33.2
1960	54,234	17,049	31.4
1965	60,815	17,299	28.4
1970	70,920	19,381	27.3
1975	76,945	19,611	25.5
1980	90,564	20,065	23.0
1985	94,521	16,996	18.0
1990	103,480	16,740	16.1
1995	110,038	16,630	14.9
1997	114,533	16,110	14.1

*Data before and after 1980 are not entirely comparable, earlier data being based on total employment in nonagricultural establishments. Data from 1980 and thereafter are based on wage and salary employment of persons, 16 years and older. **Data refers to annual average number of dues-paying members reported by labor unions, also including members of employee associations similar to a union, with exclusion of members of professional and public employee associations. ***Does not include nonmembers represented by unions.
Sources: U.S. Department of Labor, Bureau of Labor Statistics, Handbook of Labor Statistics (1980): Table 165. For l980, Earnings and Other Characteristics of Organized Workers, Bulletin No. 2105. For 1985 and thereafter, January editions (1986,1991,1996, and 1998) of Employment and Earnings.

ristown, Pennsylvania, for his knowledge and many insights over a period of years concerning current union structure and activities.

THE AFL-CIO: THE NATIONAL FEDERATION

Most of the unions in the United States are members of the AFL-CIO, a federation of fifty-two national and international unions (i.e., including Canada), plus the few local unions that do not belong to any national union. With headquarters in Washington, D.C., the AFL-CIO is primarily a lobbying and service organization, having very limited powers over its constituent national unions, although it can expel them for failure to meet prescribed standards of conduct. One traditional restriction on national unions has been the prohibition against raiding other unions for membership. Once considered a primary benefit of Federation membership, this power has lost much of its meaning nowadays, since national unions are organizing widely diverse groups. In one major city, for example, the Teamsters have organized public-service lawyers and university maintenance workers. Restrictions, still quite relevant, are prohibitions against involvement in systematic corruption; against adherence by union officers to communism or any other totalitarian ideology; and against discrimination asso-

Table 10.2
Union Affiliation of Employed Wage and Salary Workers by Selected Characteristics, 1997

	Members of unions	Represented by unions
Total employed, age 16 and over	16,110,000	17,923,000
Percent of employed	14.1	15.6
By Age		
16 to 24	5.2	6.1
25 to 34	11.7	13.2
35 to 44	15.9	17.7
45 to 54	20.5	22.4
55 to 64	19.2	20.7
65 and over	8.3	9.4
By Race, Hispanic origin, and Sex		
White	13.6	15.1
Men	6.0	17.4
Women	10.9	13.3
Black	17.9	20.1
Men	20.2	22.2
Women	16.0	18.3
Hispanic origin	11.8	13.5
Men	12.6	14.3
Women	11.6	12.2
Full or Part-time Status		
Full-time workers	15.6	17.3
Part-time workers	7.0	8.0

Source: U.S. Department of Labor, BLS, *Employment and Earnings* (January 1998): Table 40.

ciated with race, color, religion, or national ancestry. The Teamsters have been expelled more than once for reasons of corruption, and the old United Electrical Workers (UE) for being led by communists. Other unions have left voluntarily. The United Auto Workers, for example, withdrew at one time in protest against lack of AFL-CIO militancy, returning to the Federation at a later time.

Organizational Tasks

The AFL-CIO represents the United States in international as well as national affairs. It helps workers in other countries to organize and has financed resistance to communism and fascism. In recent years the AFL-CIO has been criticized for devoting too much of its energies and resources to overseas affairs. This involvement began during the cold-war period: the labor movement was co-opted by the U.S. State Department and the CIA into combating international communism by influencing labor movements in vulnerable countries abroad. The monies funneled through the labor Federation, whether government-originated or their own, went to discredit certain governments, such as that of Nicaragua, and to elect alternative worker representatives. Criticisms of these activities have focused on whether this was/is a proper realm of activity for a labor union, whether the union movement is mixing with the right "friends," and on the extent to which the AFL-CIO's limited resources should continue to be invested abroad.

Governance

The Federation is governed by its biennial national convention, but between sessions its governance consists of a president, secretary-treasurer, executive vice-president, and an Executive Council. These representatives are elected at conventions attended mainly by the presidents of the affiliated national and international unions (52 in 1998). To service its nationals the Federation has professionally staffed trades departments, such as building trades, food and allied service workers, union-label trades, maritime trades, metal trades, professional employees, and transportation trades.[3] A staff unit, headed by a deputy director, was established by the newly elected Sweeney administration in 1996 for the purpose of organizing, the platform upon which the new incumbents ran for office.

Representation of national unions in the umbrella AFL-CIO is based on the size of their membership, with every national union holding a minimum of one vote. Some nationals, accordingly, wield more influence in the Federation than others. Important policies and decisions are made at the convention; and between conventions, responsibilities fall to the Executive Council, comprised of the president, secretary-treasurer, and thirty-three vice-presidents. The president and secretary-treasurer are full-time; the vice-presidents, usually presidents of nationals, attend several yearly meetings. The Executive Council, through its standing committees, deals with matters involving organization, political education, research, and economic policy. In addition there is a General Board, with representatives from all the nationals and heads of departments of the AFL-CIO holding advisory powers only. In short, there are a series of groups through which elected and appointed AFL-CIO officials can communicate and share in decision-making with the Federation's national constituents.

Educational Facility

The Federation maintains a Washington, D.C., staff that includes economists and other research specialists, and a resource library. The central staff assumes a leadership role in coordinating lobbying efforts with those of the national unions. It also helps with organizing drives. Its special industry departments and other special-services units offer professional support and expertise to national unions and their locals. For example, the construction-industry department may do research on trends throughout the country concerning use of materials, new technologies, and building techniques. A labor education center is situated in the Washington, D.C. area.

Background History

The AFL-CIO has evolved in a series of steps, from an early federation of craft unions (AFL) established in 1886 under the leadership of Samuel Gompers, a cigar-maker whose conservative policies dominated the organization for thirty-three years. The AFL grew in numbers, as both the economy and the workforce expanded; it fell under continual attack for its unwillingness to respond to new political trends, including radical movements, and its reluctance to adapt to the changing industrial order by, for example, recruiting the unskilled workers who populated the newly developing industries.

Despite, or perhaps because of, the AFL's mainstream political stance, it succeeded in working within the system for incremental change. Some reforms that it is credited with influencing during this early period are:

1. State laws regulating the employment of women and children.
2. State laws protecting workers suffering from industrial accidents.
3. Worker-compensation legislation by many states.
4. Establishment of a national Department of Labor (1914).
5. Exemption of unions from the restrictions of the Clayton Anti-Trust Act of 1914.
6. Regulation of sailors' working conditions, the Seamen's Act of 1915.
7. The Lloyd-LaFollette Act (1915), giving the right of lobbying and unionization to public employees.
8. The Adamson Act (1916), enacting the eight-hour day for railroad workers engaged in interstate commerce.

By 1935 the internal tensions between the craft-union traditionalists and the leadership, hungry to recruit within the new industries, had grown so strong that an Organizing Committee for industrial workers was formed by AFL dissidents, which culminated in the establishment of the Congress of Industrial Organization (CIO) in 1938.[4] The labor movement remained split until its separate factions merged in 1955 to become the AFL-CIO, with a traditionalist from the AFL, George Meany from the Plumber's Union, as president.

After passage of the 1935 National Labor Relations Act (Wagner Act), which fully legalized labor organization, union membership expanded at an unprecedented pace, especially in the industrial-sector unions. By 1936, the unionized work force had risen to 3.989 million (7.4% of the total workforce); by 1946, the end of World War II, to 14.395 million (23.6%). Membership, in absolute numbers, was highest in 1980 when 22.4 million (20.9%) were in the union fold. Union density, however, was heaviest in the years from 1946 through 1960 at 23.6 percent, after which it began to fall as a proportion of the labor force. As of 1997 membership was 16 million (14.1% of employed persons). In recent years union recruitment has been most effective in the public sector; its membership as of 1997 constituted 42.3 percent of all public sector workers. Membership in the private sector, on the other hand, has fallen to 10 percent (BLS 1998, Table 42). Table 10.3 breaks down recent union-membership figures by industry.

THE NATIONAL UNION

The national unions comprising the Federation vary greatly by many dimensions, including size, membership type, membership mix, industries involved, and geographic location. It is now inadvisable to state that any particular national union represents a specific occupational group (or groups). Despite the difficulties in generalizing about the "nationals," some common characteristics pertain.

Governance

A national (or international) union is a collection of local unions operating under the same authorization, the constitution of their respective national. National unions are governed by their conventions, most of which meet annually or biennially although they are obligated only to meet every five years. The convention membership is elected by locals, with representation according to size. Local union officials tend to predominate as delegates, but larger unions may include rank-and-file members. These delegates elect the officers of the national. The social aspects of union involvement may be seen in the conventions' popularity. A prominent union president once confided to the writer that he felt an annual convention (cost: $8 million) unnecessary, and favored a biennial one; but that membership liked the beaches of Puerto Rico too much.

Between conventions, the executive board of the union makes the decisions. These officers tend to have long tenures, a circumstance believed to explain much of the moribund character of many national unions. Since delegates come from around the country, these meetings provide the members with an opportunity to exchange information. Otherwise, communication between the nationals and their locals tends to be very limited. The officers of nationals often come from the ranks of especially successful, paid officials who began as union volunteers in their local union and worked their way up to the ultimate height of a paid position in a district council or on the national staff. They are often nominated by incumbent officers. Tenure tends to be long; departure tends to correspond with retirement. This is, in part, due to dearth of attractive alternatives in the union field.

Table 10.3
Union Affiliation of Employed Wage and Salary Workers by Industry, 1995

	Members of unions (Percent of employed)	Represented by unions
Mining	13.9	14.3
Construction	18.6	19.5
Manufacturing	16.3	17.2
Transportation and public utilities	26.0	27.5
Wholesale and retail trade	5.6	6.2
Finance, insurance, and real estate	2.2	2.8
Services	5.4	6.5
Government	37.2	42.3
Agriculture	2.1	2.4

Source: U.S. Department of Labor, Bureau of Labor Statistics, *Employment and Earnings* (January 1998): Table 42, p. 217.

Major Responsibilities

A national union's major responsibilities are to give assistance to locals in the areas of organizing; bargaining; grievance; arbitration; legal advice and services; and development, operation, and dispersal of strike funds. These activities are often realized through the area council or district council. The national union constitution usually mandates the rules of operation for the local union, and addresses such matters as the amount of dues and method of collection; procedures for holding meetings; selection of officers; and discipline of membership. National unions are particularly concerned about local negotiations that might set precedents in the larger product market in which the national union operates. In other words, the national cannot permit a local to influence future negotiations in industries involving other locals of the national. It is particularly obligated to keep *wages out of competition* in a product market.[5] For this reason industrial unions tend to be more centralized than craft unions.

The national unions remain responsible for the organization of new membership, a union tradition, though recruitment is a task that must be performed at the local level. Much latter-day criticism of national unions has focused on their lack of aggressiveness in this area. As of the mid-1990s, some national unions have increased their membership efforts, with positive results; the International Service Employees Union is an outstanding example. These activist unions commonly run educational programs for membership and staff and publish newsletters. They may also attempt to reach out to the larger community to influence public opinion. For example, some unions have paid for "Buy American" ads on television.

As a source of professional expertise, a national union's support is valuable to its locals. Because collective bargaining has become so complex it, is difficult for any local to have the capability to deal with larger employers. The national union supplies needed labor-law specialists, statisticians, and seasoned negotiators, and in so doing gains considerable control over the content of negotiations. The national union also supplies professionals who help with internal union affairs, such as the settlement of grievances and matters involving arbitration. Lawyers, paid by the national, can be utilized by locals to advise them concerning legal matter, to help with aspects of labor negotiations, and to represent them in court, if necessary.

Power Relations

The constitutions of most national unions tend to give them considerable power over their locals. A local may not call a strike without its national's permission, and the national must approve any contract negotiated by a local before that contract can go into effect. Should a local defy its national by calling an unauthorized strike, the national can exert unofficial pressure by withholding strike benefits from the membership and, as a last resort, officially take over the union through a trusteeship arrangement. Persistent and unresolved corruption on the part of a local, for example, might force a trusteeship.

The primary source of financial help during strikes is to be found in the national union. It holds the funds needed to pay benefits to union membership when a strike action is called. Of course, the national can only do this as long as the strike fund has the means, though sometimes other national unions come to the rescue with loans from their treasuries. The national may give funds to a local in the midst of a prolonged strike to help with family emergencies, such as to stave off evictions or utilities cutoffs.

THE LOCAL UNION

The local union is the most common point of contact for the membership. Often the local union came into being because, at some point in time, a group of employees was dissatisfied with wages or working conditions and asked the area representative of its industry's union or its craft union to help the group organize. Ultimately the employees, as a group, received a charter from the national union of which their local is a member. In some instances, a national union takes the initiative and attempts to organize a plant's eligible employees (the nonexempt, under the National Labor Relations Act), giving them a charter once they have established bargaining rights.

Local unions tend to be closer to their nationals than the nationals to the Federation. This is in large part because of the control nationals exerts over locals, including the right to revoke the local's charter. The national controls strike funds, most available professional expertise, and the technical support needed by locals to successfully negotiate contracts and conduct strikes. Locals must secure the permission of their nationals regarding certain important decisions such as making contract demands or calling a strike. In many instances, where industry-wide bargaining is involved, the national negotiates the contract, returning it to the local for settlement of local issues. Where the product market is limited to one locality, as in the case of unions offering plumbing or maintenance services, the local can act more independently of the national; when the product market is nationwide, the national union usually takes major responsibility for decision-making, especially in the area of contract negotiations.

There are some local unions that are not associated with any national. Mostly the successors of now illegal company unions, they have declined since 1935 to join any national union. They are widely dispersed throughout the economy, and some, such as the chemical and refining unions, still play an important role in their industries.

Basically, there are two types of union locals: the *craft local* and the *industrial local*. The characteristics of a individual local will vary greatly, depending into which category it falls.

Craft Union Locals

The Craft Local. Representing the earliest known type of unionism, the craft local consists of members of a particular trade or craft (plumbing, carpentry, electrical work, cement work). They are often graduates of a union-sponsored apprenticeship program, and they obtain their work through the union's hiring hall, which covers a defined geographical area. In short, craft union workers tend to perform for many different employers a single set of tasks that usually involve specialized skills and training. A national craft union may include members of several crafts; but at the local level, membership is separated into single-craft locals. The craft union negotiates wage rates for its geographic area.

Craft union members, traditionally, have considered themselves the aristocrats of the labor movement. With their skills, which they attempt to keep in short supply, they command relatively high rates of pay. In a craft union obtaining employment is largely dependent upon the demand for work and the maintenance of a good relationship with the business agent who serves as hiring officer of the local union. Typically, employers call into the union office to obtain workers, as needed. The job may last one day or for years, but generally employment is highly time-limited. Seniority plays some part in who is sent to work and, when retrenchment is necessary, who is laid off. Craft-union members have sometimes been known to complain that they cannot obtain employment due to the racial or gender bias of the hiring official, or because they are "on the outs" with that individual. Some craft unions have been accused of attempting, as a matter of policy, to monopolize employment on behalf of members' families (or neighbors or ethnic group) by refusing to grant apprenticeships to undesired persons. During the civil-rights struggles of the 1960s, much effort was expended in attempting to influence craft unions, especially the construction trades, to change their admission practices. For the purposes of this discussion, the point is that craft-union employment is typically sporadic and emanates from the union hiring hall, not from individual employers.

The craft union contract is negotiated locally or regionally; it is a short document, because there is little to negotiate. The nature of the job has been predetermined in the apprenticeship process, with limitations strictly guarded. Craft unions have traditionally been quick to strike to maintain their job boundaries and monopolies. But more recently, they have been forced to alter their behavior because of changes in technology, changes in the political environment, and the general movement of employment away from the large cities, traditional bastions of union strength. The construction trades make for a good case study. The building trades have retained their monopolies only in a few large cities, such as New York and Philadelphia, as economic development has shifted to the union-resistant suburbs and right-to-work states of the South and West. Even within the union bastions, the craft unions may make themselves more competitive by, for example, effectively lowering labor rates by permitting employers to use a greater number of union apprentices over journeymen (apprenticeship graduates) than specified in the contract.

Industrial Union Locals

Members of industrial locals tend to be regularly employed by one firm at a single site. The local may include skilled, semiskilled, and unskilled workers who perform varied tasks, but in practice a set of permissible tasks for each category of worker is usually specified in the labor contract. In the recent past industrial-union employment was entered into with the expectancy of permanence, except when demand-deficiency brought about layoffs. Traditionally, unions have been adamantly opposed to the hiring of part-time or temporary workers; but many have been forced to concede this hiring practice to the employer.

In contrast to the members of craft unions, the generally low-skill status of industrial-union members makes them easily replaceable. They receive lower wage rates than crafts workers and receive their pensions and other benefits through the employer (who may pay into a union fund). Entrance fees and dues tend to be low. When unions were strong, the national unions were often able to negotiate a master contract for a whole industry (or a geographic region), and the document was sent to individual unions for negotiation of purely local issues (local supplements). Now, master contracts are infrequent, since few unions hold sway over a large portion of an industry.

Industrial-union contracts tend to be long and detailed. One aspect of contracts, the *work rules*, are thought to be particularly influential in stimulating high levels of resistance on the part of employers to unionism. This is the matter of *work rules*. Unions, on the other hand, generally cherish the rules. To clarify, following Katz and Kochan (1992) we refer to rules dealing with protection from arbitrary treatment (arbitrary dismissal, denial of benefits, for example); seniority rights, important because they are the basis for distributing benefits and job opportunities; and job transfer rights, in the case of job losses at a unionized plant.

Employers tend to dislike work rules because they believe that the rules raise both wage levels and number of employees, aside from limiting employer control. They especially dislike rules borrowed from Taylorism and scientific management, which specify very narrow job categories, that is, limitations upon the number of tasks that a given worker may perform. It has been claimed that work rules, rather than wage levels, have fueled high levels of employer resistance to unionism, since the work rules tend to wrest control of the workplace floor from employers. Indeed, the participative-management movement of the 1980s has been interpreted by some as an effort by management to persuade unions to give up some of the cherished rules in return for keeping plants open (Katz and Kochan 1992). The *givebacks* of the 1980s were unprecedented by their "depth and pervasiveness" in all the years since the Great Depression, and they were fueled, many labor observers believe, by determination on the part of employers to lower wage costs.

It is difficult to describe a "typical" local union, because the individual locals vary greatly. Unions officers, usually a president, vice-president, secretary-treasurer and a few lesser officers, are elected by direct membership vote, according to provisions in their union charter. Shop stewards, usually one from each department of the employing firm, are either elected or appointed, mainly for the purpose of conducting grievance investigations. They tend to be in close touch with membership. They and other union officers often work without pay, conducting union business during working hours, usually with the tacit acceptance of the employer. Typically, the shop steward serves ten to twenty workers (Katz and Kochan 1992). In craft unions large enough to afford it, the building trades, in particular, a paid business agent may visit work sites to make sure that standards are upheld and that the contract is enforced. The number of workers served by union personnel, one measure of potential effectiveness, is difficult to establish because of the differences among unions, the distinction between paid and unpaid personnel, and union sensitivity over the matter. According to the writer's communications with individual union officers, the number of workers served by one shop steward may be enormously higher than the estimate cited above.

Local Union Activities

The major activities of a local union include the following:

1. Negotiating the contract, in conjunction with the national.
2. Servicing members' grievances.
3. Disciplining members.
4. Engaging in political activities.
5. Providing educational programs for officers, present and potential.
6. Conducting social functions.
7. Participating in community affairs.

The problem of adequately servicing contracts is one of local unions' greatest problems. In large, prosperous locals, the executive officers may be paid on a full-time or part-time basis to carry out their duties. Sometimes only the president is paid. To achieve the economies of scale necessary to support a necessary range of full-time staff, locals often go together to establish district or area councils. Lack of trained, well-qualified personnel at the work site tends to be a persistent problem. With labor unions looking to expand membership by organizing ever smaller workplaces, the economics of servicing such contracts may prove to be even more critical a factor than employer resistance and employee fear.

As noted earlier, locals do not have free rein in regard to negotiations; they often have to conform to national guidelines, and local agreements must also be ratified by the national. As national unions weaken, negotiations are now more likely to be confined to the local level than ever before. But in circumstances of gross misconduct, specified in the Landrum-Griffin Act of 1959, the national unions can still resort to takeover by trusteeship, to bring locals back into line.

The local bears a legal responsibility to represent members who have grievances (complaints about violated aspects of their contract) against management. This activity takes up most of the time and energy of union leadership and is a major factor by which members judge a union's effectiveness. Grievances often present problems to the officers, who are legally obliged to service them, whether meritorious or not. This obligation may create discontent among other members, who feel that the officers are wasting most of their time on "the bums." Some union leaders feel that union-management cooperative arrangements can be helpful in lessening this problem.

The local is expected to take action against members who violate basic union rules, such as engaging in strike-breaking, going out on wildcat strikes, or misappropriating union funds. The union must provide fair judicial hearings, as specified by the Landrum-Griffin Act.

The political activities of local union officers are summarized below, following Balfour (1987):

1. The local representative or shop steward, industrial union, hears and files grievances, enforces the contract, and maintains dialogue with management.
2, The business agent or shop steward, craft union, enforces the contract and maintains dialogue with management.
3. The local president, industrial union, conducts contract negotiations or local supplements (depending on the national union's role) and represents members in the arbitration of grievances.
4. The local president, craft union, represents the craft in contract negotiations, possibly in conjunction with other craft unions.

The reader will note that it is the local union (as opposed to its national or the Federation) that performs the tasks of greatest importance to the membership. The local union also controls the purse strings in that it collects the workers' dues, usually via employer *checkoffs*, a process by which the employer deducts dues from paychecks and transmits them to local unions. The national lives off per-capita taxes paid by its locals; the AFL-CIO off per-capita payments from the nationals. Often, in the case of craft unions or where employers change frequently, the local union, sometimes in conjunction with its national, may administer the employees' pension fund.

Many local unions attempt to educate current and potential union leadership in union history, labor law, and legal obligations, with the goal of producing better service to members. Some send officers and others to a labor training school, such as the George Meany Center for Labor Studies in the Washington, D.C., area.

Union Dues

Local unions are supported by members' dues. According to Estey (1981) and Gentile (personal communication, 1996), the most democratic type of dues assessment would be the establishment of a given percentage of worker earnings, but the reality is that a flat amount is often set at the demand of the better-paid workers (older workers or full-timers versus part-timers) who emerge to vote only on occasions when money matters are on the agenda. The ideal of the nation's second-largest union, the Food and Commercial Workers of America, according to Gentile, is one hour's pay per week. Presently union dues tend to average about two hours' pay per month or about one percent of total pay, and are generally higher for craft workers than for the unskilled (Balfour 1987).

The Participation Issue

Much has been written about local union members' participation or lack thereof. The effectiveness of local unions is often said to be limited by the low level of member participation in routine union affairs, beginning with the poor attendance rate of only 10 to 15 percent at regular meetings (Estey 1981). Some labor scholars refute the widespread claim of membership apathy; they argue, for example, that the fairly frequent rejection by local membership of contracts negotiated by both national and local leaders indicates that member participation does occur when the rank-and-file is sufficiently interested. Also, the fact that local-union members regularly and vigorously contest elections and the fact that

unions experience considerable officer turnover suggest that both union participation (and democracy) prevails at this level (Katz and Kochan 1992). While
employers once claimed that reputedly low participation levels reflect a lack of
union democracy, they no longer press this issue as it is believed that more
union democracy means more difficulties for employers. The belief is well
founded: union leadership is committed to being responsive to members' needs
and desires. One common desire is for "more," a wish that leadership often believes to be unrealistic, but elected officers often are forced into making unwise
demands and even calling strikes that they do not want, to please their constituency (Filer, Hamermesh, and Rees 1996).

Competition for local leadership positions tends to be high. Motivations may
range from wanting to "do good" to aspiring to higher office (at the regional or
national levels) or gaining prestige. For a non-college-educated person, union
activities represent a rare opportunity to exercise leadership capabilities. A stint
in a union leadership position may also be a way to garner employer attention
and a promotion into management.

Organizational Support Systems: The District Council

To increase their effectiveness, local unions often belong to one or more union
organizations, beyond their connection to their national. They may join a regional organization, the district or area council, of their national. They also may
be part of an industry- or occupation-based union organization. Some national
unions have diversified their membership to the point that they cannot meet the
needs of this increasingly heterogeneous membership adequately through any
one organization. Their locals may belong to a number of occupationally or in-
dustry-based bodies in their region or area, For example, the Teamsters now include, among others, lawyers, white-collar employees, and service workers. To
better meet the needs of a diverse membership, a Teamster local might join one
district council in which service workers predominate, a second for white-collar
workers, a third for professionals, and a fourth for drivers, the Teamsters' traditional constituency.

The district or regional or area council arose from the limitations of local-
union capacity to adequately service individual members and meet organizational needs. It is largely financed by the national, with possible supplementation
by the locals involved. The district council, which includes a number of locals
of the same national union, is in a position to hire one or more full-time business agents, clerical staff, and attorneys with expertise in contract negotiations
and labor law. Each full-time agent is likely to service a number of union locals
within the district. The district council may also be able to hire full-time organizers and other support staff.

The district council facilitates communication between local unions and their
national and also serves as a vehicle for bringing together locals of the same national within a given geographical area. The financial support provided by the
national gives the district director clout with the locals, and it represents a
major source of national influence and control. District directors often become
vice-presidents of their nationals.

STRUCTURES FOR POLITICAL ACTIVITIES

The labor movement, on national, state, and local levels, has structures that facilitate political activity. At the national level, the AFL-CIO has established state-by-state, geographically oriented central labor councils, for the purpose of influencing state legislation and public opinion around matters of special interest to the union movement. Staff members and representatives from unions-within-state lobby in the state legislature around proposed legislation and attempt to arouse interest among constituent unions and their respective memberships.

Central labor councils have also been established in many cities within the country. These serve the same purposes as the state-level labor councils, but draw their resources and personnel from within the area of the city and its environs. Representatives of local unions affiliated with the AFL-CIO may become members. Traditionally, the central labor council of a large "union" city has a place among the power-brokers of the city.

Unions often engage in such political activities as efforts to elect a mayor or city-council members, a governor, state representatives, or the president of the United States. Activities may include financial contribution, especially the donation of PAC (Political Action Committee) funds; lending union facilities for various political events, and door-to-door campaigning. Financial contributions and workers are eagerly sought by political candidates.

The union movement has mainly been identified with the Democratic Party, but some unions, especially the Teamsters and many craft unions, have endorsed Republican candidates. An interesting example of the political pragmatism sometimes exhibited by unions was the persistent support lent to the late senator John Heinz (R-Pa.), the richest millionaire in the U.S. Senate, by unions in and around Pittsburgh, a Democratic stronghold. The unions' loyalty stemmed from Heinz's strong identification with the area and his total dedication to job creation in the former iron-and-steel capital of the world, where his family dominated in pickles, soup, and catsup.

LEGISLATIVE CONSTRAINTS

Standards of behavior for labor unions are regulated by the 1959 Landrum-Griffin Act, which codifies members' rights. By law, unions must represent all members of the covered workforce, regardless of whether they are union members or not. For this reason, the number of persons represented by unions is greater than union membership.

Figure 10.1 illustrates how union members relate to the organizational structures described in this chapter.

Figure 10.1
The Union Member's Relationship to the Parts of the Union Organization

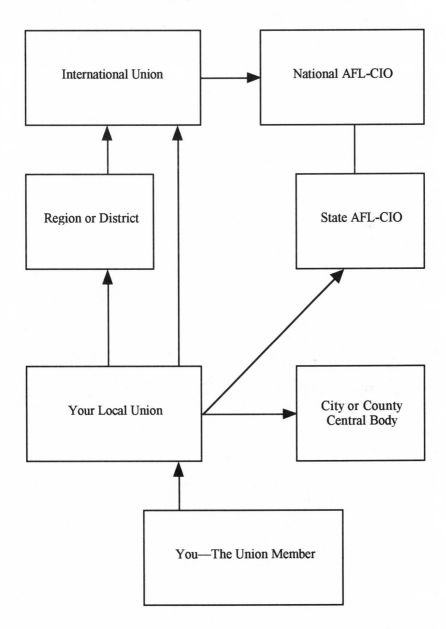

Source: The Food and Commercial Workers of America

NOTES

1. Nonexempt employees in unionized establishments cannot be forced to join the union, but must pay dues. They receive the benefits of union activities.

2. Since the workforce has expanded over the years cited, union density figures—percentage of the workforce organized—are more meaningful than absolute numbers.

3. The former industrial union department and the public-employees units no longer exist.

4. Actually, the AFL did attempt to respond to the new situation by issuing charters that included all types of workers, with special provisions for the skilled minority employed in affected firms, but these compromises with the AFL traditional crafts-only tradition were insufficient for the industrial union proponents who chose to break away.

5. This refers to the need of a union to protect the employers with whom it has contracts, to the extent that it can, from being disadvantaged by reason of having signed a labor agreement. The union has the obligation to maintain the same agreed-upon wage rates for all competitors with whom it has contracts in the same product market.

REFERENCES

Balfour, Alan. 1987. *Union-management relations in a changing economy.* Englewood Cliffs, N.J.: Prentice-Hall.

Dunlop, John. 1989. *The management of labor unions,* Lexington, Mass: D.C. Heath & Company.

Ehrenberg, Ronald, and Robert S. Smith. 1994. *Modern labor economics.* 5th ed. New York: HarperCollins College Publishers.

Estey, Marten. 1981. *The unions: structure, development, and management.* 3rd edition. New York: Harcourt Brace Jovanovich.

Filer, Randall K., Daniel Hamermesh, and Albert Rees. 1996. *The economics of work and pay.* 6th edition. New York: HarperCollins College Publishers.

Katz, Harry, and Thomas Kochan. 1992. *An introduction to industrial relations.* New York: McGraw-Hill.

Masters, Marick. 1997. *Unions at the crossroads: strategic membership, financial, and political perspectives.* Westport, Conn.: Quorum Books.

Rees, Albert. 1989. *The economics of trade unions.* Chicago: University of Chicago Press.

Sloane, Arthur, and Fred Witney. 1988. *Labor relations.* 6th edition. Englewood Cliffs, N.J.: Prentice Hall.

U.S. Department of Labor. Bureau of Labor Statistics. 1980 *Handbook of labor statistics.* Table 165, from *Employment and Earnings and Other Characteristics of Organized Workers,* Bulletin No. 2105. Washington, D.C.: Government Printing Office.

———. 1986. *Employment and earnings* 33 (January) Washington, D.C.: Government Printing Office, Table 57.

———. 1991. *Employment and earnings* 38 (January) Washington, D.C.: Government Printing Office, Table 57.

———. 1996. *Employment and earnings* 43 (January) Washington, D.C.: Government Printing Office, Table 40.

———. 1998. *Employment and earnings* 45 (January) Washington, D.C.: Government Printing Office, Tables 40, 42.

11

The Revival of Unionism
and Possible Futures

Since the mid-1990s the American organized-labor movement has experienced a resurgence, a change enhanced by new leadership at the top. After assuming office in 1996, AFL-CIO president John Sweeney launched a series of new initiatives along several fronts. Some observable outcomes of this renewed activity are noted in this chapter. The commonly offered explanations for the decline of unionism since the 1960s are spelled out and a review of unionism's new directions and some suggested alternatives to traditional union functioning that have been offered by scholars are presented.

THE ANATOMY OF DECLINE

A long series of explanations has been offered for the decline of U.S. unionism, ranging from an unfavorable external environment to aging and static internal leadership. Three types of explanations, sociological, cyclical, and political, commonly account for unionism's decline (Goldfield 1987). Sociologically based explanations imply that the decline is an inevitable accompaniment of changes in industrial technology, geographic relocation of industry, and changes in workforce composition, while cyclically oriented explanations suggest that changes in economic, social, and political conditions occur periodically, with peaks and troughs, union membership rising during the upturns and falling during the downturns. These explanations are in line with the view that unions are products of their environment and that their health shifts with environmental change (Dunlop 1989; Kochan 1980). Political explanations differ from the others in that they deal with changing relationships between the parties involved: workers, unions, employers/owners, and government. Proponents hold that workers are less interested in unionism than they have been in the past; that unions are less aggressive and less skilled in organizing; that business is more militant in rejecting the presence (or threat) of unionization; and that government is less sympathetic, if not hostile, in its response to its use of legal power in regard to union activities.

Major Explanations Offered

The following briefly summarizes the major explanations offered for the decrease of union representation:

1. Disappearance of the potential for organizing in mass-production industries, combined with the economy's shift to the traditionally unorganized service sector.
2. Changes in work-force composition, with more participants who are traditionally "hard-to-organize": women, youths, the elderly, and minorities. This explanation lacks credibility in that women and minorities are well represented in unions; but it has some force to the extent that women and youths disproportionately work part-time.
3. Weakness of labor laws and lack of enforcement by unfriendly governments, resulting in a severe drop in contracts won through National Labor Relations Board elections.[1]
4. Changes in employer attitudes and behaviors, including determined resistance, with a readiness to act illegally, to stop the organizing process. Changed attitudes include breakdown of the implicit contract between labor and management in which management accepted a role for labor organizations.[2]
5. Establishment of human resources departments with control over industrial relations, a power shift within organizations.[3]
6. Clash between employers' need to efficiently organize tasks and unions' adherence to archaic work rules.[4]
7. Slower employment growth in union-organized plants.[5]
8. Inadequate union leadership.[6]
9. Loss of the key to bargaining power, keeping wages out of competition (Mangum and Mangum 1987). This observation ties union effectiveness to ability to maintain common wage rates for all employers in an organized industry, so as not to disadvantage any employer who has signed with the union. The policy can only be implemented when organizing is industry-wide and union density very large.
10. Negative view of unions, as an institution, by workers (Lawler 1986).

Important Recent Events and Developments Eroding Labor Power: Further Explanations of Decline

Landmark events that have undercut the power of the labor movement are the following:

1. The breakdown of pattern bargaining and industry-wide bargaining.
2. Forced concession bargaining.
3. The legitimation of the use of replacement workers, during the Air Traffic Controllers' Strike (PATCO) in 1981.
4. The deregulation of heavily organized industries.
5. The downsizing practices of the late 1980s and 1990s.
6. The passage of the North American Free Trade Agreement (NAFTA) in 1992.

Pattern and Industry-wide Bargaining. Beginning in the early 1980s, as the power of unions ebbed, employers forced concessions without regard to industry standards. As unions gave in to preserve companies and the jobs that they provided, other companies began demanding concessions as well. The unions' ability to insist upon a collective-bargaining arrangement that preserved industry-wide standards failed; thus power to "keep wages out of competition" was undermined. *Pattern-bargaining*, the practice of a union bargaining with an industry "leader" with the expectation of setting a standard for the industry and keeping competitors in line, also withered.

Concession Bargaining. This practice, another indication of change in power balance, reached unprecedented heights in the early 1980s and included wage "freezes," decreases, and the giving up of wages due under existing contracts; decreases in such fringe benefits as pension payments, health insurance, vacations, and holidays; the introduction of the two-tier wage system, that establishes lower wage scales for new hires; and the modification of heretofore sacrosanct work rules which, from the union point of view, meant losing jobs to efficiency (Flanagan 1984); by 1983 new contracts for fully one-third of all unionized workers included pay cuts, sometimes as high as 20 percent the first year. Also, union wage increases in 1983 when they occurred, were 1 percent less than those of nonunion workers. Also unprecedented was the number of union contracts reopened for the purpose of concession-giving. As pointed out by Goldfield, the concession-giving continued even after the end of the early 1980s recession, indicating that the primary cause was not cyclical in nature.

Use of Permanent Replacement Workers. The permissibility of using permanent replacement workers after strikes, commencing with the Air Traffic Controllers (PATCO) Strike of 1981, put a chill on use of the strike weapon in labor negotiations. This broke the implicit understanding that, when workers went out on strike, they could return to their jobs upon completion of the action, successful or not. Although the practice would not have been illegal employers did not tend to hire permanent replacements for their striking workers. Since the PATCO strike, public employers have ceased to turn a blind eye to illegal strikes, and union efforts to abolish permanent replacement hiring have been unsuccessful.

Deregulation. Passage of the Airline Deregulation Act of 1978 set off a spate of deregulations of large union employers, reducing administrative interference in fare-setting and route determination and permitted entry and exit. Within quick succession American Telegram and Telegraph's control over local phone service and control of equipment sold to local companies was broken up by court injunction; the freight-hauling industry, the railroads, and the maritime industry were all deregulated. Faced with heretofore nonexistent competition, the deregulated companies moved to lower costs. This led to changing work rules, cutting staff, and lowering wages, all objectionable to the unions involved. To cut union employment, companies resorted to such tactics as *double-breasting.* This tactic involves moving the work of the unionized firm to a newly established, nonunionized plant that it has established for the purpose of evading its union contract commitments. The second plant pays lower wages for similar work utilizing similar equipment. Some companies have also resorted to bankruptcy, which permits divestment of union contracts. Unions, in turn, resorted to some tactics of their own. In the aftermath of airline deregulation, they have operated on the airlines' financial markets, forcing some mergers and dealing directly with some carriers' creditors. In some cases they have acquired a large proportion of the ownership of the airline in return for wage concessions.

As for railroads, the deregulatory Staggers Act of 1980 permitted the carriers to charge prices and offer service levels according to demand, leading to the elimination of 200,000 jobs between 1979 and 1987. The large number of crafts (16) and unions (13) made the restructuring necessary for rail survival difficult (Arouca 1984). The unions resisted change; they raided each other rather than cooperate with management in an effort to retrieve what could be saved. Despite some union concessions, few cases involved collaborative efforts between labor and management.

Downsizing. Corporate staff reductions, whether necessary for survival, greater profitability, or to be in vogue, are widely believed to have inhibited unionization by reducing the number of well-paying jobs traditionally organized by labor. Whether downsizing actually has led to greater unemployment is controversial. The AFL-CIO, echoed by some news commentators, claims that some downsizings are unrelated to demand, but are simultaneously accompanied by the employment of temporaries and part-timers, allegations that are difficult to prove.

NAFTA. Finally, the 1992 passage of NAFTA (North Atlantic Free Trade Agreement) exacerbated union problems, according to a 1996 report commissioned by the U.S., Canadian, and Mexican governments. Initially suppressed by the U.S. Labor Department, the report indicates that U.S. employers are using their freedom to cross borders, threatening to close plants when unions attempt to organize them; in fact, they are moving plants southward at a higher rate than ever when they lose elections (Bronfenbrenner 1996); the Bronfenbrenner study, an analysis of union elections between 1993 and 1995 by a prominent labor researcher, found that about half of employers facing representation elections threaten to close their plants and that unions are now losing about half of these elections, as opposed to about 33 percent when employers refrain from such threats. Also, a much larger number are actually carrying out their threats when they lose, 7.5 percent as opposed to 2–3 percent in earlier years.

NEW DIRECTIONS FOR LABOR—BY LABOR

Sweeney's Program

In the years prior to the 1996 election of John Sweeney as President of the AFL-CIO, industrial-relations commentators were generous in offering recommendations as to the future directions unions should take in order to be strong factors in labor affairs. Since Sweeney, the flow of suggestions has subsided. In this light the following review of possible futures for the union movement begins with the initiatives undertaken by this service-sector union chief, the first federation president from outside the old crafts or heavy industry sector of the labor movement.

Sweeney made his reputation as President of the Service Employees International Union by almost doubling membership, aggressively recruiting in a highly fragmented industry of low-wage workers who were previously thought to be unorganizable. At the onset of his AFL-CIO presidency, Sweeney injected new blood into the organization by appointing a new, fifty-four-member executive council designed to reflect the AFL-CIO's diverse membership, and by announcing a series of objectives and precedent-breaking strategies designed to facilitate organizing. These strategies included the following:

1. Setting up national training-centers for paid and volunteer (student) organizers.
2. Setting up a women's department in the federation to help female workers through out the country organize.
3. Organizing throughout every region of the country, with emphasis on the South and Southwest, which are viewed as growth areas.
4. Organizing entire industries in a given area to avoid the excuse that targeted employers would become noncompetitive if they raise wages.
5. Involving the federation directly in local unions' organizing campaigns by offering financial assistance (one dollar for every four spent by the local) and helping with organizers, both a break with tradition.
6. Using new tactics, such as corporate campaigns.

According to information gleaned from an internal memo sent by Sweeney to the national unions on February 2, 1996, and news-media reports, such as an article by Steven Greenhouse in the August 10, 1997, *New York Times*, Sweeney's strategy is to organize in growing industries (government and the services). More particularly, he is focusing on low-wage workers in such industries as poultry processing, hospitals, and nursing homes. One justification for seeking out these traditionally hard-to-organize workers is that manufacturing workers often vote against unionization in elections because they fear that their plants will be shut down. And even when elections are won, the plants often do close and move elsewhere, leaving the unions involved to wonder why they wasted their time fighting for certification. But the service jobs targeted by Sweeney cannot be moved.

Sweeney began his presidency by reactivating the union movement politically, making heavy financial contributions to national and local political campaigns and by stimulating local union memberships into action. Early 1996 efforts, consisting largely of nationally financed media advertising, were seen as impressive but ineffectual in influencing the public's voting patterns; 1997 efforts, noted the *New York Times* (November 7, 1997), succeeded in blocking acceptance of a piece of national legislation that would have authorized the president to negotiate further reductions in national trade barriers. Most significantly, success was effected through influencing membership to contact Congressmen individually, a highly significant development in view of the wide divergence in recent years in political orientation of union leaderships and their memberships. By the midterm elections held in fall 1998, the AFL-CIO strategy was "reward our friends; fight our enemies" without regard for candidates' party affiliations. This resulted in the endorsement of a number of Republican candidates, even though the majority supported by the Labor Federation were Democrats. The major union effort was, reported the October 25 *New York Times*, political education and "get out the vote" campaigns, that is, foot power as opposed to the financing of particular candidates.

In his first three years, Sweeney carried through on his pledge to reverse the twenty-year hiatus in union organizing by aggressively recruiting new organizers and increasing spending ten times over the 1994 level, an action that was noted by the September 28, 1997, *Philadelphia Inquirer*, and the November 12, 1997, *New York Times*, to cite two examples. Among Sweeney's boldest strategies, according to the November 7, 1997, *New York Times*, has been the effort to by-pass the hostile National Labor Relations Board by pressing employers to accept employee signatures on union cards as sufficient evidence for the granting of contract negotiations. Should this effort be successful, Sweeney will have removed a major impediment to new organizing. He has also attempted to influence the movement of jobs overseas by making the advantages less enticing. The April 4, 1997, *New York Times* reported that earlier that year several national labor unions participated in a U.S. government task force established to impose standards on the apparel industry in their operations abroad. In addition, Sweeney sent organizers to Mexico to facilitate union organizing in that country.

Recruiting, as of Sweeney's early years as AFL-CIO head, remains at the top of his agenda. His initiatives are often undertaken in the form of attempting to meet needs common to the less affluent community, as a whole. Reports in the *New York Times* (February 27 and March 2, 1998), have pictured the AFL-CIO president as behaving somewhat like the governor of a state, moving about New York City hearing grievances covering the gamut of problems of the poor, from lack of affordable housing to daycare and medical care.

Preconditions Facilitating Sweeney Strategies. In the several years prior to the Sweeney presidency, fresh air started blowing through the union movement, perhaps setting the stage for the administration to come. New approaches and the willingness to adapt to modern technology surfaced. Flexibility on the part of craft unions, previously inconceivable, was reported. For example, the July 10, 1995, *New York Times* reported that New York City television-news-industry unions were reportedly crossing jurisdictional lines, permitting one person to perform a number of different functions, even though this might involve paying dues to two unions. Various unions made attempts to lead their industries by devising means of making work more efficient, in order to protect jobs and raise pay by making employer plants more profitable. For example, the building-trades unions in the Philadelphia attempted to stimulate employment by such measures as developing training programs, anticipating employer needs, investing in pension funds to get projects to a start, and cooperating with drug and alcohol programs for the purpose of cutting costs and on-job accidents. Accounts of such efforts may be found in the April 7, 1997, editions of the *New York Times* and *Business Week*.

Organizers began to find new ways to reach out to the unorganized public as well. They appealed to new groups by offering services as opposed to purely economic benefits. One such effort is the ongoing campaign launched in 1997 by the 1.5 million-member strong New York City Central Labor Council, aimed at improving the lot of unorganized immigrant workers, "the most exploited workers in the City," noted the September 7, 1997, *New York Times*. These are immigrants who fill job slots in service occupations, such as garment worker, waiter, hotel maid, and nurse's aide. Central Labor Council's activities of relevance to such immigrants include lobbying to raise the state minimum wage, cooperating with ethnic groups in school-board referendums, and politicking in the state legislature to rectify a series of immigrant grievances. Another nontraditional effort involves a white-collar union (United Office and Professional Workers of America) that is organizing fashion models, reported the November 20, 1995, *New York Times*. While they earn $30,000 to $70,000 annually, these models nonetheless are independent contractors who receive no benefits such as life, medical, and dental insurance nor help for drug abuse nor Worker's Compensation coverage, and they often experience problems in collecting fees. The union's unorthodox organizing goals, beyond increasing job security and benefits, are to provide protection from exploitation for the models who not infrequently are teenaged girls preyed upon by unscrupulous photographers and clients. The union may even help them obtain safe housing. Higher wages are not, in this case, an issue.

An important organizational development has been the series of union mergers that have occurred or that are scheduled as part of an effort to mobilize greater resources and coordinate efforts in areas of common interest. Between 1956 and 1994, 133 mergers occurred, over half between two AFL-CIO national unions, about one-third between an AFL-CIO union and an independent union, and the remainder between independent unions. Most of these mergers fall into the category of *absorption*, a stronger union taking in a weaker one, which then loses its identity. Between 1984 and 1990 half of the forty-six mergers reported were absorptions by four unions, the Service Employees International Union (9), the Association of Machinists and Aerospace Workers (5), the United Food and Commercial Workers (5), and the Communications Workers of America (4). Since 1995 mergers have included some of the important unions in the "union past": the two garment-workers' unions, the International Ladies Garment Workers Union, and the Amalgamated Clothing and Textile Workers Union (itself a recent merger), all now together as the Union of Needletrades, Industrial, and Textile Employees (UNITE). The "mega-merger" of the big three metalworkers' unions, the United Auto Workers, the United Steel Workers (already merged with the United Rubber Workers, as of 1995), and the International Association of Mechanists, is scheduled for 2000 (Williamson 1995).

Great challenges remain. One is the intransigency of the South in relation to unionization. Between 1985 and 1995, the number of unionized private-sector workers in the South dropped 19 percent, the percentage of private-sector workers from 7.1 percent to 4.7 percent, according to a Bureau of National Research study reported in the February 24, 1997, *New York Times*. Membership across the nation as a whole continued to fall, although at a slower pace than in previous administrations. Sweeney has been given high grades for having recruited large numbers of young organizers, for committing ten times the revenues to organizing than done in previous years, and for jumping over the nationals to inject federation funds directly into local union treasuries. Yet, according to union leadership, as of late 1998 the organizational efforts had not produced appreciable new membership. And Sweeney himself had lost some of his luster as a new face of unionism by being uncomfortably close to the Teamsters Union's leadership, which became involved in corruption scandals.

Prospects for Union Success

A few labor scholars have offered criteria for assessing the prospects for the future success of traditional unionism. One criterion is the matter of *union density*, the extent to which union members in a given industry are organized. The possibilities for success in new organizing are thought to be associated with prevailing density (Rose and Chaison 1996). Another criterion for success is the ability of unions to innovate. According to a 1990 survey of several hundred officials of 111 national U.S. unions, the major characteristics attributable to those unions that have demonstrated ability to take new directions are the constant monitoring of events in the environment that affect the union's well-being, and the readiness to adjust the union's structure and functioning in the interests of internal efficiency and best achievement of other union goals. It was also found that unions with greater diversity in their memberships were more inclined to innovate than those that were less so (Delaney and colleagues, 1996).

Pointing out that unions cannot hope to alter the major environmental changes that have occurred, Marick Masters (1997), an industrial relations scholar, urged labor to try harder and do better in the industries and occupations they have ignored or in which they had little past success. Masters acknowledges, however, that unions do not have the necessary resources to organize effectively, noting, for example, that, according to his analysis, 6 billion dollars would be needed over a five-year period to advance 10 percent annually, a sum several times the annual income of the twenty-eight largest unions. As president of the Service Employees International Union, Sweeney took the path urged by Masters and has attempted to pursue these tactics as leader of the federation. This approach involves targeting professionals, technicians, and service employees; further pursuing women and minorities; and working to maintain gains in the public sector while stopping the losses in the original areas of strength, manufacturing and blue-collar occupations. It also requires investing a greater proportion of union income in organizing. Where organizational strength has been seriously eroded, more union mergers are required for the purpose of obtaining greater resources to apply to organization; this is another path being taken. Whether a beefing up of traditional unionism, renewed efforts at new organization, and so-called innovative measures, whatever they may be, are sufficient to make unions the powerhouses they once were remains a matter for debate, as do the possible alternatives.

NEW DIRECTIONS FOR LABOR, AS ADVOCATED BY CRITICS

Organized labor has found an energetic, activist-oriented, new-style leader for an old establishment. But some advocates for labor doubt that traditional models for labor organizational, however well utilized, can effectively achieve organized labor's fundamental objectives: union recognition, maintenance of a collective voice in negotiating wages, hours, and other conditions of work, job preservation, raising wage and benefits levels, and so forth. A series of scholars who doubt that traditional union programs and practices can be beefed up or extended sufficiently to make meaningful differences in the lives of working people have proffered a series of proposals for new directions for labor unions. The major suggestions offered are summarized here.

Labor-Management Cooperation

A popular view is that traditional, adversarial unionism is doomed because of environmental changes. John Dunlop, a seminal thinker on American industrial relations, has described national labor policy as "in a disastrous state in its bias towards conflict and against cooperation and joint problem-solving; in artificiality, legalism, and delays; in its failure to encourage mediation and negotiated rule-making; and in the lack of a serious role for labor and management representatives in industrial relations policy-making and administration" (Commission on Worker-management Relations, 1994). One remedy for the issues raised by Dunlop is the development of new types of cooperative, collaborative relationships between labor and management.

Such attempts, undertaken over the past twenty-five years, have often produced unanticipated outcomes. The first cooperative-collaborative efforts, along the lines suggested by Dunlop, began in 1973 when General Motors and the United Autoworkers Union set up Quality of Work Life (QWL) projects in which small union and management groups met together periodically to discuss workplace issues. Initially, the QWLs limited themselves to matters outside the union contract; but later, as union strength deteriorated, they also addressed negotiable items, for example, revisions of traditional work rules. These QWL programs were generally regarded as failures.

In the 1980s much corporate (and academic) attention was focused on the *quality circle* as a vehicle for worker-management cooperation on matters, again, outside the union contract. Quality circles, in the United States, consist of small groups of volunteers from the same work area who receive training in problem-solving, statistical quality control, and group process for the purpose of suggesting and implementing means of improving group productivity. More recent labor-management cooperative efforts frequently have been in the form of *participative management*, defined here as a situation in which labor and management agree to the reorganization of work and the definitions of workers' roles to permit individual workers to perform a variety of jobs, as needed; operate without supervision; and participate in organizational decision-making in a mode of cooperation as opposed to controversy (Commission 1994).[7] A series of cooperative ventures in this mode have been conducted, a celebrated one being the Saturn operation of General Motors in Spring Hill, Tennessee.

Some labor leaders support joint employer-union efforts at participative management, seeing it as a means of preserving jobs by helping employers become more competitive. Others feel that union involvement in such schemes reflect labor's weakness and that management's ultimate goal, couched in terms of cooperation, is to persuade workers that they do not need unions to serve as their voice when they can speak directly to management through an employee involvement group. The unions' "bottom line" is that no matter how successful cooperative efforts at individual plants may be, they tend not to be lasting. Even when cooperative efforts have "turned a plant around," strategic decisions made at the top of the corporate hierarchy have often resulted in plant closures for reasons unrelated to plant performance. And no amount of cooperative effort may be able to overcome the fact that some plants are dinosaurs and, from a purely economic point of view, should be closed.

Labor tends to be suspicious of management sincerity when the possibility of collaboration is raised. Sometimes sympathetic statements are made by business leadership in joint meetings staged in the national limelight, but back home company actions often belie the principles. For example, in 1991 a meeting of industry and labor leaders held under the aegis of the Collective Bargaining Forum, a prestigious national group, endorsed the need to collaborate as a means of ensuring a rising standard of living in the United States; their final statement accepted union legitimacy, in practice and as well as principle (U.S. Dept. of Labor 1991). Yet in 1993, just two years later, the long-time president of the AFL-CIO, Lane Kirkland, scathingly denounced U.S. employers for refusing to accept the basic principles of "workplace democracy," as they set up allegedly participatory programs in which workers had no real decision-making power and hired part-time and contingent workers.

Many cooperative programs have been adopted, but this has not stopped plants and jobs from disappearing. Enough failures have occurred to make cooperative efforts seem futile, even though some of the managements involved (GM, for example) have argued that job loss would have been worse without such programs. Repeated attempts by the UAW to save the GM plant in Tarrytown, New York through recourse to participative management coupled with union concessions ultimately failed. And workers are not always backing innovative leadership on the local level, leaving union reformers vulnerable to ouster from their prized union posts. Whatever their initial reactions, union members tend to be less than enthusiastic about cooperative programs when asked to share the pain of bad years as opposed to profits in the good years. And extended periods of high overtime have created tensions that sometimes lead to revolts at the local union level, irrespective of the presence of "involvement" programs.

Despite labor's ambivalence about participative management, in February 1994 a committee of thirty-one AFL-CIO union leaders, mostly presidents, recommended that the labor movement work with management to further develop such programs. They took the position that present workplace arrangements were not in the best interests of workers; that the arrangements were based on Taylorism or scientific management, the doctrine of "one man-one job," with no flexibility in work assignments or time frames, which offered economic rewards as the only basis for work motivation. The committee of presidents outlined a series of principles upon which the "new work organization" should be based, including genuine power-sharing and the continuing right of workers to be represented by unions and receive a fair distribution of the rewards of workplace productivity. Labor leadership was reported to be split on the committee's recommendations, and little was heard of them the following year at the 1995 Florida meeting of the AFL-CIO executive committee, nor since.

The failures of a series of labor-management efforts, including Eastern Airlines or LTV Steel, for example, has taught labor leadership that more than agreements between a single employer and one union are required if mutual needs are to be met. Many feel that, irrespective of good intentions, labor and management goals are likely to be antithetical. Such was the case in a British experiment in participative management, in which union members served on the board of the postal service, as follows:

After a government commission recommended that establishments' boards be composed equally of shareholders' and workers' representatives, plus independent outsiders, a group of unionists served on the Postal Service board. One outcome was to move a number of conflicts, usually resolved elsewhere, before the board, while some issues, deemed critical by management, were moved outside. Although each side had thought that worker representation would lead to better understanding of the other's problems, this did not happen. Communication between the parties was very poor, and labor representatives found themselves in constant conflict over what was good for their membership versus what was necessary for organizational goals. With several unions involved, the position of each union on specific issues often diverged or was unclear. Feedback to union membership was poor. One outcome was that rank-and-file union members became more resistant to acceptance of managerial positions, feeling they would be co-opted. Conclusion: the results of union representation on a board are difficult to predict, being dependent on many factors. (Batstone et al. 1983)

Employers want a freer hand in workplace arrangements, while unions prioritize job security. Interested readers will find accounts of basic role conflicts involved in worker representation on company boards, as experienced in fourteen different situations during the early 1980s, in Hammer and colleagues (1991). Since greater efficiency and productivity make for fewer jobs, both cooperating managements and unions require some environmental changes if their agreements are to hold. One is availability of jobs, lots of good jobs, to replace those lost to greater workplace efficiency. But, in the face of union pressures, managements are more likely to move jobs outside a given community, often overseas, to achieve cost reductions. No matter how flexible a union may be prepared to become, nor how efficient the plant, it is likely that costs could never be reduced to the point of being competitive with foreign alternatives. Recognition of this fact has led to a search for alternative options.The current pessimism concerning the possibilities for success of worker participation tend to be associated with the assumed inevitability of conflicting interests, with subsequent negative impact on the attitudes of both workers and management.

Before leaving the subject of worker participation, it is worth looking at the effects of collaborative efforts on productivity. An analysis of forty-three published studies of efforts to investigate the effects on productivity of several variations of worker participation found that profit-sharing, worker ownership, and worker participation in decision-making all were positively associated with productivity while mandated codetermination was negatively related. The strength of the correlation was greatest among labor-owned or-controlled plants than within firms owned privately or by stock owners. These latter are the firms using such participatory mechanisms as ESOPs (Employee Stock Ownership Plans) or quality circles (Doucouliagos 1995).

Employee Ownership

An alternative path, advocated by some labor scholars and union leadership, is *employee ownership*, defined as ownership of common or preferred stock of a publicly traded firm exceeding 4 percent of the total market values of these equities held by a group of employees, including substantially more than the top executives and key middle-level managers. An employee-owned company is one that is at least 51 percent owned by its employees. Most of the employees, broadly represented, must be involved. As described by Joseph Blasi and Douglas Kruse (1991), the contemporary version of employee ownership has evolved from a series of developments extraneous to union-management issues. Contrary to past policy, companies now frequently offer stock options to all employees, as opposed to restricting the offerings to the top echelon and the exempt (those not covered by the National Labor Relations Act). And, significantly, corporations are encouraging worker participation in ESOPs, a cheap, capital-raising vehicle for employers. Further, company pension funds often purchase their own stock to beef-up its value, increasing the stake of employees in ownership. Also, many companies are encouraging their employees to open 401(k) accounts and buy shares of the employer's stock. In addition, profit-sharing plans often involve payments to employees in the form of company stock. Companies may offer special employee-share plans, sometimes as part of salaries or in return for wage and benefits concessions.

Organized labor is deeply involved in ownership programs in a few large companies with whom they hold contracts. This came about for purely pragmatic reasons: for want of alternative attainable concessions, certain unions (especially the airline industry unions, following deregulation) demanded substantial shares of company stock in return for wage and salary concessions sufficient to keep their financially unstable employers alive. For example, as of 1995 United Airlines pilots, together with one other airline union, owned 55 percent of the company's stock. The agreement included assigning three of twelve board seats to union representatives and permitting establishment of a low-cost shuttle, with a lower wage scale, to enable UA to compete with small nonunion carriers. By April, 1997, however, the relationship had soured to the extent that the pilots, frustrated in their wage demands, issued a statement to the effect that they are unwilling to cooperate in trying "to foster a collegial atmosphere," reported the *New York Times* (April 6, 1997). Even more interesting, in July 1998 the passenger-service workers voted to become members of the International Association of Machinists despite their participation in company ownership, a gain of about 19,000 members for the union, the largest for private-sector unions in more than twenty years. The *New York Times* (July 18, 1998) attributed the victory to dissatisfaction of the nonunionized with their lack of representation in the ESOP plan even though they owned part of it, and with a three-tier pay plan that left them with inferior earnings and benefits, compared to union members.

The withering of a number of worker-ownership programs have prompted much head-wagging and "I told you so" reactions from industrial-relations people, because of the inherent contradictions between union and management roles. The problematic experiences of the management of a union-owned and operated hospital, described below, constitute an extreme example of the dilemmas involved in being both management and union.

The directors and administrators of John F. Kennedy Memorial Hospital, the only union-owned hospital in the United States, were in a quandary during the summer of 1995. How should they respond to a threatened strike by hospital nurses, members of the Pennsylvania Nurses Association, over management demands for more flexibility on working hours? Owned by District Council 33, American Federation of State, County, and Municipal Employees Union (AFSCME), the union's board members are also directors of the hospital. Could they, as union members themselves, cross a picket line of their own employees? And what are their choices when they have a legal obligation as directors to provide services to their AFSCME membership with whom they have contracted to provide health care? Should they bring in readily available agency strikebreakers? Aside from legal obligations, satisfactory performance is necessary for the financial survival of the hospital. Fortunately for the directors, or perhaps because of the tensions due to their "two hats," after acrimonious negotiations, the differences were settled without a strike action. (*Philadelphia Inquirer*, June 18 and August 14, 1995)

Ownership Through Pension Funds. In addition to ownership-as-concessions, unions have become involved in ownership through their pension fund investments. One of the first union "buyouts," in the 1970s, involved the United Steel Workers of America (USWA), which cooperated with the bankrupt LTV Corporation by buying its steel-bar plant, rather than have it fall into unfriendly hands and be shut down. The USWA then raised massive amounts of capital to rehabilitate the old facility. Since then, this union has bought out a series of plants, its prime motivation being job preservation. Blasi and Kruse (1991), who made the largest known analysis of the extent of employee-ownership in the United States, report that unions, at the time of their survey, believed that a properly structured employee buyout, with concessions made to one's own investment (such as employer-relief from rigid work rules), is more advantageous than offering concessions to a new owner, an "often ungrateful corporation." As of 1990 about 10.5 million union members were involved in employee-ownership schemes, about 12.2 percent of the private-sector workforce (Blasi and Kruse 1991).

During the same year (1990), reported the February 2 *New York Times*, the AFL-CIO gave its blessings to a fund established to help unions buy factories in danger of either closing or being bought by unfriendly parties. However, unions' attempts to use pension fund "power" has been exercised more in the direction of trying to change company policies than in attempting ownership of problem properties; experiences with a number of union-ownership undertakings have been influential in dampening enthusiasm for employee-ownership. The outcome of the LTV Steel experience is a good example: the *New York Times* (December 13, 1995) reported that after the Ohio- and Indiana-based company's 8,500 workers made large-scale wage concessions to keep their plants open, the company, in conjunction with two foreign partners, moved south, building a new mini-mill in Alabama. However, this has not stopped some observers from calling for continued efforts in this direction. One possibility raised is for unions to engage in buyouts of healthy rather than sick companies. This approach was taken by an activist union, the United Food and Commercial Workers, Local 1776, when it attempted to join a private investment firm in purchase of a food market chain with stores in the mid-Atlantic region; union employees were to own a 40 percent interest. The attempt failed, however, when the owner upped the price (newspaper accounts and personal communication).

An alternative route undertaken by a number of unions is to attempt to influence the companies in which their pension funds are invested. The writer has been advised by a prominent labor leader that the purpose is to prevent union jobs from being transferred overseas, but most known cases point to interest in maximizing investments on behalf of members, not to job preservation. The most prominent pioneering entity has been Calpers (California Public Employees Retirement System), which aggressively lobbies boards of directors of publicly traded corporations in which the pension fund is invested to change policies perceived unfavorable to shareholders' interests. Increasingly, unions are participating in board meetings and challenging management decisions.

Taking advantage of a 1993 change in the Securities and Exchange Commission (SEC) regulations, unions have been mounting proxy fights as stockholders to protect their members' pension and welfare fund investments. In one situation, the Teamsters, who have very few members working at Kmart but 150 pension funds with $35 million dollars invested in the company, opposed a proposed new-stock offering in June 1994. Their motivation was based on the judgment that the proposed stock offering represented a poor strategic move and would not lead to better stock-price performance. In a situation involving Philip Morris, the Teamsters and the Food Workers Union combined their voting clout, a $150-million pension-fund investment, to attempt to make their 5,000 food-service members' jobs more secure by splitting the food and cigarette units of the company, to remove potential health-associated lawsuit threats from the food-service jobs. Of reported cases, this is an exceptional one in that job protection was directly involved.

During the 1980s mergers-and-acquisitions craze involving large corporations, some unions began playing in financial markets to prevent those actions they deemed undesirable. Such efforts were denounced as unsuccessful and dangerously expensive in terms of risks to union assets by one important union, according to the *New York Times*, March 11, 1990. One example of such strategies were the actions of the Communication Workers of America, which attempted to affect the value of Bell Atlantic stock by running statements, from spokespersons from several large pension funds, expressing fear that Bell Atlantic bargaining tactics would depress stock prices. One such statement ran in the *New York Times*, December 11, 1995.

Companies' Reactions. Companies sometimes resort to complaining to the Securities and Exchange Commission that those unions that try to mix their stockholder and employee representation roles are trying to organize through the back-door. According to the Investor Responsibility Research Center, shareholders win only a tiny proportion of the proxy fights staged, but in the first six months of 1994, unions won seven of their eleven challenges. It is thought that unions will continue to intervene in board decisions in this way.

Associational Unionism

An alternative model for nonadversarial union-management relations is the *associational unionism* model, put forward by Charles Heckscher (1988). The proposed associational unionism emphasizes commonality of goals and the need for inputs by all interested parties, beginning at the work site up to national policy-making federations, laying the groundwork for ultimate systems change. The kinds of parties-at-interest envisioned are employee groupings by job type, organizational level, geographic location, gender, and race. The associationalist model accepts the existence of conflicts-of-interest, while emphasizing the reaching of constructive solutions without government involvement.

The National Education Association is cited by Heckscher as an example of an organization that could evolve into a model for associational unionism. A long-time purely professional organization, the NEA eventually began to conduct collective-bargaining activities, performing some of the functions of a union.[8] Another example of potential for associational unionism is the role of women's organizations such as Nine-to-Five, which puts pressure on both unions and employers in female-dominated industries to eliminate gender-based discrimination.This pressure and the decentralized approach are believed to have facilitated organization among clerical and service workers, both heavily female groups. A third example of associational unionism is the Yale University strike (1984–85) in which women staffers walked out over the *comparable worth* issue, which involves the ideal of equal pay for work of equal value. In Heckscher's view, the favorable outcome resulted in part from pressures from sympathetic faculty and students, whom he views as associational groups. The same view was taken by Johnston (1994), in analyzing the outcomes of two strike actions undertaken by women city workers and private-sector janitors in California during the 1980s. In analyzing these successes, as opposed to the failures of two strikes during the same period by similar, better organized workers, Johnston attributed the two successes to their unions' mobilization of support from the public, interpreted as a return to "social movement" unionism; the janitors' strike, for example, garnered widespread community support as "Justice for Janitors."

Readers may wish to consider some of the recent activities of John Sweeney and some of the individual unions, as described in this chapter, in terms of their movement in directions resembling Heckscher's suggestions.

Alternative Models for Worker Representation from Abroad: The German and Japanese Experiences

German and Japanese forms of employee representation are often suggested as alternatives to the present American model. With the inflexibility of the systems of both countries in the public consciousness in the recent period, the effectiveness of the much-vaunted labor systems have come into question. Still, the *works council*, Germany's vehicle for labor-management cooperation, and *codetermination*, the institutionalized philosophy of involving workers (actually, their representatives) in fundamental decisions concerning their work situation, are worthy of review. Easily accessible descriptions of these are contained in a 1993 Brookings Foundation publication by Katherine Abraham and Susan N. Houseman, entitled *Job Security in America: Lessons from Germany,* and in a chapter by Joel Rogers and Wolfgang Streeck,"Workplace Representation Overseas: the Works Council Story," in a 1994 Russell Sage publication, *Working under Different Rules,* a National Bureau of Economic Research Project Report, edited by Richard Freeman.

The German system of labor organization has been widely studied because of provisions embedded in federal legislation for the presence of worker representatives on the boards of larger firms (*codetermination*) and the role of *works councils,* legally mandated bodies elected by all employees of larger firms, union or nonunion, white-collar and blue-collar, including many supervisory employees. By law, these work councils have the following rights:

1. To access company information on financial matters, personnel planning, and work organization.
2. To consult with management over personnel planning and work reorganization.
3. To impose co-determination upon many issues involving human resource management.

Works-council members are not necessarily members of labor unions, but there is much overlapping, and the distinction becomes ambiguous in many instances. It is claimed that this system enjoys employer support.

Japanese labor organization is typically described as having two unique characteristics: *enterprise unionism,* and the peculiar *joint consultation council* and other labor-management information-sharing institutions. Enterprise unionism is a term used to explain the structure of unionism in Japan: each local stands alone, the functional equivalent of an American local union, completely identified with its employer and, in the case of a multi-plant employer, with the individual plant. Such unions have come to be described as "company unions," which precisely exemplifies the highly inaccurate and misleading material in circulation about Japanese unionism. The enterprise unions of Japan, far from being isolated, belong to one of two national labor organizations that cooperate together each March or April in launching a "Spring drive" (the SHUNTO). At that time the two nationals present a coordinated series of wage demands of the various industrial unions, with negotiations in the steel-heavy engineering and automobile industries serving as "point of reference" for negotiations in all other industries, including government (Schwab 1986). As for the information-sharing, that which companies disclose to their enterprise union is hardly as broad as often painted.

Although most Japanese writers have depicted the power of the union movement as diminishing, producing very low wage increases in recent years, Ikio Kume (1998) believes that the trade-union movement has been in ascendancy since at least the early 1980s, noting that it was a critical factor in the defeat of the Liberal Democratic Party in 1993. Kume's work and *Portraits of the Japanese Workplace: Labor Movements, Workers, and Managers* by Makoto Kumazawa and colleagues (1996), are readily available studies of the Japanese trade-union system.

The Education and Training-Retraining Route

A final suggestion on the future of unionism is that unions engage in reeducating or retraining of their memberships for the "jobs of the future; help with placement; and long term security." Establishment of "occupational unions" in the service sector, that, following the Swedish model, provide such services as training, job placement, and employment security (in lieu of employers offering long-term employment), is one suggestion (Herzenberg 1996). A December 1, 1997, *Business Week* editorial, "What a Modern Labor Movement Needs," urged that unions engage in improving the productivity of their workers by teaching them such skills as computer literacy, math, and English. The editorial also urged unions to engage in inventing means of raising worker productivity rather than fighting it. Readers will recall that some, but not all, of these suggestions are being attempted in the United States. An illustration was given in this chapter of how the building trades in one city are engaged in adapting their training programs to current employer needs in the interests of raising productivity and thus attracting business and jobs. One union (1199C), the Hospital Workers of America, has long been involved in a more daring program than those suggested, negotiating the payment of tuition for education and training for higher level occupations in recognition that certain occupations have finite possibilities for betterment of membership.

NOTES

1. According to the Wilson Center for Public Research (1993) , firings and engaging in illegal antiunion activities occur so frequently as to inhibit union organization. Even when unions win representative elections (50% of campaigns), in only half of these cases do they actually obtain a contract. Employers successfully use a series of tactics to avoid signing, the law requiring only that employers must bargain if a union wins a representative vote; not that they must come to an agreement. These conclusions are in line with those of Freeman (1983) and Dickens and Leonard (1985), who identified them as the primary explanation of union losses between 1950 and the 1980s

2. According to Piore (1982), unions during the 1970s operated under the delusion that the industrial-relations system established by the National Labor Relations Act in 1935 was still accepted by management as a permanent arrangement. With the rise of international competition and internal deregulation, however, the old arrangement, under which each tolerated the other, became untenable.

3. HR people have different agendas than industrial-relations personnel, appealing to all segments of the workplace by emphasizing such issues as merit pay, use of ombudsmen for conflict resolution, and Employee Assistance Programs to help employees and their families.

4.Two separate studies (Piore 1982 and Strauss 1984) based on extensive interviewing with managers, determined that pressure for efficiency was the major explanation for change in employer attitudes.

5. A pioneer study (Leonard 1992) of the effects of union employment at the plant level found that employment growth is about 4 percent less in unionized plants than nonunionized ones. Up to 61 percent of the decline in the proportion of the workforce currently unionized was attributed to the slower growth in employment in unionized plants.

6. Poor union leadership is also held responsible for lags in organizing as far back as the mid-1950s, not the 1970s, as commonly thought (Goldfield 1987). Another failure cited was unreadiness to broaden the appeal of unionism by becoming involved in issues of broad societal interest (Freedman 1989). Employers took advantage of union weakness by hiring union-busting firms to conduct their negotiations and using a series of illegal tactics in labor negotiations, such as prolonged election delays.

7. Quality circles can be considered a type of participation management, according to such a defininition.

8. In 1998 the membership strongly rejected merger with the National Federation of Teachers, an AFL-CIO affiliate, thus declining union identification.

REFERENCES

Abraham, Katharine G., and Susan N. Houseman. 1993. *Job security in America: lessons from Germany*. Washington, D.C.: Brookings Foundation.

Arouca, D. A. 1984. Railroad collective bargaining—anatomy or pathology. *Proceedings of the Thirty-Seventh Annual Meeting*, Industrial Relations Research Association, December: 429–30.

Batstone, Eric, Anthony Ferner, and Mike Terry. 1983. *Unions on the board: employee relations*. Oxford: Blackwell.

Blasi, Joseph, and Douglas Kruse. 1991. *The new owners*. New York: Harper Business, Harper Collins, paperback edition, 1992.

Bronfenbrenner, Kate. 1996. Plant closings and labor rights: final report. Ithaca, N.Y.: Cornell University School of Industrial Relations. Submitted September 30 to Labor Secretariat of the Commission for Labor Cooperation. Included in Labor Commission's June 10, 1997 report, The effects of plant closings or threat of plant closings on the rights of workers to organize. Dallas, Texas, 75201-4240.

Commission on the Future of Worker-Management Relations. 1994. Report and recommendations. Washington, D.C.: U. S. Departments of Labor and Commerce. Washington, D.C.: Government Printing Office.

Delaney, John T., Paul Jarley, and Jack Fiorito. 1996. Planning for change: determinants of innovation in U. S. national unions. *Industrial and Labor Relations Review* 49 (July): 597–614.

Dickens, William, and Jonathan Leonard. 1985. Accounting for the decline in the union movement, 1950–1980. *Industrial and Labor Relations Review* 38: 323–34.

Doucouliagos, Chris. 1995. Worker participation and productivity in labor-managed and participatory capitalist firms: a meta-analysis. *Industrial and Labor Relations Review* 49 (October): 58–75.

Dunlop, John. 1989. *The management of labor unions*. Lexington, Mass.: D.C. Heath & Company.

Flanagan, R. J. 1984. *Wage concessions and long term union wage flexibility*. Washington, D.C.: Brookings Papers on Economic Activity.

Freedman, Audrey. 1989. Unions' future is bleak. *Personnel Administrator* 34 (December): 98–100.

Freeman, Richard. 1983. Why unions are faring poorly in NLRB representation elections. Paper prepared for the M. I. T. Conference on Industrial Relations in Transition.

Goldfield, Michael. 1987. *The decline of organized labor in the United States*. Chicago: University Press.

Hammer, Tove, Steven Currall, and Robert Stern. 1991. Worker representation on boards of directors: a study of competing roles. *Industrial and Labor Relations Review* 44 (July): 661–80.

Heckscher, Charles. 1988. *The New Unionism*. New York: Basic Books.

Herzenberg, Stephen. 1996. Review of Ottoson, Gary, and Douglas Thompson, *Reducing unemployment: a case for government deregulation*. Westport, Conn.: Praeger Publishers. In *Monthly Labor Review* (September): 47.

Johnston, Paul.1994. *Success While Others Fail: Social Movement Unionism and the Public Workplace*. Ithaca, N.Y.: ILR Press.

Kochan, T. A. 1980. *Collective bargaining and industrial relations*. Homewood, Ill.: Richard D. Irwin.

Kumazawa, Makoto and colleagues. 1996. *Portraits of the Japanese workplace (social change in global perspective)*. Boulder: Westview Press.

Kume, Ikio. 1998. *Disparaged success: labour politics in postwar Japan*. Cornell Studies in Political Economy. Ithaca, N.Y.: Cornell University Press.

Lawler, John. 1986. Union growth and decline: the impact of employer and union tactics. *Journal of Occupational Psychology* 59, no. 1: 217–30.

Leonard, Jonathan S. 1992. Unions and employment growth. *Industrial Relations* 31 (Winter): 80–94.

Mangum, Garth, and Stephen Mangum. 1987. The loss of competitive shelters: another insight into union decline. *Journal of Labor Studies* 12 (Fall): 4–19.

Masters, Marick. 1997. *Unions at the crossroads: strategic membership, financial, and political perspectives*. Westport, Conn: Quorum Books.

Piore, Michael. 1982. American labor and industrial crisis. *Challenge* (March-April): 5–11.

Rogers, Joel, and Wolfgang Streeck. 1994. Workplace representation overseas: the works council story: 97–156. In Freeman, Richard, ed. *Working under different rules*. A National Bureau of Economic Research Project Report. New York: Russell Sage Foundation.

Rose, Joseph B., and Gary Chaison. 1996. Linking union density and union effectiveness: the North American experience. *Industrial Relations* 35 (January): 78–105.

Schwab, Laurent. 1986. Professional relationships and crisis in Japan. *Futures* 18 (April): 230–41.

Strauss, George. 1984. Industrial relations: time of change. *Industrial Relations* 23 (Winter): 1–15.

U.S. Department of Labor. Collective Bargaining Forum. 1991. Concluding statement, labor-management meeting.

Williamson, Lisa. 1995. Union mergers: 1985–94 update. *Monthly Labor Review* 119 (February):18–24.

Wilson Center for Public Research. 1993. *Organizing focus*. AFL-CIO Industrial Union Department Executive Board Meeting, 19 March.

Part V

Wage Determination

The matters of how wages and salaries are set—the principles on which they are based and the processes involved—is of continuing interest, since most people today are earners for a good portion of their lifetimes. Almost everyone is familiar with the concept that people are paid on the basis of the interaction of supply and demand for their particular occupation in the labor market of relevance, be it local, regional, national, or even international. Beyond this point discussions of how employers arrive at rates under various sets of circumstances tend to become highly technical.

These chapters can give only an overview, leaning toward the approach of the institutionalists. Chapter 12 gives a brief summary of the grand theories and goes on to describe how wage rates tend to differ, according to a series of dimensions. Included is a discussion of unions' impact on the wages of members and others. Chapter 13 addresses the matter of pay from the viewpoint of the firm, that is, as compensation, giving an overview as to how human-resources departments (or their consultants) establish the rates and scales that end up as specific amounts in paychecks. Chapter 14 describes special circumstances under which employers may pay wage rates above or below market wages and curtailments on the power of the employer to set rates in terms of the legally mandated wage floor — the federal minimum wage— and collective-bargaining agreements that may affect nonunion employers as well as those who signed the contracts.

12

The Major Theories
and Wage Differentials

The basis on which people get paid for their work has been a matter of continuing interest since the onset of industrialization in the 1800s. A series of grand theories have predominated thinking on wage issues until the recent era, the major ones being the wages fund theory, associated with the names of David Ricardo (1772–1823) and Thomas Malthus (1766–1843); Marxism, the theory developed by Karl Marx (1818–83); and marginal productivity theory which is associated with the name of Alfred Marshall (1842–1924), in England, and with John Bates Clark (1847–1938), in the United States. As unionism prospered during the late 1930s and 1940s, bargaining-power theory, not a grand theory, became popular with a school of economists who were preoccupied with industrial relations; and in recent years theories of market segmentation, such as dual labor market theory, also not a grand theory, have been utilized by some economists inclined toward social activism. A brief overview of these theories is offered here.

WAGES FUND THEORY

The wages fund theory was developed as England moved from its agricultural economy into industrialization, with its dependence on wage labor. The wages fund theory was built around the concept of a *natural price for labor*, defined as the price necessary for laborers to subsist and raise a family, neither more nor less. The amount of resources available for payments for labor was held as fixed, any increase in wages for one necessarily leading to lesser pay for another. Enthusiastically espoused by employers, this theory was used to persuade the British Parliament that efforts to organize unions were criminal conspiracies. Wages were also held down by legal restrictions against workers moving outside their parishes, so as to prevent labor scarcities and resultant upward movements of wages.

MARGINAL PRODUCTIVITY THEORY

Marginal productivity theory, which succeeded the wages fund theory, allows for rise in workers' wages.[1] The theory follows from the concept that when an item is in demand, the cost will rise, the price being the point at which supply and demand intersect. Wage rates are thus seen as determined by the point at which labor supply and employer demand *clear the market*, assuming markets are perfectly competitive. This may be taken to mean that the wage is the point at which all employer needs are met and no additional workers are available to work at lower rates. The *marginal revenue product of labor*, the crux of the theory, determines how much an employer can (and will) pay in wages, using a particular number of workers with a given amount of equipment. The wage paid to labor, according to this theory, depends on the employer's observations as to the number of workers that it is most advantageous for him/her to hire in terms of the value of their outputs. He or she will then pay all workers the amount produced by the last worker hired (the marginal worker, the revenue from whose work determines the wage rate). Some economists interpret the theory as explaining employer wage and hiring policies as determined by their taking on additional workers for a given amount of equipment up to the point where their marginal revenue product is sufficient to pay the going market rate. This theory, too complicated to describe in the space permitted, is heavily criticized but it remains the reference theory to this day. Readers may consult any elementary economics textbook for elaboration.

Marginal productivity theory has been highly criticized on many grounds, but especially because of its assumption of perfectly competing labor markets. Another criticism assails the assumption that employers can know the price they will receive when they hire labor. Some critics hold that the theory can explain the hiring policies of small, *price-taking* employers, whose hiring and selling is too small to have any impact on labor or product markets, but that larger employers, *price-makers* or *concentrated employers*, operate on the basis of other principles, that is, they can impose prices on the public and therefore have more power over the wage rates that they pay (see the discussion of oligopolies and monopsonies respectively; also Ehrenberg and Smith 1994; Rima 1981).

It should be noted that some critics of Marxism have interpreted marginal productivity theory as a refutation of Karl Marx's theory, in that it holds that workers are indeed paid the value of their productivity. Critics of marginal productivity theory have pointed out that this is not so, since according to marginal productivity theory, workers are paid only the value of the product of the last worker hired, not according to *average* value of each worker's revenue product.

MARXISM

Marxism, which was developed about the same period as marginal productivity theory, takes the position that workers are exploited by wage systems because they are always paid less than the full value of their labor, no right to profit being conceded to their employers. In insisting that workers are always exploited, Marx followed earlier classical writers who saw capital as stored up labor (Bellante and Jackson 1983). Marx was pessimistic about the possibilities for raising wage rates above subsistence levels because he felt that "a reserve army of the unemployed" would always exist to compete for existing jobs. But he thought they would be paid subsistence levels because to do otherwise would create inefficiency in workers.

BARGAINING POWER THEORY

During the 1940s and 1950s, theorists influenced by John Maynard Keynes (1883–1946) took the position that various forces outside the economic system have an influence on wages. These "bargaining power" theorists hold that even while demand falls, wage rates tend to be "sticky," that is, they often do not decrease, at least not in the short run. According to this way of thinking, wage rates are largely determined by the relative strength of the actors, who are identified as employers, unions, government, and the public. Unsurprisingly, these economists focused on collective bargaining and industrial relations. Problems for bargaining-power theorists are first, that the influence of unions on wages is controversial; second, that unions no longer influence a large portion of the economy; and third, that unions are no longer focusing on wages, but on job retention. Nonetheless, the labor economists' methods of analysis remain insightful.

DUAL LABOR MARKET THEORY

In the 1970s the concept of labor-market segmentation as explanatory of wage rates came to the fore, propelled by an influential work by Doeringer and Piore (1971) that described wages as being determined by the *internal labor markets of employers*. They described *dual labor market*, differentiating the internal labor markets of large establishments from those of smaller employers. The first, they said, pay high wages, attractive benefit packages, and often invest in job training, which creates an incentive for policies aimed toward worker retention, even during recessionary periods. Small establishments are described as hiring easily replaceable workers at low pay and low level of benefits, if any, beyond those legally required. Some labor-market segmentationists have characterized the two types of firms as price-makers and price-takers; as oligopolistic versus competitive in nature. This means that larger firms have the ability to control prices, and are therefore able to pay better wages than smaller firms whose activities are so minor that their actions have no impact in either product or labor markets, and who therefore must charge market rates for their products and, subsequently, pay wages according to the going market for labor. The concept has been used, for example, by Barbara Bergmann (1971, 1974, 1991), an economist influential in establishing directions for the women's movement in the 1970s, to explain women's and minorities' inferior earnings.

CONTEMPORARY THINKING

Mainstream economists today tend to avoid attempts at grand theory. Rather, they attempt to explain aspects of employment-associated behaviors, dealing with such topics as job-search frictions, the matter of asymmetric information and signaling, unions and collective bargaining, efficiency wages, the reservation wage, and health benefits, most of which are discussed throughout this book in other contexts. A great deal of attention is paid to the role of imperfect information.

With this background, the matter of *wage differentials*, systematically observed differences along several commonly used dimensions —interpersonal, inter-plant, and by occupation, industry, and region of the country — is taken up. Also discussed are pay differentials by size of firm. Finally, conflicting theories on the impact of unions on wage rates are described. None of this material provides direct information as to *how* wage rates are arrived at, but it describes the situations under which differences are observable.

Interpersonal Differentials

The type of wage differential of greatest interest to employees is that occurring between individuals within the firm. Employers are keenly aware that workers are concerned about what persons at the same level and those just above and below them are receiving in their pay envelopes. Employee concern over personal equity overrides such concerns as the increasing disparity between average pay and executive pay. For reasons of plant morale, employers tend to work toward eliminating pay differentials between persons occupying the same job titles within the same plant. Most large employers today develop their wage and salary schedules on the basis of job-evaluation schemes The goal is to establish consistency in wages and salaries within the various employee groups (blue-collar, white-collar, managerial, etc.) within the organization.

The following case study involving railroad-track workers, reported in the December 2, 1995, *New York Times*, illustrates the interpersonal differential.

A small group of railroad track workers, members of Teamsters Local 808 in New York State, shut down part of the North-South Commuter Railroad for several hours December 1, 1995, reputedly over a dispute with management (Conrail) over several days of sick leave and vacation pay. The shutdown occurred despite resolution of all major contract issue differences through hard negotiations. According to union spokespersons, the willingness to engage in a shutdown over relatively trivial grievances stemmed from years of bitterness on the part of this small group, over being treated differently than fellow workers on the commuter line. The disparate treatment exists because of historical factors, a number of small lines with different labor contracts having been merged into one line in 1976. Over the years most differences in pay and benefits have been removed, but the bad feelings and remaining frustration over minor differences fueled the decision of the trackers to stage an action.

Inter-Plant Differentials

Many large employers own plants at different locations and in different parts of the country or beyond its borders. The parties most interested in the possibility of differentials between plants belonging to the same firms are unions. When plants are widely dispersed throughout the country, it is often difficult for unions in one plant to obtain information concerning rates at other plants, making efforts at wage-rate uniformity problematic. In recent years some companies have resorted to *whipsawing*, promoting competition for concessions, to induce local unions to undercut other locals of the same national union. Inter-plant differentials defy a prime union objective, keeping wages out of competition, which is a necessity for unions if they are to succeed in keeping union employers competitive.

In the era of the global economy, with large employers dispersing their plants throughout the world, inter-plant differences have become more important than ever. The issue tends to push into the political arena the matter of free trade and the ability of goods to cross borders freely, as was the case in the 1992 battle over passage of the North American Free Trade Agreement (NAFTA).

Occupational Differentials

The fact that members of different occupations receive different monetary rewards is commonly known. Differences in return according to educational degree have already been pointed out. Although investments in education may be equal, whether measured in terms of number of years invested or level of degree obtained, returns on degrees in different subjects may be unequal. The same pertains to occupations. Some of the reasons for differentials in earnings between occupations are variations on the following:

1. Costs of acquiring entry-level skills.
2. Individual preferences concerning time factors.
3. Relative attractiveness of non-wage dimensions, including prestige, conditions of work, upward mobility potential, and so forth.
4. Individual tastes.
5. Instability of earnings, that is, riskiness.
6. Readiness to accept risk. (Bellante and Jackson 1983)

Differences in earnings, by major occupational groups, are shown on Table 12.1.

Relative Costs of Skill Acquisition. Costs of occupation entry have been found to affect its financial rewards. If cost of entry to one occupation is greater than to alternatives, a premium must be paid to induce potential occupants to invest in required skill preparation. The size of the premium will depend upon the level of demand at any given time. Were costs of entry to lessen, more persons would probably enter the occupation with higher entry costs.

A premium sufficient to attract people into a high-cost occupation theoretically must be enough to compensate interested parties for their loss of time, that is, be equal to their rate of return on the free time involved in skill preparation for that occupation. As of 1998 the supply of potential entrants is relatively *elastic*, that is, supply can be influenced by some change in rate of return. Should the rate of return increase, persons considering career opportunities in lesser-paid occupations will be more likely to enter the more lucrative occupation. Under such circumstances, wages for less attractive occupations will rise (lesser supply), while wages for the more desirable occupation will tend to fall (greater supply). At some point wages for the more desirable occupation will fall sufficiently until the formerly financially superior occupation is no longer sufficiently attractive to lure undecided individuals to it. Movement between the alternative occupations will then tend to cease.

Table 12.1
Median Weekly Earnings of Full-Time Wage and Salary Workers, by Occupation, 1997

	(in dollars)
Managerial and professional specialty	738
Executive, administrative, and managerial	725
Professional specialty	750
Technical, sales, and administrative support	456
Technicians and related support	582
Sales occupations	482
Administrative support, including clerical	419
Service occupations	313
Protective service	550
Services except protective service	293
Precision production, craft, and repair	548
Operators, fabricators, and laborers	401
Machine operators, assemblers, and inspectors	390
Transportation and material moving occupations	498
Handlers, equipment cleaners, helpers, and laborers	**329**

Source: U.S. Department of Labor, Bureau of Labor Statistics, *Employment and Earnings* 45 (January) 1998: Table 43, 218.

Time Preferences as a Factor. People differ in the importance that they assign to time, which leads to great variations in rates of return to individuals. Aside from differences in individual temperaments, life circumstances may also play a factor. A family man with a wife and two children to support will probably require a higher rate of return on time involved in preparation for a higher level occupation than a nineteen-year-old college freshman.

Tastes as a Non-Wage Factor in Attracting Occupational Aspirants. In the real world people differ greatly in their evaluations of the relative attractiveness of occupations. Therefore, people who enter a low-paying occupation when they have the possibility of entering a higher paying one do so because they probably place a very low value on the nonfinancial aspects of the better paying occupation. A good example of how nonwage aspects of occupations affect movements into occupations is the difficulty in attracting clerical and retail sales workers into higher-paid blue-collar work, or blue-collar workers into white-collar work, even when traditional blue-collar opportunities are drying up. Also, to the surprise of profit-maximizing economists, many able and competent people in the real world work for low-paying nonprofit organizations, such as universities, charitable organizations, and health-care institutions.

Earnings Variability Between Occupations. An important occupational-choice consideration is the likelihood of being able to maintain stable income upon entering the occupation, that is, the occupation's riskiness. Such occupations as acting, music, creative writing, dance, painting, and sculpting notoriously fail to offer any likelihood of regular income. Faced with two possible occupations, most people will choose the less risky one, even if mean average wages for both are the same. Most people tend to avoid risk, doubting that they are likely to be the lucky high earners who skew the average and conceal the small, irregular financial returns experienced by the many.

Wage Differentials by Industry

Earnings data for the United States and other advanced countries consistently show marked differences in earnings according to industry of employment. According to mainstream theory, there should be no differences in pay rates across industries. *Average* wage rates may differ because occupational mix differs, of course; but why does a secretary earn more in one industry than another? Various explanations have been suggested, including the idea that the size of a plant affects the employer's ability to pay; larger employers have the ability to pay more, that is, offer *efficiency wages*, wages above market level, for the dual purposes of attracting and retaining superior staff (Filer, Hamermesh, and Rees 1996; Allen 1995) Better explanations are awaited. The clearly observable differences in wage averages paid, by industry group, are shown on Table 12.2.

Some further explanations offered for variation in occupational pay within industries are the following:

1. Public sector and nonprofit employers can afford to pay noncompetitive wages.
2. Companies operating under conditions of monopsony or concentration pay according to a different set of considerations than other employers.
3. Jobs in some industries are more dangerous, working conditions less pleasant, and employment less stable than in others.
4. Some locations, regions of the country, are more desirable than others.
5. Levels of skill of the employee-mix differ.

Public-Private Sector Differentials. Empirical data have partially substantiated the claim that public-sector pay rates can be above those for identical persons in the private sector due to absence of the profit motive. However, higher wage rates are evident only in the Federal Civil Service and not at the highest levels there. Occupants of the highest level Federal positions earn far less than their private-sector counterparts, offering their services at personal financial sacrifice. In recent years, as the status of government employment has fallen, the differentials between public and private employment have lessened. At the state, county, and municipal levels, job occupants have tended to earn less than identical persons in the private sector.

Geographical Differentials

It is often stated that wage and salary rates vary considerably throughout the country. In an earlier period empirical evidence was produced to substantiate this belief. Today it is held that while average wages may be lower in some areas than in others (as in the South versus the rest of the country), wage rates for similar occupations and industries are now basically the same. Although this position is difficult to document because of the limitations of Federal statistics-gathering, the primary reason for the seeming regional differences in wage rates is the different mix of industries existing within different geographic areas. Other factors are thought to be interregional differences in the cost of living; a relative

Table 12.2
**Median Weekly Earnings of Full-Time Wage and Salary Workers, by Industry,
1997**

	(in dollars)
Agricultural wage and salary	306
Mining	475
Construction	504
Manufacturing	507
Durable goods	533
Nondurable goods	466
Transportation and public utilities	596
Transportation	527
Communication and public utilities	693
Wholesale and retail trade	380
Wholesale trade	503
Retail trade	343
Finance, insurance, and real estate	521
Services	456
Government workers	592

Source: U.S. Department of Labor, Bureau of Labor Statistics, *Employment and Earnings* 45, no.1
(January) 1998: Table 43.

labor surplus in the South, stemming from a higher rate of reproduction; and
right-to-work laws that render union-organizing difficult if not impossible in
many states in the South and Southwest.

According to BLS statistics, average annual wages differ sharply throughout
the United States. For example, in 1992 average annual earnings for workers in
sixteen states were from $18,000 to $21,999 annually; in eighteen states, from
$22,000 to $24,999; and, in sixteen states, including the District of Columbia,
$25,000 and above. But this data cannot be interpreted as indicative of geo-
graphic wage differentials (*Statistical Abstract of the U.S., 1994*, Table 663).
Economists deny the possibility of permanent geographical wage differentials because, in such a situation, both capital and labor would migrate to areas of advantage. During the early 1900s Southern workers moved north in large
numbers, but Northern employers constantly moved jobs and capital south.
Over time these two movements are thought to have had the effect of lowering
wages in the north, because of the withdrawal of capital and addition of Southern
labor supply, most of it unskilled and willing to work at very low rates. As
mentioned previously, labor is now moving south more than in any other direction, presumably for job opportunities at attractive levels of pay.

According to this thinking, migration of capital southward resulted in increased demand for labor in the South at a time when the labor supply was
tightening due to the out-movement. The dual circumstances, greater demand for
labor in the South amid lesser supply, are believed to have pushed Southern
wages upward, while northern rates have been falling. In some industries wage
rates are actually higher in the South than the North. This occurs because the
new, "runaway" plants in the South tend to be highly automated, while the par-

ent plants in the North are "dinosaurs." In such situations union leadership in the old industrial cities of the North often accept low wages as the price for keeping decaying, inefficient plants open. A good example of this development are paper mills, which once paid 15 percent less in the South, but now pay higher wages there than in the North.

Whether a regional state of equilibrium, so logical in theory, has actually been reached is another matter. It is generally believed that regional wage rates, to the extent that they may exist, are narrowing. A seminal study by Douty (1968) found that differentials in many industries had already disappeared as of the mid-1960s, but opined that they would not disappear completely in the foreseeable future, primarily because of the labor surplus in the South. Another view is that imperfect information and the cost of mobility would drag out the movement toward equilibrium over a long period of time (Bellante and Jackson 1983). However, Bellante (1979) found in the 1970s that a study of real wage rates, as opposed to money wages, would demonstrate that regional differences had ceased to exist, in that Southern wages reflected a lower standard of living.

Operationally speaking, the major reasons given for decreasing regional wage gaps are the need of employers to raise wage rates in low-paying areas to attract desired categories of workers and company policies. However automated a new Southern steel plant may be, the company will have to import some management personnel and administrative support, engineers, and skilled workers, including foremen, who know the business. To make relocation attractive, the firm will have to offer wage and salary incentives. It will also need to attract local skilled personnel away from present employers. All this leads to the practice of paying wage premiums to both imported and local skilled staff. This accounts for early findings that Southern wage differentials for skilled versus unskilled workers were higher than in the North. This makes sense in view of the South's generally low levels of education and its large pool of unskilled labor due to high birth rates.

As national and, recently, international companies have spread into the less-industrialized parts of the United States, they have had to make decisions concerning their wage policies. Their options include paying the going rate in the local community; being the best-paying local employer; or maintaining a national wage schedule, irrespective of location. According to one source, many employers choose the latter option for want of information concerning local rates (Regional BLS economist, in private communication).

OTHER VARIABLES EXPLAINING WAGE DIFFERENTIALS

Size of Firm

In recent years size of firm (as measured by number of employees) has been found to be associated with wage rates. One study found that firms hiring fewer than twenty-five employees pay less than larger employers: small employers with twenty workers pay an average of $10 per hour, while large companies with 1,000 workers pay $11 to $11.50 per hour. These differences are observed for similar workers in the same industries, job categories, and areas of the country (Brown and Medoff, 1989; Medoff, Brown, and Hamilton 1990). A second set of investigators have speculated that the greater job stability (longer duration of jobs; 25% fewer resignations) that exists in larger plants (company size rather than plant size, in their study) was the important variable. A higher proportion of married workers were found to be working in the larger plants, while single women, teenagers, and older workers tended to be drawn to the smaller firms that experienced more variable growth rates and more failures. These investigators also concluded, overall, that larger plants obtain superior workers (Evans and Sleighton 1988).

One outcome of these studies is a challenge, reported in the May 27, 1990, *Philadelphia Inquirer*, to the current assumption that increases in the numbers of small businesses are desirable. Pointing out that small businesses, defined as those with fewer than 500 employees, enjoy competitive advantages over larger employers due to political clout (which would render them exempt from some workplace safety regulations and antidiscrimination laws, for example), Harvard economist James Medoff holds that the less-advantaged employees of the smaller plants are paying the price of mistaken governmental policies as average pay is 30 percent higher in the larger plants. The widespread belief, fueled by a 1987 study based on Dun and Bradstreet data (Birch 1987) that small business is responsible for 80 percent of the new job creation in the United States, is rejected by Medoff's group, which claims the figure was closer to 56 percent for the period 1969–73. About half of the U.S. workforce is employed by firms with fewer than 500 employees.

Impact of Unions

Unionization is another factor that must be considered in explaining wage differentials. It is often assumed that unions raise wage rates for their members. The matter is usually investigated by exploring the extent to which workers in the same industry and area of the country are organized.

Crowding vs. Threat Effects. Theorists take two contradictory positions on the impact of unions on wages. The first, labeled the *crowding* or *spillover effect*, is that successful union wage negotiations result in a loss of jobs by some union members; and lowered wages for both the job-losing union members and the work forces of nonunionized competitors. This follows from the need of unionized employers to lower labor costs through elimination of marginal workers, based on the assumption that the productivity of fewer workers is higher per worker than that of a larger workforce. The higher wages will be covered by the increased productivity of the workers remaining on the payroll.

As for union workers laid off after a wage increase, their wages will fall because they will attempt to obtain similar work from nonunion employers. Ultimately, wages for all workers in the nonunion sector of the same industry will tend to fall because of the increased competition for jobs, that is, the increase in labor supply. Sometimes it is argued that laid-off union workers will leave the primary labor market for the secondary labor market, with the same outcomes. This implies that there often is no replacement employment in the same or similar industries and that laid-off workers are likely to have to move from the high-paid to low-paid sectors of the economy. In some cases the job-losers may stay out of the labor force, waiting for new opportunities in the union sector

(Summers 1990). In such cases the withholding of the labor of these persons has the effect of lessening pressures for reduction of wages in the nonunion sector.[2]

A contrary school of thought is that when unions, which pose a threat to unorganized employers, secure raises for union members, they cause all wages within an industry to rise. This is believed to occur in two ways. In one scenario firms that are unionized adjust the salaries of their nonunionized (exempt) employees upward whenever they negotiate wage increases for their union workers; these exempt employees are sometimes known as "free-riders." The second scenario is that nonunion competitors raise wage rates to the same level as, or slightly above, negotiated raises of their unionized competitors, to forestall organizing drives in their own plants. How the turbulent environment of the 1990s has affected these practices is unknown; however, the problem occurs much less than previously due to the decline in unionism and diversion of union attention to issues other than wages.

Which theory of union impact on wages is correct? Various studies have produced these contrary theories. Analyses by cross-sectional data focusing on one point in time have tended to support the threat-effect hypothesis, the notion that unions raise wages in both union and nonunion sectors of an industry. A recent study, which investigated the matter in a more detailed way, however, produced mixed findings. Looking at wages by industry and city across occupations, over time—using CPS data for 1973 to 1989 and analyzing longitudinal studies on the percentage of organized workers by industry and city—this study challenges earlier conclusions. It noted, first of all, that the impact of unionization, industry by industry, appears predominantly to take the form of the crowding (or spillover) effect. An increase in the percentage organized within an industry has resulted in a lowering of the nonunion wages within that industry. When the union effect was studied in terms of percent organized, city by city, however, the threat effect predominated. Wages of nonunion workers in the same industry rose when unions obtained increases in wages.These findings might be explained, according to the researchers, by anecdotal evidence that locally organized unions in the service sector are more influential within a geographical area than national unions within industries (Neumark and Wachter 1995). But when looking at the effect of unionism on wages of the unorganized in the same industry by still another dimension, type of worker organized, the researchers found that when one type of employee, blue-collar, professional, managerial, was organized, wages and salaries of other categories of workers in the same industry tended to fall, indicating the presence of the crowding effect. The data also suggested that other issues are involved, such as complementarity—or lack of mutual substitutability—of workers.

The Extent of the Union Wage Effect

While most observers agree that unions have some influence on wages, how much is almost impossible to ascertain because of the union influence on wages of nonunion employees. Most estimates of union/nonunion wage differentials put them at between 10 to 15 percent, varying over time and differing by industry, greater for the unskilled than the skilled, greater for women than for men, and for African Americans than for whites. These latter estimates are particularly interesting because of accusations that unions have tended to discriminate against women and minorities. It has also been found that union power to affect wage rates is less in times of prosperity than in deflationary periods (Lewis 1963), as rising demand for labor in an industry pushes nonunion wages higher without the need for union intervention.

Important studies on relative differences in union/nonunion wages have been done by H. G. Lewis (1963) and Richard Freeman and James Medoff (1984). Recently Neumark and Wachter (1995) have done an analysis of the union effect on the earnings of nonunion workers by occupation and industry. They show some relationship between the percentage of workers organized and the size of the wage differential by industry, but not consistently for all industries. The topic of union influence on wages is of less interest than formerly because unions have not been emphasizing wage raises in recent years; they have been diverting energies to damage control, fighting against wage concessions and for retention of benefits, especially health care, and job security.

Alfred Marshall's Laws on Conditions Under Which Wages Can Rise

At this point it is appropriate to recall Marshall's four famous laws or conditions under which wages can rise, often presented as conditions under which unions can obtain wage increases. Marshall's theory is based on the premise that the demand for labor is a derived demand, that is, it stems from a demand for the product that labor produces. As such, prices for the product and, therefore, for its labor inputs can rise if demand is relatively *inelastic*, which means that people will purchase the product without regard to price. In a situation of inelasticity, the producer can raise wages to meet union demands without accompanying increase in productivity; job losses need not occur (Marshall 1923, 3rd ed.). Such inelasticity may occur under the following circumstances:

1. It would be technically difficult or impossible for the employer to substitute other inputs for labor.
2. The demand for the product that labor produces is itself price-inelastic.
3. The ratio of labor cost to total cost is low.
4. The supply of a substitute or complementary input is relatively inelastic.

Union Wage Concessions

Unfortunately for unions, circumstances in recent years have not led to the exploitation of Marshall's laws. To the contrary, many unions have been under intense employer pressure to write "give backs" into their contracts. During the period 1980–87, the employers most likely to receive concessions were those doing poorly, as opposed to those doing well, as measured by stock prices and employment growth; smaller firms; firms paying high wages; and firms with relatively low levels of unionization (Bell 1995). The impact of imports and a changing market structure have been cited as reasons that some high-paying employers were pressed to lower their pay levels to industry norms and in turn pushed their unions for relief. Extensive deregulation of a series of monopolistic or oligopolistic employers, such as some public utilities and airlines, also played a role.

NOTES

1. "Wages" may be taken to mean payment for services rendered, usually by a period of time, day, week, or month. For present purposes, it includes salaries.

2. Actually, there are some limited circumstances, such as in cases of oligopoly or concentration, under which unions can obtain higher wages and maintain employment levels, at least for a while, as such employers may be able to pass on costs to consumers by raising prices to cover the additional labor costs. See Ehrenberg and Smith (1994), for elaboration of the effects of oligopoly and concentration on wages.

REFERENCES

Allen, Steven G. 1995. Updated notes on the inter-industry wage structure, 1890–1990. *Industrial and Labor Relations Review* 48 (January) 305–21.

Bell, Linda. 1995. Union wage concessions in the 1980s: the importance of firm-specific factors. *Industrial and Labor Relations Review* 48 (January) 208–75.

Bellante, Don. 1979. The North-South differential and the migration of heterogeneous labor. *American Economic Review* 69 (March): 166–75.

———, and Mark Jackson. 1983. *Labor economics: choice labor markets.* New York: McGraw-Hill.

Bergmann, Barbara. 1971. The effect of white incomes on discrimination in employment. *Journal of Political Economy* 79 (March/April): 294–313.

———. 1974. Occupational segregation, wages, and profits when employers discriminate by race or sex. *Eastern Economic Journal* 1 (April/July): 103–10.

———. 1991. Does the market for women's labor need fixing? 247–61. In Reynolds, Lloyd, Stanley Masters, and Colletta Moser. *Readings in labor economics and labor relations.* 5th ed. Englewood Cliffs, N.J.: Prentice Hall.

Birch, David. 1987. *Job creation in America: how our smallest companies put the most people to work.* New York: Free Press.

Brown, Charles, and James Medoff. 1989. Employer size and the payment of factors. *Journal of Political Economy* 97: 1027–59.

Doeringer, Peter and Michael Piore. 1971. *Internal labor markets and manpower analysis.* Lexington, Mass.: Heath Lexington Books.

Douty, H. M. 1968. Regional wage differentials: forces and counter forces. *Monthly Labor Review* 91 (March): 74–81.

Ehrenberg, Ronald G., and Robert S. Smith. 1994. *Modern labor economics: theory and public policy.* New York: Harper Collins College Publishers.

Evans, David, and Linda Sleighton. 1988. Why do smaller firms pay less? *Journal of Human Resources* 24, no. 2: 301–19.

Filer, Randolph, Daniel Hamermesh, and Albert Rees. 1996. *The economics of work and pay.* 6th edition. New York: Harper Collins College Publishers.

Freeman, Richard, and James Medoff. 1984. *What do unions do?* New York: Basic Books.

Lewis, H. G. 1963. *Unionism and relative wages in the United States.* Chicago: University of Chicago Press.

Marshall, Alfred. 1923. *Principles of economics.* Eighth ed. Chapter 6. London: Macmillan and Co.

Medoff, James, Charles Brown, and James Hamilton. 1990. *Employers, large and small.* Cambridge, Mass.: Harvard University Press.

Neumark, David, and Michael Wachter. 1995. Union effects on nonunion wages: evidence from panel data on industries and cities. *Industrial and Labor Relations Review* 49 (October): 20–36.

Rima, Ingrid. 1981. *Labor markets, wages, and employment.* Chapters 6 and 7. New York: W. W. Norton & Company.

Summers, Lawrence. 1990. *Understanding unemployment.* Cambridge: MIT Press.

U.S. Department of Commerce. Bureau of the Census. *1995 Statistical abstract of the United States.* 114th ed. Washington, D.C.: Government Printing Office, Table 663.

U.S. Department of Labor. Bureau of Labor Statistics. 1998 *Employment and Earnings.* 45 (January). Washington, D.C.: Government Printing Office.

13

The Setting of Compensation

The subject of compensation, as opposed to wage theory and differentials, is a relatively neglected topic. This chapter identifies conventional forms of compensation—a combination of money wages and benefits—and what employers hope to achieve through the use of each form; and describes how compensation specialists develop pay schedules, that is, the mechanics of wage and salary-setting, a much-neglected topic, and some closely associated issues. The processes of decision-making and implementation are not very scientific, with traditional assumptions and practices shifting with environmental change. The immensity of the topic precludes anything more than an outline of the processes involved. The importance of both external and internal equity is discussed, followed by an overview of the processes by which each is achieved. The best-known innovative pay schemes are described and the peculiar matter of executive pay discussed, due to current interest in this topic. The chapter ends with a description of what is known about the receipt of *benefits*, or nonmonetary compensation.

MONEY WAGES

The phrase "money wages" refers to those aspects of compensation that involve payments for work performed (as opposed to benefits, incentives, and perquisites). Money payments for hourly employees, usually blue-collar and nonexempt (covered by the National Labor Relations Act) are commonly referred to as wages; while payments to both exempt and nonexempt employees in white-collar situations and to middle-level managers in blue-collar situations are referred to as salaries. Larger employers may offer all these categories of payments, while smaller ones may offer no more than base pay or some type of incentive pay, such as commission.

A series of employer considerations determine the form of payments offered to employees; they include relative costs of hiring, risk to the employer, beliefs as to the motivational power of the particular form of payment, the payment's impact on quality of work done, and the impact on morale of fellow workers. For example, costs of hiring are less when workers are hired by *piece rate*, once thought the most appropriate means for extracting maximal production from factory workers, but some disadvantages exist: the quality of output suffers and equipment often deteriorates through rough usage. Also, suspicious workers have often engaged in slowdowns, motivated by fear that employers will lower rates if production rises too much. When workers are hired on the basis of time, that is, by *flat rate*, more careful selection and subsequent supervision are necessary. This method of payment raises costs and necessitates greater worker productivity.

To motivate workers, employers may use commissions, bonuses, profit-sharing, and gain sharing, the latter three schemes aimed at making the workers identify their welfare with that of the employer. Commissions are usually payments associated with sales, a portion of the sales price of an item or service going to the salesperson (and sometimes his/her superior). Bonuses are payments to individuals, usually associated with recognition for measurable output. Such schemes are often used because companies lack adequate information upon which to make good decisions in the recruitment and hiring phases. The tools of personnel departments (testing, interviewing, gathering letters of recommendation) are inadequate when it comes to predicting the future contributions of a new hire to an organization.This is most often true in situations where supervision is inappropriate or impossible and thus cannot provide the information necessary for good compensation decisions. In such situations compensation schemes are directed toward minimizing the present and future costs incurred by the lack of adequate information, by turning to methods that involve employee motivation. Approaches to employee motivation may be individually oriented, such as the use of bonuses and commissions, or group-oriented, such as profit-sharing or gain sharing.

To encourage employees to stay with an employer, compensation setters traditionally have scheduled wage rates in such a way over time that workers find staying with the employer to be the most profitable of their options. An *age-based payment scheme* is thought to be particularly useful in situations where the employer cannot closely supervise workers for purposes of maximizing work effort. It is believed that this is done by paying workers less than their marginal revenue product (MRP) during the early years of their employment and more during their later years. This offers an incentive to work hard, impress the employer with one's ability, and collect the rewards (higher wages than their MRP) during their later tenure (their preretirement years). Of course, the employer can only do this if the lower-than-MRP initial wage is at least market level; otherwise, the worker would be attracted elsewhere. This scheme essentially assumes lifetime employment, a fading concept.

Do employers actually skew wage/salary payments to the lifetime employment model as just described? It is unlikely that compensation specialists will admit to it. And are employers firing older people as a matter of policy because they are, indeed, more expensive than the value of their productivity, or because they are more expensive than more youthful employees who are hired on a productivity-related pay schedule? Since the matter of the extent of current employment instability as opposed to that of the recent past remains unsettled, despite popular beliefs on the subject, the question cannot be answered for lack of empirical evidence. And no employer would admit to a policy of firing older workers because of anti-discrimination legislation.[1]

Today, with the decline in manufacturing, distinctions between blue-collar and white-collar work are lessening, with many employers moving toward putting former wage workers on salary. Sometimes this is motivated by the belief that "punching the time clock" lowers workers' status in their own eyes, as well as in the eyes of the *exempt*. Companies that have moved into the *team approach*, described later in the chapter, often eliminate the time clock and hourly wages as part of their changeover strategy. Recall that nonexempt workers (those covered by the Fair Labor Standards Act of 1938) are entitled to overtime payments when working beyond the legal work-week, nights, or weekends. However, some employers voluntarily pay overtime to exempt workers (those said to be associated with management, although many do not have direct managerial responsibilities) for time worked beyond official hours.

The setting of compensation begins with philosophy, the matter of what the employer hopes to achieve by payment plans, short-term and long-term. It is generally believed that employers want to develop pay schemes that make it possible for them to attract the employees of choice. In other words, pay policies begin with a list of employer goals and philosophies about how to attain them. Some employers aim for the most competent workers; others may be satisfied by mediocre workers; both are usually concerned about turnover. The pay policies of companies with different objectives are likely to differ. Some employers actually develop wage policies designed to encourage high turnover. Very often wage strategies are discussed in terms of another dimension, *employee motivation*, the assumption that worker performance can be altered by a company's wage policies, which is a hotly debated issue.[2]

Traditionally, advancement within an organization has been associated with both good performance and seniority. Accompanying this association is the concept of *merit pay*, additional remuneration for ever-improving performance, based on a yearly evaluation. Administration of merit-based pay schemes is widely recognized to be highly problematic and will not be dealt with in this chapter. Many factors interfere with the ideal of pay for merit; the primary factor being difficulties in securing realistic evaluations from supervisors, who are cautious about offending their subordinates. *Pay for performance*, a current vogue discussed in this chapter, should not be construed as a manifestation of traditional merit-pay practices (which are thoroughly discussed in Lawler 1990).

The Importance of External Equity

Employers are necessarily concerned about the going market prices for their employees. If they are not cognizant of these prices, they may end up unable to attract desired personnel and actually lose current workers, which can be both disruptive and expensive. Nevertheless, employers do not necessarily pay the going rates. Their pay strategies are usually characterized as *lead, match*, or *lag* (Milkovich and Newman 1996).

Leading:The Efficiency Wage Approach. It is believed that some employers voluntarily pay above-market rates for workers when it is unnecessary to do so.

Economists explain this phenomenon on the basis that the practice expedites hiring and attracts superior employees. According to this thinking, employers are tremendously concerned about reducing the heavy costs of recruitment and turnover. [3]For a more thorough discussion of efficiency wages, see Ehrenberg and Smith (1994); for an overview of theory, see Murphy and Topel (1990). Long-time tenure has always been seen as desirable in situations where employers invest heavily in worker training, which is likely to be the case in such situations. Of course, as economists admit, there are limitations on employers' ability to pay above-market wages. Annual *raises*, a cultural expectation, may bring the costs of labor to a level exceeding returns. For the employer to maximize profits, the wage cannot exceed the point at which the marginal costs exceed the marginal revenues. The logic behind the apparent willingness of employers to pay more than necessary in hiring and in benefits, aside from the savings in recruitment and turnover costs, according to economists, is embedded in the belief that superior personnel are more productive. The case study below, a 500-employee engineering company's rationale for an above-market pay policy, exemplifies this belief.

A small, East Coast environmental-engineering firm with 500 employees finds it impossible, with a staff of only three human-resources personnel, to use "scientific methods," such as the point-factor system, to establish wage/salary rates. Instead, they watch the want-ads of local newspapers for indications of what competitors of similar size and industry are paying. The firm maintains a file of such ads, adjusting for inflation over time. In line with their desire to be an "industry leader," the company pays 10 percent above what they believe to be the prevailing rate when they make an offer. The company believes that this *benchmarking* helps them stay competitive and that the additional 10 percent premium helps reduce turnover. The company has a degree of freedom in wage-setting in that they are not unionized and company policy forbids employees from discussing compensation with each other. They know that the latter policy is "a farce" but, as the company president commented, it "actually works well." (Student report)

Another circumstance under which above-market wages are often paid workers is where working conditions are generally considered to be undesirable. Such payments are known as *compensating differentials*. Good examples of work circumstances for which such differentials are commonly paid are jobs involving the use of dangerous equipment, work taking place in highly adverse physical circumstances, and second or third shifts. Economists take the position that the differential is the amount necessary to persuade the worker to give up preferred conditions for the amount of the bonus (Ehrenberg and Smith 1994).

Lagging: The Low Wage Approach. Some employers choose a strategy of paying the lowest possible wage or salary and abandoning the offering of discretionary benefits. This occurs even during periods of low unemployment. In some situations employers actually desire high levels of turnover for the purpose of maintaining a majority of the personnel at the entry-level wage and ineligible for benefits that might accrue from longer tenure. This approach is often used in situations where recruitment, training, and placement are relatively inexpensive and the employee is readily replaceable. In recent years it has been speculated that the widespread adoption of low-wage policies, despite minimal unemployment levels, has become possible because of a cowed workforce that is unprotected by unions and demoralized by reports of wholesale exports of jobs to low-wage countries. Other reasons commonly proffered are the ready availability of cheap labor, explained by the high levels of unskilled immigration, legal and illegal, in recent years; the increasing proportion of the population entering the labor force; increased hours of work, often experienced in the form of two or more jobs per person; and through the existence of more two-income families, all of which swell the labor force. The low-wage employer may sound quite similar in description to that of a secondary labor market employer; nonetheless, many large employers are using the low-wage approach. They do so partly by outsourcing to smaller, competitive employers; or they might engage in wage-depressing practices within their own internal markets. An example of this latter practice is *double breasting*, manifested when a unionized firm opens a second, lower-paying, nonunionized firm to which it diverts its work.

Though we hear much about U.S. employers choosing to go the low-wage route, not much is written about this matter except in terms of growing wage inequality. One outstanding textbook on labor economics, for example, limits itself to stating that employers using the low-wage approach must expect higher training costs because of greater turnover than employers willing to recruit at higher levels (Ehrenberg and Smith 1994). Examples such as the low-wage, high-turnover policies of a large service-industry employer, below, are seldom stated as openly as below.

A food service company, with several hundred thousand employees internationally, maintains a low-wage policy at the service-worker level, deliberately designed to encourage high turnover. The objective is to dissuade workers from staying long enough to qualify for raises. The policy has been so effective that annual turnover reached 300 percent, a level the firm desired to reduce to 90 percent. One inducement offered by the firm to encourage employees to stay for an average of almost a year is a daily "square meal," believed to be meaningful to the personnel involved. (Regional vice-president, large food-service company, in personal communication)

Signaling. Some explanations offered for companies paying lower-than-market wages take an entirely different turn. According to one account the decision to *lag* market wages is the chosen compensation strategy of some companies which works as follows: employers use wage offers to *learn* about the intentions and characteristics of prospective employees, since few can be expected to be frank in their job interviews and the information gleaned by interviewers is likely to be neither sufficient nor accurate enough to let the employer know what the firm is getting. Thus, willingness to accept a sub-market wage, accompanied by the offer of a generous bonus if the recruit is successful in meeting employer expectations, is thought to *signal* to the prospective employer that the person intends to stay with the firm a while and is a go-getter. Basically, users of such a strategy are said to be looking for a different type of person than one who prefers the certainty of a fixed pay check (Milkovich and Newman 1996).

Matching. Most employers, it is thought, tend to pay the going market rate for their area, industry, and occupation. This is the simplest, most straightforward approach, but in certain situations this practice may create problems within the firm if current market rates are higher (or lower) than wages levels currently incorporated into the organization's wage structure. Ill will on the part of the current employees is likely to be engendered by inconsistent pay levels, a situation with which human-resources departments often have to contend.

The Importance of Internal Equity

Human-resources departments invest considerable energy in developing compensation schedules that incorporate *internal equity*. Robert Livernash (1957) specified three dimensions of internal equity: number of levels, size of pay differentials between levels, and criteria used (job vs skill/competency vs performance). Establishing internal equity is a major challenge to managers motivated by the desire to establish a feeling of fairness within the workplace, since it is widely believed that employee morale is affected by perceptions of the schedules, most particularly in regard to the pay of their equals and those just above and below them in their job cluster (Milkovich and Newman 1996); Livernash (1957) located the focus of employee comparisons as being the *job cluster* of the employee. (The groups used for comparisons, those within individual's job cluster, are known as *reference groups*.) Given this focus, a major test of internal equity is whether the scale is widely accepted by the employees involved (Milkovich and Newman 1996), an important criterion for scholars who believe that perceptions concerning equity affect employee behavior (Livernash 1957). Because of the touchiness of the equity issue many employers attempt to avoid bad feelings by forbidding employees to discuss their paychecks with each other.

Edward Lawler III has pointed out that obtaining internal equity can be very expensive if every aggrieved employee's desire to receive the equivalent of superior performers is met; Lawler therefore advises firms to emphasize external equity (1981). Despite the widespread view that internal equity is critical to good functioning, some companies still choose to pay according to the going market price. As to how this affects morale, performance, and turnover, not much is known, but according to early research on the subject, companies with a good fit between wage strategy and pay systems do better than others (Montemayer 1994; Milkovich and Newman 1996).

The Role of the Implicit Contract

The factor underlying traditional employer-employee relationships in primary labor markets has been the *implicit contract*, the informal, legally nonbinding understanding between employer and employee that in a situation of good performance and job availability, employment would be indefinite, that is life-long, an understanding that bonds the worker to the organization and encourages staff stability. The objective is (was) to motivate the employee to reward the employer with superior work effort and organizational loyalty. Because workers value the prospect of long-term employment, larger employers traditionally offered this prospect. The widespread belief that employers are abandoning this practice is probably the most significant development in worker expectations and management-employee relationships of the past quarter century in the United States, especially for the managerial and professional groups that traditionally have most heavily benefited from this practice. Compensation practices are believed to have been heavily influenced by this widespread implicit understanding.

THE PROCESSES OF WAGE AND SALARY DETERMINATION

The descriptions that follow of how wage/salary scales are translated into dollars and cents are limited to *job-related*, as opposed to *skill-related*, systems, as little is known about the administration of the latter. The complex tasks involved, about which only an overview is provided here, are often performed by a consulting agency specializing in compensation. Broadly speaking, wage/salary rates are the products of a series of information-gathering efforts, scale constructions, and policy decisions that involve reconciliation of going rates in relevant, external labor markets with the internal wage structures designed for the individual establishment by its human-resources department or authorized agents. Because of a multitude of considerations and lack of solid data, the outcomes reflect a series of best judgments.

The major steps of the complex process of compensation-setting are outlined below. [4]

1. Perform preliminary tasks:
   a. Group all jobs into job clusters (also referred to as job families).
   b. Analyze each job, evaluate, and write job descriptions.
   c. Rank each job title according to its level of importance, relative to the *key job*, the best known job in the job cluster (group of closely associated jobs).
2. Establish external equity:
   a. Develop an information base to ascertain current rates for key jobs in relevant labor markets.
   b. Decide upon establishment wage policy: lead, match, or lag.
3. Establish internal equity:
   a. Choose a method for building a wage structure for the establishment. Methods may be quantitative, such as point-factor or factor-comparison; or qualitative, such as job classification, ranking, or market pricing. Major steps involved in the use of the point factor system, the most popular system, are
      (1) analyzing key jobs.
      (2) deciding upon the compensable factors to be used in each group of job families.
      (3) deciding upon the degree (or extent) of importance of each factor to the key job.
      (4) utilizing the above, calculation of the weights to be accorded each.
      (5) explaining the process in writing for use by staff.
      (6) calculating the dollar values of non-key jobs in each job cluster or family of jobs.
   b. Establish grades in which to group jobs with similar values.
   c. Establish wage ranges within each grade.
4. Reconcile the two wage structures (the attempt at market simulation and the attempt to establish internal equity).
   a. Compare by constructing wage curves and examining for "good fit" (not a necessity).b. Adjust the internal wage structure to match going market rates, if deemed desirable.
5. Based on the resulting internal wage structure, calculate individual paychecks.

Learning the External Wage Structure

The tasks listed above may be performed in-house or by consultants. The information base may be obtained through self-generated surveys or through sharing with local competitors, a swap that comes about as the result of relationships developed informally over time. Major methods used in data-gathering are personal interviews, telephone inquiries, or questionnaires sent through the mail. Supplemental sources of information often used are Bureau of Labor Statistics and Census Bureau publications, Chambers of Commerce reports, and surveys conducted by consultant groups.

A few comments on major elements in the various processes are in order. The role of *key jobs* in compensation-setting is critical. Because job titles vary between organizations, only through identification of commonly used titles can reliable data on going wage rates be collected. To cope with these difficulties, compensation specialists review the job titles on their rosters and organize them into job clusters. They choose the most commonly used job title within each cluster and rank all other jobs within each cluster (or job family) in relation to their relative value, above and below the key job. The entire process is known as *benchmarking* and is illustrated in Table 13.1.

Once data on the value of each key job in the external labor market is obtained, dollar values on the worth of all other jobs in each cluster can be calculated, using the *bench marking* calculations. The "assigned dollar values" do not represent the amounts actually paid to the establishment's employees. Rather, they represent the best wisdom that the compensation specialists have been able to compile as to what the current going rates for these jobs are in the external markets of interest.

In establishing the internal wage structure of an organization, the builders can use one of several qualitative or quantitative methods, the point factor being the quantitative measure used most frequently. It is important to understand how much judgment is involved in development of these scales. The establishment of the weights used to calculate the values of individual job titles is arbitrary and based on best judgments which themselves are heavily influenced by custom and tradition (Byars and Rue 1984).

Table 13.1
A Hypothetical Clerical-Job Cluster of an Establishment
Key Job Title: Secretary

Job ranking	Value ratio	Assigned dollar value
Office manager	1.50	30,000
Secretary	**1.00**	**20,000**
Stenographer	.90	18,000
Typist	.75	15,000
Data entry clerk	.60	12,000
File clerk	.55	11,000

Building the Internal Wage Structure

Quantitative Methods. In establishing the internal wage scale, using the *point factor system*, the factor sets used most frequently are listed below.

1. Skills required
2. Effort required
3. Responsibility
4. Physical working conditions
5. Problem-solving capabilities required
6. Necessary knowledge base
7. Accountability expected
8. Visual/mental demands
9. Responsibility for material
10. Responsibility for the safety of others
11. Incidence of health and accident problems
12. Manual skills

Within the same organization the factors used for different job families may differ. Although research has shown that a relatively small number of factors are sufficient to establish wage rates highly comparable to those derived from use of large numbers, sometimes a larger number are used to satisfy all parties involved (DeLuca 1993).

Once the factors are chosen, they must be defined and a scale must be developed to determine the extent or level (degree) of the compensable factor existent in the jobs that are to be analyzed. The next step involves assigning point values to each level or degree of the factor. These are assigned according to the best judgment of the analyst (or analysts, often a committee) as to the value of each degree to the employer. This must be done for each factor.[5]

At this point, a set of numerical values exist which can be used to establish internal equity for job titles within the organization. The compensation specialists are now at the stage where they require job descriptions for all the key jobs involved. Job descriptions emanate from job analysis, a process that involves detailing all the tasks associated with a job title: the skills involved; relative dependence on others, individual or group; the level of technology involved; working conditions; and traditions impacting the status of the job, including pay rates. Good job descriptions, together with the accurate ranking of job titles, are key to establishing the final pay scale. The job description must be unique enough to differentiate the job title from all others. Once developed, the process can move into the phase of assigning dollar values to each job (see DeLuca 1993).

Qualitative Methods. Job ranking is the simplest of all of these methods, but is the least often used. Job classification is best known for its use by the U.S. Civil Service and the *Dictionary of Occupational Terms* (U.S. Department of Labor 1965); it depends upon the detailed knowledge and judgments of experts and does not deal with the relative value of each job title. As for market pricing, a third qualitative method, personnel departments simply look for whatever indicators that exist to determine what is currently being paid for specific jobs in the labor markets of interest. Often they prove to be as simple an indicator as a newspaper classified ad (DeLuca 1993). The difficulty connected with the use of this increasingly popular method is in choosing *which* market is relevant, since wage rates differ by industry, occupation, and region of the country. As of 1994 over 20 percent of jobs were estimated to be paid on the basis of market pricing (Oak 1994). The effect is to deemphasize internal consistency (Milkovich and Newman 1996).

Testing and Using the Wage Scale for the Establishment

Compensation specialists may attempt to test the validity of the wage scales they have constructed for internal use against the scales they believe to be the going rates in the external labor market, by plotting wage curves for the two sets of data. Theoretically, if the two wage curves fail to correspond closely, corrections will be made in the internal wage structure. In fact, internally generated rates found to be higher than market rates are sometimes maintained in the interests of internal equity and the maintenance of office morale. Eventually, job titles with similar rates are organized into grades, a grouping in which each title will have approximately the same number of points (where the point factor system is used). Wage rates for each grade will probably overlap with the grades above and below them, since different rates for learning phases and experience within the same grade must be accommodated.

Once final decisions have been made concerning the pay schedules to be associated with job titles within the organization, these rates must be translated into wages and salaries for individuals. The human-resources staff now calculates where each individual employee falls within the wage range for the job title involved, grade by grade. Traditionally, decisions have been influenced by such considerations as years of experience, supervisory evaluations (merit record), and interest in acquiring or retaining the individual. Human-resources staffs have been reluctant to admit it, but evidence has been produced to show that other considerations are also involved in assigning values to factors, namely dominant race and gender of the occupants of job titles (see chapter 16).

Criticisms of Compensation-Setting Practices

Before leaving this very broad and simplified overview of compensation-setting, some thoughts on the effectiveness of the standard methods are in order. It is generally believed that, despite all the efforts made to achieve accuracy in job evaluation, end results are often less than satisfactory. The point factor system has been criticized as basically unsatisfactory because of implementation problems, which include identifying appropriate factors, assigning values to each, and establishing the degrees within each factor (DeLuca 1993). The entire process of wage determination has been criticized by Lawler, a leading behaviorist, as being basically subjective, even though, through a series of proceedures and use of mathematics, it is made to appear scientifically objective. Although Lawlor (1986; 1990) criticizes use of the method for multiple reasons, his basic objection is that it represents an obsolete way of thinking about work, some examples of which are discussed in the next portion of this chapter.

Another criticism of current compensation-setting practices pertains to the widespread policy of using different criteria in establishing pay ranges for different job families. For example, job titles in the manufacturing, office/clerical, and sales occupations are placed in lower wage ranges than job titles in managerial, sales, technical, and executive jobs. The explanation for this, offered by an authoritative manual on compensation (DeLuca 1993), is that "each [job] family has different work characteristics and unique compensable factors." The rationale is that the qualities demanded for some job families are worth more to employers than the same qualities in others. When it is said that wage determination consists of a series of often arbitrary judgments, this is a case in point. Such rationales may go far in explaining the "different labor market experiences" of women and minorities.

Factors that Limit Compensation-Setting

Compensation-setters are limited by a series of factors outside their control. In unionized firms the *threat effect* must be taken into account. Though statistics are nonexistent on current employer policies around this issue, intermittent news reports, such as those that appeared in the November 12 and 13, 1993, *New York Times*, tell of white-collar and executive discontent in situations where employers have broken with the tradition of raising the salaries and wages of exempt employees when the organization's unionized workers obtain raises through collective bargaining. Also, the expectation of a yearly raise tends to distort the wage scale, leading to a practice of setting the entry-level wage lower than the actual productivity of the person hired. Further, in periods of strong labor demand, wages and salaries of new hires may be higher than those of an establishment's long-time employees, making for bad feelings and an internally inconsistent wage-salary schedule. In such situations the compensation-setter has to decide to either let an inflation-induced   ripple effect occur, with raises throughout the organization, an expensive decision; or learn to live with an internally inconsistent set of wages and salaries and employee discontent. Finally, there is the matter of federally and sometimes state-mandated minimum-wage floors.

INNOVATIVE PAY SCHEMES

Alternative pay schemes—*pay-for-performance, skill-based pay, profit-sharing,* and *gain-sharing*—may be characterized as placing risks on employees. No longer can employees under such schemes be secure in the knowledge that they will receive a fixed wage or salary each pay period. A portion of their earnings are subject to the meeting of certain goals, either by the individual, the work group, or the company (or some unit of it, such as one plant or one division). To clarify, the risk under alternative pay schemes involves basic pay, not bonuses on top of the base. The underlying motivation is more to trim costs than to share the rewards accruing to the employer from superior performance by employees. However, in view of the assumption of risk by workers, employers using such schemes may ultimately pay *more* than the going market rate for a job when specified objectives are reached.

These alternative pay schemes, together with the *two-tier wage system*, testify to the fading away of traditional merit systems. This trend is due, in part, to perceptions that merit systems do not work and widespread skepticism concerning the validity of supervisory evaluation programs, the heart of the traditional merit system. The skepticism is especially strong among nonmanagerial employees. Frequent complaints are that clear links between pay and good job performance are missing; rather, the merit system is seen as a zero-sum game, with one worker profiting at another's expense. The relevance of the merit system, as we have known it, is also under question because traditional career paths are disappearing.

Pay-for-Performance

Among the schemes being utilized by employers who are disenchanted with their traditional merit-pay systems for exempt employees is *pay-for-performance*, which puts basic pay at risk, while still utilizing merit as a basis for compensation. A survey by Hewitt Associates found that in 1995 about two-thirds of medium and large-sized companies had some form of incentive pay system, up from one-half in 1990; while a Towers-Perrin survey found incentive schemes to have increased by 40 percent between 1993 and 1995. (*Business Week* 1995)

In a pay-for-performance, system employer and employee agree on carefully defined job performance goals for the year, as well as specifying specific areas for improvement. Systematic evaluations take place annually, with rewards allocated according to the end-of-year evaluation. Although one goal is to increase employee motivation by making merit evaluations more rigorous and objective, these programs have been introduced mainly to lower payroll costs. In a period of payroll-cutting and cost reductions, reducing the raises of mediocre (or poor) performers is one way of making more funds available for rewarding top performers. The approach is not foolproof, as DuPont's experience demonstrates:

A 13-member committee at the DuPont Company, the chemical giant, spent two years designing an "Achievement Sharing" plan for 20,000 employees in its fibers division, 6 percent of annual salary being tied to annual profits of the division. When the division failed to meet its profit goals in 1990, the company declined to exercise its right to withhold the 6 percent for fear of creating morale problems in a division already shaken by the dismissal of 7,000 workers during the early 1980s. The leadership's decision was influenced by their observation that people had been working harder than previously because of earlier downsizing.

The lesson taken from this experience is that, for a pay-for-performance plan to be successful, it is necessary for goals to be so designed that they are within the individual worker's control and are so perceived. To do so, some companies are reporting designing a large number of small plans, utilizing the suggestions of the persons who will be involved, work group by work group (*Business Week* 1995).

In recent years pay-for-performance has figured strongly in the controversies concerning the sharp rise in executive pay since the 1970s. For a thorough discussion of this issue, see the most definitive work on the subject, George Milkovich and Alexandra Wigdor's *Pay for Performance: Evaluation Performance*

Appraisal and Merit Pay, a compilation of articles for the Committee on Performance Appraisal for Merit Pay, Commission on Behavioral and Social Sciences and Education, and the National Research Council, (1991); Enslow (1991); Blair (1994); and Zajac and Westphal (1995).

Skill-Based Compensation

Skill-based compensation, a relatively new compensation scheme for blue-collar workers, pays individual workers for their knowledge of specific workplace skills of interest to the employer, as opposed to the level of control that they exert and their place in the organizational hierarchy. It tends to be associated with work-restructuring, employee-involvement programs, the team approach, and participative-management plans. Compensation modes for skill mastery vary, with some companies giving a pay increase for each skill learned, while others, to contain costs, offer an initial bonus for entry into the program and then give permanent pay raises when more involved skills are learned (Wagel 1989). Pay is usually calculated by estimating the value of a group of skills constituting a job in the external labor market (Bunning 1992). Another method is to set minimum and maximum wage levels, according to the external market, and add wage steps to the entry-level wage as new skills are acquired (Lawler and Ledford 1985; Ledford, Tyler, and Dickey 1991). How to price skills, as opposed to jobs, is problematic, since little precedent exists and base pay may end up higher than market price, by job-pricing standards (see Schuster and Zingheim 1992). To receive a raise the worker must pass a competency test or go through a peer review.

From an economic point of view, raises under the skill-based pay scheme should be more than customary merit increases, because team workers are more efficient than individuals in a traditional workforce. Since each team requires only a limited number of skills, one might question how team members will be raised subsequent to their mastering all the skills called for within the team. Reports differ as to how many skills are required by typical teams and how many each worker is permitted to learn. Moreover, little has been reported on the breadth and depth of these skills, a matter impacting on the levels of pay that could be expected from such arrangements. Although efficiency may be greater in a team situation, whether the contribution of each individual becomes more or less valuable than before is unknown. In the early 1990s the use of skill-based pay by large companies increased enormously, jumping from 40 percent to 60 percent among the Fortune 1000 firms between 1987 and 1993. However, only about 1 to 20 percent of the employees of these firms are included in such pay plans (Ledford, Lawler, and Mohrman 1995).

Profit-Sharing and Gain-Sharing

Profit-sharing and gain-sharing are relatively familiar alternative payment schemes, each having been used by a few employers for decades They are closely related: the goal of each is to tie wages more closely to productivity. They are differentiated here.

Profit-sharing. Profit-sharing attempts to accomplish the stated goal by making a portion of the regular paycheck dependent upon the level of company profits. (See Weitzman and Kruse 1990, and Weitzman's seminal 1984 book, *The Share Economy,* which made the case for profit-sharing as a major strategy for maintaining economic stability.) It does not involve the allotment of bonuses above and beyond standard wage levels; on the contrary, the worker may be guaranteed even less than the customary wage. Usually, some formula exists that specifies at what point guaranteed pay ends and the profit-based portion of the paycheck begins. Because of the risk involved to the employee, total pay may rise above the customary or market level wage for the position held, in a situation of company profitability. In both scholarly works and the media, the scheme is often discussed in association with innovative pay practices, as an antiunion tactic, and as a means of controlling labor costs by keeping base wages at market levels or below (Ledford, Lawler, and Mohrman 1995).

Exactly what constitutes profit-sharing is still unsettled, except for agreement that payments are based on economic returns, that is, on company performance (Jones, Kato, and Pliskin 1994). There may or may not be a specific formula determining the amounts to be distributed. Payment plans vary: some payments are made in cash, while others are deferred, perhaps assigned to a pension-plan trust. Sometimes both a cash payment and deferred contribution are made. And despite the previous statements, sometimes plans that are labeled "profit-sharing" make payments independent of the company's profitability (Kruse 1991).

How prevalent is profit-sharing? According to BLS (1998), in 1995 about 20 percent of the 13.6 million full-time employees of medium and large private establishments in the United States participated in some type of deferred profit-sharing plan, 13 percent through a defined contribution plan that offers deferred profit-sharing, and 7 percent through a combination of cash and deferred arrangements through a (401(k) plan.[6] A survey that focused on Fortune 1000 firms (500 of the largest manufacturing and 500 largest service firms) found between 21 to 40 percent of the employees in these large firms to be involved in profit-sharing schemes (Ledford, Lawler, Mohrman 1995). As for smaller private employers (those with fewer than 100 workers), 13 percent of those in defined contribution retirement plans participate in deferred profit-sharing (*Statistical Abstract* 1998). What all of this reveals about profit-sharing as an innovative motivational tool is, unfortunately, almost nothing. The fact that profit-sharing is reported by BLS exclusively in the context of retirement programs suggests that most profit-sharing schemes are not associated with active motivational programs.

Gain-Sharing. Gain-sharing differs from profit-sharing in that a portion of the paycheck is linked directly to improvements in productivity (the ratio of labor costs to output), irrespective of whether profits are generated (Driscoll 1979). Employees share in the value of the gains, usually awarded as a supplement to the paycheck as soon as possible after determination. Amounts are calculated by a set formula and usually cover all hourly employees in an entire plant. These plans usually coexist with an employee-participation plan. Gain-sharing plans tend to be based on the Scanlon Plan, the Rucker Plan, or Improshare, with almost half customized by users.

The Scanlon Plan, famous for its Depression-era origins (1938), is best described today as an exercise in participative management (Gomez-Mejia 1988).

Management first establishes a payment formula that compares current productivity, usually measured in terms of its ratio to revenues, net sales, or sales value of production, to a historically based ratio. Other costs may be included, such as materials, overhead, and rejects. An agreed-upon percentage of the gains stemming from the productivity increases or cost savings are shared with the workers when the observed ratio is less than the historical ratio (Lawler 1990). The Rucker Share-of-Production Plan is similar to the Scanlon scheme, but derives its bonus payments from more elaborate analysis, sometimes involving observation of operations ("an economic engineering audit") for several years prior. Based on value-added gains, it pays a bonus when gains are achieved. The "value added" is defined as sales minus raw materials and services secured outside the company. The Improshare scheme differs from the other gain-sharing plans by rewarding employees for work-time saved for a given number of units produced. The value of the hours saved (hours allotted for the task minus actual hours used) is shared between management and work force on a 50-50 basis (Fein 1991). For more detailed discussions of gain-sharing, see Doyle (1983) and Graham-Moore and Ross (1990).

How popular is gain-sharing? Apparently, gain-sharing plans are used far less frequently than profit-sharing plans. In 1992 a survey of Fortune 1000 firms found 39 percent to be using some form of gain-sharing, but with only a small portion of the work force covered (Lawler and Cohen 1992). A series of other small surveys report similar findings. More impressive is Lawler's comment that "the most important thing we know about gain-sharing plans is that they work" (1990). This is high praise indeed, coming as it does from a proponent of people-based plans.

The Two-Tier Wage Scale

This is a relatively new but already widely used type of compensation that compels attention because of the many reverberations to its usage. It is usually seen as a vehicle for concession-making by unions, a strategy that maintains union leadership's popularity with present membership at the expense of future union members. In two-tier systems, new hires are paid lower rates for the same work than present union workers; often they also receive lesser benefits and job security. There may or may not be provisions for a closing of the gap over a period of years. In addition, some firms have punctured traditional union job security by assigning the new hires status as *contingent workers*, to be discarded in times of shrinking demand, without prospect of permanent employment. In such situations, benefits are also likely to be absent.

After the first few large concession-making contracts were signed, it was widely speculated that worker resentment would force the abandonment of two-tier arrangements within a few years. Because of the morale factor, some companies have terminated their two-tier system by providing for the merger of wage rates after a period of years. For example, according to the *PR Newswire*, October 10, 1995, because of the bitterness aroused, American Airlines agreed, in its 1995 contract negotiations, to end its two-tier plan in five years rather than the originally agreed-upon eight. But the advantages to the employer encourage the conclusion that two-tier plans will be around for the foreseeable future.

To conclude this description of variable pay plans, the best that can be said is that, for all that has been written and/or claimed about them, relatively little is known about their effectiveness. While the variable wage trends described are touted as the wave of the future, convincing documentation is lacking as to their prevalence. To demonstrate that income volatility has increased since the 1980s does not establish variable pay plans as a root cause. Most of the variable pay schemes described are thought to be motivational in nature, but whether monetary rewards actually increase employee motivation is a subject for books on organizational behavior. All that will be noted here is that a minority of observers reject the arguments usually presented on behalf of the variable pay concept, that rewards bring better results for the employer. One contrarion argument is that rewards to individuals create competition, undermining the most advantageous employer strategy, the team approach (Kohn 1993).

EXECUTIVE PAY

The special case of executive compensation currently commands great public interest. While it has long been known that top executives are treated differently than other employees, the size of disparity has been increasing, while the links to performance have been lessening and often tend to be indiscernible. The level of executive pay is unique among the advanced industrial nations, far out-pacing compensation habits in Europe and Japan, though American practices are now beginning to affect recruiting costs of foreign nationals in Europe and Asia (*Business Week*, April 19, 1999). The continuing exceleration in executive pay in the U.S. is suggested by the facts that average U.S. executive pay in 1990 was $2 million and 13.6 million in 1998, up 36 percent from the prior year (1997). [7] The average increases for white collar and blue collar workers between 1997 and 1998 were 3.9 and 2.7 percents respectively. [8] Put another way, the average top company executive earned 419 times the average blue-collar wage in 1998. In view of the wide-spread skepticism about the relationship between earnings and performance, *Business Week* compared 1998 executive pay with company profitability for the year. Among their findings: two of the three highest-paid executives of the year were among the five top executives who produced the *least* returns, according to two measures, shareholder return and average return on equity (as measured by the relative index). [9]

Base pay has become relatively unimportant in the total executive compensation picture and perquisites less important than formerly, with long-term incentives (stock options) the major enricher. Tax considerations have heavily influenced the composition of the total compensation package. With the multiples of disparity accelerating since the early 1980s and pressures mounting from pension plans and other ownership groups, Congress wrote a provision (162m) into the 1993 Omnibus Budget Reconciliation Act which forced the disclosure of executive compensation in publicly owned companies and established an annual million-dollar cap on tax exemptions for executive compensation unless directly tied to performance by a quantifiable measure previously agreed-upon by shareholders. As one observer pointed out, this action effectively established the figure of $1 million as the annual "minimum" for top executives (Byrne 1995).

The great increase in corporate pay during the 1990s has been fueled by the spectacular stock market rise which pushed the value of the stock option portion of the executive pay package upward. Stock options permit the holder to purchase a specified number of shares of stock at a specified dollar figure without regard to market price whenever they choose to exercise their rights; the employer may then claim the difference between the "strike" price and the market price as an expense.[10] In the past the sizes of options offered to corporate leadership were closely associated with annual compensation, with different multiples for different job levels and different industries (Minow 1992). In the early 1980s standards began rising. While the highest paid executives in 1983 made $2 to $3 million, Michael Eisner in 1994 took away $204 million "without complaint" because of his success in increasing the market value of Disney stock (Byrne 1995); and, in 1998, $575.592 millions in total pay (*Business Week*, April 19, 1999).

The general public has exhibited perplexity and annoyance, but only relatively modest protest to the growing pay gap between executives and other workers. Organized resistance, such as has occurred, has been largely confined to groups with direct financial interests, such as pension funds. When the business community has deemed it necessary to justify executive pay, it has couched explanations in terms of contributions to shareholder profits rather than involving itself in income disparity issues. Its stance has been that if the public could only be helped to understand the role of the executives in enhancing the wealth of the corporation, controversy would evaporate; in other words, the problem is poor communication (Patrick 1992).

As for alleged unrest among shareholders, as opposed to the public, as a whole, according to a prominent business spokesman, even the most vocal critics of executive pay want only "more comprehensive and more consistent disclosure, with explanations of corporate goals and how companies define performance" (Minow 1992), although another spokesperson conceded that shareholders need to be convinced that the executives are entitled to their takings (Brindisi 1992). The April 1999 *Business Week* report cited stated it's longtime opposition to the escalation of executive pay, pointing out that, when stock prices fall severely, the same corporate executives who argue for stock options as the most logical form of reward have turned to repricing of stocks (for themselves, not share-holders) as a means of restoring the value of their options, i.e., lowering the cost of the shares to themselves, Or, in a prolonged bear market, as occurred during the 1970s, they may turn to a bonus system which reacts to some internally–determined goals that are rewarded by cash payments or restricted stock that retains its value even when the market price falls.

Perhaps the United States' historical experience accounts for the uniquely high pay levels for its CEOs. According to one scholar, American business has incorporated into its compensation practices aspects of the Puritan work ethic, according to which personal achievement and accumulations of wealth are indications of God's blessings and of personal salvation.[11] Current executive pay levels may be interpreted in this light as expressions of a "pay-here-and-now" philosophy (Peck 1995). Another explanation of public acceptance of high-level executive pay, popular among economists, is the *tournament mentality*, a "winners-take-all" attitude on the part of employees. In this view workers are motivated to work hard throughout their company careers by the possibility, however remote, of winning the top executive position. The great disparity between earnings of the average top executive and his immediate subordinates can hardly be attributed to ability, but rather to possession of the job itself. Another explanation of the increased importance of stock options reportedly stems from boards' belief in their effect on executive behavior. One such effect, according to human-resources theory, is the attraction of top-notch leadership to the firm. However, the prevailing view ("agency theory") is that when share ownership by top executives is encouraged the interests of management become more closely aligned with those of shareholders. This line of thought has allegedly led companies to emphasize long-term over short-term salary incentives (Zajac and Westphal 1995). Questions have been raised about this rationale, however. Is too much stock ownership necessarily a good thing? Might executives be impelled to refrain from making new investments because they would drain resources and lower their own stock values (Enslow 1991)? Thus far, this is not seen as a major problem. Meanwhile, companies are moving in the direction of encouraging a broad spectrum of employees, not just top executives, to join in ownership.

Other explanations for the extraordinary rise in executive pay are that most boards are still picked by CEOs and are anxious to please them. In view of the greater mobility of CEOs, use of stock options as an incentive to retain the chief executive is reportedly another factor One who leaves a position tends to immediately receive a huge boost in pay in the new position. This tendency is thought to be in line with a current belief that only a few people are talented enough to run a big company successfully.

Most of the pay schemes discussed above are described by their advocates as motivational in nature, with only a minority of observers rejecting the common assumption on which they are all built: that rewards bring better results for the employer.

BENEFITS AS PART OF TOTAL COMPENSATION

A much valued portion of total compensation, benefits are both voluntary and involuntary. Employers are obligated by law to make Social Security payments for all acknowledged employees and to pay for Workers' Compensation and Unemployment Compensation. But the provision of health insurance, life insurance, pensions, tuition payments, paid vacations, and day care for employees' children are discretionary on the part of the employer.

Unsurprisingly, larger employers offer more categories of benefits and cover a larger proportion of their employees than smaller ones. As shown on Table 13.2, larger employers (those with 100 or more employees, as of 1995) offer paid vacation leave to almost all full-timers and paid holidays to most employees. About three-quarters receive medical insurance, but only about one-third on a noncontributory basis (based on a 1993 survey). The proportion of full-timers now covered by defined benefit pension plans is down to about one half (52%), while a slightly larger proportion (55%) participate when a defined contribution plan is offered. A large majority (87%) are covered by a life insurance plan (in 1993, largely noncontributory). The data shown reflect, of necessity, selective reporting, with some exceptions, reporting the benefits received by the largest numbers. More detailed data may be found in BLS 1998.

Small employers (those with fewer than 100 full-time workers) offer a smaller range of benefits to fewer of their workers; it should be noted, however, that the data for smaller and larger employers is not always parallel, so comparisons of specific benefits offered and   relative levels of coverage are not always possible. Although most full-timers in small firms receive paid holidays and vacations; two-thirds, medical insurance; and almost two-thirds, life insurance, coverage for other benefits is drastically less than that offered by the larger establishments. More detailed data on small employers may be found in *Statistical Abstract* 1998. Data on the cost of benefits to small employers is provided in BLS 1997.

Benefits for Full-Time Workers

The widely reported shrinkage in employee benefits is shown on Table 13.3. The fall in health-care coverage for full-time employees (private, medium, and large-sized establishments) is particularly noteworthy, dropping from 97 percent in 1980 to 83 percent by 1991 (*Monthly Labor Review* 119, no. 10 [October 1996]: Table 25, "Current Labor Statistics," 116). The shrinkage has continued, at least in regard to small businesses, since the 1991 BLS survey. According to a nationwide 1998 survey of small employers by Dun & Bradstreet Corporation, only 39 percent of small employers offer health-care benefits, as opposed to 46 percent in 1996 (Koretz 1998).

Even more dramatic than the erosion of health-care coverage is the shrinking-away of employer-defined benefit pension plans. Basically, these are the plans through which employers traditionally expressed their long-term commitment to their employees. Participation by full-time employees dropped from 84 percent to 59 percent within the eleven years reported upon by BLS. Interestingly, participation in defined contribution plans—plans with no employer commitment as to the amount of the pension—has also fallen, from 54 to 48 percent, according to available data (1985 through 1991 only). The Dun & Bradstreet survey confirms the trend: small businesses are continuing to retrench on retirement benefits and paid vacations for full-time workers. Nineteen percent in 1998, as opposed to 28 percent in 1996, said they offer retirement benefits, while only about half offer paid vacations for full-time workers.

It is true that the proportion of full-timers who participate in tax-deferred savings plans has increased steeply during the 1980–91 period, but still fewer than half of all full-time employees are involved in these publicly subsidized, self-financing arrangements. Such arrangements, the most prominent being the 401(k) account, offer the advantage of being *portable*, a crucial factor in today's atmosphere of impermanence, and some employers do make voluntary contributions to them. Nonetheless, since workers must take contributions out of their pay envelopes, in practice, such plans effectively tend to preclude the participation of low-wage earners in pension plans. Thus, these plans reflect the increasing disengagement of employers from the expectation of long-term relationships with their employees. A rare look at the subject by Bloom and Freeman (1992) corroborates the BLS's overview, particularly insofar as it observes that coverage began to fall during the 1980s and increasingly excludes young, less-educated males.

Benefits for Part-time Workers

Only very recently has detailed information concerning benefits for part-time workers become available. The data indicate that when medium and larger employers offer benefits to part-timers (about one-sixth of their 40.2 million employees), they do so at a lower rate than to full-timers, even when inferior wage and salary rates are taken into account. Part-timers are only about half as likely to be covered by retirement plans and rights to unpaid family leave as full-timers, and one-quarter as likely to be covered by a medical plan and to participate in a life insurance plan. The benefit most available to part-timers is paid time off (vacations, holidays, and jury duty). Less than one-fifth receive paid sick leave and only 42 percent of the part-timers can claim unpaid family leave. About one-fifth have access to the various insurances, such as health, life, and short-term disability, and about one-third are eligible for job-related educational assistance (BLS 1998).

Total compensation costs for all full-time workers in the United States as of March 1997 averaged $20.37 per hour; for part time workers, $9.60 (47% of full-timers' compensation), while total benefits costs averaged 28.6 percent versus 19.2 percent of total compensation. A larger proportion of the benefits paid for part-timers are mandated by law (10.9% vs 8.8%), while the larger portion of benefits' monies spent for full-timers goes to voluntary coverage, such as insurance and retirement benefits (BLS 1997a).

Current trends in employee benefits include reductions in both the proportion of employers offering certain highly valued benefits and the extent of employer contributions for those covered (a subject outside the scope of this chapter). For these reasons, employee benefits are likely to be the focus of considerable interest in the coming period. These realities have led to benefits playing a curious role in the economy, as the following case study demonstrates.

Establishments have been under pressure to cut costs since the beginning of the 1990s, and have begun with reductions in benefits programs. This has had the effect of increasing the number of two-earner families, according to a J.C. Penney manager. As of the mid-1990s there have been a large number of women employed on the J.C. Penney sales force who work mainly for the benefits. To be eligible they must work a minimum of 25 hours weekly. The majority of these women accept employment at Penney's because the store's benefits package is superior to those which are available to their husbands. In most cases the husbands earn a larger salary, but have suffered significant cuts in benefits. Regarding health insurance, the Penney Managed Care System is above average. Thus, the J.C. Penney benefits package helps attract qualified employees who might otherwise choose to not work or to work for a higher-wage employer. (Personal communication)

Interested readers will find a good nontechnical description of major methods of compensation in Byars and Rue's *Human Resources and Personnel Management* (1984) and DeLuca's *Handbook of Compensation Management* (1993). Ed-

Table 13.2
Selected Employee Benefits, Full-Time Workers in Private Establishments, 1994 and 1995

	*Medium and Large Private Establishments, 1995		**Small Private Establishments, 1994
Percent of participants in			
Paid time-off			
Vacations	96	Vacations	88
Holidays	89	Holidays	82
Sick leave	58	Jury duty	58
Family leave	2	Funeral leave	50
Unpaid time-off			
Family leave	84	Family leave	47
Insurance plans			
Medical care	77	Medical care	66
Life	87	Life	61
Retirement and savings plans (all)	80	Retirement plans (all)	42
Defined benefit pension	52	Defined benefit plans	15
Defined contribution pension	55	Defined cont. plans	34
Educational assistance (job-related)	65	Educ. assistance (job-related)	37
Child care	8	Child care	1

*Medium and large employers are defined as those with 100 employees or more.
**Small employers are defined as those with fewer than 100 employees.
Sources: U.S. Department of Labor. Bureau of Labor Statistics. 1998. *Employee Benefits in Medium and Large Private Establishments, 1995*, Bulletin 2496, Table 1, 7–8; 1997. *Employee Benefits in Small Private Establishments, 1994*, Bulletin 2475, Table 1, p. 6. Washington, D.C.: Government Printing Office.

Table 13.3
Percentage of Full-Time Employees Participating in Employer-Provided Benefits Plans, Selected Years, 1980–91

	Medium and large private establishments*				Small private establishments**	State and local governments***	
	1980	1985	1989	1991	1990	1987	1990
Time-off plans	10	10	10	8	8	17	11
Paid. rest time	75	72	71	67	48	58	56
Paid. funeral time	--	88	84	80	47	56	63
Paid. holidays	99	98	97	92	84	81	74
Paid. personal leave	20	26	22	21	11	38	39
Paid. vacations	100	99	97	96	88	72	67
Paid. sick leave	62	67	68	67	47	97	95
Unpaid. maternity	–	–	37	37	17	57	51
Unpaid. paternity	–	–	18	26	8	30	33
Insurance plans							
Medical care	97	96	92	83	69	93	93
Life insurance	96	96	94	94	64	85	88
Long-term disability.	40	48	45	40	19	31	27
Sick./accident	54	52	43	45	26	14	21
Retirement plans							
Defined benefit pension plans****	84	80	63	59	20	93	90
Defined contribution	–	53	48	48	31	9	9
Tax-deferred savings	–	26	41	44	17	28	45
Other benefits							
Flexible benefits	–	–	9	10	1	5	5
Reimbursement accts.	–	–	23	36	8	5	31

The historical data is not entirely comparable. *Includes 50 to 250 employees up to 1986; thereafter, private establishments with 100 or more employees. **Private sector employers with fewer than 100 workers. *** 1987 data excludes local governments with fewer than 50 employees; 1990 data includes all state and local governments. ****Coverage for persons with defined benefit pension plans varied over the years. Note: Dash indicates that data was not collected that year.
Source: Monthly Labor Review. 1996. 119, no. 10 (October): Table 25, p. 116.

ward Lawler III's *Strategic Pay* (1990) discusses the pros and cons of the alternative methods from the viewpoint of a behaviorist. Ehrenberg and Smith's *Modern Labor Economics* (1994) and Filer, Hamermesh, and Rees' *The Economics of Work and Pay* (1996) can contribute heavily to one's understanding of broader issues. Such BLS surveys as *Employee Benefits in Medium and Large Private Establishments 1997* (1998) and *Employment Benefits in Small Private Establishments 1994* (1997) together with periodic Department of Labor news bulletins offer broad-based, detailed information on employee benefits as a part of total compensation.

NOTES

1. For further discussion of age-based pay policies, see Ehrenberg and Smith (1994), 385–93.

2. See Kohn (1993) for a discussion of employee motivation and a denunciation of the reward concept.

3. These facts reflect a problem of *asymmetric information* in the hiring process, that is, knowing less about job applicants and their intentions than it would be desirable to know.

4. For general proceedings regarding job analysis, see Milkovich and Newman (1996); and DeLuca (1993).

5. For a nontechnical illustration of the point factor system, see Milkovich and Newman 1996.

6. Five percent involve a combination of employer contributions and salary reductions and 2 percent participate in deferred profit-sharing not involving salary reduction.

7. *Business Week* studied the compensation packages of 365 of the largest companies in the United States

8. *Business Week* secured this figure from the Bureau of Labor Statistics Employment Cost Index.

9. Stock price at the end of 1998, plus dividends reinvested for three years, divided by stock price at the end of 1995, a technique used by Standard & Poor's COMPUSTAT.

10. The force behind the movement into stock options for top executives is the Financial Accounting Standards Board rulings, which permit high executive pay and liberal use of stock options without hurt to company profits (Blair 1994).

11. Max Weber provides a full discourse on the Puritan ethic in his classic work, *The Puritan Ethic and the Spirit of Capitalism.*

REFERENCES

Blair, Margaret. 1994. CEO pay: why such a contentious issue? *Brookings Review* 12 (Winter): 22–27.

Bloom, David, and Richard Freeman. 1992. The fall in private pension coverage in the U.S. *American Economic Association Papers and Proceedings* 82 (May): 539–45.

Brindisi, Louis J. 1992. Cash flow impact on stock price and stock compensation plans. In Brothers, Theresa, *Rethinking corporate compensation plans.* New York: Conference Board.

Bunning, R. L. 1992. Models for skill-based pay plans. *HR Magazine* 37 (February): 62–66.

Business Week. 1995. Bonus pay: buzzword or bonanza? 14 November.

————. 1999. Special report: executive pay. 19 April:72, 3, 78, 81, 84, and 89.

Byars, Lloyd, and Leslie Rue. 1984. *Human resources and personnel management.* Homewood, Ill.: Richard Irwin.

Byrne, John. 1995. Why executive compensation continues to increase. In *Compensation: present practices and future concerns, a conference report.* New York: The Conference Board, Inc.

DeLuca, Matthew J. 1993. *Handbook of compensation management.* Englewood Cliffs, N.J.: Prentice Hall.

Doyle, R J. 1983. *Gain-sharing and productivity: a guide to planning, implementation and development.* New York, N.Y.: AMACOM.

Driscoll, James W. 1979. Working creatively with a union: lessons from the Scanlon plan. *Organizational Dynamics* 8 (Summer): 61–80.

Ehrenberg, Ronald, and Ronald Smith. 1994. *Modern labor economics: theory and public policy.* 5th edition. New York: HarperCollins College Publishers.

Enslow, Beth. 1991. Up, up, and away. *Across the Board* 28 (July/August): 18–25.

Fein, Mitchell. 1991. IMPROSHARE: a technique for sharing productivity gains with employees. In Rock, M. L.,and L. A. Berger, eds., *The compensation handbook.* 3rd edition. New York: McGraw-Hill.

Filer, Randall, Daniel Hamermesh, and Albert Rees. 1996. *The economics of work and pay.* 6th ed. New York: HarperCollins.

Gomez-Mejia, L.R. 1988. Evaluating employee performance: does the appraisal instrument make a difference? *Journal of Organizational Behavior Management* 9, no. 2: 155–70.

Graham-Moore, Brian, and Timothy Ross. 1990. *Gain-sharing plans for improving performance.* Washington, D.C.: Bureau of National Affairs.

Jones, Derek C., Takao Kato, and Jeffrey Pliskin. 1994. *Profit-sharing and gain-sharing: a review of theory, incidence, and effects.* Annandale-on-Hudson, N.Y.: Jerome Levy Economics Institute of Bard College, Working Paper 125 (September).

Kohn, Alfie. 1993 *Punished by rewards: the trouble with gold stars, incentive plans, and praise and other bribes.* Boston: Houghton Mifflin.

Koretz, Gene. 1998. The widening health care gap. *Business Week* (October 12): 28.

Kruse, Douglas. 1991. profit–sharing and employment variability: microeconomic evidence on the Weitzman theory. *Industrial and Labor Relations Review* 44 (April): 437–52.

Lawler III, Edward. 1981 *Pay and organization development.* Reading, Mass.: Addison-Wesley.

————. 1986 What's wrong with point-factor job evaluation. *Compensation and Benefits Review* 18, no. 2: 20–28.

————. 1990. *Strategic pay: aligning organizational strategies and pay systems.* San Francisco: Jossey-Bass.

————. and S. G. Cohen. 1992. Designing a pay system for teams. *American Compensation Association Journal* 1, no. 1: 6–19.

Lawler III, Edward, and G. E. Ledford. 1985. Skill-based pay. *Personnel* 62, no. 9: 30–37.

Ledford, Gerald, W. R. Tyler, and W. B. Dickey. 1991. Skill-based pay; case number 3: Honeywell ammunition assembly plant. *Compensation and Benefits Review* 23, no. 2 (March/April): 57–77.

Ledford, Gerald, Edward Lawler III, and Susan Mohrman. 1995. Reward innovation in Fortune 1000 companies. *Compensation and Benefits Review* 27 (July-August): 76–81.

Livernash, Robert. 1957. The internal wage structure. In Taylor, George, and F. C.

Pierson, eds., *New concepts in wage determination.* New York: McGraw Hill.

Milkovich, George, and Alexandra Wigdor, eds. 1991. *Pay for performance: evaluating performance appraisal and merit pay.* Washington, D.C.: National Academy Press.

———. and Jerry Newman. 1996. *Compensation.* 5th edition. Chicago: Irwin.

Minow, Sol. 1992. Is there runaway executive compensation? In Brothers, Theresa, ed., *Rethinking corporate compensation plans.* New York: Conference Board.

Montemayer, E. 1994 Realigning pay systems with market systems. *ACA Journal* (Winter): 44–53.

Murphy, Kevin, and Robert Topel. 1990. Efficiency wages reconsidered: a review of theory and evidence, 204–44. In Weiss, Yoram, and Gideon Fishelman, eds. 1990. *Advances in theory and measurement of unemployment.* London: Macmillan.

Oak, Frederick. 1994. Compensation survey. *Compensation and Benefits Review* (September/October): 19–22.

Patrick, Stewart. 1992. Developments and trends in executive compensation. In *Rethinking corporate compensation plans.* New York: Conference Board.

Peck, Charles.1995. *Pay and performance: the interaction of compensation and performance appraisal.* In Hall, Thomas, ed. *Compensation: present practices and future concerns: a conference report.* New York: The Conference Board, Inc., 8–9.

Schuster, J. R., and P. K. Zingheim. 1992. *The new pay.* New York: Macmillan.

Statistical Abstract.of the U.S., 1997. 1998. 117th edition. Washington, D.C.: Government Printing Office.

U. S. Department of Labor. Bureau of Labor Statistics. 1996. Current labor statistics. *Monthly Labor Review* 119, no. 10: Table 25.

———. 1997. *Employee benefits in small private establishments, 1994.* Bulletin 2475. Washington, D.C.: Government Printing Office.

———.1998. *Employment benefits in medium and large private establishments, 1995.* Bulletin 2496 (April): Washington, D.C.: Government Printing Office, Table 1 and Chapter 9, 146–7.

———. Manpower Administration. Bureau of Employment Security. 1965. *Dictionary of occupational titles.* 3rd edition. Washington, D.C.: Government Printing Office.

Wagel, W.H. 1989. Sola ophthalmics. *Personnel* 66 (March): 20–24.

Weitzman, Martin. 1984 *The share economy.* Cambridge, Mass.: Harvard University Press.

———. and Douglas Kruse. 1990. Profit-sharing and productivity, 95–140. In Blinder, Alan, ed., *Paying for productivity.* Washington, D.C.: Brookings Institution.

Zajac, Edward, and James Westphal. 1995. Accounting for explanations of CEO compensation: substance and symbolism. *Administrative Science Quarterly* 40 (June): 283–308.

14

Curtailments on the
Power of the Market

This chapter identifies and describes situations in which usual employer practices concerning wages differ or are widely believed to differ from the norm. These situations are referred to as oligopoly and monopsony. The chapter also discusses a limitation on the power of employers to set pay rates, the minimum wage, and the issues surrounding that phenomenon in view of widespread concerns about the consequences of raising the rate. The fact that some unionized employers must also be given cost of living increases (COLAs) as specified in their collective bargaining agreements, and the necessity of paying a premium for employees working more than the standard work week, under certain circumstances, are also noted.

WAGES IN SITUATIONS OF NONCOMPETITIVE LABOR
AND PRODUCT MARKETS

Economists have long speculated that wage rates are affected by situations in which employers do not have to compete in the product market. The influence of two such situations, those involving oligopoly and monopsony, upon wage levels is briefly reviewed here. Such discussions assume that labor markets operate under conditions of imperfect competition, that is, situations prevail in which some sellers can and do exert control prices.

Oligopoly

Oligopoly usually involves a situation in which a very few employers in certain industries control the supply of a desired product. If only one employer controls access to a product, which has been the case in public utilities until recently, the establishment would be termed a *monopoly*. Most economists insist that monopolists pay the same wages as competitive firms for the same types of workers with the same education in the same local labor markets, but that they hire fewer workers than competitive firms. The lower hiring levels are attributed to oligopolies maximizing profits on a different basis than competitive firms. In the view of economists, the problem of oligopoly with reference to social welfare is that of reduced hiring and the pushing of would-be workers into lower wage industries (Bellante and Jackson 1983). They admit that this is counter-intuitive, but point out that there is no evidence that oligopolies share their monopoly-associated profits with their workers by paying above-market rates.

Regulated Industries. What about monopolies that enjoy special protection from competition because of government regulation? Some economists claim that where government regulation is involved, employers enjoying monopolistic or oligopolistic status behave much as described above. They hire fewer employees than competitive firms, but pay wages at the same going market rates as competitive firms, since they have to compete for workers in the same local labor markets (Bellante and Jackson 1983). Another school of thought, however, proffers that regulated monopolies pay higher wages than other employers (Long and Link 1983; Heywood 1986). Basically, the argument of these researchers is that those who choose to share a part of the profits derived from their product market monopoly do so because they can pass on the added costs to consumers who have no choice if they wish to obtain the product—it is precisely for this reason that the electricity industry is being deregulated. But according to Ronald Ehrenberg and Robert S. Smith (1994), evidence is mixed as to the effect of regulation on wage levels.

Concentration. Oligopolistic firms are also said to be *concentrated.* The concentration ratio of a firm in an industry dominated by a few large players is its percentage of the total sales made by the four leading firms. One reason sometimes given for the fact that higher wages are paid by concentrated employers is that they are more likely to be unionized than others. But since both unionization and oligopoly are associated with large-sized employers, the extent to which each factor, concentration or unionization, is responsible for the payment of higher wages is unclear.

The views of economists concerning the pay policies of oligopolistic employers may be surprising in view of public impressions about the superior pay levels for semiskilled and low-skilled workers in now-fading oligopolies, such as the automobile industry. Are not pay levels for automobile workers (members of the United Auto Workers of America) above market level for the skill levels involved? If not, what is the identity of competitive firms that pay the same rates? As noted previously, large employers tend to pay more than smaller ones for the same type of worker, and unionization may or may not raise wages. Does size of employer explain the superior pay? Recent research says yes, but it is also true that no one has been able to explain satisfactorily or offer proof as to exactly why large firms pay more. Does the effect of unionization need to be re-examined? This is of more than academic interest: current economic discussion includes considerable mention of the search for "good jobs" and "bad jobs" and describes desirable, potential employers who might offer to persons of very modest skills levels the "good jobs" previously supplied by such industries as the automobile-makers.

Monopsony

Another scenario in which an establishment may pay lower-than-market wages involves *monopsony*, the circumstance in which an employer is able to hire, but still pay less than the value of employees' marginal revenue product (MRP), that is, the value of the product they produce. The phenomenon can exist in the following situations: when (1) only one buyer or very few buyers of certain types of labor exist in a given location, (2) only one or very few employers exist for a certain type of occupation, or (3) several employers collude to maintain an artificially low level of wages. In such situations workers are paid less than their MRP.

If theory holds true, in a situation of monopsony, the employer can underpay the workers who are actually hired because there will always be some people who have no choice but to accept whatever is offered. Meanwhile, job slots remain vacant. Sometimes, to persuade workers to accept jobs at wages lower than marginal revenue product, an inducement such as flexible hours may be offered to compensate for poor pay. However, some potential workers will withdraw from the labor market rather than agree to be underpaid; others may shift to other occupations; or workers may pursue unionization. It has been suggested that the markets for teachers and nurses have the characteristics of monopsony. The example of professional baseball players prior to 1978 is described by Filer, Hamermesh, and Rees (1996); the case of hospitals depicted as discriminating oligopolistic employers of nurses, by Schramm (1983). Awareness of the practices of oligopolistic employers is necessary for understanding the nature of the periodic "shortages" of certain types of personnel who withdraw from the labor force or take up other occupations that do not require much training or investment. Such awareness would lead one to see the folly of starting "drives" to train more teachers or nurses, for example, when such "shortages" periodically occur, rather than taking measures to bring back already trained personnel—wasted human capital investment—by offering more adequate wages and salaries.

LIMITATIONS ON EMPLOYER FREEDOMS

Three major impediments to employer freedom in wage-setting are the minimum wage, overtime pay, and COLAs. The first is mandatory upon almost all employers; the second in certain circumstances; the third comes into play only when it is included in a union contract. However, employee expectations of annual raises amounting to at least the equivalent of the yearly rise in the cost-of-living keep this subject in the forefront.

The Minimum Wage

A legally mandated minimum wage represents an attempt to establish a wage floor for the least competitive, poorest paid workers in the society, the ultimate objective being the elimination of family poverty. Upon adoption of the Fair Labor Standards Act of 1938 (commonly referred to as the Wages and Hours Law), the national minimum wage was initially set at $.25 per hour. Table 14.1 shows the subsequent rises of the nominal federal minimum wage since its

Table 14.1

Value of the Federal Minimum Wage, 1954–96, in 1996 Dollars, Adjusted for Inflation Using the Consumer Price Index for All Urban Earners

Year	Nominal Dollars	1996 Dollars	Year	Nominal Dollars	1996 Dollars	Year	Nominal Dollars	1996 Dollars
1954	0.75	4.37	1969	1.60	6.84	1984	3.35	5.06
1955	0.75	4.39	1970	1.60	6.47	1985	3.35	4.88
1956	1.00	5.77	1971	1.60	6.20	1986	3.35	4.80
1957	1.00	5.58	1972	1.60	6.01	1987	3.35	4.63
1958	1.00	5.43	1973	1.60	5.65	1988	3.35	4.44
1959	1.00	5.39	1974	2.00	6.37	1989	3.35	4.24
1960	1.00	5.30	1975	2.10	6.12	1990	3.80	4.56
1961	1.15	6.03	1976	2.30	6.34	1991	4.25	4.90
1962	1.15	5.97	1977	2.30	5.95	1992	4.25	4.75
1963	1.25	6.41	1978	2.65	6.38	1993	4.25	4.61
1964	1.25	6.33	1979	2.90	6.27	1994	4.25	4.50
1965	1.25	6.23	1980	3.10	5.90	1995	4.25	4.38
1966	1.25	6.05	1981	3.35	5.78	1996	4.75	4.75
1967	1.40	6.58	1982	3.35	5.45			
1968	1.60	7.21	1983	3.35	5.28			

Source: U. S. Department of Labor web site, www.dol.gov/dol/esa/public/minwage/chart2.htm (July 22, 1998).

inception, and its value in 1996 dollars between 1954 and 1996. The table indicates a steady fall in value since 1968. By 1996 the Minimum (nominally $4.75) was worth only two-thirds of its value in 1968 when the fall began (nominal value, $1.60; value in 1996 dollars, $7.21). Since 1996 the second phase of the Congressionally authorized raise took effect, bringing the hourly Minimum to $5.15 .

Lowest Wage Group Profile. As of the third quarter of 1998, that is, after the second increase (to $5.15 per hour) authorized by Congress as of September 1997, about 5.5 million hourly wage workers were reported to be earning the new hourly minimum wage or less. That is, 2 percent of the hourly work force was at the $5.15 minimum; an additional 5.6 percent was below it. As shown on Table 14.2, minimum-wage and sub-minimum-wage workers are predominantly young, concentrated in the age sixteen to nineteen-year-age category. Unsurprisingly, they are disproportionately part-time as opposed to full-time workers; they are also more female than male, more minority than white, and more likely to be in the services than in manufacturing or the public sector (BLS, unpublished data, 3rd quarter, 1998).

The Minimum Wage Debate. Calls to raise the national minimum are heard periodically, usually after purchasing power has been seriously eroded, and the legal minimum is found to be trailing the actual minimum being paid most low-level workers. The discussion typically involves costs of the proposed raise, and whether it would harm rather than help the least competitive workers through loss of employment. A rise in the minimum wage causes the weakest to lose their jobs, the argument goes, as employers would invest in labor-saving equipment or move the jobs out of the area or out of the country altogether (Becker 1995). Common wisdom has been that a 10 percent rise in the national legal minimum results in about 1 percent loss in jobs. In cases where individual states have minimum wage standards higher than the national level, the same discussion prevails: employment will be moved out of state should the current minimum be raised. Impetus for adoption of minimums by some states began fairly recently, spurred by the severe depreciation of the national minimum, unchanged for ten years (Card and Krueger 1994).

Debate About the Collapse of the Wage Floor. Consensus exists that the real earnings of low-skill, poorly educated men fell drastically after 1973 and throughout the 1980s. Between 1979 and 1989 the proportion of persons with "low earnings," defined as less than the poverty line for a family of four, almost doubled, rising from 8 percent to 15 percent for employed male high-school graduates, and from 13 percent to 30 percent for male school drop-outs, (high-school and earlier). The situation of minority males worsened even more severely, soaring to a quarter of all employed black school-drop-outs and about 40 percent of all Hispanic school drop-outs earning less than poverty level, far above 1979 levels (Acs and Danziger 1993). The most dramatic declines in earnings during the 1980s were among poorly educated males, male school drop-outs losing 25 percent of their value between 1973 and 1990; male high-school graduates, 16 percent. The trend began during the 1970s, but it accelerated in the 1980s, occurring during a period when college graduates' real earnings declined only slightly (2.4%). The real earnings of those with advanced degrees were the exception; they rose during this period (Gittleman 1994; Howell 1996). However,

Table 14.2
Proportion of Hourly Workers Paid at or Below the Minimum Wage, Selected Characteristics, 1998, 3rd quarter*

	Percent of all workers paid hourly rates at or below $5.15		
	Total	At $5.15	Below $5.15
N=72,702,000			
Total, 16 and over	7.6%	2.0%	5.6%
16-24 years	16.9	5.0	11.8
16-19 years	26.2	8.2	17.9
25 years and over	4.8	1.2	3.6
Males	5.8	1.9	3.9
Females	8.8	2.3	7.2
White	7.5	2.0	5.4
Black	8.8	2.6	6.1
Hispanic Origin	8.6	2.3	2.0
Full-time workers	4.3	1.1	3.2
Part-time workers	19.1	5.6	13.5
Private sector	8.1	2.2	5.9
Goods-producing	3.4	1.0	2.4
Service-producing	10.4	2.6	7.6
Public sector	4.0	1.5	2.5

* Excludes the incorporated self-employed; are not seasonally adjusted.
Source: U.S. Department of Labor, Bureau of Labor Statistics.Unpublished data, third quarter,1998

as reported by Topol (1993), during the 1980s and the "white collar recession" of 1990–91, degrees were not fool-proof means of securing a better life as many college graduates were forced to compete for lower-skilled jobs, contributing to overcrowding and wage depression.

A series of explanations have been offered for wage deterioration of the low-skilled, the most widely circulated being that technological changes in the industrial sector lessened demand for low-skill workers, creating oversupply and lowering wages (Bound and Johnson 1992). Rejecting the traditional supply-and-demand scenario, a series of other economists insist that the collapse has to be viewed in a larger context (Card and Krueger 1995). Alternative explanations include widespread adoption of low-wage policies by employers, implemented by their human resources departments (Kochan, Katz and McKersie 1994); the role of increased low-skill immigration (Borjas, Freeman, and Katz 1996); the consistent loss of value of the minimum wage since the early 1970s, plus the decline in the level of unionism (Blackburn, Bloom, and Freeman 1990; DiNardo, Fortin, and Lemieux 1994); and the effects of foreign trade on high-wage workers in concentrated durable goods industries (seen as the primary source of growing wage inequality, although how this occurs was not understood by the investigators (Borjas and Ramey 1993).

Advocates for raising the minimum wage challenge the accepted wisdom that the curtailment of employment for the most vulnerable would necessarily follow. The conventional wisdom that a rise of 10 percent in the minimum wage results in a 1 percent loss in employment was upheld in a study by Currie and Fallick (1996), which involved the experiences of youths affected by minimum-wage rises in the years 1979–80, using data from the National Longitudinal Survey of Youth; but a widely reported study of employment levels in the fast-food industry in New Jersey following a rise in the state minimum in 1994, concluded otherwise (Card and Krueger 1994). Using employment levels in the neighboring state of Pennsylvania as a control group, Card and Krueger found that employment rose subsequent to the 1994 rise in the minimum wage, instead of falling, as predicted. These findings were savagely attacked by opponents of raising the minimum and just as stoutly defended by fellow advocates. Alan Blinder (1996), for example, in addition to defending Card and Krueger's research methodology, the basis for some attacks, also noted that most of the older studies collapse when 1980s data is introduced, no longer producing "job-killing" conclusions. Despite the support of Blinder and others, however, to refute criticisms Card and Krueger (1998) confirmed their original findings by making a second study of the New Jersey fast-food industry, using representative payroll data.

Another recent attempt to ascertain the effect of rise in the minimum wage on employment, a telephone survey of a nationally representative sample of 568 small businesses (defined as having fewer than 1,000 employees), conducted during the winter of 1998, found that 89 percent of the employers contacted reported that the recent rise in the minimum wage (to $5.15 per hour) had not affected their decisions to hire, with 76 percent stating that a further rise to $6.00 per hour would not affect overall hiring or employment decisions (Levin-Waldman and McCarthy 1998).

As to why a mandatory wage rise might *not* impel employers to fire minimum-wage workers and substitute a smaller number of higher-paid, presumably more productive employees, Blinder (1996) offers three possibilities:

1. A rise in wages might help reduce turnover enough to pay for the increase, leaving employers without incentive to reduce payroll.
2. The recruitment process is expensive, and employers would have to raise every one's wages eventually if they pay more for "better" employees, again, a disincentive for hiring at a higher wage.
3. The proportion of minimum wage labor is often only a small and relatively fixed part of total business costs, not being very important to the employer.

As one of the nation's preeminent liberal economists, Blinder admits to being unsure as to whether the above theories are correct, and whether some employment might not indeed be lost; but he believes that if that is the case, the amount of lost employment would be small and the risk worth taking. Blinder's convictions stem from his concerns for the 40 percent of minimum-wage earners who are the sole wage earners in their households, followed by the two-thirds of the teenaged earners who live in homes with below-average incomes.

Another reason for supporting periodic rises in the minimum wage is less publicized. Some economists believe that rises help the lowest level earners, in that they have the effect of increasing total productivity and thereby improving the economy. One hundred and one prominent U.S. economists, including a dozen Nobel Prize winners, supported this position in a letter to the *Philadelphia Inquirer*, December 19,1995.

Limitations of the Minimum Wage. In recent years conviction that the minimum wage can serve as an eradicator of family poverty has lessened among policy-makers as it becomes ever clearer that this goal, the original objective for passage of the legislation, is beyond current public resolve. According to BLS, in 1996 a rise to $7.80 per hour would have been necessary to lift a single-earner family of four to $15,600, at the time the poverty level for a family of this size. Moreover, it was thought that raising the minimum wage from $4.25 to $5.15 would affect only 20 percent of poor families. While the minimum-wage increases occurring during the first half of the 1990s affected about 7 percent of all workers and helped lower the poverty rate in families with at least one worker, it did not affect poverty within the population as a whole. On the other hand, a rise in minimum wage does not cost taxpayers anything.

Sectional Advantages of Rise. Other little discussed consequences of the 1996 rise in the national minimum wage were anticipated by some advocates. One was an increase in the competitiveness of areas of the country that pay higher-than-average wages, such as the Northeast. The *New York Times,* May 12, 1996, commented that it was no wonder that the Republicans who broke ranks to vote for the mid-1990s rise were from high-wage states. Economists believe that a higher minimum might possibly help stem the flight of jobs to the South and other lower-cost areas. Higher minimums may also force wage increases in the underground economy. On the other hand, they may influence some employers to move into underground operations; even so, it is thought that a small wage increase would be necessary there, too.

Early Outcomes. In view of the pessimism concerning the instrumental value of the minimum wage, the short- term evidence, interestingly enough, provides good news on two fronts. First, according to BLS statistics,   unemployment rates for sixteen- to nineteen-year-olds fell, hardly surprising in view of an exceptionally strong economy, but still contrary to opponents' predictions regarding an inevitable rise if the the minimum wage rose. For example, in December 1996 the unemployment rate for sixteen- to nineteen-year-olds was 16.8 percent; one year later, December 1997, it was 14.3 percent (BLS, August 1998). By June 1998, at 14.6 percent, it had hardly moved despite a second mandated rise in the official minimum that took place September 1997 (Current labor statistics 1998). Second, between 1989 and mid-1998, the share of the national income going to the bottom 20 percent of the workforce rose more than any other segment in the work force. By mid-1998, reported the *New York Times* (July 19), the poorest fifth of the employed were earning 20 percent more (adjusted for inflation) than in 1989 when economic expansion ended and the nation went into recession.

Alternative Strategies. In recent years pessimism as to the potential of the minimum wage as an antipoverty weapon has caused policy-makers to shift to an alternative strategy, the "earned income tax credit" (EITC). This tax credit is associated with family income and does not interfere with market forces. But unlike the minimum wage, the EITC shifts the burden of higher income from employers to the tax-paying public. A consensus appears to exist that neither the minimum wage nor any other single measure can eliminate poverty, but that a variety of approaches are needed. On this basis, interest in maintaining a minimum wage remains, as does periodic interest in raising it to make up for the erosion caused by inflation. For example, Bluestone and Ghilarducci (1996) argue that antipoverty strategists need both the minimum wage and the EITC as tools for maintaining income adequacy. Each has its own weaknesses as an antipoverty weapon, but they can be combined to help stabilize low-level incomes in a period of increasing uncertainties. Bluestone and Ghilarducci find the minimum wage, as an antipoverty device, weak on three criteria—income adequacy, target efficiency, and labor supply employment effects—but strong by other criteria—labor demand, productivity enhancement, fiscal impact, and limited moral hazards [the likelihood that income protection against loss causes people to reduce their efforts to protect themselves from the loss, a problem of insurance]. The EITC is the preferred program, as measured by the first three criteria).

One negative concerning the EITC that is usually ignored by advocates is the incentive it offers employers to refrain from raising wages. This fact explains the vigorous leadership taken by important groups within New York State's business community for increasing the state's tax credit, using the budgetary surplus generated by the good economy to pay for it. New York State is one of nine states that have their own tax credit in addition to the federal EITC program. Advocates for the poor, reported the *New York Times* on March 1, 1998, also tend to support the EITC on grounds that the credit makes low-paying jobs more attractive to the poor.

As of the close of 1999, pressures for raising the minimum to $6.30 per hour over a two- to three-year period were being heard within both major political parties, making it likely that some adjustment will be mandated during 2000. And, as reported by Louis Uchitelle in the *New York Times* of November 19, 1999, forty cities and counties in seventeen states have adopted *living wage* ordinances which require that employers who do business with government pay a higher-than-current minimum wage and, sometimes, benefits, as well. Los Angeles, for example, has had a mandated *living wage* of $8.76 per hour since March 1997; Tuscon, $9.00 per hour since May 1996.

Overtime Payments

To spread work during the Great Depression, the 1938 Congress included in the Fair Labor Standards Act of that year a provision that all work for nonexempt employees over forty hours must be paid for at a premium rate, usually 1.5 times the normal rate. It is generally believed that this policy decision has backfired, with many employers finding it cheaper to pay overtime than take on additional workers. Between 1994 and 1997 overtime hours for full-time manufacturing workers, paid for at premium rates, averaged a little above 10 percent of total hours worked.

Cost-of-Living Adjustments (COLAs)

Since the early 1900s organized workers have sought periodic cost-of-living adjustments to maintain the value of their earnings. Use of COLAs tends to be associated with government interventions in the economy during major wars or national crises, such as the two World Wars and the Korean War. Despite governmental efforts to maintain wage and price stability, increased demand brings about both wage and price pressures during such periods and, with them, union demands for some easing of the squeeze on workers' buying power. During World War II, the instrument of the COLA made concessions to workers' wage demands possible without officially reopening wage-price formulas set by the Wage Stabilization Board. Technically, the COLA could be said to offer a catching up with lost buying power, not a raise. The popularity of the COLA has been highest during inflationary periods, but some unions have clung to them during periods of deflation, such as the early 1980s. More recently, however, unions have begun to put less emphasis on COLAs, as opposed to job preservation and retention of pensions for their aging members.

The COLA has not raised wages to the level of price rises, has covered a relatively small portion of the work force (10% to 20%), and has been associated with long-term union contracts, guaranteeing industrial peace for a number of years, with the increase typically subject to periodic review. Between 1970 and 1985 the trend was away from built-in ceilings and toward the use of city-specific Consumer Price Indexes rather than the use of a national figure (Hendricks and Kahn (1983.) At their height of popularity, about 60 percent of all unionized workers were covered by COLAs; by 1994 only about one in four (24%). According to a U.S. Labor Department official (via personal communication), since the mid-1980s COLAs have either "faded away" or "remained in the back ground" due to wage stagnation. Some major unions, such as the Teamsters,

Table 14.3
Workers Under Cost-of-Living Adjustment (COLA) Clauses in Major Collective Bargaining Agreements in Private Industry, Selected Years, 1968–94

Year*	Workers covered by union contracts (Numbers in millions)	Workers with COLA coverage	
		Number	Percentage**
1968	10.6	2.7	25
1973	10.2	4.0	39
1976	9.8	6.0	61
1978	9.5	5.6	59
1982	8.3	5.0	60
1988	6.1	2.4	40
1993	5.5	1.3	24
1994	5.4	1.3	24

(preliminary***)
*Data is for December 31 of each year. **Percentage coverage computed on actual rather than rounded employment numbers ***Data relate to information available September 30, 1994.
Source: Sleemi, Femida.1995. Collective bargaining outlook for 1995. *Monthly Labor Review*, 118 no. l, January: 3–22.

have removed them from their contracts. Table 14.3 gives historical data on the level of COLA coverage in recent years.

REFERENCES

Acs, Gregory, and Sheldon Danziger. 1993. Educational attainment, industrial structure, and male earnings through the 1980s. *Journal of Human Resources* 28, no. 3: 618–48.

Becker, Gary S. 1995. It's simple: hike the minimum wage, and you put people out of work. *Business Week* 6 (March): 22.

Bellante, Don, and Mark Jackson. 1983. *Labor economics: choices in labor markets.* New York: McGraw Hill Book Company.

Blackburn, McKinley, David Bloom, and Richard Freeman. 1990. The declining economic position of less-skilled American men. In Gary Burtless, ed. *A future of lousy jobs: the changing job structure of U.S. wages.* Washington, D.C.: The Brookings Institution,. 31–76.

Blinder, Alan S. 1996. The $5.15 question. *New York Times* (May 23).

Bluestone, Barry, and Teresa Ghilarducci. 1996. Making work pay: wage insurance for the working poor. Public Policy Brief No. 28. Annandale-on-Hudson, New York: Jerome Levy Economics Institute, Bard College.

Borjas, George, Richard Freeman, and Lawrence Katz. 1996. Searching for the effect of immigration on the labor market. *American Economic Review* 86, no. 2 (May): 246–51.

———, and Valerie Ramey. 1993. Foreign competition, market power, and wage inequality: theory and evidence. Manuscript (May). Quoted in David Howell, 1994, The collapse of low-skill male earnings in the 1980s: skill mismatch or shifting wage norms? Working Paper No. 105 (March). Annandale-on-Hudson, N.Y.: Jerome Levy Economics Institute, Bard College.

Bound, John, and George Johnson. 1992. Changes in the structure of wages in the 1980s: an evaluation of alternative explanations. *American Economic Review* 82 (June): 371–92.

Card, David, and Alan B. Krueger. 1994. Minimum wages and employment: case study of the fast-food industry in New Jersey and Pennsylvania. *American Economic Review* 84 no. 4: 77–93.

———. 1995. *Myth and measurement: the new economics of the minimum wage.* Princeton: University Press.

———. 1998. A reanalysis of the effect of the New Jersey minimum wage increase on the fast food industry with representative payroll data. Working Paper No. 6386. Washington, D.C.: National Bureau of Economic Research.

Currie, Janet, and Bruce Fallick. 1996. The minimum wage and the employment of youth: evidence from the NLSY. *Journal of Human Resources* 31, no. 2: 404–28.

DiNardo, John, John Fortin, and Thomas Lemieux. 1994. Labor market institutions and the distribution of wages, 1973–9: a semi-parametric approach. Unpublished manuscript, University of California-Irvine.

Ehrenberg, Ronald, and Robert S. Smith.1994. *Modern labor economics.* 5th edition. New York: HarperCollins.

Filer, Randall, Daniel Hamermesh, and Albert Rees. 1996. *The economics of work and pay.* 6th edition. New York: HarperCollins.

Gittleman, Maury. 1994 Earnings in the 1980s: an occupational perspective. *Monthly Labor Review* 17, no. 7(July): 16–27.

Hendricks, Wallace, and Lawrence Kahn. 1983. Cost-of-living clauses in union contracts determinants and effects. *Industrial and Labor Relations Review* 36 (April): 447–60.

Heywood, John S. 1986. Labor quality and concentration earnings hypothesis. *Review of Economics and Statistics* 68 (May): 342–46.

Howell, David. 1996. The collapse of low-skill male earnings in the 1980s. Working Paper No. 178. Annandale-on-Hudson, N.Y.: Jerome Levy Economics Institute, Bard College.

Kochan, Thomas, Harry Katz, and Robert McKersie. 1994. *The transformation of American industrial relations.* Ithaca, N.Y.: ILR Press.

Levin-Waldman, Oren, and George McCarthy. 1998. Small business and the minimum wage. *Policy Notes*, no. 3. Annandale-on-Hudson, N.Y.: Jerome Levy Economics Institute, Bard College.

Long, James, and Albert Link. 1983. The impact of market structure on wages, fringe benefits and turnover. *Industrial and Labor Relations Review* 36 (January): 239–50.

Medoff, James, Charles Brown, and James Hamilton. *Employers, large and small.* Cambridge, Mass: Harvard University Press, 1990.

Schramm, Carl J. 1982. Economic perspectives on the nursing shortage. In Aiken, Linda, ed., *Nursing in the 1980s: crisis, opportunities, challenges.* Philadelphia: J. Lippincott, 42–56.

Sleemi, Femida. Collective bargaining outlook for 1995. *Monthly Labor Review* 118 (January): 3–22.

Topol, Robert. 1993 Wage inequality and regional labor market performance in the United States. Paper presented at NBER Labor Studies Meeting, Cambridge, Mass., November.

U.S. Department of Labor. Bureau of Labor Statistics. 1998. Current labor statistics. Washington, D.C.:Government Printing Office. *Monthly Labor Review* (August): Table 6.

———. 1998. *Employment and Earnings* 45 (January): Washington, D.C.: Government Printing Office. Table A–9.

Part VI

The Different Labor Market Experiences of Women and Racial and Ethnic Minorities

It is clear to everyone who has ever held a job in an organization that the workplace is not a level playing field in terms of the human factor. Women and minorities tend to be distributed unevenly across industries and occupations and within job categories. As one gazes up organizational hierarchies women and minorities become less and less visible, with African Americans and other racial or ethnic minorities usually less observable than women in general in the more desirable areas of the organization. If the organization is at all typical, few women and minorities will be in positions of authority and will tend to be more heavily supervised than male workers. The observer will also quickly notice that white males tend to earn more than women and minority employees.

Despite demonstrable differences in occupational distribution and earnings between the genders, races, and ethnic groups, many economists, perhaps the majority, are reluctant to attribute the disparities to discriminatory treatment. Instead, they point to differences in group characteristics which impact work experience. In this light, the subject of unequal treatment in employment and earnings is now politely referred to as "differences in labor market experiences," rather than as discrimination. A leading economist, for example, claims that a review of the literature on the subject shows that most of the earnings gap between black and whites during the 1990s can be explained by *pre-market* factors, mainly differences in skills (Heckman 1998). A minority of economists, and some others in the social sciences, insist otherwise, proclaiming that discrimination is alive and flourishing. The following chapters reflect the view that discrimination persists, both within and without the employment arena, and that it has a profound impact on the experiences of women and minorities. The terms *race* and *ethnicity* are used with reference to the two largest minorities in the United States. The terms are used to denote social and cultural identities only, in recognition of the fact that, biologically, most African Americans and Hispanics possess European blood and that, according to one analysis, perhaps as much as 25 percent of the white population probably has some African or Native American ancestry (Simpson and Yinger 1985).

Chapter 15 presents statistical data on inferior earnings status and presents the major theories used to explain the different outcomes. Chapter 16 focuses on earnings and employment inequalities from the viewpoints of the *occupational segregationists*, those investigators who study segregation of employment, by occupation and job title. Finally, chapters 17 and 18, respectively, offer historical perspectives on the factors affecting employment opportunities and wage rates for women and African Americans, with comments on remedial strategies, past and present.

15

Employment-Associated Discrimination

EMPIRICAL EVIDENCE OF DIFFERENT EMPLOYMENT OUT-COMES OF WOMEN AND MINORITIES AND THE EXTENT TO WHICH DISCRIMINATION IS INVOLUNTARY

Women workers now comprise 46.5 percent of the civilian labor force; African Americans, 11.3 percent; and persons of Hispanic origin, 9.2 percent. African Americans are the largest U.S. minority group, the civilian, noninstitutional population standing at 24 million in 1997, with Hispanics following at 20 million. However, BLS predicts that Hispanics will shortly move into first place. A rough overview of income disparity may be seen on Table 15.1, which shows full-time women workers still earning on average only about three-quarters of male wages; black workers three-quarters of white earnings; and Hispanic workers, on average, about two-thirds as much. Women in each racial and ethnic groups earn less than males of their group. Concerns about discriminatory treatment of these large groups in our population follow from the knowledge that despite the efforts of the last thirty years, the disparities remain and result in serious social problems. Most BLS data, upon which this book heavily depends, reports on males versus females and whites versus blacks, and only sometimes Hispanics. Reports on persons of Asian or Native American background are rare. This is because national sampling procedures result in data bases too small to be statistically reliable. Budgetary limitations are another factor.The African-American workforce will usually be referred to as "black," the designation used by the U.S. Bureaus of Labor Statistics and the Census.

Another set of statistics often used to illustrate current income disparities is the occupational distribution of the workforce by race and ethnicity, with accompanying wage levels. Distribution by broad occupational categories is shown on Table 15.2. Current efforts to explain income disparity focus heavily on how women and minorities are dispersed *between* and *within* occupational categories, topics that will be developed later in this chapter.

Table 15.1
Ratios of Median Weekly Earnings of Full-Time Women Workers to Males, Blacks, and Persons of Hispanic Origin to Whites, and Women of Each Group to Men of Their Group, 1997

Females to males	74%	White female to white male	75%
Blacks to whites	77	Black female to black male	87
Hispanic origin to white	68	Hispanic female or Hispanic male	86

Source: U.S. Department of Labor. Bureau of Labor Statistics. *Employment and Earnings*, January 1998.

This data tells us that women and minorities are continuing to earn appreciably less than white males, but it does not tell us how much is due to discrimination and how much to other factors, termed *pre-labor market experience.* This means that women and minorities may be less attractive to employers than white males because they have invested less in human capital or in less lucrative types of training. For example, it is argued that women receive lesser returns from a bachelor's or master's degree because more men take engineering or business courses of study while more women go in for teaching or nursing. While such a statement is factually correct, whether it explains differences in earnings outcomes is another matter. In other words, are the economic outcomes of engineering or business school careers greater than in careers in elementary or high-school teaching because the former involve greater knowledge and skills or is the superior pay due to the fact that the first two occupations are male-dominated and the latter two, primarily occupied by females?

In regard to African Americans, a *pre-market* factor often mentioned as explaining African Americans' lesser appeal to employers is the inferior education believed to be prevalent in many center-city public schools. In these chapters the continuing efforts of economists to separate out the factors contributing to lesser productivity and those directly stemming from discrimination, a favorite exercise, are reported. However, the disparities are treated here as being heavily associated with continuing discriminatory practices.

A major problem in the body of work on discrimination and on the so-called different experiences of women is one of measurement and methodology. It is very difficult to establish conclusively the contribution of personal (and group characteristics) to inferior positions and earnings. Data used in studies dependent upon regression analysis tends to be inadequate and not always applicable to particular individuals and groups studied; and broad-based BLS data have other limitations. Also, certain decisions made by the researchers themselves influence the outcomes of studies. For example, one alternative method, the *audit study*, or use of matched pairs—black and white, male and female—who are trained to present themselves as identical in job interviews, has been denounced on various grounds, among them, that the persons sent out rarely replicate reality.

Reports of Discrimination in the Late Twentieth Century

Evidence Secured Through Statistical Techniques. A review of evidences of current employment-associated discrimination by William A. Darity, Jr. and Pa-

Table 15.2
Distribution of the Employed Labor Force, 16 Years and Older, by Occupation, Gender, and Median Weekly Earnings, Full-Time Workers, 1997

	Percent		Median Weekly Earnings	
	Male	Female	Male	Female
	100.0	100.0		
Managerial and professional specialty	28.0	30.9	$908	$644
Technical, sales, and admin. support	19.9	40.8	595	408
Service occupations	10.2	17.5	381	286
Precision prod., craft and repair	18.5	2.1	562	389
Operators, fabricators, and laborers	19.8	7.7	447	313
Farming, forestry, and fishing	3.6	1.0	296	271

Source: U.S. Department of Labor. Bureau of Labor Statistics. *Employment and Earnings,* January 1998.

trick Mason (1998) reveal persisting patterns of widespread discrimination. First, they reported on evidence produced through different statistical procedures: regression analysis and the Blinder-Oaxaca decomposition procedure. Regression analysis involves setting up an equation with earnings or occupation as the dependent variable, and various factors, including race, gender, education, and experience used to explain the contribution of each to the outcome, that is, earnings or occupation. If the coefficients for race or gender are statistically significant and negative, and other factors' contributions have been accounted for, the researcher assumes that discrimination is involved. In the Blinder-Oaxaca decomposition procedure, the experiences of all groups under study are compared with the experiences of a reference group, for example, all males, all females, or all whites. The value of the total earnings or occupational share of the reference group is estimated by the researchers. The method enables researchers to distinguish between the contributions of education and other factors to outcomes for the group under study, compared to the reference group, and then see where the discrepancies occur and to what extent. These are the two methods most utilized by professional researchers.

On the basis of studies made by use of regression analysis, Darity and Mason report that progress in narrowing the male-female wage gap occurred during the 1980s and 1990s. The earnings of full-time women workers rose from 59 percent of male earnings in 1970 to 71 percent in 1995 (Blau, Ferber, and Winkler 1998); 74 percent, according to 1997 figures. With a portion of the differentials attributable to differences in worker characteristics, only part of the differentials can be attributed to discrimination. This shrinkage in wage gap is attributed to three causes: (1) a rise in female wages in all points of the range, with women in midrange making the largest gains combined with shrinkage in the wage rates of all men below the 79th percentile (Gottschalk 1997); (2) less of a human-capital gap between men and women, especially in the area of work experience (Blau, Ferber, and Winkler 1998); and (3) the success of legal pressures designed to open up better opportunities for women (Blau and Kahn 1997).

The Darity-Mason review found two major areas of persistent difficulty. The first is known as the *family gap*, wherein women with children are earning about 10 to 15 percent less than childless women (Waldfogel 1998). Possible explanations proffered by the researcher are less motivation on the part of mothers, employer discrimination, and lack of day care and other support systems. The second area of difficulty is the persistence of occupational segregation, with women remaining clustered in the low-paid jobs. Again, there has been improvement since 1970; but still, the *index of occupational dissimilarity*, the best measure for determining occupational segregation, is 53 percent (as opposed to 68 percent in 1970). Over half of all male employees (or women employees) would have to change jobs for the sexes to be evenly distributed throughout the ranks.[1]

Using regression analyses, explorations of differences in employment outcomes by race, analysts have determined that black males' earnings were depressed by at least 12 percent to 15 percent of earnings in 1980 and 1990 by reason of continuing discrimination (Darity, Guilkey, and Winfrey 1996; Gottschalk 1997). Using race and different shades of skin color, a unique series of studies have shown that a combination of being black and having dark skin color resulted in 52 percent less possibility of being employed (after controlling for age, education, and criminal record; Johnson, Bienenstock and Stoloff 1995). Similar results were found in other such studies (Keith and Herring 1991; Johnson and Farrell 1995) and in studies concerning Hispanics (Arce, Murguia, and Frisbie 1987).

Periodically, studies are produced that make the case that differences in education and training, that is,. human capital accumulation, are responsible for differences in employment outcomes of minorities (or women). If so, this places the onus for inferior life situations (type of employment, promotion possibilities, earnings) on the individuals involved (or on their parents or communities), and removes responsibility from the employer community. Perhaps because of economists' fondness for "rational" answers for social problems, there has been considerable reaction to the 1996 finding that black scores on the Armed Forces Qualifying Test (AFQT)—that is, inferior educational preparation—could explain all (or the major portion of) indications of discrimination in the earnings of black males. This conclusion has triggered considerable controversy, especially since a series of investigators (O'Neill 1990; Ferguson 1995; Neal and Johnson 1996) concurred. The argument then became one of whether the AFQT adequately reflects human-capital investment. The controversy reached the popular press, with a letter in the *Wall Street Journal* from Abigail and Stephen Thernstrom, authors of a controversial 1997 book on discrimination (*America in Black and White: One Nation, Indivisible*. New York: Simon and Schuster), which essentially calls discussion of discrimination a dead issue. Rather, the Thernstroms implied, better pay for the better endowed and better prepared is the proper employer response. The argument over where the blame lies for undeniable differences in employment experience may be expected to continue.

Evidence Secured Through Audit Studies. Through the use of the *audit method*, patterns of discriminatory behavior by employers in the recruitment and employment processes have been documented. The Urban Institute project found, after sending out matched pairs to interview for the same jobs, that the rejection rate for black males was triple that for white males chosen for similarity of characteristics (Darity and Mason 1998). Hispanic males also experienced rejection at triple the rate of white males (Fix, Galster, and Struyk 1993). An audit study by the Fair Employment Council of Greater Washington, D.C., found blacks and Hispanics to be discriminated against in more than 20 percent of the cases. Discrimination was evident throughout the whole employment process: interview, receipt of a job offer, level of job offered, and pay offered (Bendick, Jackson, and Reinoso 1994). According to the results of a Russell Sage and Ford Foundations study conducted in several large cities, employers exhibited decided preferences in favoring white males over white women; Hispanics over blacks; and black females over black males (Holzer 1997). These results have been replicated in other studies; among the most unusual is the upsurge in the hiring of female orchestra players, when the auditions are conducted behind a screen (Goldin and Rouse 1997).

Evidence Secured Through Legal Actions. Large corporations, including multinationals, continue to be brought before the courts because of alleged violations of Equal Employment Opportunity legislation. The testimony produced in these suits, according to the Darity and Mason review, show that large corporations are still engaging in racial and gender discrimination in all aspects of the employment process, from recruitment and hiring, training, assignment, and lay-offs. They emphasize the persistence of pervasive occupational segregation.

THEORIES OF EMPLOYMENT DISCRIMINATION

The theories presented in this chapter are those most commonly utilized to explain continuing differences in labor-market experiences, but none of them can satisfactorily explain the differential group outcomes. Recent studies may be found that uphold or refute some portion of each theory. Nevertheless, each major theory adds some new insight. Discussed first are two theories of employment discrimination in the neoclassical economics mainstream: Gary Becker's *tastes and preferences* and Barbara Bergmann's *crowding hypothesis*. Becker's theory represents a seminal work on the economics of prejudice, emphasizing the role of *tastes* (prejudice) in hiring and payment; while Bergmann focuses on how the clustering of women and minorities into a relatively few occupations creates conditions for inferior outcomes. A second theory of Becker's, *household economics,* attempts to explain how the different employment outcomes of women follow rationally from individual decision-making on the part of family members.

Becker's Tastes Theory

In his ground breaking *Economics of Discrimination* (1957), Becker was the first to discuss employment discrimination in terms of costs to employers and to attempt to quantify these costs. Becker explained employers' will to discriminate in terms of *tastes* and *preferences,* without attempting to explain the basis for them. According to his theory, employers as individuals are driven by considerations other than profit-maximization. One is the desire to avoid contact with minorities in the workplace. In economists' terms, employers maximize utility as opposed to profits. Part of the employer's satisfaction (or utility) is a minority-free workplace, for which the employer is willing to sacrifice a certain amount of profit. Although Becker focused on discrimination against African Americans, he held that the model could be used to analyze the treatment of women or other ethnic or racial minorities.

Becker introduced the concept of the "discrimination coefficient" to measure the strength of an employer's desire to discriminate. He allowed for a nominal cost and a *psychic cost* (the pain of dealing with minorities). For purposes of his analysis, Becker assumed perfectly competitive labor markets and a supply of both white males and equally qualified minorities. For example, suppose that an employer must pay $10 an hour to hire white males to work in his firm, and that a supply of equally qualified minorities exists who are willing to perform the same work for $6.50 an hour. The cost of discrimination to the employer per employee (employer *tastes*), according to Becker's theory, would be $3.50 per hour.

According to Becker, employers place limits on indulgence of their tastes (for discrimination). In the example given above, the limit may be $3.50 or even more. The nominal cost is $10; the psychic cost of discrimination, $3.50. At whatever point the psychic costs exceed the strength of the taste for discrimination, the employer will begin to hire from minority labor pools. In other words, employers tend to be willing to only go so far to gratify their biases. If an employer believes that the $10 an hour is in excess of the white male workers' marginal revenue product, then the difference between their MRP and the wage they are paid may be said to be the premium paid white workers, and the employer may be said to be engaging in nepotism on behalf of the white male workers. Whether or not the $6.50 represents the actual MRP of equally qualified black employees, they are being discriminated against because, though equally qualified, they receive less than members of the white male group for doing the same work. Becker also analyzed the effect of size or density of the disliked group upon wages. He posited that the greater the number of minorities in a labor market, the lower the wages.

Role of Employee and Customer Tastes. Although this theory concentrates first and foremost on the role of employer tastes, it also assumes a role for the the feelings of employees and customers in who is hired and for which jobs. Employee tastes are held to influence hiring and job allocations because white male employees believe their jobs are worth less when they share employment with low status groups. Therefore they may leave such jobs or refuse to work in an integrated workplace; at least, employers believe they may do so. Such a situation has been described in a study of a suburban Illinois steel mill (Williams 1987), a good thirty years after Becker introduced his theory in his doctoral dissertation. The steel-mill management was found to be discouraging the recruitment of needed city blacks for fear of being unable to attract (and retain) skilled white workers, as a consequence of becoming known as a heavy employer of minorities.

Customer tastes are the focus of the following case study: An employment agency in Philadelphia runs a valet parking service, recruiting both college students and casual workers to staff city parking garages. Hires are completely dependent on tips for remuneration. A university student who collected an average of $100 nightly, reported that customers, black as well as white, tipped white parking attendants more generously than black ones (personal communication).

Becker borrowed concepts from international trade theory to demonstrate that, overall, all parties (communities) are poorer because of employment discrimination. According to trade theory, societies (here seen as the black and the white communities) trade factor inputs—not final products—between themselves in a situation of perfect competition. It is assumed that each exports to the other its plentiful factors, resulting ultimately in equality of income. Each community is enriched. Due to tastes for discrimination, however, the returns for each community on labor and capital inputs are lessened because black employers have less capital to work with and white employers less labor than would be the case in the absence of discrimination. Again, Becker emphasized that discrimination *costs*. He broke new ground by arguing that the costs of discrimination to an employer must inevitably bring discrimination to an end, because in the perfectly competitive labor markets that he assumed, employers who wish to compete successfully with discriminating firms have only to hire women and minorities at lower wages. With lower costs per unit, money for expansion would be available. Consequently the discriminating firms would inevitably be driven out of business. Becker thought that discriminatory practices of white firms opened up doors of opportunity for black entrepreneurs.

The leading critics of Becker's theory express the following: (1) evidence of the continued existence of discrimination, despite Becker's prophecies; (2) widespread disbelief, even among neoclassical economists, in a perfectly competitive labor market; and (3) rejection of the idea that employers *lose*, not gain, by practicing discrimination. Some also disagree with the assumption that women and blacks, in the real world, tend to be perfect substitutes for white male workers in terms of productivity.

Arrow's Theory

Kenneth Arrow, one of the nation's most distinguished economists, developed a revised version of Becker's theory, emphasizing employer concerns about the *mix* of their employees. Arrow predicted that employers would eventually segregate women and minorities in the workplace, while paying the same wages, since he believed that differentials could not be sustained in the long run. According to this newer version of *tastes*, such a situation is slow in developing because employers hesitate to pay the costs of change (Arrow 1972, 1973).

Arrow also believes that discrimination is a moral issue and cannot be discussed solely in terms of markets. Criticizing all economic theories that assume market considerations will eventually lead to the elimination of discrimination, Arrow argues that in all stages of the employment process, racial attitudes influence employer behavior and alter outcomes. Therefore, since racial discrimination has not been eliminated, he recommends looking for nonmarket factors that influence economic behavior, and he posits *social interaction theory* and *networks theory* as the most promising ones (1998).

Bergmann's *Crowding* Hypothesis

During the 1970s, when women activists were looking for explanations of why female workers, on average, always seemed to earn less than male workers, Bergmann (1971, 1974, 1991) came up with an answer. She said that the labor market consists of noncompeting groups. Women tend not to compete directly with male workers because of *sex segregation in the workplace*; similarly, blacks tend not to compete to directly with whites. Since the majority of women and minority workers have traditionally been limited to a relatively few occupations, this makes for over-supply and wage depression. This situation persists because few alternatives exist for women and minority job-seekers outside these occupations.

The concept that different groups of workers face constraints when they attempt to move outside traditional areas of employment was offered as an explanation for unequal earnings as far back as 1874 (John E. Cairnes).The idea of women trapped into overcrowded occupations as the primary reason for low earnings, however, propelled Barbara Bergmann into the fore as a guru of the women's movement. The widespread acceptance of this explanation by women's groups set, for at least a decade, their action-agenda: the capturing of a fair share of male-monopolized "good jobs."

Bergmann drew on human-capital theory for explanations of lower pay in the female-dominated (and minority-dominated) occupations, which she described in terms of labor market segmentation. Workers in such occupations receive less employer training and have little incentive to invest in their own educations; for these very reasons they may well be less productive than workers in male-dominated occupations. Also, since labor costs are artificially low, employers have little incentive to invest in labor-saving equipment that would raise the MRP of individual workers while reducing total employment. Bergmann and others also assume that many of the workers in women-dominated occupations have poor work habits and poor attitudes, a further reason for considering them to be inferior employees, and a partial justification for lesser wages. In contrast to Becker's *tastes* theory, Bergmann's theory holds that the sexes and races are usually *not* perfect substitutes for each other. Though Bergmann's influential theory is considered to be in the neoclassical tradition, it has much in common with the thinking of the occupational segregationists.

Bergmann's writings encouraged the women's movement to go after jobs in the male-dominated industries and occupations, and invest in educational preparation that would enable penetration of the male labor market monopoly. The Bergmann approach implied that women should not waste time on slogans such as "equal pay for equal work," as such strategies would get them nowhere, as their grandmothers' generation had learned. Much evidence exists to indicate that Bergmann's advice has been taken.

Statistical Discriminations

A very different explanation of "different labor market experiences" comes from *statistical discrimination theory* (Arrow 1972, 1973; Phelps 1972; Aigner and Cain 1977). Two versions of this theory exist (Darity 1982). The first holds that blacks and whites, and men and women, are on average equally productive; but blacks' abilities vary more than whites', and women's more than men's. This could be the basis on which risk-averse employers prefer to hire from white labor pools even though black-white capabilities may be equal; the same pertains to employing women. The second version of statistical discrimination theory posits that blacks and whites do not differ in distribution of abilities, but that employers, when they engage in testing to determine which job candidates to hire, secure more accurate test results for whites than for blacks; for men than for women. On this basis, risk-averse employers will tend to hire whites or males only, depending on the job categories. This will be true, even when candidates of both races or genders achieve the same scores. Either version of statistical discrimination purports to explain the depression of black and female wages on the basis of lowered demand. It has also been suggested that employer perceptions, over time, may actually cause behaviors that they find unattractive. For example, black youths who know that they are unlikely to be hired by employers may not invest in educational preparation (Darity and Mason 1998; Arrow 1973; Coate and Loury 1993).

As readers who have some knowledge of human-resources management are aware, the processes involved in recruitment and hiring are very expensive. Even more costly are the consequences of mistakes made by decision-makers. Even the best of interviewers are believed to have high levels of error in choice-making, that is, they tend to choose less qualified candidates and reject better ones. To minimize risks and avoid costly screening procedures, cautious recruitment personnel may resort to using rule-of-thumb guesses in making their choices. This leads to ascribing group characteristics to individuals, which equates to the stereotyping of individual job candidates to make up for inability to fathom "unobservable differences," such as how candidates may behave in various types of situations. Examples of stereotypical thinking that leads to statistical discrimination include the belief that women tend to quit to have babies, and are therefore not worth an investment of training; or that black youths don't stay on a job as long as white youths, so they should be rejected if alternative prospects are available. More complicated situations arise, as well: for example, out of a group composed of black and white women who achieve equally on a typing test, the employer hires white women with average scores, but only those blacks with superior ones. In short, while some economists claim that statistical discrimination grows out of the costs of imperfect information, others hold it to be another form of pure prejudice in disguise—out-and-out discrimination that cannot be rationalized as discrete business practice. Statistical discrimination is thought to be the most common form of current employment discrimination.

Dual Labor Market Theory

The dual labor markets approach of Peter Doeringer and Michael Piore, another variant of *crowding-monopoly power theory*, became very popular after the writers' *Internal Labor Markets and Manpower Analysis* was published in 1971. In this influential book white males are seen to exercise a monopoly over primary labor-market jobs, with women, youths, and minorities relegated to the secondary sector. The outstanding contribution of this theory lies in its detailed description of how racial and gender discrimination is implemented within the workplace.

The foundation for Doeringer and Piore's theory consisted of the concepts of primary and secondary labor markets. Primary labor market employers, usually described as oligopolistic, are said to offer employees relatively high wages, job training, stable employment, and advancement possibilities. Secondary labor market employers, usually identified with competitive establishments, are characterized as paying low wages, offering little or no job training nor possibilities of promotion, providing poor working conditions, and anticipating high turnover. Escape from secondary labor market jobs is seen as ranging from improbable to impossible.

According to dual labor markets theory, employers deliberately design their workplaces with the intention of discriminating. Employers place more valued workers in favorable ports of entry (career ladders) and treat them in a privileged manner. Discriminatory behavior is advantageous both to the employer and selected employees. Once hired, the favored workers enjoy job security and advancement opportunities, while the employer gains from the economies of a stable body of employees. While the employees benefit from their monopoly over the "good jobs," employers enjoy the minimized costs of recruitment, hiring, and training.

Embedded in dual labor markets theory is employer concern about the maintenance of implicit contracts, the notion of an implied understanding between employers and their favored employees as to conditions of work. Employer violation of long-standing customs and tradition-based practices would adversely affect worker cooperation and morale. Valued employees might go so far as to leave the establishment, causing loss of human capital investment. Among the most zealously guarded practices often identified as pertaining to implicit contracts are job tenure for primary labor-force workers and a monopoly of employment for present incumbents, their friends, and their families. This translates into the exclusion of outsiders, women and minorities, from the privileged job categories.

Operationally, employers engage in three types of discriminatory practices, according to dual labor market theory: entry decisions; internal allocation of jobs; and wage practices. The theory has long been assailed as unproven and itself based on stereotypes; in fact, some recent research (Boston 1990) has produced some empirical support for the existence of two noncompetitive labor markets segregated by race, gender, and age, with movement from secondary to primary severely constricted for some groups. Boston's work supports the notion that primary labor market jobs require some degree of preparation, and secondary, much less so. Nonetheless, BLS has produced 1990s data that tends to refute Doeringer and Piore's claim that employers do not invest in female and minority employees. For example, BLS (1993) reports that 44 percent of employer investments in paid training go to women (51% of all payrolls) while 7.7 percent go to blacks (11.7% of total payrolls); perhaps these do not amount to a fair allocation of training investments, but the figures do not support dual labor market claims of total exclusion, either. The reality of dual labor markets as it may pertain to job-segregation research requires further clarification.

Thurow's Monopoly Power Theory

Another approach to employment discrimination (Thurow 1969) is to look at how white workers, the dominant group, profit from their monopoly power over conditions of employment. Thurow pointed out that unequal opportunities for employment and inferior earning power leads to the deterioration of all aspects of life, and increases possibilities for the white population to continue discriminatory policies. Thurow espoused social-distance theory to explain why whites decline to share jobs with blacks and women, holding that whites are willing to have blacks and women occupy jobs that do not challenge white position, status, or self-esteem.[2] Were whites to share jobs with persons of lower status (women and blacks), their jobs would be worth less in their own eyes.

Becker's Household Economics Theory

The father of the economics of employment discrimination, Becker himself abandoned his *tastes and preferences* theory for one based on *family economics* (1981)[3] In Becker's new model persisting discrimination is the consequence of rationally based investment and consumption decisions of family households. Families, he posits, look at the earnings potentials of wives versus the demands of unpaid household duties, the household division of labor, and the earnings potentials of male versus female children. The end result, according to this theory, are often family decisions to keep the wife at home or to have her engage in paid employment outside the home on a part-time basis only. In the economists' lingo, preference is given to the choice of *leisure* (meaning time spent with children and home duties than paid work.)

For the economists who insist that behavior is rational, perhaps the most powerful aspect of Becker's household economics theory is that it describes how parents perpetuate occupational segregation by socializing their children to select occupations with optimal payoffs according to gender. Such decisions are said to be reinforced by the levels at which they are willing to invest in the education of sons versus daughters, as noted above. If parents believe that sons will earn more than daughters over a lifetime they will invest more heavily in sons. They may also perpetuate sex segregation in employment by urging their daughters to enter traditional female-dominated occupations or by declining to help them enter traditionally male-dominated ones. In other words, Becker blamed inferior female job and earnings status on socialization patterns that result in lesser human-capital investment and, ultimately, on situation in low-paying occupations.

According to Becker, women often deliberately choose lower paying occupations because they desire immediate returns.[3] He also suggested, without offering proof, that some women deliberately enter dead-end job categories with relatively high entry pay rates (no training costs involved), since they expect to be in and out of the labor force throughout their lifetime and do not expect to reap rewards from job continuity or experience. Because of Becker's status in the economics profession, somehow he has never been asked to provide proof for any of his theories of discrimination, so lack of proof in regard to women's alleged readiness to enter dead-end occupations does not appear to be a problem.[4]

Social Interactions and Networks Approach

Declaring that economists' attempts to explain employment discrimination on the basis of market-based theories are inadequate, Nobel Prize–winner Kenneth Arrow has pointed to the study of social interactions and networks as a more productive path (1998). Alluding to extensive research that shows that most employment takes place as the result of social contacts (referrals of friends and relatives, for example), Arrow observes that many outcomes with economic implications are the result of a large number of individual decisions, and that these are unfiltered by price levels or any impersonal market influence (Rees and Schultz 1970; Granovetter 1974, 1988; White 1995). Beliefs and preferences may themselves be the product of social interactions as opposed to economic determinants (Blume 1997; Durlauf 1997). Basically, Arrow's position is that employment discrimination is best studied (and dealt with) in terms of the influence of a multitude of individual decisions made without significant interference from impersonal "markets."

Also questioning the validity of purely demand-oriented approaches, Glenn Loury argues that inequalities in labor-force experience indicate not discrimination per se, but mainly the persistence of a substantial skills gap between blacks and whites (1998). The gap, he explains, reflects social and cultural inequalities, such as the quality of educational experiences, geographic segregation, and de-structive social norms and peer influences, all supply-side determinants. Although Loury believes that an educational and socialization problem, not a discrimination problem, accounts for racial differences in employment experi-ence, he agrees that societal action is required to remedy this situation.Loury points out that opportunities follow social networks and that black youths suffer from lacks in their parents' backgrounds, in their communities' lacks, in geo-graphic isolation from jobs, and so forth. Various studies are cited by Loury to bolster his argument that environmental factors play an important role in re-stricting employment opportunities for black youths (Anderson 1990; Waldinger 1996; Cutler and Glaeser 1997).

Other Nontraditional Theories

Several alternative theories that include both pre-market and in-market dis-crimination have been described by Darity and Mason (1998). The first is that of the *self-fulfilling prophesy:* if employers consistently reject certain groups, mi-nority youths, for example, in the belief that they have inferior preparation, the youths may cease efforts to secure educations in the belief that the effort would be futile (Elmslie and Sedo 1996; Borjas 1994; Darity 1989). A second is the *non-competing groups hypothesis,* another type of monopoly theory advanced by Le-wis (1979): one group manages to infiltrate the more desirable jobs and upper levels of the occupational hierarchy within an establishment and then maintains its control through such devises as controlling hiring and entry into desired job ladders, educational and training opportunities, and promotion policies. The group keeps itself in gatekeeper capacity to maintain its monopoly. Criticism of this theory lies in the necessity of the gatekeepers to maintain group solidarity and in the questionable notion that employers would accept an arrangement that raises its costs. As Darity points out, this theory, dependent on power and so-cial control, renders in-market discrimination unnecessary: the undesired groups never penetrate the internal labor market of the establishment nor its desired ar-eas. A third alternative theory is a nontraditional analysis of the outcomes of competition, in which competition is seen as encouraging the equalization of rates of profit, which in turn encourages a monopoly in desired jobs. In this con-text pay rates are determined by both worker and job characteristics. Racial and gender identity are also used to exclude the persons involved from better posi-tions (Darity and Williams 1985). This approach has been adopted by the re-searchers whose work is reported upon in the chapters that follow.

NOTES

1. The percentage of one group needing to be replaced by others to eliminate oc-cupational segregation is the criterion upon which the index of occupational dis-similarity is based.
2. Position refers to a monopoly-hold on the better-paying and higher status jobs. Higher status jobs may be low paying; for example, there was once a long-standing ban on hiring black women as clericals (Myrdal 1944).
3. Becker based his new theory on women's alleged willingness to accept inferior employment as a means of avoiding the *opportunity costs* associated with acquisi-

tion of education, such as tuition, baby-sitting, and experience associated with prior education, or learning on-the-job.

4. Nevertheless, Becker's original thesis remains heavily quoted and his 1957 book is still sold in bookstores.

REFERENCES

Aigner, Dennis, and Glen Cain. 1977. Statistical theories of discrimination in the labor market. *Industrial and Labor Relations Review* 30 (January): 175–87.

Anderson, Elijah. 1990. *Streetwise: race, class, and change in an urban community.* Chicago: University of Chicago Press.

Arce, Carlos, Edward Murguia, and W. Parker Frisbie. 1987. Phenotype and life chances among Chicanos. *Hispanic Journal of Behavioral Studies* 9, no. 1: 19–33.

Arrow, Kenneth. 1972. Models of job discrimination and some models of race in the labor market. In Pascal, Anthony, ed., *Discrimination in economic life.* Lexington, Mass.: D.C. Heath and Co.

———. 1973. The theory of discrimination, 3–33. In Ashenfelter, Orley, and Albert Rees, eds. *Discrimination in labor markets.* Princeton, N.J.: Princeton University Press.

———. 1998. What has economics to say about racial discrimination? *The Journal of Economic Perspectives* 12 (Spring): 91–100.

Becker, Gary. 1957. *The economics of discrimination.* Chicago: University of Chicago Press.

———. 1981. *A treatise on the family.* Cambridge: Harvard University Press.

Bendick, Marc Jr., Charles Jackson, and Victor Reinoso. 1997. Measuring employment discrimination through controlled experiments, 294–313. In James B. Stewart, ed., *African-Americans and post-industrial labor markets.* New Brunswick, N.J.: Transaction Publishers.

Bergmann, Barbara. 1971.The effect of white incomes on discrimination in employment. *Journal of Political Economy* 79 (March/April): 294–313.

———. 1974. Occupational segregation, wages, and profits when employers discriminate by race or sex. *Eastern Economic Journal* 1 (April/July): 103–10.

———. 1991. Does the market for women's labor need fixing? 247–61. In Reynolds, Lloyd, Stanley Masters, and Colletta Moser. 1991. *Readings in labor economics and labor relations.* 5th edition. Englewood Cliffs, N.J.: Prentice Hall..

Blau, Francine, and Lawrence Kahn. 1997. Swimming upstream: trends in the gender wage differential in the 1980s. *Journal of Labor Economics* (January): 1–42.

Blaug, Francine, M. Ferber, and A. Winkler. 1998. *The economics of women, men, and work.* 3rd edition. Upper Saddle River, N.J.: Prentice Hall.

Blume, Lawrence. 1997. Population games. In Arthur, W. B., S. Durlauf, and D. Lane, eds. *The economy as an evolving complex system.* Menlo Park, Cal.: Addison Wesley Longmans.

Borjas, George. 1994. Long-run convergence of ethnic skill differentials: the children and grandchildren of the great migration. *Industrial and Labor Relations Review* 47 (July): 553–73.

Boston, Thomas. 1990. Segmented labor markets: new evidence from a study of four race-gender groups. *Industrial and Labor Relations Review* 44 (October): 99–115.

Cairnes, John Elliott. 1967. *Some leading principles of political economy newly expounded.* New York: A. M. Kelley (Reprint; original publication London, 1864).

Coate, Stephen, and Glenn Loury. 1993. Anti-discrimination enforcement and the problem of patronization. *American Economic Review Papers and Proceedings* 83, no. 2: 92–98.

Cutler, David, and Edward Glaeser. 1997. Are ghettos good or bad? *Quarterly Journal of Economics* 112, no. 3: 827–73.

Darity, William A., Jr. 1982. The human capital approach to black-white earnings inequality: some unsettled questions. *Journal of Human Resources* 17, no.1: 72–93.

———. 1989. What's left of the economic theory of discrimination? 335–74. In Shulman, Steven, and William Darity, Jr., eds. *Question of discrimination: racial inequality in the U.S. labor market.* Middletown: Wesleyan University Press.

———, and Rhonda Williams. 1985. Peddlers forever? culture, competition, and discrimination. *American Economic Review* 75 (May): 256–91.

———, David Guilkey, and William Winfrey. 1996. Explaining differences in economic performance among racial and ethnic groups in the U.S.A.: the data examined. *American Journal of Economics and Sociology* 55 (October): 411–26.

———, and Patrick Mason. 1998. Evidence of discrimination in employment: codes of color, codes of gender. *Journal of Economic Perspectives* 12 (Spring): 63–90.

Doeringer, Peter, and Michael Piore. 1971. *Internal labor markets and manpower analysis.* Lexington, Mass: D.C. Heath and Co.

Durlauf, Stephen. 1997. The memberships theory of inequality: ideas and implications. Working Paper, Department of Economics, University of Wisconsin.

Elmslie, Bruce, and Stanley Sedo. 1996. Discrimination, social psychology, and hysteresis in labor markets. *Journal of Economic Psychology* 17 (August): 465–78.

Ferguson Ronald. 1995. Shifting challenges: fifty years of economic change toward black-white earnings equality. *Daedalus* 124 (Winter): 37–76.

Fix, Michael, George Galster, and Raymond Struyk. 1993. An overview of auditing for discrimination, 1–68. In Michael Fix and Raymond Struyk, eds. *Clear and convincing evidence: measurement of discrimination in America.* Washington, D.C.: Urban Institute Press,.

Goldin, Claudia and Cecilia Rouse. 1997. Orchestrating impartiality: the impact of "blind" auditions on female musicians. Unpublished manuscript. Harvard University, June.

Gottschalk, Peter. 1997. Inequality, income growth, and mobility: the basic facts. *Journal of Economic Perspectives* 11 (Spring): 21–40.

Granovetter, Mark. 1974. *Getting a job: a study of contacts and careers.* Cambridge, Mass.: Harvard University Press.

———. 1988. Economic action and social structure. In Wellman, Barry, and S. D. Berkowitz, eds. 1988. *Social structures: a network approach.* Cambridge, U.K., and New York: Cambridge University Press.

Heckman, James. 1998. Detecting discrimination. *Journal of Economic Perspectives* 12 (Spring): 101–16.

Holzer, Harry. 1997. *What employers want: job prospects for less-educated workers.* New York: Russell Sage Foundation.

Johnson, James H., Jr., Elisa Bienenstock, and Jennifer Stoloff. 1995 An empirical test of the culture capital hypothesis. *The Review of Black Political Economy* 23 (Spring): 7–27.

———, and Walter Farrell, Jr. 1995. Race still matters. *The Chronicle of Higher Education* 42 (July 7): 48–56.

Keith, Verna, and Cedric Herring. 1991. Skin tone and stratification in the black community. *American Journal of Sociology* 97 (November): 760–78.

Krueger, Anne. 1963. The economics of discrimination. *Journal of Political Economy* 79, no. 2 (March/April): 481–86.

Lewis, W. Arthur. 1979. The dual economy revisited. *The Manchester School*, no. 3: 211–29.

Loury, Glenn C. 1998. Discrimination in the post-civil rights era: beyond market interactions. *Journal of Economic Perspectives* 12 (Spring): 117–26.

Madden, Janice. 1975. Discrimination: a manifestation of male market power. In Cynthia Lloyd, ed. *Sex, discrimination, and the division of labor*. New York: Columbia University Press.

Myrdal, Gunnar. 1944. *An American dilemma: the Negro problem and American democracy*. New York: Random House.

Neal, Derek A., and William R. Johnson. 1996. The role of pre-market factors in black-white wage differences in urban labor markets. *Journal of Political Economy* 104, no. 5: 869–95.

O'Neill, June. 1990. The role of human capital in earnings differences between black and white men. *The Journal of Economic Perspectives* 4 (Fall): 25–45.

Phelps, Edmund. 1972. The statistical theory of racism and sexism. *American Economic Review* 62 (September): 659–61.

Rees, Albert, and George Schultz. 1970. *Workers and wages in an urban labor market*. Chicago: University of Chicago Press.

Simpson, George, and J. Milton Yinger. 1985. *Racial and cultural minorities: an analysis of prejudice and discrimination*. 5th edition. New York: Plenum.

Thernstrom, Stephen, and Abigail Thernstrom. 1997. *America in black and white: one nation, indivisible*. New York: Simon & Schuster.

Thurow, Lester. 1969. *Poverty and discrimination*. Washington, D.C.: Brookings Foundation.

U.S. Department of Labor. Bureau of Labor Statistics. Various years. *Employment and Earnings* (January; November). Washington, D.C.: Government Printing Office.

Waldfogel, Jane. 1998. Understanding the "family gap" in pay for women with children. *Journal of Economic Perspectives* 13 (Winter): 137–56.

Waldinger, Roger. 1996. *Still the promised city: African Americans and new immigrants in post industrial New York*. Cambridge: Harvard University Press.

White, Harrison. 1995. Social networks can resolve actor paradoxes in economics and in psychology. *Journal of Institutional and Theoretical Economics* 151, no. 1: 58–74.

Williams, Bruce. 1987. *Black workers in an industrial suburb*. New Brunswick, N.J.: Rutgers University Press.

16

Occupational and Job Segregation

This chapter elaborates on the argument that segregation of women and minorities in the workplace is responsible for inferior employment and earnings. A historical overview of employer practices is given, together with an analysis of how the human-resources departments of large corporations further such policies. The special case of occupational and job segmentation in professional/technical groups is described, with opinions on the impact on earnings. Failure of civil-rights legislation to adequately deal with the earnings issue is explained, and the weapon of choice of the past quarter-century, the *comparable worth* doctrine, is explained and evaluated.

EXPLANATIONS OF OCCUPATIONAL SEGREGATION

Women and minorities have always been excluded from many occupations and jobs. The allocation of work between the sexes is traditional and culturally determined, and it has differed according to time and place. Occupations and jobs considered male or white at one point in time may be occupied by females and blacks at another. And, sometimes the gender and racial identity of a job has reversed itself more than once over the past 200 years.

According to the occupational segregationists, both men and women who work in female-dominated occupations earn lower wages than males and females in male-dominated occupations. Within an occupation, each job category brings the same pay for men and women who hold the same job title. The interpretation of gender-associated pay rates differs among economists. Bergmann (1974), who introduced the concept of *occupational crowding* into economic discussion, concluded that women workers are paid their marginal revenue product, but that for the female-dominated occupations, the MRP is lower than it would have been if the occupation was gender-neutral or male-dominated. Pay in the male-dominated occupations, Bergmann thought, was higher than in a nonsegregated environment. Others believe that women and minorities are paid less than their

MRP (Goldin 1990). A review of findings concerning wage differentials between males and females and whites versus minorities found estimates ranging from 10 percent to 30 percent (Sorenson 1989). Using alternative methodology, the same investigator later produced an estimate of a 23 percent wage differential due to occupational segregation (Sorenson 1994). The segregationists have also tended to challenge the justifications of inferior black earnings proffered by human-capital and dual labor market theorists on the basis of lower productivity (Galle, Wiswell, and Burr 1988). The work of the occupational segregationists is particularly provocative because of the light they shed on the very processes that produce occupational segregation. The interested reader will find more material on women than minorities, possibly because women's segregation is easier to document than that of minorities (who constitute smaller groups within the total population) and because so many of the occupational-segregationist school are women who are drawn to this area.

Roles of Custom and Tradition

Systematic undervaluation of women's work is thought to stem from several longstanding beliefs and practices (Sorenson 1994), the first of which is that women's natural sphere of activity is within the home. This has resulted in the stigmatizing of work associated with care-taking (nursing, teaching) and shunning of such work by men. Second, since the onset of the industrial revolution in the late 1700s, employers have treated women as a cheap, docile, alternative labor force. As agricultural work declined, men forcibly drove women (and children) out of the early factories and entrenched themselves in formerly female-and-child-occupied jobs. Men maintained their employment monopolies through unions, legislation, and social coercion. Since then, other occupations and jobs have been observed to shift gender-identity with changes in economic environments; office-clerical occupations, for example, have been vacated by men and filled by women.

During the 1920s (the so-called Progressive Era), unions and well-intentioned humanitarians joined forces to pass protective legislation that ultimately, according to many women's advocates, had the effect of removing women from many better-paying jobs. It is believed that the goal of unions was exclusion, not betterment of women's employment opportunities. It is also alleged that unions used the "family wage" concept to idealize the role of the man as family head for the purpose of justifying lower wage rates for women.

According to social historians the ideologies surrounding the male's role in the family must be understood to comprehend the establishment of historical male-female wage differentials. Alice Kessler-Harris (1990) notes that up through the mid-1850s a family wage for every man was a widely held societal goal. This led to public acceptance of two separate, gender-associated wage scales unrelated to job content. As heads of families men had to be accorded a wage sufficient to support all members of the household. Women, having lesser needs, could (and should) be paid less. The woman who had to support herself or the widow with a houseful of children was seen as an aberration, and her needs were disregarded.

The movement for a living wage, backed by the church, made the possibility of women becoming self-sufficient even more remote. Men had the privilege of supporting their families. Employed women, on the other hand, were perceived as needing only a living wage for themselves, and the amount was conceived to be the least possible to support the most spartan livelihood. Women's wages were, in fact, so low that they had to be supplemented by family contributions.

Beginning about 1900 social reformers who expressed concern over the extreme hardships experienced by single women and women with dependents adopted the goal of a minimum wage for women as a remedy. In attempting to establish a reasonable norm, they found consensus among employers and economists that women were being paid according to perceptions of their needs, unrelated to value of work produced, which was the basis upon which men were paid (Butler 1909). Budgets proposed by reformers were extremely low, since it was believed that too much money might encourage frivolity or immorality. At this time women constituted about 25 percent of the workforce; over one-third in urban areas lived apart from their families; and three-quarters of those at home contributed to the support of other family members. But the social mythology guiding public policy was that women are always dependents. Among other justifications for the low wages paid women were first, a belief in the wages fund theory—if women's wages were raised, men's would have to be lowered; second, the idea that productivity-related wages might tempt women to neglect their families (Alfred Marshall, quoted by Baker 1969); and third, the sentiment that since women were "sensitive" beings, they required especially tactful supervision (Shuler 1923).

Traditional beliefs and practices are often shaken up during social upheavals such as wars. Such occurred during World War I, when women were able to penetrate men's jobs, although they did so at lower wage rates that nevertheless, were higher than traditional pay for women's work. Black women were able to obtain some factory work, but at lower wages than those paid to white women. Although they were largely driven out of male-identified jobs after World War I, women continued to enter the labor force throughout the 1920s; they were motivated largely by the desire to contribute to family needs, now redefined to include the new spirit of consumerism that pervaded the burgeoning postwar economy. Momentum grew for the adoption of the long-advocated minimum wage for women, accompanied by opposing arguments that depicted women as morally inferior, less productive, and in need of protection from themselves as well as from the wider society. Reformers as well as employers were ready to accept a dual wage standard. This wage drive movement died in 1923 at the hands of the U.S. Supreme Court, a development welcomed by employers who then turned to the marginal productivity argument to justify the lower wages paid to women.

During the waves of struggle on behalf of the living wage, family wage, and the minimum wage for women, the issue of equal pay for equal work arose periodically.The advocates were an unlikely combination of women's advocates and trade unionists. The women's groups wanted to raise the depressed earning power of women, while the unionists wanted to maintain the male monopoly on higher paying jobs. Because of the sex segregation of jobs, women's leadership understood that few women would be helped by equal pay legislation and that it might actually lead to the hiring of fewer women. This self same point interested the trade unionists, who believed that employers would hire few women if they were forced to pay them wages equivalent to men's. Nevertheless, the two groups presented themselves to the public as advocates for working women.

During the years following World War I, the struggle for equal pay tended to be framed more in terms of individual rights than family rights. Pressures during the Great Depression drove many married women out of the labor force, but some remained at work outside the home, since women on the whole were in greater need than ever of employment. Female-identified jobs became more plentiful than male as the economy gradually began an up-turn cycle in the early 1940s, stimulated by activities associated with World War II. More equitable wages for women, at this point, were seen as benefiting the family as a whole as well as representing an individual right.

Role of Human-Resources Departments

The occupational segregationists take the position that isolation of female and black employees by occupation or job classification is a way of life within large modern corporations (Sorenson 1989). Their case is summarized in the following statements: corporations maintain internal labor markets for the purpose of reducing training and turnover costs. They reward their favored (primary labor force) employees with increased security, promotional opportunities, and benefits in return for workforce stability and employee motivation. Women and minorities, on the other hand, are hired mainly for jobs that either have no *career ladder* or, at best, a very truncated one. The reader will recognize a similarity to the description of secondary labor market jobs. The major difference is that the employers being described are often large and are price-makers. In other words, the occupational segregationists take the position that employers effectively operate two different labor markets; one for the favored group (white males) and the other for the less desirable, women and minorities. While the case might be made that smaller employers cannot afford to pay the relatively high wages and benefits received by favored white male groups in larger corporations, the occupational segregationists make the case that larger employers deliberately offer different job (career) opportunities, wages, and benefits to white males as opposed to women and minorities.This is accomplished through their personnel departments' use of criteria reflecting societal norms and the social values of the larger community *(status closure)* to institutionalize a series of everyday, routine practices that result in occupational and job segregation.

Occupational segregationists trace the condition of lower pay for women and minorities to the separation of the sexes and races in internal labor markets. They believe that a number of ethnic groups are treated similarly, but, for lack of adequate data, tend not to include Hispanics and others in their investigations.

Human Resources Department Tactics. The following practices have been identified as commonly used by human-resources departments of corporations to institutionalize occupational segregation.

1. Different job ladders for white males, females, and blacks, which limit promotion and wage improvement for the latter two groups (already noted).
2. Reliance on the current employees for recruiting, resulting in work forces reflecting the ethnic, gender, religious, and racial character of the incumbent workforce.
3. Job-posting practices that limit information concerning available jobs to the imme-

diate work group, even though widespread incorporation of the policy of job posting was meant to open up desirable employment to all groups

4. Anti-nepotism rules that limit employment to one family member, often precluding any desirable work in a given community for a second available family member, usually the wife.
5. Formal promotion systems that restrict women's potential in that they cannot go beyond the few jobs for which they can apply within their career tracks.
6. Traditional tool design, which deprives women of opportunities because much equipment was built for use by men. (Reskin and Hartmann 1986)

Some occupational segregationists go further to identify job segregation *within occupations*, including those that are female-dominated and black-dominated, as an even more effective means of removing women and minorities from the more desirable employment opportunities. The argument of the job segregationists is that, over time, the resultant separation of the workforce into different occupational/job categories and sometimes different departments or even plants, by gender, race, and ethnicity, becomes standard practice to the extent that the pattern is zealously defended as a gender or racial-ethnic monopoly by those who benefit. This standardization may be accomplished through the use of a proliferation of job titles produced by human resources departments. Men and women doing similar work often are given different job titles and are employed in different firms and geographic locations with different opportunities and rewards (Bielby and Baron 1986; Groshen 1991).

Methods of devaluing the jobs allocated to women and minorities (*status composition*) have been identified through a rare study that analyzed employment throughout a state (North Carolina) by *job title* (Tomaskovic-Devey 1993). The following criteria were found to be used to determine the qualities of jobs to be assigned by gender and minority identity.

1. Closeness of supervision: the degree to which the worker's tasks are overseen.
2. Task complexity: the variety of task experiences included in the job.
3. Degree of internal labor market opportunity: the placement of the job on a scale ranging from deeply entrenched in the internal labor market to dispensable according to market shifts.
4. Managerial authority: the ability to make decisions concerning the organization's products, services, budgets, or major purchases.
5. Supervisory authority: the degree to which the worker has direct control of his or her own labor.

These means (or processes) all serve to limit the possibilities for women and minorities within the organization, primarily for the benefit of the employer, though white male workers also benefit.

Informal Barriers Within the Establishment: Women's Experiences

When women attempt to breach the barriers to male monopolized jobs within the firm, they meet informal barriers as well as the formal ones described above, according to the comprehensive Reskin-Hartmann review. The barriers are familiar ones, including male hostility, resistance by incumbent workers to offering essential on-the-job training to unwanted newcomers, and exclusion from informal networks. As a result, women have been found to do better in situations where work can be performed independently, as in real-estate sales, bus driving, and office machine repair. In the recent past exclusion from professional organizations and unions has been a problem. Whether women have more difficulties in obtaining mentors than men has not been well documented. Another problem in women's career progress is that doing a job well does not help unless the work is visible and can be assessed by objective standards.

Informal Barriers Within the Establishment: African Americans' Experiences

Aspiring African Americans tend to echo these complaints. A series of studies of black managers in white corporations (Fernandez 1987; Irons and More 1985; Davis and Watson 1985) reveal common experiences, emphasizing status issues and persistence of racial stereotypes. Findings include the following: whites in internal labor markets have a problem accepting blacks other than as menial workers; blacks' presence in management is seen as breaking up the corporate value system; low ceilings exist, with blacks being placed in less powerful departments and line positions (EEOC positions, for example); little confidence in blacks' capabilities exists; mentors are hard to find; and informal networks are closed to them.

OTHER FACTORS ENCOURAGING OCCUPATIONAL AND JOB SEGREGATION

Most explanations of occupational/job segregation include reference to factors that influence the occupational choices that women make, most particularly the oft-mentioned *socialization* of females. The comprehensive 1986 review by Barbara Reskin and Heidi Hartmann concluded that the influence of socialization and the formal education system on women's occupational behavior is unknown. This review of education focused on vocational programs because they most directly affect occupational choice.

Actual or anticipated domestic responsibilities of women, often said to factor into their occupational decisions, have been utilized to account for women's concentration in jobs of lesser responsibility or stability. The Reskin-Hartmann review found little evidence to sustain such claims, but did find that the availability of opportunities was a critical factor in determining job choice. Most people, aided by informal information and job contacts, take the jobs that are available. The human-capital school's predictions, that women who work intermittently because of family obligations will be more likely to hold female-type jobs than those who work consistently, was not upheld in the body of research reviewed, nor was evidence found that women who work intermittently fare better in female-dominated occupations than in male-dominated ones, a claim of Becker's household economics school. In other words, the mainstream theorists have not been able to produce consistent evidence substantiating their claims that women's inferior employment and wage position can be rationally explained by women's preferences and their reputed "special needs."

The great movement of women into paid employment after World War II was into female-type jobs for which there was expanded demand, opportunities that had never existed before (Oppenheimer 1970). Thus expanded demand and rising wage rates (Cain 1966; Mincer 1962) created the supply. It is not known whether there are currently large pools of women presently available for male-dominated jobs.

Blacks were also able to take advantage of the expanded demand during the post–World War II boom, securing many well-paying low-skill jobs in heavy industry, but not necessarily in new occupations (Smith and Welch 1987). The consequences of the disappearance of these "good jobs" is believed to be causing much of the distress in African-American communities.

The conclusions of the Reskin-Hartmann review of sex-segregation studies, to summarize, are that women's choices, preferences, and preparation have had little impact on the continued sex-segregation of occupations. Women's inferior workforce situation is not one voluntarily chosen. The series of studies have produced evidence of persisting, oft-cited but unsubstantiated stereotypes. Blacks also did better as the result of increased demand during the post–World War II period but, as in the case of women, basic segregation patterns within internal labor markets remained unchanged. There is room in scholarship for the creation of a comprehensive survey of contemporary black experience in labor markets for research purposes, such as the Reskin-Hartmann survey has provided concerning women's experiences.

JOB SEGREGATION WITHIN THE PROFESSIONAL/ TECHNICAL OCCUPATIONS

The job segregationists have directed considerable attention to job segregation within professions and technical occupations, the most desired in the occupational hierarchy. The term *professions* is used here as it is utilized by the Bureau of Labor Statistics, and includes jobs calling for college or requisite technical education. Extant studies tend to focus on the circumstances under which women and minorities have penetrated previously closed, higher level occupations.

According to the studies on professional entry, when women and minorities enter jobs formerly monopolized by white males, it is usually because males are exiting from the field for more desirable opportunities or because demand is so high that there is room for some of the formerly excluded groups (Higginbottom 1987; Glenn and Tolbert 1987; Simpson 1990; Dill, Weber, and Vanneman 1987; Malcolm 1989). Legal pressures associated with Affirmative Action programs have also contributed to opening up entry possibilities. But legalities cannot save the newly occupied job titles from subsequently losing status, autonomy, and income, which is often the result. This devaluing of an occupation leads to resegregation, with women or minorities dominating in the vacated job titles and white men in the higher status and higher paid job titles within the occupational hierarchy; in short, these findings substantiate the hypothesis of the job segregationists.

A rare look at the process of female penetration into previously male-dominated professional occupations during the 1960s and 1970s is provided by Natalie

Sokoloff (1992) who traced the movements of white and black women within thirty large professional and technical categories (about four-fifths of all professional-technician occupations). Sokoloff described these thirty large occupational categories as "newly penetrated occupations characterized by departing male incumbents." Prominent among the thirty professional/technical occupational categories are accounting, design, and nonspecific college teaching. All are in the lowest average income brackets for large male-dominated professions, except the ministry. Other examples are vocational and educational counseling, social work, and editing and reporting, all occupations deteriorating in desirability in terms of autonomy, control, skill requirements, working conditions, and income.

As noted earlier there has been less investigation of the experiences of African Americans than of women, but it has been established that blacks have had less success in penetrating the professional/technical fields, as a group, than white women. Upwardly mobile African-American males have tended to enter gender-neutral job titles previously closed to them, such as personnel work, labor relations, and vocational and educational counseling, while black women found the largest number of opportunities in job titles vacated by white women (social work, prekindergarten and kindergarten teaching, elementary education, and clinical lab work). Other examples of resegregated occupations are systems analysis, pharmacy, and public relations (Malcolm 1989). Although some job titles become integrated, with women and blacks being represented according to their proportion of the workforce, most do not.

The most prestigious and high-paying job titles within each occupation tend to remain occupied by white males. Black men advanced within most engineering specialties, chemistry, and medicine during the twenty years (1960 to 1980) studied by Sokoloff, while black women tended to enter professions formerly dominated by white women. However, most of the prestigious professions remain dominated by white males. A review of occupancy of professional/ managerial titles between 1983, the first year this data was published, and 1997 shows the percentage shares held by blacks and persons of Hispanic origin, in relation to their representation in the workforce, to have risen modestly and, in the case of Hispanics, to have fallen in some instances. This latter development may be explained by the heavy immigration of uneducated Hispanics between 1983 and 1997.

Professional job segregation has been found to be characterized by type of employer. For example, from 1960 to 1980, black physicians and nurses, male and female, worked mainly in municipal clinics and public hospitals as salaried workers, serving the poor. Most black women professionals and technicians are likely to be clustered in the public sector (Higginbottom 1987). Black women lawyers, five years or more after graduation, have been found to be primarily employed by government (59%), with only a few finding places in private law firms (13%) (Simpson 1990). Those entering law firms have seldom been promoted. Such data tends to reinforce the widely held belief that most blacks with middle-class status work in the public sector.

Finally, opinions appear to differ as to the progress of American women in professional/technician employment. One study (Sokoloff 1992) reported that despite apparent progress in the professional-technical occupations, the relative share of women appears to have fallen, with white males increasing their representation and black women losing ground. On the other hand, another recent study shows women to be increasing their representation in the elite professions (Goldin 1990).

Comparison of BLS statistics on the proportion of women in the elite occupations between 1983, the first year that these statistics were gathered, and 1997 give the impression of progress in some occupations. Absolute numbers rose, as did the proportion of women in the various occupations and the proportional share in relation to women's representation in the workplace (BLS 1984 and 1998).[1]

When social scientists discuss workplace segregation by gender or race they are usually reporting on findings developed from studies of differences by *occupational* category, often broken into as narrow groups as available data permit. Good examples are reports of women and minorities in the professions or in managerial occupations. In recent years some researchers have raised the question of job segregation *within* occupations as being key to understanding the employment outcomes of women and minorities. Study by *job title*, as opposed to occupation offers the possibility of gaining a more realistic picture of what is, in fact, happening within establishments than can be obtained through comparisons of work experiences by occupational category, however narrowly defined. The findings of Tomaskovic-Devey (1993) who accessed a unique body of data by job title for the state of North Carolina are therefore of particular interest. They suggest that further explorations by the job title approach might lead to a better understanding of the dynamics of employment inequality, position and earnings than the paths conventionally taken. The major findings and problems associated with this approach found by Tomaskovic-Devey are therefore reported here.

In general, Tomaskovic's findings tend to indicate that women and African Americans are more likely than white males to be in the lower-skilled, low-power job categories *within* each occupational group. Looking at gender segregation in job titles within the managerial occupations, for example, 41 percent of the positions in the North Carolina workforce, taken as a group, are occupied by women (53 percent of North Carolina workforce). On the surface it appears that the managerial occupational group is not badly skewed, gender-wise. More detailed analysis reveals otherwise. When the occupancy of individual managerial *job titles* is examined, *the index of dissimilarity* (internal segregation index) is found to be sixty, meaning that, on average, sixty out of every 100 managerial employees would have to leave their jobs to be replaced by members of the opposite sex for the managerial job titles to contain as many women as men. Using the "gender-integrated index," Tomaskovic-Devey's analysis shows that only about 15 percent of all the managerial job titles have between 1 to 99 percent occupancy by one sex or the other, that is, *any* presence in those job titles. And only about a tenth of the job titles are "gender-balanced," a more rigorous measure.This is taken to mean that, though women heavily populate the managerial occupations, as a whole, men and women are severely concentrated in separate job titles and rarely occupy the same ones.

Racial segregation within the managerial occupations is more severe than gender discrimination. With about 22 percent of the North Carolina workforce African American, only 10.9 percent of all managerial positions are black-populated; the index of dissimilarity is 89, meaning the overwhelming majority of blacks (or whites) would have to change jobs to have an equal distribution within each job title. Only about one-tenth of all managerial job titles have between 1 to 99 percent black (or white) occupants, that is, any presence at all in each of the job titles. No managerial title is "racially balanced," that is, occupied by between 11 to 33 percent by blacks, a "ball-park" reflection of the actual representation of blacks in the community. This is interpreted to mean that blacks are overwhelmingly excluded from most managerial jobs

EFFECTS OF OCCUPATIONAL AND JOB SEGREGATION ON EARNINGS

Ultimately, the occupational segregationists must offer proof that the occupational (and job title) segregation that they so diligently attempt to document results in lower wages for women and minorities. This has not been easy, nor satisfactorily accomplished. Claudia Goldin, an economic historian (1990) who offers both empirical data and a historical perspective on female wage rates obtained through study of old payroll records, found that the extent of the wage gap has varied over the past 200 years. The notion that economic and technological progress brings about linear progress in women's employment experience is not necessarily true, according to her calculations. The female wage gap rose, from a top of about 20 percent in clerical work in 1900 to 55 percent in manufacturing in 1940. Goldin attributes this rise to changes in employer policies. In 1900 women in manufacturing, while segregated, were paid more in accordance with the market value of their work than the clerical workers of the 1940s. The 1940s clerical wages were determined by personnel departments that, having acquired control of hiring and wages, barred women by employer policy from many jobs and paid primarily according to gender identity instead of productivity.

In the contemporary period the largest finding of wage discrimination by reason of sex segregation, located through major reviews of the evidence (Cain 1986; Madden 1985; Tomaskovic-Devey 1993), was 56 percent of the wage gap. However, the inclusion of other contributing variables, such as education (college major, in particular) in subsequent studies lowered the unexplained portion of the gap (customarily attributed to wage discrimination by researchers) to 23 percent (Daymont and Andrisani 1984). As discussed above, Tomaskovic-Devey's study of employed adults in North Carolina is especially valuable in that he was able to limit his comparisons to narrower, and therefore, more similar, groups, making his findings more reality-based.[2] Tomaskovic-Devey's major finding, concerning gender differentials, is that over half (56%) of the male-female hourly earnings gap in North Carolina ($3.46 in 1989) could be explained by the gender identification of the job; whether whether male or female, persons who work in male-dominated occupations tend to earn more than persons who work in female-dominated ones. The converse was also true for both men and women. But the researcher acknowledged the existence of other factors, such as the type of degree undertaken, level of market demand, and years of experience.

Investigation of occupational and job segregation by race lags behind that done in regard to gender, leaving the question of impact on earnings of African

Americans unanswered. For this reason, Tomaskovic-Devey's rare look at racial segregation by *job title*, in the study mentioned above, is of particular interest. Tomaskovic-Devey's opinion is that racial segregation of jobs appears to have less consequence for the black-white wage gap than does gender segregation for male-female differentials. His figure for the impact of segregation of job titles by race in North Carolina, accounts for at least 21 percent of the black wage gap ($2.30) during the period studied (1989). Other factors, mainly job characteristics (the meaning of which he does not define) (36%) and human-capital factors (29%), were found to be more significant. However, Tomaskovic-Devey admitted that study of the black experience is more difficult than of gender issues because of measurement problems: numbers, in terms of population and employed persons in specific job titles, are smaller than for females, which makes generalization problematic.

Existing legislation, as interpreted by the courts, is inadequate to the task of eradicating gender pay differentials. In 1963 an Equal Pay Bill passed Congress, but only after backers removed a clause providing for equal pay for "work of comparable quantity and quality." Despite the passage of much stronger anti-discrimination legislation the following year, the Civil Rights Act of 1964, the majority of women remain in sex-segregated occupations and cannot benefit from the protections offered in either pieces of legislation. Affirmative-action programs do not appear to have affected the basic employment patterns of women; the employment shares at various levels are the same among employers monitored by the Federal Contract Compliance Program and those not monitored (Leonard, for the Glass Ceilings Commission 1994). Meanwhile, seen from the perspectives of the women's rights movement, the struggle for higher wages/salaries for women continues, mainly in the framework of the *comparable worth* movement.

As for African-American progress, the general belief exists that a sizable black middle-class has been created, but that it is mainly dependent upon government employment. The majority of African-American males, it is believed, are more drastically affected by the collapse of manufacturing, that is, the unavailability of high-paying jobs requiring low levels of skills in the economy as a whole and in center-city areas where most African Americans still tend to reside. Other factors affecting African Americans without higher education are increased competition from recent immigrants, legal and illegal; the globalization of the economy, which drains work out of the country and sucks in cheap goods, further removing possibilities for employment in goods-producing jobs; and the presence of the vast alternative work force, women.

During the late 1980s and 1990s, the determined low-wage approach of U.S. employers, seemingly accepted as unstoppable by the American public, resulted in little action on the part of either women or minorities to improve their status, other than through investment in higher education, now seen as the surest road to a better life. Political and community efforts in both African-American and women's organizations on behalf of greater shares in employment and earnings have been remarkably muted. Rarely has the use of the favored strategy of the women's movement to produce equity in earnings, described below, been documented during the 1990s. In the black community the major efforts of the past few years have been to defend Affirmative Action (AA) programs against attacks on the state level. Various efforts have been launched on the state level to eliminate preferences offered racial minorities through AA programs in schooling: two states, as of this writing, have been forbidden via state referendums to admit students to institutions of higher learning on the basis of racial identity.

Comparable Worth: The Women's Movement's Change Strategy

The tactic adopted by the women's movement to force gender equality on reluctant employers, in light of the bankruptcy of the equal pay for equal work approach, is use of the *comparable worth* doctrine, which holds that an employer must pay employees in jobs held predominantly by women the same as employees in jobs held predominantly by men if the jobs require comparable skills, effort, responsibility, and working conditions, that is, if the jobs are of equal value, social characteristics of the workers aside (Feldberg 1986; Sorensen 1994). The immediate goal of the comparable worth approach is to raise women's earnings, but one outcome would be to discourage sex segregation of jobs by taking away the profit incentive.

In the United States implementation of comparable worth principles has occurred largely in the public sector. Of the state governments who have adopted comparable worth, most have limited themselves to examining only a few occupations and have spent relatively little on adjustments. It is believed that a considerable number of private employers have examined their personnel policies in light of comparable worth principles and that some have made pay adjustments, but the extent is unknown.

Criticisms of the Comparable Worth Strategy. Although comparable worth has held sway as the strategy of choice of women's advocates for over a quarter-century, a number of analysts (Tomaskovic-Devey 1993; Killingsworth 1990; Acker 1989) cite serious limitations in the policy. One problem is that it is ineffectual in the majority of situations because of job segregation. Another limitation is that employers who accept comparable worth tend, under sufficient pressure, to adjust wages upward, because it would be politically infeasible to reduce male wages. This raises the total wage bill. In some states all employees received raises as an outcome of job reclassification. Implementation of comparable worth programs in ten states studied by Acker (1989) varied considerably: for example, state payroll costs rose between .6 percent (New York) and 8.8 percent (Iowa). States that adjusted only the women's jobs spent less; those who reclassified all jobs spent more. In some states gender gaps were eliminated; in others, they were reduced.

The major conclusion concerning comparable worth is that, while it has some potential for removing inequities among women who have managed to obtain jobs in male-dominated fields, it cannot help the majority of women who are in sex-segregated, low-skill jobs since the courts have ruled that Title VII of the Civil Rights Act pertains only in cases of *intentional* discrimination by employers. Otherwise, the defense that prevailing wage rates reflect market forces is likely to be accepted. Since the unexplained pay gap in the private sector can be explained entirely on the basis of prevailing wages (according to such researchers as Sorensen), current Supreme Court decisions do not permit redress for private-sector women (or minorities). Because public sector employers have been amenable to consideration of the principles involved, mainly because of the political power of women and the heavy presence of labor unions in government (Smith 1988), comparable worth might be a viable policy for removing wage inequities for women (and minorities) on public payrolls.

NOTES

1. Unfortunately, comparable data offering detailed occupational distribution by race is not published by BLS.

2. Examples of use of job title as opposed to occupational category are: secretary as opposed to clerical worker; welders and cutters as opposed to operators, fabricators, and laborers; furniture-sales work as opposed to sales occupations.

REFERENCES

Acker, Joan. 1989. *Doing comparable worth*. Philadelphia: Temple University Press.

Aldrich, Mark, and Robert Buchele. 1989. Where to look for comparable worth: the implications of efficiency wags. In Anne Hill and Mark Killingsworth, eds. 1989. *Comparable worth: analysis and evidence*. Ithaca, N.Y.: ILR Press.

Baker, Elizabeth F. 1969. *Protective labor legislation: with special reference to women in the State of New York*. Studies in History, Economics, and Public Law, Columbia University. New York: AMS Press (originally published 1925).

Bergmann, Barbara. 1974. Occupational segregation, wages, and profits when employers discriminate by race or sex. *Eastern Economic Journal* 1 (April/July): 103–11.

Bielby, William, and James Baron. 1986. Men and women at work: sex segregation and statistical discrimination. *American Journal of Sociology* 91, no. 4 (January): 759–99.

Butler, Elizabeth B. 1984. *Women and the trades: Pittsburgh, 1900-1908*. Pittsburgh: University of Pittsburgh Press (originally published 1909).

Cain, Glenn. 1986. The economic analysis of labor market discrimination: a survey, 693–785. In Ashenfelter, Orley, and Layard, P. *Handbook of labor economics*. Amsterdam: New Holland.

Davis, George, and Gregg Watson. 1985. *Black life in corporate America: swimming in the mainstream*. Garden City, N.J.: Anchor Press.

Daymont, Thomas, and Paul Andrisani. 1984. Job preferences, college major, and the gender gap in earnings. *Journal of Human Resources* 19 (Summer): 409–28.

Dill, Bonnie T., Lynn Weber, and Reeve Vanneman. 1987. Race and gender in occupational segregation. In *Pay equity: an issue of race, ethnicity, and sex*. Washington, D.C.: National Committee on Pay Equity.

Feldberg, Roslyn. 1986. Comparable worth: toward theory and practice in the United States, 163–80. In Gelpi, Barbara, N. Hartsock, C. Novak, and M. Strober, eds. *Women and poverty*. Chicago: University of Chicago Press.

Fernandez, John. 1987. *Survival in the corporate fish bowl: making it in upper and middle management*. Lexington, Mass.: D.C. Heath and Company.

Galle, Omer R., Candace Wiswell, and Jeffrey Burr. 1988. Racial mix and industrial productivity. *American Sociological Review* 50 (February): 20–23.

Glenn, Evelyn, and Charles M. Tolbert II. 1987. Technology and emerging patterns of stratification for women of color: race and gender segregation in computers, 319–31. In Wright, Barbara, et al., eds. *Women, work, and technology transformations*. Ann Arbor: University of Michigan Press.

Goldin, Claudia. 1990. *Understanding the gender gap: an economic history of American women*. New York: Oxford University Press.

Groshen, Erica L. 1991. The structure of the male-female wage differential. *Journal of Human Resources* 26, no. 3 (Summer): 457–72.

Higginbottom, Elizabeth. 1987. Employment for professional black women in the twentieth century, 73–91. In Bose, Christine, and Glenna Spitze, eds. In *Ingredients for women's employment policy*. Albany: SUNY Press.

Irons, Edward, and Gilbert Moore. 1985. *Black managers: the case of the banking industry*. New York: Praeger.

Leonard, Jonathan. 1994. Use of enforcement techniques in eliminating glass ceilings barriers. Prepared for the Glass Ceiling Commission, U.S. Department of Labor, Washington, D.C.

Kessler-Harris, Alice. 1990. *A woman's wage: historical meanings & social consequences*. Lexington: University of Kentucky Press.

Killingsworth, Mark, 1990. *The economics of comparable worth*. Kalamazoo, Mich.: W. E. Upjohn Institute.

Madden, Janice. 1985. The persistence of pay differentials: the economics of sex discrimination. *Women and Work: An Annual Review*: 76–114.

Malcolm, Shirley. 1989. Increasing the participation of black women in science and technology. *Sage: A Scholarly Journal on Black Women* 6 (Fall): 15–17.

Mincer, Jacob. 1962. Labor force participation of married women: a study of labor supply. In H. Gregg Lewis, ed., *Aspects of labor economics*. Princeton, N.J.: Princeton University Press.

Neal, Derek, and William Johnson. 1996. The role of pre-market factors in black-white wage differences. *Journal of Political Economy* 104, no. 5: 869–95.

Oppenheimer, Valerie. 1970. *The female labor force in the United States: demographic and economic factors governing its growth and changing composition*. Westport, Conn.: Greenwood Press.

Reskin, Barbara, and Heidi Hartmann. 1986. *Women's work, men's work: job segregation on the job*. Washington, D.C.: National Academy Press.

Shackett, Joyce R., and John Trapani. 1987. Earnings differentials and market structure. *Journal of Human Resources* 22 (Fall): 518–31.

Shuler, Marjorie. 1923. Industrial women confer. *Woman Citizen*, 27 January.

Simpson, Gwyned. 1990. Black women in the legal professions. Unpublished manuscript, New York.

Smith, James, and Finis Welch. 1987. Race and poverty: a forty year record. *AEA Papers and Proceedings* 77, no. 2 (May).

Smith, Robert S. 1988. Comparable worth: limited coverage and the exacerbation of inequality. *Industrial and Labor Relations Review* 41, no. 2 (January): 227–39.

Sokoloff, Natalie. 1992. *Black women and white women in the professions: occupational segregation by race and gender, 1960–1980*. New York: Routledge.

Sorensen, Elaine. 1989. The wage effects of occupational sex segregation: review and new findings. In Hill, Anne, and Mark Killingsworth, eds. Colloquium on Comparable Worth. Cornell University. *Comparable worth: analysis and evidence*. Ithaca: ILR Press.

———. 1994. *Comparable Worth: Is it a worthy policy?* Princeton: Princeton University Press.

Tomaskovic-Devey, Donald. 1993. *Gender and racial inequality at work: the sources and consequences of job segregation*. Ithaca, N.Y.: ILR Press.

U.S. Department of Labor. Bureau of Labor Statistics. 1984. *Employment and Earnings* 31, no. 1, (January) Table 22, 178–82.

———. 1998. *Employment and Earnings* 45, no. 1, (January) Table 11. 174–79.

17

The Uniqueness of the African-American Experience

The continuing inferior position of African Americans, as measured by wage rates, is no more satisfactorily explained by mainstream economic theories than are women's earnings differentials. Perplexity has increased as more recently arrived minority groups have made marked economic progress in relatively short periods of time. Although a black middle-class has emerged since the civil-rights era of the 1960s, the economic situation of the unskilled and semiskilled, the majority, has deteriorated. Many African Americans have fallen to the level of *underclass* (Wilson 1987), a group all but eliminated from the mainstream economy. To gain insights into this puzzling state of affairs, this chapter reviews the explanations most often offered for the different labor-market experiences of African Americans in the context of the unique employment history of the United States' largest minority group, now approximately 12 percent of the labor force. Where racial or ethnic comparisons are relevant, the discussion concentrates on black-white issues, as detailed data concerning other ethic minorities is unavailable. The historical material is largely drawn from classic studies by Du-Bois (1899) and Myrdal (1944), supplemented by the more recent work of Hacker (1992) and other more specialized analysts, particularly Green and Pryde (1990).

EXCEPTIONAL ASPECTS

Roles of Custom and Tradition

Exclusion, Confinement, Displacement. In the 1940s an explanation of the persistence of racial discrimination against African Americans was offered by Gunnar Myrdal, the famous Swedish economist who was imported by the Carnegie Foundation to make a definitive study of reasons for the chronically depressed condition of the racial minority. Comments here on Myrdal's monumental work are limited to aspects relevant to employment and earnings. After surveying, through intensive interviews, the racial attitudes of a broad spectrum of Americans of all ages and regions of the country and making an exhaustive review of historical records, Myrdal concluded that the tradition of job segregation of African Americans was a deep-rooted, integral part of a U.S. caste system that emerged in the post–Civil War era for the purpose of controlling the group. Myrdal saw historically based customs and traditions as the major determinants of both job segregation and wage differentials. He viewed the racial discrimination prevalent in the early 1940s as a manifestation of this caste system, and as an example of how institutionalized patterns of behavior persist long after the original reasons for their adoption disappear.

Myrdal argued that Americans were, at the time of his survey, torn between their views of African Americans as immutably inferior and their deeply incorporated sense that all human beings are of equal value, an ideological contradiction he termed the "American dilemma." He noted that fears of economic competition were bobbing near the surface, but insisted nonetheless that the necessary starting point for an understanding of the black experience in America resided in an awareness of these deeply held social values.

According to Myrdal, the situation of the African-American labor force deteriorated a few years into the post-bellum period because of the following, conscious policies by white employers that were backed by community sanction: (1) exclusion from jobs traditionally filled by whites, (2) confinement of blacks to traditional "black work," and (3) displacement from such work when it became attractive to whites. These policies were justified by the development of an American caste system, buttressed by new legislation entrenching segregation through law. These new segregation policies, adopted during the 1880s, dictated an inferior position for the African-American community, placing constraints on economic development that generated the black-white wage differentials persisting even today in the U.S. economy. The intense competition for the types of work available to African Americans pushed wages down.

The forces of custom and tradition, so evident in the setting of women's wages, have also established inferiority in wage rates as the norm for employment associated with African Americans. Myrdal identified economic discrimination, an inhibitor of accessibility to jobs and other means of earning a living (land purchase, rental, credit), as an integral part of post–Civil War discrimination policies that still prevailed in the consciousness of the citizenry of the 1940s. Myrdal also believed that the relationship of working-class whites and blacks has always been one of competition and antagonism. In his view much of the employment discrimination against blacks on the part of owners was influenced by, and originated out of, the struggle between impoverished whites and blacks for wage jobs and opportunities.

Exclusion from most employment was achieved by both formal and informal means, with the informal—the inaccessibility to blacks of the social networks that feed the recruitment and hiring pools of employers—more prevalent. Formal exclusion through union charters and denial of apprenticeship opportunities also played an important role in barring opportunities in the most lucrative fields, especially construction. As craft unionism became stronger in the late 1800s, many unions excluded blacks formally by charter, although some segregated locals were formed. Strong social pressures tied to the majority value system and employer and employee resistance converged to bar access by blacks to most jobs above the menial level. The unwillingness of white workers to offer on-the-job training to black recruits was another factor. Myrdal interpreted white employee resistance to black coworkers to reflect a desire to limit the supply of available labor for the purpose of maintaining wage rates, and to stem from status considerations, the belief that working on the same job with a black person carried social stigma.

The second process used to delimit black employment was *confinement* to a very limited number of occupations that then became known as "Negro occupations." As of the 1930 Census, the most common characteristic of all black jobs was that they were undesirable and carried stigma because they were black-dominated. Many of the male jobs involved outdoor work and were intermittent in nature, involved repetitive movements, and were particularly dangerous or otherwise disagreeable; two examples are logging and work in the turpentine industry. Black women were confined largely to domestic work, although black males secured the better jobs, which included cook and steward. Black women were barred from clerical work; only .7 percent held clerical jobs in 1930.

The third process, unique to black experience, is *displacement.* As "Negro jobs" became more desirable due to industrialization (movement of work from home to factory) or technological changes, job-hungry whites—poor whites in the South and new immigrants in the North—drove blacks out of their traditional employment. For example, black males lost most of their barbering work shortly after the Civil War; their enterprises became limited to black neighborhoods. Black women lost their laundress positions to white-staffed industrial laundries. In the North employers gave preference to new immigrants over long-resident blacks (Hershberg 1971).

In the process of mechanization, typical "black jobs" were eliminated at a faster rate than the totality of manual jobs for the general population. The number of skilled black craftsmen in the North increased during the 1920s, but this probably represented a gain from migration, not more craftsmen in general. Beginning in the 1920s the remaining skilled blacks in the South continued to lose ground, partly due to the increased presence of craft unions and the opposition of white members to black coworkers. Again, the process of exclusion reared its head, in the form of denial of apprenticeship opportunities.

The Philadelphia Studies. Two important studies of the black experience in America before and after the Civil War, which focused on the African-American community in Philadelphia, offer some interesting insights as to the nature of black progress, as well as clarification as to the nature of the forces interfering with advancement. As with women's.progress movement toward black economic betterment has not been linear. The original data for the first case study cited was collected between 1830 and 1856, that is, prior to the Civil War, by Philadelphia Quakers whose goal was to ascertain the progress of the free African-American community. A reworking of the data, using modern methodology, was performed by Theodore Hershberg (1971). The second study, renowned as a pioneering type of investigation for its sociological underpinnings, is W.E.B. DuBois' *The Philadelphia Negro,* published in 1899. Hershberg's study, written later than DuBois' and of lesser renown, is described first because his database is pre–Civil War, while DuBois' is post-bellum.

As Hershberg notes, historians of the African-American experience often pose the following question: do continuing impacts of the slave condition or other factors account for the continuing depressed socioeconomic condition of a disproportionate portion of the black population? Most prominently mentioned as an alternative explanation is the negative influence of big city life on predominantly rural families that left the South for the cities of the North in successive waves after 1865, and especially after the Great Migration of the 1920s. Utilizing a rare set of data collected by Abolitionist Friends over a quarter century commencing in 1830, Hershberg (1971) compared the economic conditions of ex-slaves and freeborn blacks in Philadelphia in the pre–Civil War period to ascertain the impact of slavery on subsequent socioeconomic conditions. He also investigated changes in the employment status of black workers during this time period. Philadelphia was a model city to study as it had a free black population of 22,000 persons in 1860, second only to Baltimore outside the Slave South.

Findings. Hershberg smashed the "slavery impact" argument by producing evidence that freed slaves fared better in pre–Civil War Philadelphia than black persons born free. They had larger families; a greater likelihood of two-parent households; a higher church and beneficial-society affiliation rate, which was a symbol of status attainment in the black community; sent more of their children to school; lived in less densely inhabited sections; were wealthier, owned more real estate; and had slightly better jobs than freeborn blacks. They were also more likely to be part of the small black middle-class.

Hershberg showed that Philadelphia blacks have been systematically excluded from desirable employment from the period prior to the Civil War, even losing black-segregated jobs to successive waves of white immigrants. Although the Society of Friends of that time thought that the Philadelphia black community was making progress, Hershberg's present-day computer-based analysis of their data shows a continuing deterioration in black socioeconomic status between 1830 and 1860. Blacks were largely confined to the most menial occupations: 70 percent were laborers, porters, seamen, carters, and waiters; another 10 percent worked in similar unskilled occupations. Denied access to factory jobs, while at the same time losing much of their traditional dominance in semi-skilled and unskilled jobs to the newly arriving Irish immigrants, the socioeconomic situation of free blacks in Philadelphia was deteriorating during the pre–Civil War period. For example, according to the 1850 Census, blacks held 5 percent of all hod-carrier and stevedore jobs, which were considered well-paying, in 1847, but only 1 percent three years later. Skilled black craftsmen complained of being forced out of their trades and of being unable to obtain apprenticeships for their sons. Unemployment among this skilled group rose from 23 percent in 1838 to 38 percent by 1856. The great majority (80%) of black women in Philadelphia were limited to domestic service. About one in seven (14%) worked as seamstresses; another 5 percent in low-level white-collar work, mostly selling food and clothing.[1]

Studying contemporary statistical data, Hershberg noted that the African-American employment situation declined between the two world wars. Where blacks had entered new occupations during World War I, they tended to be driven out when it was over, more evidence that the tradition of exclusion was still alive. The entrance of African Americans into better employment opportunities during World War II was facilitated by the Fair Employment Practices Committee, established by President Franklin D. Roosevelt through Executive Order 8802, a forerunner of current equal employment opportunity legislation.

DuBois' Philadelphia Story. The second case study of Philadelphia is W.E.B. DuBois' now classic work, *The Philadelphia Negro* (1899), an investigation made at the request of concerned aristocrats of the city's establishment. In this work, which secured DuBois' position as a " founding father of American sociology,"[2] the young DuBois reported on the circumstances of 9,000 black inhabitants of Philadelphia's Seventh Ward[3] in the last years of the 1890s.

DuBois found that it was difficult for a black man, irrespective of education or training, to find work except as a "menial servant." Black men were excluded from clerical, supervisory, instructional, or crafts work ("mechanics"), and any unionized work. Black women were confined to three occupations: "domestic service, sewing, or married life." Black residents of the ward under study were found to have difficulties in retaining the jobs that they held, being replaced in the better domestic positions due to "changes in fashion." In general, they were "the last hired and the first fired." Entering new lines of work was also difficult due to objections by the public. Intense competition for jobs, in DuBois' view, was responsible for prevailing wages, lower than those for whites doing similar work. This vignette of Philadelphia life in the 1890s, predating Myrdal's 1940s nationwide survey, indicates that little progress had been made in the almost half-century between.

Reinforcement of the Displacement Hypothesis. One largely unknown fact of the immediate post–Civil War era is that the majority of the skilled workers of the South were black, approximately 100,000 out of an estimated 120,000. According to Davie (1949), African Americans began the post-bellum period with a near monopoly of existent craft-type jobs in the South. They were prominent as cabinetmakers, blacksmiths, painters, masonry workers, and shipbuilders, and they occupied many other craft positions. The situation of this skilled group soon deteriorated as employers, faced with the necessity of paying wage labor, lost incentive to train blacks, thus beginning a tradition of regarding African Americans as an alternative labor force. Initially, in the early period following the Civil War, the few highly educated blacks who migrated North were able to find suitable work fairly easily; but later, education ceased to be a vehicle for advancement. The employment "lid" was not movable. One reason was the antagonism of the white working class whose wage levels had long been depressed because of the presence of the captive black labor force (Genovese 1961). This information is invaluable in that it redefines the problem from lack of skills, often identified as the nature of the problem, to systematic *de-skilling*, that is, discriminatory policies for which employers and the public are responsible.

The Great Migration. After the Civil War the impoverished Southern black labor force, perceiving no possibilities for betterment, began migrating to the large cities of the North and West, a movement that lasted more than 100 years (1865–1970). Mass migration began about 1916 and varied thereafter, becoming larger during periods when poor crops and low labor demand in the South converged with increased opportunities in the North. Such occurred during the two World Wars. During the last period of great migration, 1940–70, many of the migrants came to the great cities of the North and West without the intermediate step of urbanization in southern cities, a factor that made their adjustment to the industrial economies of their destinations more problematic.

Despite burgeoning industry in the North, most black migrants were unable to escape the discriminatory practices described above, which limited jobs to unskilled, manual work and employment in the domestic servant category, for which demand was strong. During industrial disputes black men were often in demand as strikebreakers, which exacerbated racial tensions between working-class whites and incoming blacks. As late as 1900 about 95 percent of all black workers were still manual workers.

One of the paradoxes of black progress has been that, as things have appeared to be getting better, they have often worsened. Repeatedly, color prejudice and the marketplace have interacted to limit black possibilities and thereby depress wages (Anderson 1996, discussing DuBois' relevance to the present-day problems of the African-American community). For example, during World War II unskilled African Americans obtained a toehold in such factory-based employment as metalworking, meat packing, and automotives. Although the new internal migrants were crowded at the bottom of job hierarchies, factory employment represented progress in terms of escape from traditional confinement to the most undesirable, unstable employment. And when progress began to be made, the jobs began to disappear.

POST CIVIL-RIGHTS ERA DEVELOPMENTS

Although the mid-1960s represented a period in which opportunity seemed to be opening up as never before, evidence of a situation getting worse just as it seemed to be getting better reemerged. The period was relatively prosperous and saw passage of long-sought civil-rights legislation (Title VII of the Civil Rights Act of 1964), which was designed to facilitate entry of blacks into heretofore closed occupations. A public now sensitized to the injustices and economic consequences of racial discrimination was more willing to accept blacks into mainstream employment. When legislation alone proved insufficient to the task, equal employment opportunity practices were introduced through court order during the Kennedy Administration; employers with Federal contracts were obliged to include racial minorities (and women) in their workforces, at minimum to the extent that they would be representative of the surrounding population. But even in this hopeful environment, deterioration in black employment was already apparent.

Explanations for Deterioration in the 1960s

Most explanations of the reasons for post-1960s African-American employment deterioration focus on the exodus of jobs from center-city areas and the ravages of efficiency, developments that have largely eliminated the need for unskilled and semiskilled labor. The motivations commonly given for this job migration were noted in an earlier chapter: more available land in the suburbs or *exurbs*, cheaper rents, local tax concessions, less unionism, high utility costs in cities, and cheaper labor abroad.

An alternative explanation proffered by Bruce Williams (1987), who studied racial attitudes in industry, is that white workers' aversion to working with blacks is a major factor in plant relocation. When a plant becomes too black, management will often pick up and move to exurbia. Whichever explanation one favors, it was already clear by the mid-1960s that the jobs that offered middle-class status to relatively unskilled workers of either race were vanishing. Many white workers followed surviving jobs, but blacks did not, largely because housing segregation limited them to central city areas. Meanwhile, in the 1990s many of these jobs no longer exist, whether because of job export abroad or shrinkage at home due to technological developments; this development was predicted in the 1960s by Myrdal, who said that blacks would be the first candidates for job displacement under such circumstances (1962; in introduction to a reissue of *The American Dilemma*).

Seen retrospectively, African Americans arrived in the North as opportunities for the unskilled were shriveling due to processes of industrialization and mechanization. Blacks entered the manual sector during a period in which employment first began shifting from manual to nonmanual, blue-collar to white-collar. Until Roosevelt's New Deal, they were shut out of the most obvious source of employment, the Federal government. In other words, blacks suffered from the same job stagnation and losses as the unskilled and semiskilled white population, but to a greater extent because their entry was so much later, penetration so much shallower, and ability to enter newer fields less likely. The downhill trend in jobs for African Americans in the "promised lands" of the North and West started in the 1960s, although deindustrialization did not cause black incomes to fall for at least another twenty years (Kornweibel 1976).

Reverse Migration. When the Northern economy deteriorated during the 1970s, some reverse migration began, with African Americans moving south in the hope of obtaining better opportunities there. The now rapid industrialization of the South, together with the outward movement of the population, was the dominant force in breaking the iron grip of the caste system on Southern blacks. By the 1970s going south became a viable option in terms of employability, but the issue of black-white wage differentials remained. Table 17.1 shows the uneven distribution of African Americans among the occupational structure, as well as earnings levels for each occupation. The costs of occupational segregation are high for blacks (as well as for women of all groups).

Black Professionals and Managerials

Until the civil-rights era, education had little possibility of payoff for African Americans; this was due to the ban on employment of African Americans in positions above the menial level. Although education was highly valued and sought after by black families throughout the post–Civil War era, until the 1960s it was difficult for aspiring African-American professionals or managerials to obtain employment in their fields of preparation. Barriers to advanced preparation included legally or de facto segregated public-school systems, chronic underfunding of black-associated educational institutions, exclusion from many white colleges and universities, and personal finances. Still, custom and tradition are thought to have constituted the major barriers to black entry into white-collar,

Table 17.1.
Distribution of Full-Time Workers, by Occupation and Race, and Median Weekly Earnings of All Full-Time Wage and Salary Workers by Occupation, 1997

	White	Black	Median weekly earnings* (*dollars*)
Total Employed, 16 and over (*percent*)	100.0	100.0	503
Managers and professional specialties	30.3	20.5	738
Executive, administrative, and managerial	14.9	9.5	725
Professional specialty	15.4	11.0	750
Technical, sales, and administrative support	29.8	29.5	456
Technicians and related support	3.2	2.8	582
Sales occupations	12.7	9.5	482
Administrative support, including clerical	13.9	17.2	419
Service occupations	12.4	21.9	313
Private household	.6	1.0	215
Protective service	1.7	3.0	550
Service, except private h.h. and protective service	10.1	17.9	296
Precision production, craft, and repair	11.3	7.7	548
Operators, fabricators, and laborers	13.5	19.5	401
Machine operators, assemblers, and inspectors	5.7	8.3	390
Transportation and material handling occupations	4.1	5.8	498
Handlers, equipment cleaners, helpers, and laborers	3.7	5.4	329
Farming, forestry, and fishing	2.6	.9	295

*Earnings are annual averages for 1997.
Source: U.S. Department of Labor. Bureau of Labor Statistics. 1998. *Employment and Earnings* (January): Tables 17 and 39.

professional, or managerial employment. Should blacks somehow acquire an advanced education, jobs appropriate to their degrees and credentials were almost impossible to locate. Sizable numbers of master's degrees and doctorates actually were obtained by blacks during the 1930s and 1940s, but most of the recipients ended up as railroad dining-car redcaps and the like (Drake and Cayton 1945).

By 1930 only 6 to 7 percent of the black labor force could be said to be in business or professional categories, most of these as teachers or ministers, the majority of the latter holding second jobs to support themselves. Black professionals such as doctors and lawyers had great difficulty because of the poverty in the black community, their only source of clientele. There were a few social workers, but their numbers were limited because of unwillingness to permit them to disperse funds. Positions in black-owned business were rare, for reasons discussed later in this chapter. Job competition, the poor funding of black institutions that could offer employment, and the low income of black community members all combined to depress salaries for the educated class (Sokoloff 1992).

By 1960, the beginning of the civil-rights era, just 4.7 percent of all black workers were classified as professionals as opposed to 12 percent of whites. Black male professionals were still largely limited to the black community and the segregated public sector. Black women professionals were confined, as in earlier times, mainly to teaching in segregated systems. Some worked as nurses and social workers. Since 1960 many walls have been breached. However, studies in the 1980s showed that black professionals still experienced discrimination in their occupations, being situated mainly in lower-level job categories than similarly qualified whites (Farley 1984; Landry 1987; Gelman et al. 1988).

The extent of black progress at the upper end is controversial. The impact of Affirmative Action on minority employment at its peak period of effectiveness (1965–80) was modest, accounting for possibly 1 percent faster growth in the minority share of employment than growth among non-Federal-contract compliance-monitored employers (Leonard 1994, for the Glass Ceiling Commission.) Since the collapse in 1980 of political support for the program, Affirmative Action has had no particular, observable impact. It is often said that the present black middle-class largely owes its enlargement to government employment.

This data tells us that women and minorities are continuing to earn appreciably less than white males, but it does not tell us how much is due to discrimination and how much to other factors, termed *pre-labor market experience.* The industries in which African Americans find their niche is of some relevance since some industries tend to pay higher level wages for the same work. In Table 17.2, data on black distribution by broad industrial categories shows that African Americans are more heavily represented than whites in two relatively well-paying fields: public administration, and transportation, and public utilities. Although blacks are likely to be in the lower job categories, their presence in these industries still works to their advantage, because higher paying industries tend to pay more for all job titles. On the other hand, these industries have been downsizing due to current political and economic currents, which does not bode well for the relatively new black middle-class community.

Table 17.2
Distribution of the Employed Labor Force, by Industry and Race and Median Weekly Earnings of All Full-Time Employed Wage and Salary Workers, 1997

	Employed labor force (percentages)		Median weekly earnings (dollars)
	White	Black	
Portion of total employed work force, 16 and over	84.7*	10.8	
Total	100.0	100.0	503
Mining	0.5	0.2	680
Construction	6.9	4.0	518
Manufacturing	16.0	15.4	517
Transportation and public utilities	6.8	9.8	617
Wholesale and retail trade	21.0	17.0	391
Finance, insurance, and real estate	6.5	5.7	546
Services	35.3	40.3	475
Public administration	4.1	6.8	605
Agriculture	2.9	0.8	306

* Includes some persons of Hispanic origin
Source: U.S. Department of Labor. Bureau of Labor Statistics. 1998. *Employment and Earnings* (January): Tables 39 and 43.

Failure of Black Entrepreneurship and Black Capitalism

In light of the difficulties in breaking out of limited employment possibilities in the larger society, the question arises as to why African Americans have not emulated generations of immigrants by turning to self-employment or to established employers within their own community. The answer is that many have resorted to self-employment on a very marginal level, but black business have not developed to the point of becoming a major source of employment. This remains the case today. Currently most African-American-owned businesses are local and basically mom-and-pop enterprises, only 70,000 (15%) having any paid employees. Of 425,000 black-owned businesses (2.4% of all U.S. corporations, partnerships, or sole proprietorships reported by the 91–92 Census), annual receipts averaged only $50,000. So opportunities for employment through family or community sources of employment are almost as rare as in the past (Hacker 1992).

Explanations. One view as to why black business has failed to develop is the lack of a culture of entrepreneurship, brought about by the exclusionary atmosphere in which most African Americans have lived (Myrdal 1944). The most prominent black leaders saw the need to encourage the development of business enterprises, but were not successful in convincing their constituencies or in creating circumstances that might have facilitated such a movement Booker T. Washington, in his role as advocate for a trained black labor force, in *The Negro in Business* (1907), called for the development of qualities involving the work ethic (hard work, thrift, learning of new skills, and so forth) that must arise spontaneously in communities as necessary preconditions for the development of entrepreneurship. He viewed the crowded ghettos of Black America as offering a peculiar advantage to potential black businessmen as they could offer services not available elsewhere. As a pioneer activist on behalf of black enterprise, Washington extolled business as a preferred occupation for young, educated black men, but did not succeed in convincing his target group, who perceived government—especially the postal service and teaching positions in the public schools—as the source of its best opportunities.

A second explanation of the failure of black enterprise to develop and expand was the hardening of segregationist tendencies after the Civil War. A large number of black-owned businesses existed in the North and the South, before as well as after 1865, but they failed to prosper and eventually disappeared, an outcome of abandonment by white customers and lack of buying-power on the part of poverty-stricken blacks. Blacks were driven out of areas they had dominated, catering and the building trades, and those where they had had some modest success, such as shoemaking, barbering, and sail making. After the Panic of 1875, few black businesses remained (Lee 1973).

Third, the operations of the black businessman were constrained by discriminatory legislation. For example, after the Civil Rights Act of 1875 was declared unconstitutional by the Supreme Court, black businessmen in the South were banned from "white" enterprises, such as hotels, barbershops, eateries, and theaters. Fourth, even more important, the sparsity of black-owned financial institutions, banks and insurance companies that could help with financing, discouraged entrepreneurship. Resources in existent black-owned banks were very limited; most disappeared by the time of the Great Depression, with only a few organized thereafter. Fifth, those businesses that did survive tended to attract only black customers. In the bind between impediments presented by the caste system and the lack of funding resources within black communities, most black businesses that existed prior to 1900 perished (Irons 1971).

A revisionary view of the potential of black enterprise for jobs for the African-American work force was expressed by Myrdal (1944), who concluded that black entrepreneurship could not serve as a significant source of black employment. For example, although most black stores at the time of Myrdal's 1940s survey relied solely on black customers, they captured only 5 to 10 percent of black consumer dollars. Limitations of size, type, location, and problems of obtaining credit were cited by Myrdal as reasons for the unlikelihood of significant black business expansion. The smallness of the great majority of black enterprises that contributed to inability to train the generations of managers deemed critical by Washington was another reason for Myrdal's pessimistic view of the future of black business. Business development in urban ghettos, frequently called for to retain the energies of the brightest and the best for community betterment (Foley 1968; Bates 1985), simply did not happen.

E. Franklin Frazier (1949), who studied how African Americans assimilated into the larger culture, agreed with DuBois and Myrdal that the success of black business was impeded by a scarcity of commerce-oriented skills; but he identified black business culture as the core problem, without discounting the handicaps caused by racism. A later analysis that focused on the relationship of urbanized ghetto dwellers of the North to the larger economy during the first half of the twentieth century (Bates and Fusfeld 1984) concluded that African Americans had remained poor and immobile economically because they were a good source of cheap labor that remained cheap because of intense competition for jobs. In other words, it suited the purposes of the larger community that African Americans might remain confined to the lowest levels of employment, a situation that discourages, perhaps even precludes, skill acquisition and upward mobility. In this environment social factors have an impact on young people and contribute to their unattractiveness to employers.

Rise of the Black-Capitalism Movement

Out of the ferment of President Lyndon Johnson's 1960s Great Society effort to eradicate poverty, the black-capitalism movement arose. Focused on community development, black capitalism defined the economic stagnation of black ghettos in term of lack of self-determination. Black capitalism strove for black control of business enterprises in African-American communities, a rejection of earlier leadership's goal of integration of black enterprise into the larger community. As explained by Theodore Cross (1969), black capitalism called for investment in ghetto areas and development of black entrepreneurship within these areas through private-enterprise efforts, in adamant rejection of direct governmental interventions. Financing, Cross proposed, would be through tax deductions.

Twenty years after the onset of the Great Society program, Bates and Fusfeld (1984) diagnosed the historic black entrepreneurship problem as being one of poor credit access, low educational and training possibilities, and rejection by the larger community. They concluded, however, that patterns were beginning to change: that emerging businesses were growing larger, bringing greater returns, and becoming more integrated into the larger economy.

According to a Small Business Administration report on the 1982–87 period, during these five years the number of black-owned companies rose about 38 percent to 424,000, receipts rising by 118 percent to $19 billion. This was interpreted by a prominent black industrialist in *Business Week,* November 6, 1996, as reflecting the perceptions of experienced black managers that they could rise higher through entrepreneurship than by attempting to climb within mainstream U.S. corporations. And by 1992, five years later, the number of black-owned firms climbed to 620,912, according to the *1992 Black Economic Census* (Census Bureau 1995). The down side of this situation is that most of the firms continue to be small in size. Only 10 percent of them have any employees and these collect 70 percent of total receipts. Most are in the services, especially professional services, or retail trade.

The Census Bureau attributes the increase in numbers of start-ups, mostly sole proprietorships, to the movements of a group of African Americans who are retiring at relatively young ages into self-employment. Since over half (54%) of these endeavors earned less than $10,000 in 1992 and a large number of entrepreneurs were early retirees (46%), the data suggest that in the face of downsizing, blacks along with whites are resorting to self-employment, and they are struggling. So it is that the way in which one interprets the surge in entrepreneurship within the black community depends upon whether one wishes to see the glass half empty or half full. In any case, the struggle is far from over, as the following report from the December 12, 1995, *Philadelphia Inquirer* will demonstrate.

Black Entrepreneurship in Greater Philadelphia

Philadelphia entrepreneur Carter Borden publishes a directory of black-owned business in the Greater Philadelphia area.The first directory, released in 1991, identified 300 such companies; the 1995 edition, 810. According to Borden, few of the 300 companies listed in 1991 still existed in 1995. According to an official of the West Philadelphia Enterprise Center, a training center set up to help small-business owners gain know-how, problems include undercapitalization and lack of "real business experience, sometimes resulting in inferior customer service." Companies that need small loans either for purposes of survival or expansion, usually fail to find such resources.

A Contrarion View

Despite the range of explanations offered and historical background provided about the relative absence of black entrepreneurship, the totality is not persuasive: it is widely observed that, especially since the post–World War II period, other ethnic and racial minorities have resorted to self-employment and have established and expanded businesses, some into the larger society. What has impeded African Americans? Perhaps some of the standard explanations are faulty, or perhaps the situation of African Americans is exceptional and therefore incomparable with the experience of others. Rejecting cultural explanations, Hacker (1992) suggests that both white and black men are less likely to be entrepreneurs than men belonging to more recently arrived ethnic groups. As evidence, Hacker points out that, of thirteen different ethnic groups, Korean men are most likely to be self-employed (16.5%), with whites ranking fifth (7.4%) and blacks eleventh (3.0%). Curiously, Vietnamese immigrants, highly conspicuous in the restaurant field, ranked at the bottom (2.1%) as the least likely to be self-employed.

Hacker's data suggests that present-day entrepreneurship is mainly a part of the immigrant experience. Immigrants, many believe, are a self-selected group with atypical energy and aggressiveness. The very qualities that enable their break from the home country and subsequent journey into uncertainty are the ones that drive them to self-employment in a country where their chances of obtaining mainstream jobs with the potential for upward mobility are low.

Although it has long been assumed that the unavailability of bank credit to African Americans has been a major hindrance to business development, the necessity of such credit sources for the establishment of businesses is now being questioned. Arguing against the credit-exclusion explanation, Green and Pryde (1990) point out that other minority groups have managed to start businesses without access to bank credit; they generated funds informally from family loans, clubs of friends, and rotating credit associations. And while various scholars, such as Washington, Myrdal, and Frazier, stressed the lack of business skills as a major impediment to black entrepreneurship, there is no evidence that self-employed immigrants possessed such experience at onset. In this light, it is unlikely that bank credit has been as critical a factor as it was previously supposed to be.

A development of some interest, reported anecdotally in the July 10, 1998, *New York Times*, is a trend on the part of large U.S. corporations to expand their position in the African-American community by purchasing successful black firms. This reported trend was explained as an easy way for large corporations to penetrate a growing market with considerable purchasing power. While their relinquishment of ownership was likely to be highly profitable to a few black individuals, it was denounced by Rev. Jesse Jackson, whose Rainbow Coalition campaigns for more black capitalism as a potential source of jobs for the black community. In the August 11, 1998, *New York Times,* Rev. Jackson characterized the purchases as cases of "the alligator eating the goldfish."

What is the role of the Federal government with reference to black capitalism? The government's "set-aside" program, designed to help African Americans (and other minorities and women) secure public contracts, is thought to have had little overall effect on the level of business activity among African Americans; still, according to Hacker, few beneficiary companies have been able to shed their dependence on this program.[4]

"BLACK WAGE" RATES

As already observed, jobs identified as "Negro work" traditionally bring lower wages than comparable occupations populated by whites. Myrdal interpreted these wage differentials as the outcome of the slavery system and an economic climate in which all workers were exploited by inefficient employers who needed cheap labor to survive. He wrote,"The economic backwardness of the South must be [attributed] to the rigid institutional structure of the economic life of the region which is derived from slavery, and, psychologically, rooted in the minds of the people." As late as the 1920s, African-American migration from the South was actively discouraged by agricultural interests because of the need for low-wage labor. Blacks wishing to leave often did so surreptitiously in the middle of the night. Even relatively successful blacks, such as prosperous black farmers, felt pressure to leave because any manifestation of prosperity on the part of an African American might invite violence against the person, his family, or his property. The "Negro wage" was not only a consequence of job segregation and the stigma attached to black-dominated work, but also a buttress that preserved the white superiority demanded by the caste system.

Various means were used by the Southern establishment to insure a cheap, docile, and plentiful black labor supply. Among the legal means were the vagrancy laws in eight Southern states, which permitted the police to act as labor agents for employers, such as planters, mine owners, road contractors, and turpentine farmers. If a black person were to refuse to accept an offer, he could be sentenced to a chain gang, which was rented out to a local employer at a low rate. Some employers depended on such labor, a practice wiped out by the time of Myrdal's 1940s study. However, forms of peonage remained to force blacks to remain on jobs to pay off nonexistent, concocted debts created by court fines that could not be paid. Where blacks and whites occupied the same job titles (teachers in segregated public-school systems, for example), a dual wage scale usually existed, with blacks being paid less for the same work, a practice justified as "custom." Myrdal reported that the status quo was widely practiced, rarely defended, but rationalized. Example: A university report on dual wage scales for teachers noted that the custom was "almost universal, maybe wrong but could not be ignored by the practical school administrator" (Myrdal 1944).

Black incomes rose considerably during the forty years (1940–80) following Myrdal's study, according to data from five successive national Censuses. This wage progress reflected (1) increases in the quantity and quality of human capital investment accumulated by African Americans; (2) the migration factor, the movement from South to North, rural to urban; and (3) the resurgence of the Southern economy. Average number of years and quality of black education, relative to white education, rose during this period and the wage return on black educational investments also increased over time.The equalization of years of education, however, would still not close the wage gap (Smith and Welch 1987).

Economic development in the South between 1940 and 1980 opened up opportunities for the newly urbanized black populations. Although many of the new industries were runaway plants from the North, they offered more steady, wage-paying employment than seasonal agriculture and casual work had provided. While Southern wage rates tended to be about 10 percent less for white males and 30 percent less for black males than in other areas during this period, this nevertheless represents improvement and suggests that wage discrimination was starting to fade in the South.

A dark side of the picture that possibly contributed to the narrowing wage gap was the marked withdrawal of black males from the labor force in the middle of their careers and the increasing rates of unemployment for young blacks during the 1970s and 1980s. Removal of the lowest wage earners increased the average wage rates of blacks and provided a misleading picture of African-American circumstances. Affirmative action programs greatly increased the presence of blacks in affected establishments, but it is not believed to have influenced wage differentials. Most of the wage increases occurred among younger workers and the more skilled black workers in professions and management occupations. Black college graduates made larger gains than others.

In the 1980s the African-American wage trend changed. Older blacks (those in their 30s and 40s) continued to improve their relative wage positions, but youths began to lose ground. These wage losses, together with the fall in black youths' participation in the labor force, have attracted widespread attention concerning the future of the black community.

According to 1997 BLS data, full-time black males are now earning 73 percent of white male workers' median weekly income, only a slight improvement since 1979. Black women have lost in relation to full-time white women workers, their earnings falling from 92 percent in 1979 to 84 percent in 1997. This period was one of deterioration in earning power for all men, white males losing 10 percent in real wages and blacks, 8 percent. Contrary-wise, the income of white women rose by a tenth, while that of black women, 8 percent. (Recall that both white men and women started from a higher base.) The good news is, however that as of 1997, the percentage of college-educated black males holding executive, administrative, and managerial jobs almost equals that of white college graduates, 28 percent versus 30 percent.

School Enrollment

Potential for better future earnings is contained in reports of educational attainment and trends in Black American school enrollments. According to a Census report (School Enrollment-Social and Economic Characteristics of Students, 1992), the percentage of African-American youths (18 to 24) now attending college (four-year and two-year institutions; full-time and part-time) almost doubled between 1967 and 1992, from 13 percent to 25.2 percent. With attendance for similar whites at 35.2 percent, this shows a narrowing of the gap. Bearing in mind the association of education with earned income, these CPS survey figures tend to affirm the earlier opinion of Smith and Welch that the wage gains of blacks with college degrees are responsible for the increase in black middle-class status. It should be added that Hispanics are also attending institutions of higher learning at a much higher level than in 1972, when data-keeping for Hispanics first began.[5]

Do Current Wage Differentials Indicate Continuing Wage Discrimination?

William Julius Wilson, in *When Work Disappears: the World of the New Urban Poor* (1996a), has argued that average black income (in real dollars) is falling because blacks, with the disappearance of central city manufacturing employment, must compete with women and new immigrants for available employment in the low-paying service sector.[6] Complaints about limitations on black potential remain prevalent among highly motivated black professionals and managerials, according to a series of studies made during the 1980s. Major points made by several prominent black writers on African-American professionals' and managerials' experience within U.S. corporations are enumerated below:

1. Each ethnic and minority group suffers from stereotypes within the corporation, blacks the worst. Almost all blacks think a great deal of racism existed within their plants (Fernandez 1987).
2. Most minority and female middle-level managers feel that they are "tokens" in less powerful positions than their white peers, with greater educational investment unrewarded (Fernandez 1987).
3. Blacks have to be superior performers to succeed; achieve less power and authority than white counterparts; and tend to be excluded from informal groups (Fernandez 1987).
4. Affirmative Action is seen by whites as breaking up old, shared values and the "old boys network," forcing the retirement of the "myth of the corporation as a meritocracy" (Davis and Watson 1985).
5. Both black and white managers suffer culture shock as the result of association; in addition, blacks often feel estranged from their own communities (Davis and Watson 1985).

It is clear that while some progress may be noted, African Americans with educational investments beyond the high school level continue to have employment experiences that diverge from the norm for their educational level. What to do about this situation depends on how the problem is defined. If the primary problem is continuing discrimination in hiring, job segregation, and dual pay scales, stronger enforcement of present civil-rights legislation is called for. Extension of civil-rights laws to cover plant relocations has been suggested as a measure to preserve employment (Williams 1987). If statistical discrimination is seen as a major problem, the Equal Employment Opportunity Commission needs to work more aggressively with human-resources departments to eliminate such practices as can be shown to be illegal. How attitudinal problems might be dealt with is a matter for black community organizations to deal with. If job segregation is seen as a major factor, here again pressures need to be exerted upon human–resources departments to alter discriminatory practices that have perhaps become institutionalized to a new level through their policies and practices. However, if the bottom line is that job segregation exists because it remains highly profitable to owners, then other strategies would be required.

The job segregationists have suggested that approaches involving *comparable worth* strategies be applied to racial as well as sexual wage discrimination. But, as shown earlier, the outlook for the success of the comparable worth strategy does not seem hopeful. For those whose major employment impediment is defined as inadequate human-capital investment, renewed efforts would need to be directed in the realm of education area on all levels, from improving public-school education to putting more resources into scholarship-and-work programs for able youths (of all races), which have proved successful in the past, when properly funded.

Wilson(1996a) argues for a race-neutral approach to black economic betterment, stressing the importance of renewing policies directing Federal money towards big cities for social betterment programs and of expansion of the Earned Income Tax Credit—which did occur during the late 1990s. He also pushes for Federal Reserve policies favoring expansion of the economy over curtailment of inflation as the best hope for jobs appearing for the less employable.

Wilson's call for race-neutral policies have been taken up by some black conservative; for example, a leader in the move to end racial preferences in college admissions is a black businessman. However, race-neutral approaches have not been proposed by major black community leadership. Meanwhile, since 1998 the strong economy and the tight labor market it created have buoyed black incomes up to the extent that many black family incomes have been lifted above the poverty line.[8]

NOTES

1. Readers interested in additional   pre–Civil War accounts of the black labor force experience will find a wealth of material in the Appendix in Volume 2 of Myrdal's *American Dilemma*.

2. Elijah Anderson refers to DuBois's position on the interplay between between prejudice and market pressures in his introduction to the 1996 reprint of *The Philadelphia Negro*.

3. The Seventh Ward was a political division of the city inhabited mainly by African Americans.

4. An excellent review of the issues surrounding black business establishment is offered by Shelly Green and Paul Pryde in *Black Entrepreneurship in America*.

5. Although it is sometimes stated that the good news is mitigated by the fact that a disproportionately large number of black students are in two-year institutions, this is not borne out by the facts as the percentage of black and white students (18 to 24 years of age) enrolled in two-year institutions is almost identical, about 11 percent (Census Bureau 1996).

6. In this competition they often end up without jobs altogether as employers appear to prefer other groups (women, immigrants, white youths, the elderly). The phenomenon is known as *statistical discrimination*, discussed in a previous chapter. While Wilson agrees that capable young black youths are being denied employment because of employer preferences, he does not consider employers to be motivated purely by racism, but also by their perceptions of black youths as being damaged by their environments and failed institutions (inferior education, few skills, poor work habits).

7. The Earned Income Tax Credit is discussed in a coming chapter.

8. The 1998 poverty guidelines, for a family of three, were $13,650 and for a family of four, $16,450, in the forty-eight contiguous states and D.C. (*Federal Register* 63, no. 36 [February 24]: 9235–38).

REFERENCES

Bates, Timothy, and Daniel R. Fusfeld. 1984. *The political economy of the urban ghetto*. Carbondale: Southern Illinois University.

DuBois, W. E. B. 1899. *The Negro in business*. New York: AMS Press, 1971. (Reprint).

Cross, Theodore. 1969. *Black capitalism*. New York: Athenaeum.

Farley, Reynolds. 1984. *Blacks and whites: narrowing the gap?* Cambridge, Mass.: Harvard University Press.

Fernandez, John. 1987. *Survival in the corporate fish bowl: making it into upper and middle management*. Lexington, Mass.: D.C. Heath and Company.

Foley, Eugene. 1968. *The achieving ghetto*. Washington, D.C.: National Press.

Frazier, E. Franklin. 1949. *The Negro in the United States*. New York: Macmillan.

Gelman, David, and colleagues. 1988. Black and white America. *Newsweek*, 7 March.

Genovese, Eugene. 1961. *The political economy of slavery: studies in the economy and society of the slave South*. New York: Vintage Books.

Green, Shelley, and Paul Pryde. 1990. *Black entrepreneurship in America*. New Brunswick, N.J.: Transaction Publishers.

Hacker, Andrew. 1992. *Two nations: black and white, separate, hostile, unequal*. New York: Charles Scribners Sons.

Hershberg, Theodore. 1971. Free blacks in antebellum Philadelphia: a study of ex-slaves, freeborn, and socioeconomic decline. *Journal of Social History* 5 (Winter):183–209.

Irons, Edward D. 1971. Black banking problems and prospects. *The Journal of Finance* 26, no.1 (March): 407–26.

Kornweibel, Jr., Theodore. 1976. An economic profile of black life in the twenties. *Journal of Black Studies* 6 (June): 307–20.

Landry, Bart. 1987. *The new black middle class*. Berkeley and Los Angeles: University of California Press.

Leonard, Jonathan. 1994. Use of enforcement techniques in eliminating glass ceilings barriers. Prepared for the Glass Ceiling Commission, U.S. Department of Labor. Washington, D.C.: U.S. Dept. of Labor, Glass Ceiling Commission (April).

Lee, Roy F. 1973. *The setting for black business development*. Ithaca: Cornell University Press.

Myrdal, Gunnar. 1944. *An American dilemma: the Negro problem and modern democracy*. New York: Harper & Row Publishers (Anniversary Edition. 1962. New York: Random House).

Smith, James P., and Finis Welch. 1987. Race and poverty: a forty-year record. *AEA Papers and Proceedings* 77, no. 2 (May).

Sokoloff, Natalie J. 1992. *Black women and white women in the professions: occupational segregation by race and gender, 1960–1980*. New York: Routledge.

U.S. Department of Commerce. U.S. Bureau of the Census. 1992. School enrollment: social and economic characteristics of students. *Current Population Reports* (October).

———. 1995. *Black economic census, 1992*. Washington, D.C.: Governmen Printing Office.

———. 1995. *Characteristics of the black population*. Washington, D.C.: Government Printing Office.

U.S. Department of Education. National Center for Education Statistics.1996. *The .condition of education. Washington, D.C.: Government Printing Office.*

U.S. Department of Labor. Bureau of Labor Statistics. 1997. *Employment and Earnings* 44 (January): Table 37.

———. 1998. *Employment and Earnings* 45 (January): Table 10, Employed Persons by occupation, race, and sex; Table 17, Employed Persons by industry, sex, race, and occupation;Table 39, Median weekly earnings of full-time wage and salary workers by selected characteristics; Table 43, Median weekly earnings of full-time wage and salary workers by union affiliation, occupation, and industry (total work force figures only).

Washington, Booker T. 1907. *The Negro in business.* Chicago: Afro-American Press, 1969 (Reprint).

Williams, Bruce. 1987. *Black workers in an industrial suburb.* New Brunswick, N.J.: Rutgers University Press.

Wilson, William Julius. 1987. *The truly disadvantaged: the inner city, the under class, and public policy.* Chicago: University of Chicago Press.

———. 1996a. *When work disappears: the world of the new urban poor.* New York: Alfred A. Knopf.

———. 1996b. The Levy Report interview. In *The Report*, Jerome Levy Economics Institute of Bard College, (February): 6–11.

Part VII

Unemployment

The subject of unemployment commands interest for two reasons: its effect on the welfare of individuals and its impact on the economy. The focus of public and professional interest has shifted over the past 60 to 70 years from concerns about the human toll to concerns for business stability. When the nation was basically concerned about impact on people, public policies were designed to stimulate the economy, while simultaneously attempting to ease the pain of the unemployed and their families through social programs. In recent years economists and associated policy-makers have focused on how to maintain a level of unemployment necessary to forestall an undesirably high level of inflation. During the mid-1990s people-oriented interest in unemployment was revived briefly by news media reports of massive layoffs in large corporations during "good-times." As unemployment fell to levels previously considered unattainable in a situation of economic stability (i.e., without accompanying inflation), however, interest in joblessness again was reduced mainly to how to maintain the moratorium on wage and price escalation.

Since this book's focus is on the labor force, the discussion of unemployment emphasizes employment impacts as opposed to broader economic issues. Chapter 18 offers some statistics on the extent and distribution of unemployment by various dimensions and describes several different types of unemployment. How unemployment is measured and some deficiencies in this area are also commented upon. Chapter 19 discusses the matter of whether people feel less secure in their employment than formerly and presents a series of suggested remedies for unemployment.

18

The Distribution, Types, and Measurement of Unemployment

THE EXTENT AND DISTRIBUTION OF UNEMPLOYMENT

Unemployment is a phenomenon that exists at all times, but to varying extents, both in terms of time periods and groups affected. The most horrendous period of unemployment during the period of modern record keeping occurred in 1933, the height of the Great Depression, when 24.9 percent of the workforce was out of work; the least unemployment, 1.2 percent, in 1944, during World War II (BLS 1993). Table 18.1 shows the upward and downward swings of the unemployment rate between 1929 and 1998 (second quarter).

Differential Distribution by Gender, Race, and Ethnicity

Unemployment tends to be unequally distributed among groups. Until recently economists blamed much of the rising unemployment of the 1970s and 1980s on new groups coming into paid employment, especially women. However, a comparison of male-female unemployment rates shows them to be basically converging. Some years men experience less joblessness than women; other years, more. Race, ethnicity (Hispanic origin), and age are more important variables in terms of describing relative joblessness. Blacks experience roughly double the unemployment of whites; persons of Hispanic origin, 65 to 90 percent more, depending on the year. See Table 18.2 for figures for selected years.

Differences by Industry and Occupation

The industry in which an individual is employed appears to have an effect on the probability of unemployment. Some industries consistently report higher unemployment rates than others, construction and agricultural work (wage and salary) being the leaders. Each reported between 9 to 10 percent unemployment

Table 18.1
Annual Unemployment Rates from 1929 to 1998*

(Percentages)

Year	(14 years and over)	Year	(16 years and over)	Year		Year	
1929	3.2	1947	3.9	1965	4.5	1983	9.5
1930	8.7	1948	3.9	1966	3.8	1984	7.5
1931	15.9	1949	5.9	1967	3.8	1985	7.2
1932	23.6	1950	5.3	1968	3.6	1986	7.0
1933	24.9	1951	3.3	1969	3.7	1987	6.2
1934	21.7	1952	3.0	1970	4.9	1988	5.5
1935	20.1	1953	2.9	1971	5.9	1989	5.3
1936	16.9	1954	5.5	1972	5.6	1990	5.6
1937	14.3	1955	4.4	1973	4.9	1991	6.8
1938	19.0	1956	4.1	1974	5.6	1992	7.5
1939	17.2	1957	4.3	1975	8.3	1993	6.9
1940	14.6	1958	6.8	1976	7.6	1994	6.1
1941	9.9	1959	5.5	1977	6.9	1995	5.6
1942	4.7	1960	5.5	1978	6.0	1996	5.4
1943	1.9	1961	6.7	1979	5.8	1997	4.9
1944	1.2	1962	5.5	1980	7.0	1998	4.4**
1945	1.9	1963	5.7	1981	7.5		
1946	3.9	1964	5.2	1982	9.5		

* Not seasonally adjusted. ** Second quarter

Source: U.S. Department of Labor. Bureau of Labor Statistics. *Employment and Earnings* Various volumes (January); *Monthly Labor Review* 121, no. 9 (September 1998): Table 1.

Table 18.2
Unemployment Rates by Race and Hispanic Origin and Gender, Selected Years*

	1982	1987	1992	1997
Total, 16 years and over				
(Percentages)				
White	9.7	6.2	7.4	4.9
Males, 20 years and over	8.4	5.3	6.5	4.2
Females, 20 years and over	7.8	4.8	6.3	3.6
	7.3	4.6	5.4	3.7
Blacks	18.9	13.0	14.1	10.0
Males, 20 years and over	17.8	11.1	13.4	8.5
Females, 20 years and over	15.4	11.6	11.7	8.8
Hispanic origin	13.8	8.8	11.4	7.7
Males, 20 years and over	N.A.	N.A.	N.A.	6.1
Females, 20 years and over	N.A.	N.A.	N.A.	7.9

*Civilian noninstitutional population, 16 years and over, unless otherwise specified.
Source: U.S. Department of Labor. Bureau of Labor Statistics. *Employment and Earnings* (January): 1983, Tables A-44; 1988, Tables A-34; 1993, Tables A-34; 1998, Tables D-16.

during 1996 and 1997, while two broad fields—finance, insurance, and real estate; and government employment—reported the least, no more than 3 percent (*Monthly Labor Review* 1998). Unemployment has also tended to be particularly high in certain areas of manufacturing, such as the apparel and textile products industries (near 10 percent), and, some years, in the services industries (except professional services), near 8 percent in December 1997 (BLS 1998). These 8 to 10 percent levels of unemployment occurred during a period when overall unemployment was 5.5 percent. Because of the big differences in job stability, industry of previous employment is believed to be an important variable in explaining job search behavior of the unemployed, that is, the hesitancy of many displaced workers to seek work in another industry.

In regard to occupational differences in unemployment, traditionally, the higher employed persons are on the hierarchy of occupations, the less likely they are to suffer unemployment. Despite the tremors set off by the 1990s downsizing of the elite, this still holds true. Persons in the managerial and professional occupations have unemployment rates roughly 40 percent of the overall rate and persons in white-collar occupations (technical, sales, and administrative support), about 80 percent. And skilled craftsmen (precision production, craft, and repair workers with the exception of construction laborers) also have less than average unemployment, in some cases, as low as 2.5 percent. The high unemployment occupations are the services (other than protective services); the relatively unskilled blue-collar group (operators, fabricators, and laborers); and farming, forestry, and fishing occupations. For example, the service occupations, in the extraordinarily low overall unemployment environment of 4.4 percent of December 1997, reported 5.7 percent out-of-work; the operators, fabricators, and laborers; 6.6 percent, and farming, forestry, and fishing, 9.7 percent (BLS 1998).[1]

Other Factors: Age and Female-Headed Households by Race

Age Factors. Age and gender are factors that further affect an individual's employment stability. Young people ages sixteen to nineteen tend to experience very high rates of unemployment that have the effect of distorting the overall picture. For example, in December 1997, when the overall unemployment rate was 4.4 percent, the unemployment rate for sixteen to nineteen-year-old blacks was 29.4 percent; for youths of Hispanic origin, 18.8 percent; for white youths, 8.4 percent. It is for this reason that BLS, in reporting unemployment rates, includes the rate for persons twenty years and over (BLS 1998).

Gender, Race, and Household Status. Women as a group are actually experiencing less unemployment than men. Those who are heads of households (widowed, divorced, separated, or never married, as opposed to married women with spouse present), however, suffer relatively high rates. For example, in December 1997, when overall unemployment among women was 4.2 percent, unemployment among female heads of households ranged from 4.8 percent among the widowed, divorced, or separated to 6.9 percent among single women, never-married (BLS 1998).[2]

The same body of data showed the unemployment among African-American women (16 and over) to be far higher than for white women in all categories, as shown here:

	White	Black
Married, spouse present	2.3%	4.7%
Widowed, divorced, or separated	4.2%	7.2%
Single (never married)	5.4%	12.7%

These figures on unemployment by race and household status are cited as background for a subsequent discussion of "welfare reform" and the potential for success of the women involved in achieving economic independence, which is addressed in a later chapter.

Educational Attainment and Unemployment

Since education has become the favored instrument for social remedy in U.S. society, its impact on the unemployment rates of disadvantaged groups is necessarily of interest. As noted above, although the increased presence of working women is often proffered as a reason for increasing overall-unemployment levels, this does not seem to be the case. The same is true in regard to the impact of additional education on female unemployment. In 1996, for example, for persons twenty-five and over, the unemployment rates for males with bachelor's degrees or above were 2.1 percent and for females of the same attainment, 2.4 percent. The gender gap is no longer a great issue in terms of impact on unemployment. Educational attainment makes a great difference, however, in reducing unemployment when ethnicity and race are involved, as shown on Table 18.3. While African Americans and Hispanics experience more joblessness than whites at all comparable levels, their gain from human-capital investment is more significant. For example, while the unemployment rates of black adults (those 25 and older) who hold high-school diplomas only was 9.1 percent in 1996, the rate for those with college degrees was 3.1 percent, not far from the rate for whites, which was 2.1 percent. Put another way, black college graduates experienced only one-third as much unemployment as high school graduates. Greater educational investment also markedly helps Hispanics increase their employment stability. In 1996, 6.6 percent of all Hispanic adults over twenty-five who were limited to high-school education were unemployed, but only 3.8 percent of those who were college graduates were jobless. In other words, four-year degrees halved the unemployment of Hispanics who held them. For reasons unclear, black high-school graduates experience more unemployment than Hispanics, but when they possess a bachelor's degree (or more), they experience a slightly lower unemployment rate.

The often remarked-upon extraordinarily high unemployment rates of black and Hispanic youths are also shown on Table 18.3. The rates do fall with age, but this does not necessarily mean that they are gradually absorbed into the workforce. Many may be out of the labor force altogether by their mid-twenties. Note that the statistics given are for those who are not enrolled in school, that is, school dropouts and those who do not go beyond high school. The issues involved are beyond the scope of this book, but point to the differences that credentials, if not education itself, make when determining an individual's chances for economic stability.

Table 18.3
Unemployment by Educational Attainment, Race/Ethnicity, and Age, 1996

Race/Ethnicity and Highest Degree Attained	Percent Unemployed 1996*		
	16–19 years**	20–24 years**	25 years and over
White***			
All educational levels	14.2%	7.8%	3.7%
Less than high school graduate	17.0	16.0	8.0
High-school graduate, no college	12.2	8.9	4.0
Associate degree	14.5	3.9	3.0
Bachelor's degree or higher	2.9	5.1	2.1
Black***			
All educational levels	33.6	18.8	7.7
Less than high-school graduate	37.6	38.2	12.6
High-school graduate, no college	31.5	20.0	9.1
Associate degree	—	10.0	5.5
Bachelor's degree or higher	—	6.0	3.1
Hispanic Origin***			
All educational levels	23.6	11.8	7.1
Less than high-school graduate	26.1	11.8	7.1
High-school graduate, no college	20.7	11.5	6.6
Associate degree	—	7.5	4.9
Bachelor's degree or higher	—	8.0	3.8

* The unemployment rate is the percent of individuals in the labor force who are not working, and who made specific efforts to find work sometime during the prior four weeks. ** Excludes persons enrolled in school. *** Includes persons of Hispanic origin. ****Persons of Hispanic origin may be of any race.
Source: U.S. Department of Education. 1990. National Center for Education Statistics. *Digest of Education Statistics* NCES 98-015. Washington, D.C.: Government Printing Office, Table 377.

TYPES OF UNEMPLOYMENT

Readers who are accustomed to hearing about *the* unemployment rate may be surprised to learn that economists differentiate joblessness into several categories, all of which are lumped together in one published figure. These categories, or types, are: *cyclical, seasonal, frictional,* and *structural.* Sometimes *seasonal* and short-term *frictional* unemployment are lumped together and labeled *normal unemployment.* And cyclical unemployment is often termed *demand-deficit* unemployment. Most economists and the public as a whole direct most of their attention to *cyclical* unemployment, with the other types attracting consideration only during periods when the country is agreeable to active policies aiming for amelioration or remedy. Brief explanations of the four major types are summarized below. Readers will see that agreement does not always exist as to the nature of observed unemployment.

Cyclical (Demand-Deficit) Unemployment

Cyclical (or *demand-deficit*) unemployment occurs periodically when employers' need for workers is lower than the number of persons who desire employment. Economists may express this in terms of the numbers of vacancies being fewer than the number of persons seeking employment. When need falls, according to theory, employers can either reduce the number of persons employed or reduce wages. It is generally believed that employers faced with these choices tend to reduce the number of persons on their payrolls. Discussions of *demand-deficit* unemployment generally include comments on the *downward rigidity of wages,* that is, how difficult it is, in practice, to reduce wage rates. Economists have also noted that *durations* of *unemployment* are becoming longer than during earlier periods, adding to the sufferings associated with this type of unemployment (Summers 1990); Baker 1992). Varying explanations for the existence of the *business cycle* (periodic fluctuations in demand) may be found in texts on macroeconomics and in such popular works as Paul Krugman's *Peddling Prosperity* (1994).

The levels of cyclical unemployment have been rising since the 1950s, especially since 1973. This is true not only of the United States, but throughout the industrialized countries of the West. The reasons most often advanced (but not necessarily agreed upon throughout the economics profession) are:

1. Slowing economic growth since 1973, reasons for which are hotly debated.
2. Demographic factors, that is, more youths and women are in the labor force, a questionable statement with reference to the latter group.
3. The increasing difficulties of individual countries using traditional methods (e.g., Keynesian) to stimulate their economies in view of globalization.[3] Kuttner (1997) argues that the current lack of a world regulatory system (such as the Bretton Woods system which lasted until 1973) causes economies to contract and discourages growth.
4. The belief in the importance of maintaining the *natural rate of unemployment* (discussed below), which also discourages growth. The Federal Reserve Board's adherence to the concept of the *natural rate of unemployment* in making its decisions as to interest rates is seen as antigrowth by liberal commentators, such as

Eisner (1995), Kuttner (1997), and Krugman (1994). Put another way, willingness to permit more inflation, some liberal economists predict, would likely generate more jobs and thus lower unemployment rates. Conservative economists, the majority, prefer to concentrate on economic stability. Not all conservative economists, however, are necessarily convinced that they can pinpoint the exact level at which unemployment should exist (i.e., the *natural rate*).

Another Explanation for Rising Unemployment. Some insightful investigations have been performed by Summers (1990). Using data from BLS's *Employment and Earnings* for the period July 1953 to July 1986, Summers found business cycles over this period to be exhibiting new characteristics. Not only have the troughs (worst phases) of recent recessions been worse than previously, but unemployment in the peaks (most robust periods) of each business cycle have also been rising. The peaks and troughs that Summers observed during the exemplary 33 years between July 1953 and July 1986 indicate that unemployment rates in the "best of times" actually rose after 1979 and became as high as unemployment in the "worst of times," during most earlier several cycles within the period observed. Summer's basic data is summarized below:

Unemployment rate (%)

Cycle (peak to peak)	Peak	Trough
July 1953–July 1957	2.5%	5.7%
Aug. 1957–Mar. 1960	4.0	7.2
Apr. 1960–Nov. 1969	5.1	6.7
Dec. 1969–Oct. 1973	3.4	5.7
Nov. 1973–Dec. 1979	4.8	8.4
Jan. 1980–June 1981	6.2	7.7
July 1981–July 1986	7.1*	10.6*

* Not fully observed at time of writing.
Source: Summers, 1990. *Understanding Unemployment*, Chapter 9, Table 9, p. 289.

On the basis of his study of the 1953-1986 period, Summers concluded that a large number of mature men (ages 35–44) who had held high-wage jobs and who remained unemployed for a long period of time (more than 26 weeks) accounted for most of the unemployment throughout the thirty-three-year period. Summers speculated that one reason for the increasing length of unemployment spells might be reluctance to accept low-wage replacement jobs, thus rejecting as without basis in fact the oft-used explanation that the changed composition of the labor force (that is, the inclusion of more women, youths, and minorities) is responsible for persistently higher levels of unemployment.

A second study by Summers of variations in state and regional unemployment rates for the period 1970–85 led him to the same conclusions: that the persistence of high levels of unemployment was rooted in a drastic restructuring of the economy, which lessened the number of available high-wage jobs and increased the proportion of low-wage ones. Summers again attributed the prolonged unemployment of the period, which raised overall unemployment levels, to laid-off workers' persistence in seeking their reservation wage. In other words, Summers emphasizes the role of *duration of unemployment spells* to help explain rising unemployment.

Generally speaking, extant data continues to be insufficient for an understanding of the increasing levels of unemployment as well as other developments. During the late 1970s and 1980s a new phenomenon occurred that is not supposed to happen, according to standard theory: high levels of price inflation accompanied by high levels of unemployment. Dubbed *stagflation*, this new development defied the belief that high levels of inflation are accompanied by low levels of unemployment. And economists are unable to explain the long recovery following the 1990–91 recession in which annual unemployment dropped as low as 4.4 percent without attendant rise in inflation rates. One possible explanation sometimes offered is that the Federal Reserve Board has amassed enough foresight, cleverness, and know-how to tame the business cycle once and for all. Not many bets have been placed on this one thus far.

The NAIRU. In a discussion of unemployment and inflation, it is impossible to avoid the subject of the NAIRU, the acronym for the "non-accelerating inflation rate of unemployment," the mystical figure alluded to above that represents the amount of inflation necessary to maintain an acceptable level of inflation or business stability. Since the late 1950s when an English economist, A.W. Phillips (1958), produced a curve showing a historical association between unemployment and inflation, mainstream economists have tended to take the position that low unemployment *causes* inflation and, subsequently, that the amount of unemployment required to keep inflation at a low level needs to be maintained as a matter of public policy. This necessary amount of unemployment, labeled *the natural rate of unemployment*, is usually set at 5 to 6 percent or slightly above. Insofar as levels of unemployment during the post 1990–91 recovery receded *without* an accompanying rise in the level of inflation, the whole concept has been brought into question. However, except for a few liberals who favor emphasis on the human side of the unemployment-inflation relationship, mainstream economists, as of this writing, have not yet thrown in the towel on the NAIRU as their guiding principle, a subject discussed further in the next chapter.

Normal Unemployment: Seasonal and Short-Term Frictional

Some unemployment exists in the best of times. Termed *normal unemployment*, joblessness so characterized elicits little concern unless it becomes prolonged. There are two types of normal unemployment: *short-term frictional* and *seasonal* unemployment.[4] *Short-term frictional* unemployment describes situations such as that of students who are looking for jobs after graduation and the job-search period of people who have left jobs voluntarily to seek new ones. The employment status of a woman seeking to reenter the labor force after a spell of exclusive motherhood would be that of *short-term frictional* unemployment. There are also those persons who are hired to sell ice cream in the summer; farm laborers; and those who work in the apparel industry, which responds to needs sporadically during different periods of the year. Such persons are said to be subject to *seasonal* unemployment.

The level of *normal unemployment* (the sum of *seasonal* and *short-term frictional*) has been rising since World War II when it was thought to be 2 percent. In the 1950s it rose to 3 percent; in the 1960s, to 5 percent; and, since the 1970s, up to 6 percent or more at some points in time. Although economists have developed *job search* theories to explain the continuing high rates of unemployment attributed to these two types of joblessness, the public's attention in recent years has not been directed toward reducing or ameliorating normal unemployment.

Short-term Frictional Unemployment. Economists attribute the existence of what they call *short-term frictional* unemployment to imperfect information on the part of job seekers and prospective employers. If all job-seekers knew exactly where vacancies existed and which employers were ready to meet their *reservation wage* demands, no time would have to be spent in job search. However, in lieu of perfect information, time elapses as job-seeker and employer find each other. In the best of times, there will always be some frictional unemployment. The level of frictional unemployment depends upon the extent to which individuals enter and leave the labor force and the pace at which job-seekers reenter employment (Ehrenberg and Smith 1994).

The economists' focus on the issue of job search in discussing short-term frictional unemployment is in line with the belief of current mainstream economists that there would be no unemployment if everyone would accept existing jobs, irrespective of wage level. Most unemployment is considered essentially voluntary by the frictionalists, who see job-seekers as constantly weighing the costs and returns of further job search versus acceptance of jobs immediately available. In contrast, the involuntary nature of (cyclical) unemployment is emphasized by earlier theorists.[5]

Seasonal Unemployment. Although overall normal unemployment may be rising, the seasonal portion has been falling. According to recent BLS studies (Rydzewski, Deming, and Rones 1993), a little-noticed dramatic decline has occurred over the past thirty years (1960–90). In 1960, 40 percent of workers who were employed within a given year were seasonal workers, whereas by 1990 this had fallen to 31 percent. This is true throughout all of private industry and all demographic groups. Changing technologies that minimize the need for seasonal labor are one explanation proposed. A second is the greater use of part-time workers to meet seasonal requirements. This proposed explanation raises the question of whether the statisticians are engaging in a relabeling game. Has seasonal unemployment actually fallen? It is unclear. A third possibility is women's growing preference for full-time work, a prerequisite for higher earnings and a career. Another proposed explanation is a shift of population toward temperate climates, which reduces employment swings in weather-sensitive industries. Another contributory factor may lie in the decline of the garment industry in which many seasonal workers were employed in the recent past.

Why workers accept seasonal work when they know it will lead to periodic unemployment is a question that defies definite answer. The fact that jobs with limited duration sometimes pay higher than usual wages for comparable year-round jobs [6] is sometimes cited as suggestive that the seasonal status of such person's unemployment spells is voluntary in nature (Ehrenberg and Smith 1994). It has also been argued that generous Unemployment Insurance benefits (discussed in the final section of this book, encourage acceptance of seasonal work (Topel 1984). The argument that seasonal unemployment is at least partially involuntary has been made on the basis that most persons, once on a job, prefer to remain (Ehrenberg and Smith 1994).

Structural Unemployment

The fourth type of unemployment is termed *structural*. Since around the 1960s evidences of unemployment loosely lumped together under this umbrella term have interested economists. Technically a form of *long-run frictional* unemployment, structural unemployment includes the job losses that follow basic changes in the characteristics of the economy. Structuralists tend to explain this type of unemployment as being primarily caused by variations in demand for certain types of workers over time, the high cost of geographic relocation from areas of falling demand to those where openings exist, the high costs of retraining, and the failure of wages in faltering industries and occupations within geographic areas to fall to levels where demand might reappear. Perhaps the most important structural change (already alluded to) is loss of manufacturing jobs, especially in the durable-goods industries, which paid high wages to workers with relatively low level skills.

Unemployment Among the Disadvantaged. Inner-city residents of large, old urban centers are often included among the low-end of the structurally unemployed, their plight being attributed to human-capital deficits and movements of large-scale, basic industries out of big cities of the United States. Some analysts would add racism as a factor. During Johnson's War on Poverty period, these groups were often labeled *the disadvantaged,* and special programs were devised to help them into mainstream unemployment. Particular concern focuses on the persisting high unemployment rate of black youths, which is 30 percent among sixteen-to nineteen-year-olds, as opposed to 11.4 percent for whites and 17.6 percent for Hispanic youths during a period of overall prosperity (fourth quarter 1997; BLS 1998).

Unemployment among the Advantaged. During the 1980s and early 1990s, the suspicion arose that a new type of *structural* unemployment, was evolving that could not be explained in terms of the above concepts. In the period prior to the 1990–91 recession, large companies began to lay off thousands of employees on all levels. This continued unabated throughout both the recession and during at least seven years of the subsequent recovery period. Public reaction was strong, partly, it has been speculated, because managerials and professionals were affected; heretofore, unemployment was seen by this articulate group as an affliction reserved for blue-collar workers. Perplexity about the new "unemployment of the recovery" was exacerbated by continuing layoffs by large, prospering firms that do not appear to be related to *deficit demand* nor to *structural* issues.

As early as 1982 Barry Bluestone and Bennett Harrison, in the *Deindustrialization of America*, a report commissioned by Congress, charged that large companies were moving work overseas, not because their businesses were unprofitable to operate in the United States, but to reach some higher level of profitability desired by the company, for example, 22 percent versus a U.S.-based 15 percent. And, after the official close of the 1990–91 recession (July 1991), a confused public was perplexed by reports of continuing staff cuts, numbering into the tens of thousands in some cases, by the industrial giants. This led to a public outcry as to why a "jobless recovery?" (Mishel and Bernstein 1993). Why so much unemployment in "good times?" As for the unemployment rate, after the close of the 1990–91 recession it was *above* the 1990–91 rate for three years before it began its downward trend—which continued to spectacularly low levels (Refer to Table 18.1 again).

The following are some of the major explanations given during the early *downsizing* period.

1. Factory work, including many of the so-called good jobs and some service jobs, as well, were being moved overseas; and some of the exodus may have been facilitated by the passage in 1992 of NAFTA, the North American Free Trade Act.
2. American industrial giants, no longer protected oligarchies, were shrinking their bloated managerial staffs.
3. Changes in job *status* were occurring for the purpose of reducing labor costs by laying off employees and replacing them by workers in alternative work arrangements, sometimes the same workers (an undocumented allegation discussed in an earlier chapter).

Other explanations for large scale reductions in staff by large corporations include staff curtailments due to corporate mergers; losses experienced as conglomerates have returned to their core businesses; and losses due to financial excesses, such as the bank and savings and loan scandals of recent years. By 1997 much of the profits to be squeezed out of downsizing had occurred, with employers moving on to new methods of raising profits. However, by late 1998, with the threat of a recession in the air, large-scale layoffs by large corporations again commenced, some directly attributable to impacts of recessions in progress in Asia and other areas. The actual impact on overall employment is unknown, as of this writing.

Location as a Factor. Some current structural unemployment has been attributed to regional variations in demand for labor. The right-to-work states of the South and Southwest have attracted runaway industry from the Northeast and Midwest, leaving behind experienced blue-collar workers who lack the skills needed in many of the available service-sector jobs. Other factors, such as age or union histories, may also interfere with these workers being absorbed into the lower-paying service-sector jobs. The same is occurring within areas. As discussed in an early chapter, the trend is for business to leave the big cities and move to suburbs, if not farther. City-suburban moves have tended to leave central-city workers, especially minorities, geographically isolated from available opportunities. This exodus leaves only a mix of high-paid and low-paid service-type jobs, with the better-paying service-sector jobs now requiring enough education to exclude a large portion of the city population. The situation is often described as involving skill-mismatch, considered to be a major factor in structural unemployment, and it has not responded to remedial efforts.

Relocation as an Option. Although relocation is difficult for older workers and migration on behalf of job opportunities was shown earlier to be largely an option undertaken by the young, a high level of state-to-state movements for the purpose of employment does take place. Though unemployment rates among the states may differ markedly short-run, *long run*, the mobility statistics show that they tend to even out as states with greater-than-average unemployment tend to move toward the national average within a few years. This is taken to indicate that enough of the unemployed and new entrants move away from states with high levels of unemployment and into states with high levels of demand for persons of their occupations or educational preparation to even out the state unemployment averages towards the national norm (Blanchard and Katz 1992). However, another view, while not contesting these findings, is that some amount of difference in unemployment persists because of varying industries and mix of occupational opportunities in different locations (Filer, Hamermesh and Rees 1996; Marston 1985).

*Wage Rigidities and Retraining Costs.*The tendency of wages for occupations with falling demand to be rigid or to fall insufficiently to permit retention of present staff or hiring of more personnel is generally held to be one of the major causes of structural unemployment (as is the case with cyclical unemployment). A second cause is the high cost of retraining for more sought-after occupations, a possibility often untenable for older persons whose future work life would be too short to justify such a human capital investment. It is also unlikely that such persons would be considered for available openings by would-be employers, laws against age discrimination to the contrary.

MEASUREMENT OF UNEMPLOYMENT

The History

This portion of the chapter deals with how unemployment is measured. Few statistics are more widely followed than those on unemployment. An administration's popularity is often influenced by the public's perceptions of economic prosperity, these statistics being one gauge. Many questions have been raised about the quality of Labor Department data and presentations, what they tell us, what is omitted. Also of concern is whether all of those unemployed, according to BLS definitions, are being included in the count. During the Great Depression Federal policy-makers developed unemployment policies without accurate information. To remedy this situation, during the late 1930s a systematic effort to gather unemployment statistics through the device of a *monthly household survey* was initiated, the original agency evolving into the present Census Bureau, now located in the Department of Commerce. The Census Bureau, together with the Department of Labor Statistics, located in the Department of Labor, are responsible for gathering the statistics upon which we mainly depend for basic knowledge of the population, the labor force, and wages and hours data. The Bureau of the Census conducts what is known as the Civilian Population Survey (CPS) while the Department of Labor collects *establishment data* through a Current Employment Statistics (CES) survey. Efforts have been made, over the years, to keep both these data-collecting agencies highly professional and non-political. The quality of sampling has been state-of-the-art. However, with repeated budget cuts, some deterioration has been reported. And, complaints are made periodically as to how these agencies interpret the data they collect and omissions in data collection.

Data Collection. For the Civilian Population Survey (CPS), the Census Bureau sends trained interviewers door-to-door to about 50,000 households, considered to be a representative sample of the nation, as a whole, each month to gather desired information from a household member available when the interviewer comes. *Establishment data*, employer reports on numbers on payrolls and wages and hours, are collected by the Bureau of Labor Statistics, in cooperation with state agencies, by mailing questionnaires to a representative sample of about 390,000 employers who report on their 48 million nonagricultural wage and salary workers. This data provides the basis for the Current Employment Statistics (CES), reports on employment levels, hours, and weekly earnings for all full-time and part-time workers. The data for both CPS and the CES pertain to the situation existing on the calendar week of the interview including the twelfth day of the month. Data from the CPS probability sample is analyzed by the Bureau of Labor Statistics (BLS).

The sampling techniques of the Census Department used in making the Current Population Survey of households for the nation, as a whole, do not lend themselves to satisfactory analysis by smaller units (by state or city, for example). Reports for states and localities are based on other models, involving use of data from the CPS, state employment agencies, and Unemployment Insurance reports. Unemployment statistics may or may not be labeled *seasonally adjusted* In seasonally adjusted data, the amounts of seasonal unemployment occurring during various months is spread evenly throughout the year (BLS *Handbook of Methods* 1992).

Definitions and Categories. In making the count the CPS survey categorizes persons considered to qualify as unemployed into three groups: (1) *part-time* workers who consider themselves part of the full-time labor force, but who are working part-time for "economic reasons" (i.e., involuntarily); (2) presently unemployed full-time workers who are seeking full-time replacement jobs; and (3) unemployed part-time workers who are seeking part-time replacement jobs. *Duration* of *unemployment* is also reported, the term *long-term unemployed* being the designation for persons without work more than twenty-six weeks. CPS utilizes the following categories to identify the unemployed by cause: (1) *job losers*, (2) *job leavers*, (3) *reentrants*, and (4) *new entrants. Job losers* are persons who lose jobs or are laid off who immediately start to seek replacement jobs. *Job leavers* are those who leave jobs voluntarily and who commence immediate job search. *Reentrants* are persons who previously worked full-time for at least two work weeks who lost their jobs and have been out of the labor force for some time prior to initiating their job search. *New entrants* are persons who have never been employed full-time who are seeking work.

Students of unemployment believe that understanding *which* categories the unemployed fall in, at any particular point in time, is critical to understanding the nature of unemployment. One criticism of the interviewing job done by the Census Bureau's CPS workers is that distinctions between these four characterizations of the unemployed are often blurred and incorrectly reported, severely reducing the value of the data. Norwood (1993), long-time director of the BLS, advocated for years for better differentiating between the employed, unemployed, and and those out of the workforce.

Conceptual and Methodological Problems. The extent of unemployment at any given time is controversial because of conceptual and methodological problems in data collection. Some 1993 changes are expected to result in increase in the reported unemployment rate. This change is expected to have political significance in view of the importance attributed to the published figures. For example, in October 1993 BLS's quarterly unemployment index, which included *discouraged workers*, was 10.2 percent, as opposed to the widely publicized 6.8 percent (*New York Times*. November 17, 1993). Recall that a *discouraged worker* is a once employed person who has ceased job search because of morale reasons. Whether such persons should be included in the overall unemployment count is always controversial. BLS does *not* include them in most reports, but data can be obtained from the *Employment Situations News Release*, obtainable from any BLS office, or on the Internet (BLS Internet address: stats.bls.gov.).

The goal of the 1993 changes (and other changes) is to leave less to the judgment of the interviewer. In addition to the discouraged worker problem, unemployed women at home during the survey visit, for example, have often been mistakenly classified as *housewives* without further questioning. And persons who reported permanently lost jobs as *layoffs* have mistakenly been classified as "waiting to be recalled." It is expected that CPS treatment of the *contingent workforce* will also be refined to deal more realistically with inclusion of statuses, such as *temporary* worker and *lessee*, which have become more prevalent since the 1967 survey design.

Among the 1993 changes in the way surveys are conducted is how Civilian Population Survey interviewers ask crucial questions, modifications recommended since 1979! Since 1993 (1) the status of *discouraged worker* is limited to persons who have failed to look for a job more than one year prior to the interview date; (2) women found at home by the CPS interviewer are to be asked *directly* whether they are in the labor force or outside (i.e., in the housewife category); and (3) the term *layoff*, which originally described a temporary job loss, but which is now popularly used to describe permanent job separation, is clarified. Still not met is remedy for lacks pointed out by a 1979 Commission, namely, that CPS data does not include information on variables such as *potential* for *job entry* nor on *reservation wages*. Neither does it include a *hardship* index. Completely lacking are data on *job vacancies*. These data cannot be generated because there is no obligatory job-opening registration requirement for employers in the United States, as in some European countries.

NOTES

1. The matter of differences in occupational stability is thought to be an important factor in occupational choice, especially in the decision to invest in educational preparation. However, down the occupational ladder, where long-term educational investment is not a factor, it is not known how much people consider the job stability issue in deciding which occupations to enter or for which jobs to apply. It is known that people are loathe to shift from blue collar to white collar occupations and vise versa, but just how much they factor in the stability issue of an occupation into job search behavior is unknown.

2. The figure for males in December 1997 was 4.5 percent, slightly above the overall female rate.

3. According to Kuttner (1997), countries that attempt to stimulate their economies are likely to experience serious inflation and destabilization of their financial markets. Kuttner refers to use of Keynesian methods, that is, use of both monetary and

fiscal policies to stimulate the economy. Keynesian-type *monetary* policies involve increasing the nation's money supply to make money cheaper and encourage investment, while Keynesian *fiscal* policy involves using taxing power to provide funds for starting up large public employment projects or loans to business to absorb the unemployed and *jump-start* the economy. Actually, any policy considered expansionary today is called Keynesian.

4. Note that *normal unemployment* is not to be confused with the *natural rate of unemployment*, discussed above. They represent two different concepts.

5. Earlier theorists of the modern era were followers of John Maynard Keynes(1883–1946) who first explained the concept of the business cycle in *The General Theory of Employment, Interest, and Money (1936).*

6. An example is that of construction workers who are paid more than manufacturing workers of similar level of skills who work more hours per year.

REFERENCES

Baker, Michael. 1992. Unemployment duration: compositional effects and cyclical variability. *American Economic Review* 82, no. 1 (March): 31–21.

Blanchard, Oliver J. and Lawrence F. Katz. 1992. Regional evolutions. *Brookings Papers on Economic Activity* Washington, D.C.:Brookings Institution, (1): 1–75.

Bluestone, Barry and Bennett Harrison. 1982. *The deindustrialization of America.* Basic Books, Inc. New York: Free Press..

Ehrenberg, Ronald and Robert S Smith. 1994. Modern labor economics. New York: HarperCollins College Publishers.

Eisner, Robert. 1995. Our NAIRU limits: The governing myth of economic policy. *The American Prospect.* no. 22 (Spring): 58–64.

Filer, Randall, Daniel Hamermesh, and Albert Rees. 1996. *The economics of work and pay.* Sixth Edition. New York: HarperCollins College Publishers: 321–25.

Keynes, John M. 1936. *General theory of employment, interest, and money,* London: Macmillan.

Krugman, Paul. 1994 *Peddling prosperity: economic sense and nonsense in the age of diminished expectations.* New York: W.W. Norton.

Kuttner, Robert. 1997. *Everything for sale: the virtues and limits of markets.* New York: Alfred Knopf. Twentieth Century Fund Books.

Marston, Stephen. 1985. Two views of the geographic distribution of unemployment. *Quarterly Journal of Economics* 100 (2): 57–80.

Mishel, Lawrence and Jared Bernstein. 1993. The jobless recovery deteriorating wages and job quality in the 1990s, Briefing Paper. Washington, D.C.: *Economic Policy Institute*, August.

Norwood, Janet. 1993. The statistics corner: interpreting the unemployment statistics, *Business Economics* 28 (1) January : 56–60.

Phillips, A. W. 1958. The relationship between unemployment and the rate of change of money wager rates in the United Kingdom, 1861–1957. *Economica* 25, no. 97. (February): 285–99.

Rydzewski, L. G., William Deming, and Philip Rones. 1993. Seasonal employment falls over past three decades. *Monthly Labor Review* 116, no. 7 (July): 3–15.

Summers, Lawrence. 1990. Why is the unemployment rate so very high near full employment? *Understanding Unemployment.*Cambridge, Mass.: MIT Press.

Topel, Robert.1984. Equilibrium earnings, turnover, and unemployment: new evidence. *Journal of Labor Economics* 2 (October): 500–522.

U.S. Department of Education. 1977. National Center for Education Statistics. *Digest of Education Statistics.* NCES 98–015. Washington, D.C.: Government Printing Office. Table 377, 421.

U.S. Department of Labor. Bureau of Labor Statistics. 1992. *BLS Handbook of Methods*, Bulletin 2414. Washington D.C., :Government Printing Office.

———. 1983. *Employment and Earnings*. 30, no. 1 (January) Washington, D.C.: Government Printing Office, Table A-44, 42.

———. 1988. *Employment and Earnings*. 35, no. 1 Washington, D.C.: Government Printing Office, (January) Table A-34, 45.

———. 1993. *Employment and Earnings*. 40,. no. 1 (January) Washington, D.C.: Government Printing Office, Table A-34, 45–46.

———. 1998. *Employment and Earnings*. 45, no. 1 (January) Washington, D.C.: Government Printing Office, Tables 1, A-15, A-26, A-28, and D-11.

———. 1998. *Monthly Labor Review*. 121, no. 9 Current labor statistics. Washington, D.C.: Government Printing Office, Table 1, 66.

———. Regional Office, Greater Philadelphia Area. Personal communication. November 22, 1998.

———. *Employment Situations News Release*. Available from any BLS office, or on the Internet (BLS Internet address: stats.bls.gov. Washington, D.C.

19

The Job Security Issue

During the mid-1980s, a series of popular and scholarly articles have been published posing the question of whether employment security for Americans is lessening. Concerns have also been expressed about the lesser earnings being experienced as a result of replacement jobs being inferior to those lost. This job security issue has been investigated and debated in its many aspects throughout the later 1980s and the 1990s. Whether the general public is (and has been) as worried about job security as the academics is unclear, the outcomes of two national elections (the 1996 presidential and the 1998 mid-term elections) suggesting otherwise. Nevertheless, the questions raised by labor force scholars are too important to be ignored. This chapter deals with two matters concerning unemployment. The first is the issue of whether one's lifetime employment prospects are as secure as in an earlier era, discussed here in terms of the experiences of *displaced workers*, persons many of whom had been relatively secure who lost jobs and sought to reestablish themselves. This section depends heavily on DOL's displaced workers surveys and on Fallick's 1996 review of the literature on displaced workers. The second matter discussed in this chapter is commonly suggested remedies for unemployment.

HAS JOB INSECURITY RISEN? REEMPLOYMENT EXPERIENCES OF DISPLACED WORKERS

Background

Unemployment and job security has traditionally been thought to concern only "the working class," professionals and managerials being exempt from layoffs except in very extreme situations, such as collapse of an industry (loss of defense contracts by airplane manufacturers during the 1950s, for example). This immunity vanished during the 1970s and 1980s, beginning with large-scale plant closings throughout the 1970s and the large numbers of permanent separations that followed, succeeded by the recessions of 1980–82 and 1990–91, each of which resulted in unusually high levels of permanent losses of "good jobs" in large corporations, heretofore regarded as bedrock employers (Bednarzik 1983; Browne 1985; Hamermesh 1989; Fallick 1996). The concept that workers are now regarded by employers as commodities, rather than in human terms, has been exacerbated by the large-scale layoffs by prospering companies throughout the 1980s and 1990s, dubbed *downsizings,* which also included managers and professionals. Much of the concern regarding the layoffs of this period stemmed from observations that they were proceeding throughout the "good years "as well as the "bad."

The Labor Department (DOL) has responded to the concerns about job insecurity by initiating Displaced Workers Surveys (DWS), beginning in 1979, for the explicit purpose of obtaining data that could be used for investigation of the issue. The concept of *displaced workers* was developed to provide a means of identifying the job-losers of interest. Following Fallick (1996), there is general agreement that job-losers who qualify as *displaced persons* share four characteristics: they (1) were not fired for just cause, (2) were victims of some *structural* change, (3) are unlikely to be able to obtain a similar job in the near future, and (4) are strongly attached to the industry in which they had been employed.

In attempting to get an informed picture of the experiences of the body of persons who are thought to constitute such a group, the problem has been to find them. Some researchers has attempted to do so by studying a relatively small group of workers in a specific setting; for example, Ong and Lawrence (1993) studied the experiences of aerospace workers in southern California during a specific time period (1989–92), when the industry crashed due to changes in governmental policy, that is, creating structural unemployment. In such a situation the possibilities of locating individuals who fit the criteria of *displaced worker* are very high. The generalities that can be drawn from such a study are very limited, however. Therefore, most researchers turn to Labor Department data, that is the most inclusive available as it covers the entire country and is statistically representative. Unfortunately, the data obtained does not necessarily fit the criteria for displaced persons well. As noted above, DOL's definitions specify that to be considered a displaced worker, the job-loser must (1) be at least twenty years of age, (2) must have job tenure of at least three years, and (3) have lost the job due to inadequate work being available, removal of the position or shift, or a plant closing or relocation. Because of lack of good alternatives, researchers use the DOL displaced persons data, hoping that the persons included are the same ones they have in mind, particularly in regard to job losers' ability to return to their old jobs and whether the job loss experienced was actually *structural* in nature.

According to DOL's Displaced Workers surveys, based on the definition given above, about 5.1 million persons were displaced from their jobs between 1979 and 1983 (a recessionary period) and 4.3 million from 1985 to 1989 (a period of strong growth). The nature of the worker displacement was counter-cyclical, with job losers looking more similar to the general population than did the unemployed of earlier years (Flaim and Sehgal 1985; Horvath 1987; Herz 1990 and 1991; Gardner 1993).

The unemployment rates between 1979 and 1989 appeared to be moving into levels uncomfortably high for a country with an official policy of "full employment." According to Hamermesh (1989), the extent of plant closings increased between the late 1960s and early 1980s. The 1970s experience, which included very high levels of plant closings and permanent job losses, was thought by Hamermesh to explain the heightened public concern. Evidence does not exist, however, that the high 1970s' level of plant closings persisted throughout the 1980s, though the effects on the 1970s' displacements may have endured. During the 1980s unemployment was between 9 and 10 percent two years out of the ten, and in the range of 7 to 8 percent for five years. And the 1990s experienced one year of recovery (1992) with 7.5 percent unemployment, a rate higher than during the 1990–91 recession already noted. (The rates for 1990 and 1991, respectively, were 5.6% and 6.8%.)

Recent Findings. The findings of the most recent data on worker displacement (1995–97 Displaced Workers Survey, released August 1998), appear below. As of this writing they have not not yet been subjected to scholarly analysis. The major findings of the survey are:

(1) During the January 1995–December 1997 period, one of very strong employment, 3.6 million workers with job tenure of at least three years lost or left jobs under circumstances that qualfy them as *displaced workers.* [1]
(2) About three-quarters of all long-tenured displaced workers reported finding employment by February 1998; about 10 percent remained unemployed; and the remainder withdrew from the labor force. Of the prime age group (25–54), 82 percent were reemployed. Of older workers, 60 percent of those age fifty-five to sixty-four and 35 percent of those age sixty-five and over were reemployed, with many of the remaining elderly displaced having withdrawn from the labor market. Differences in reemployment by gender, race, and Hispanic origin were modest: males, 79 percent to females, 73 percent; and whites, 76 percent, to blacks, 73 percent, and persons of Hispanic origin, 72 percent.
(3) Almost half (47%) of the displaced reported plant or company closings as the reason for job loss; about one-fifth (21%), insufficient work; and one in three (32%), the shutdown of shifts or the abolition of positions.
(4) The proportion of job loss among workers formerly in manufacturing was higher than manufacturing's share of total employment, though less than during the previous 1996 survey.
(5) More than half of the previously full-time displaced workers lost 20 percent or more of their earnings. Of the 2 million displaced workers who found full-time work, over half (55%) reported earnings equal to or more than previous earnings from the last job, while one-quarter suffered losses of 20 percent or more. The gains were greater (by 7%) than those found in the previous DWS survey; the losses smaller, having been almost one-third in the 1996 survey.
(6) Although advance notice of job termination (as required by the Worker Adjustment and Retraining Notification Act of 1988) was received by a large portion of the workers (44%), it did not appear to affect the probabilities of their being reemployed by the time of the February 1998 survey.

Conclusions Concerning Employment Outcomes for Displaced Workers, 1979–97

Despite all the public discussion and research concerning the worker displacement–job security issue, no consensus exists. The DOL tends to the position that no evidence exists to uphold the contention that job security (the possibilities of long-term job tenure) has diminished markedly. For example,

BLS economists Thomas Nardone, Jonathan Veum, and Julie Yates, in a 1997 article that specifically addressed this issue, stated that the studies of this issue "generally find little, if any, decline in job stability in the last two decades." [2] Scholars outside the Labor Department, however, hold divergent views, sometimes after massaging the same data and using the same methodologies.

The following offers a sampling of the divergences in conclusions. First, let us consider the conclusions of those who see no evidence of lesser job security. Paul Osterman (1992), a prominent labor economist, compared job tenure accumulation by U.S. workers between May 1979 and May 1988 using the DWS data, and concluded that there had been *no strong differences* in the stability of employment over this period from that of the past, for the population as a whole. He found some decline in the percentage of prime-age (25–54) men in jobs lasting six or more years, however, while women did somewhat better than traditionally in this regard. An analysis of 1979–91 data by a group of well-established economists, Francis X. Diebold, David Neumark, and Daniel Polsky (1996a) resulted in the same general conclusion, that is, that overall job stability did *not* decline substantially during the 1980s, even though some decline in job stability for blacks, young workers, and the less educated was found. Henry Farber (1994), another distinguished practitioner, reported similar findings, concluding that reports of the demise of job security were premature or blown out of proportion.

Another group of researchers, however, using the same basic data as Diebold and colleagues, came to the opposite conclusion concerning job instability during the same years (May 1979–May 1988). Kenneth A. Swinnerton and Howard Wial (1995), looking at the experiences of all displaced workers during the 1980s, concluded that workers with low seniority experienced increases in tenure between 1979 and 1987, but declines thereafter (1987–91), and that these developments could not be related to the business cycle. Even during relatively mild recessions that occurred during these periods, retention rates were lower than during harsher recessions of earlier periods. Swinnerton and Wial did not claim to have *proved* that job stability is decreasing, but that their findings strongly suggest this to have been the case. Their calculations disclosed differences between *accumulated* and *eventual tenure* distribution, which suggested increasingly fewer long-term employment experiences in the coming period. According to the scenario their work evokes, over time, fewer workers will join the fortunate group that has a relatively high level of tenure (eight years or more). The 1987–91 period had the highest proportion of workers with eight-year tenure or more, but also the smallest proportion of those who would eventually occupy their jobs for up to this length. Comparisons of the two time periods under study implied to these researchers that few workers would have long-term job security.[3]

Earnings Outcomes. The second question most often addressed by analysts of displaced-worker issues is the matter of earnings provided by replacement jobs. This is of utmost importance since, if little loss occurs, the whole matter of displacement is less consequential. Following Fallick (1996), on the basis of pre-1992 experiences, earnings loss by displaced workers in their new situations is likely for four reasons: (1) loss of human capital directly associated with the job or sector, (2) loss of a high-quality match between the worker and the new

job, (3) loss of wage premiums offered by certain of the retrenching or disappearing industries and by unionized employers. and (4) loss of seniority advantage.[4]
One researcher (Ruhm 1991) estimated pre-1992 displaced workers' weekly earnings to be 16 percent less than those of similar workers in the year subsequent to
displacement and 14 percent less four years later. Another study (Jacobson, La-
Londe, and Sullivan 1993), using Pennsylvania Unemployment Insurance data,
found quarterly earnings of the displaced as compared with non-displaced to
show a severe drop upon reemployment, and that five years later, average quarterly earnings amounted to about 75 percent of previous earnings, without expectation of betterment. Since restructuring of industries is also likely to reduce
the wages of workers who were retained on payrolls, another study (Babcock,
Benedict, and Engberg 1994) explored the relationship between the earnings of
the displaced to the nondisplaced in the same structurally pressured firms, using
Allegheny County Labor Market data. Despite reduced (estimated) earnings for
the nondisplaced, the researchers found that the displaced lost an additional 25
percent of previous annual earnings upon reemployment. Still another study by
Farber (1993), using a control group "constructed" from the reports of nondisplaced workers in the CPS survey (of which the DWS is a supplement), found
wage losses of 11 percent over the first two years after displacement.

Several researchers, comparing displaced workers with one another, have
found that each year of previous job tenure possessed by a displaced worker reduces his/her subsequent earnings about one percent additional (Farber 1993;
Kletzer 1989; Carrington and Zaman 1994). The latter two researchers observed
that the amount varies sharply by occupation and industry. Other conclusions
researchers came to are: first, that if one must suffer displacement, it is better to
do so during an expansionary period (Farber 1993; Kletzer 1991; Topel 1990);
and, second, that good labor conditions in the locality of the worker's residence
tends to reduce losses (Howland and Peterson 1988; Jacobson, LaLonde, and
Sullivan 1993). In general, the more experienced workers, irrespective of tenure,
were found to be suffering the most severe earnings losses, possibly because they
come from states and industries that are doing poorly (Topel 1990; Carrington
1993a.)

Human capital losses constitute an additional factor responsible for much of
the drop in replacement earnings, according to several analysts (Addison and
Portugal 1989; Kletzer 1991). This follows from the likelihood that some of the
individual's accumulated human capital is transferable; some is not, the person
becoming worth less to the replacement employer than the prior employer. Human capital loss is thought to be especially important in accounting for earnings
losses of 16 to 20 percent when a displaced worker leaves one industry for
another (Addison and Portugal 1989; Carrington 1993b). A series of other researchers have concurred. Another research endeavor found that when high-tech
workers were retained by the same firm or went to another high-tech firm, they
maintained their previous earnings levels (Ong and Mar 1992), while those who
found jobs in other industries experienced 27 to 36 percent less annual earnings
than those who reentered high-tech employment (Ong and Lawrence 1993).

Another analysis supporting the notion that human capital tends to be transferable within a specific industry was done by Derek Neal (1995) who found that
earnings losses for an added ten years of tenure for displaced males who found

work outside their previous industry increased by 21 percent for industry switchers; while losses for those who reentered within the same industry were about 11 percent (controlling for inter-industry wage differences.) It was also found that when workers were previously employed in an industry that required only a few general occupations or occupations highly specific to the industry, workers are much less inclined to cross industries than others (Kletzer 1992 and 1995). However, many workers are apparently forced to do so. For example, study of the 1984 Displaced Workers Survey revealed that only about one-quarter of the displaced workers who found reemployment during the two years studied reported being in the same industry as previously (Devens 1986). According to Fallick (1993) this high level of inter-industry mobility indicates job-hunters' realistic perceptions of where the job growth was at the time of their search.

Movements between occupations and areas of the country also have been found to account for greater losses for those who made such moves, as opposed to those who did not (Jacobson, LaLonde, and Sullivan 1993; Addison and Portugal 1989). The biyearly DWS surveys contain detailed information on these movements.

What Does All This Add Up To?

How should one read the findings of these surveys and the interpretations presented? We have learned that about three-quarters of the displaced find new jobs, often in different industries and in different occupations than their former employment; that considerable earnings losses are experienced; and that, after about four years, the unemployment rates are about the same as for the general population, but earnings losses persist and some of the displaced have withdrawn from the workforce altogether. Overall the characteristics of the displaced are increasingly similar to those of the general population. It also appears, from the body of survey data, that tenure offers less protection than previously, since the number of years of tenure reported by the displaced has been rising (taken to mean that a greater proportion of the current workforce has relatively low levels of tenure). Academic analysts have massaged the best data available and disagree as to whether it all adds up to the conclusion that job stability is less than it was in the recent past and whether, therefore, it is reasonable to conclude that "life is less secure" than previously, as is the common wisdom. Whether the "common wisdom" is the creation of the news media and academics or actually reflective of the mood of the public is also controversial. The outcomes of two national elections (1996 and 1998) have been interpreted by the popular press as indicating that the electorate "feels good," economically speaking.

Some readers are unlikely to accept the conclusions of that portion of the economics profession that dismisses the notion of decreased job security in the United States. Skeptics may recall earlier reportage on the newly popular forms of employment, such as *on-call work* and *independent contracting*, and the questions raised as to whether these phenomena mask unemployment and/or underemployment. Yet, according to remarks by Alice Munnell, a member of the Clinton Council of Economic Advisors (1996), policy-makers were persuaded by BLS surveys of persons in alternative work arrangements that these work statuses are largely voluntary arrangements and do not represent hidden unemployment. Two possible resolutions to the controversy over the state of job security in this country are (1) that the news media has created an unfounded atmosphere of fear, based on anecdotal accounts of large corporate-downsizings, or (2) that BLS statistics (and other databases) are inadequate for the purposes desired. This latter position has been taken by sociologist S. M. Miller (1999), Director of the Poverty and Inequality Institute at the Commonwealth Institute, who denounced the BLS findings on the basis that the survey offends common sense by polling job *survivors* concerning their length of tenure. Polling on the job security issue needs to include persons representative of the unemployed as well as the employed sectors of the labor force, in Miller's view, if findings are to reflect reality. Miller also questions BLS' interpretations of the job tenure data cited.

Conclusions are that available data is inadequate; research methodology leaves something to be desired; and people continued to lose jobs during the very "good times" of the late 1990s, but unemployment, as a whole, hit a remarkable low during 1998. Perhaps we would have better understanding of the meaning of employer terminations and joblessness if researchers could afford to interview large samples of the unemployed directly concerning their experiences, as opposed to massaging masses of data in the hope of being able to make inferences concerning the subjects' experiences. No, we still do not know whether large numbers of persons unemployed over the past quarter-century could be said to have lost their *sense* of employment security along with their jobs.

PROPOSED REMEDIES FOR UNEMPLOYMENT

The remainder of this chapter deals with the most commonly proposed remedies for unemployment. To begin, the official policy of the United States concerning unemployment, as stated in the Full Employment Act of 1946, should be noted. The Full Employment Act of 1946 states that any American who wishes to work should be able to do so and that it remains the duty of government to continually use all practical means to promote maximum employment, production, and purchasing power (quoted by Alice Munnell, May 1–2, 1996, and Paul Krugman 1994). And the much less well-known Humphrey-Hawkins Act of 1978 specifically requires the Federal government to seek to achieve a 4 percent unemployment rate. The first proposal calls for abandonment of maintenance of a particular level of unemployment (the NAIRU) as the major concept for determining employment policy; the second outlines a broad-based government program for reaching full-employment without inflation; the third deals with a means of "sharing the pain"; the fourth represents an attempt to make workers more competitive; the fifth represents an effort to reduce frictional unemployment.

Ditching the NAIRU

The first suggestion for dealing with unemployment calls for a change in point of view by policy-makers, roughly capsulized as "putting people first" and "taking a chance on inflation." Perhaps the strongest expression of this view has been taken by University of Texas economist James Galbraith (1997), who, in calling for people-oriented governmental policies, derides both the values underlying current rigid adherence to anti-inflationary policies at the expense of human suffering and the effectiveness of the policy. Galbraith summarizes his main arguments as follows: (1) the theoretical case for adhering to the NAIRU is not strong; (2) that the empirical evidence that lowering unemployment below the level of the NAIRU results in intolerable levels of inflation is dubious and has become more so in the last ten years; (3) that just what the precise level of unemployment represents the NAIRU is unclear, making the whole concept "a professional embarrassment"; and (4) that adherence to policies based on the concept of the NAIRU have heavy costs and result in only minor benefits.

Galbraith calls for policies favoring raising employment to the highest possible rates compatible with a reasonable level of price stability. He suggests use of Okun's Law, that is, that an extra point of growth can bring unemployment down by half a point annually, which he sees as a more reliable guide than the NAIRU. Basically, economists of Galbraith's school of thought believe that societal well-being is best favored by having the maximal number of people working and earning and that such "human" considerations outweigh possible inflationary costs.

Major support for such proposals stems mainly from liberal economists, such as Robert Kuttner, who wrote a letter to *Business Week* (November 4, 1996) declaring that there was nothing " natural" about 5 percent unemployment and later reiterated his stand in *Everything for Sale* (1997, 93–95); and Medoff and Harless, in their book, *The Indebted Society* (1996, 72–89). Yet, the august and conservative Federal Reserve Board Chairman, Alan Greenspan, is also said to be dubious about the existence of such a rate (*New York Times*, January 30, 1997).

Government as "Employer of Last Resort": A Proposed Government Jobs Program

A proposal much in the spirit of Galbraith's policy-change ideas has been made by several scholars at Bard College. The proposal has two basic components and involves attempting to create a situation of full employment while building in safeguards against inflation. The first component would be an announcement by the federal government that employment in the public sector is available to all who want to work at a specified wage. (This employment would be separate and distinct from present government functioning.) The intent would be to abolish all involuntary unemployment by making work available to all who are willing to work at the announced wage and who are unable to find anything in the private sector. Only those persons who choose to remain unemployed would be. Papadimitrious and colleagues claim that the plan's high costs would be offset in part by reductions in other areas of social spending, such as unemployment compensation, food stamps, and other "welfare" payments. Funding would be federal, while the programs themselves would be run by states and localities.

The plan's second component would be *wage-setting* by government. Maintaining that aggregate demand is too low, evidenced by the fact that millions are out of work even in the best of times, Papadimitrious and colleagues essentially express an unwillingness to write off the well-being of millions of unemployed persons on behalf of their theoretical value as a reserve pool in suppressing infla-tion. Their argument is that spending money on supporting public employment would result in more spending by the public and would generate greater de-mand. Inflationary pressures, they contend, could be avoided by the fixed wage level that would not rise. At the same time, in its role as "benchmark" for wag-es in the private sector, the fixed rate might force some very low-wage employers to raise their rates. This would be a one-time thing and would likely motivate some of these employers to aim for greater productivity and accept lower profit levels. Although some prices might rise, they do not believe that inflation would develop. The program would also help reduce the human capital loss that results from prolonged unemployment. Basically, the Bard scholars argue that the creation of an inflationary spiral can be avoided by means of this program be-cause there would be no possibility of raising wages, affirming that only govern-ment can offer an "infinitely elastic demand for labor without setting an infla-tionary situation."

OTHER SUGGESTIONS INVOLVING GOVERNMENTAL ACTIONS

Alice Munnell (1996), a member of the Clinton Administration's Council of Economic Advisors (CEA), while stating that the Council had been in agree-ment with those who doubt the purported drop in job stability, has recom-mended federal government intervention in terms of policies supporting basic education and job training, the encouragement of portable-benefit development, and the utilization of the unemployment system (employment services and un-employment compensation) to facilitate job search and counsel job-seekers, all standard approaches of those who favor activist government approaches to social problems. The remaining proposed remedies for unemployment are essentially proposals to diminish suffering of the laid-off or to-be-laid-off. For the unem-ployed, these proposals would help accelerate movement into reemployment as opposed to actually increasing the demand for labor per se. [5]

Job-Sharing

Sometimes referred to as *short-time*, job sharing is essentially a tactic that in-volves spreading a given amount of available employment among a workforce that faces reductions in numbers. In other words, job-sharing involves sharing the pain in situations where some staff reduction is deemed necessary by man-agement. Instead of firing a portion of the pay-roll, all members work reduced hours. This lessens everyone's earnings somewhat, but leaves no one totally out of a job. Proponents of this approach also hope that the practice will open up ad-ditional jobs for presently unemployed workers or new entrants. Labor unions in the United States have traditionally opposed short- time, but some states have encouraged the adoption of this strategy by providing for the payment of unem-ployment compensation for time lost. France and Germany have experimented, as a last resort, with various ways of implementing short-time, according to the November 9, 1993, *New York Times*, which also fleshed out such a situation in a November 26 issue, as follows: "Volkswagen and the metal-workers union agreed to put workers in their six German plants on a four-day work week, with

20 percent decrease in hours and 10 percent decrease in pay. The goal is to avoid loss of 30,000 jobs out of 100,000. Both union members and the German public appear to support the strategy."

While short-time appears to be supported by both the German and French publics and a number of other European countries as a way out of the long-term unemployment that has plagued Europe, some economists express doubts about this approach. One problem is that often the workers are reluctant to give up any pay for the privilege of working fewer hours. Another problem is the high level of benefits costs that still pertain to each worker on a payroll. And for a standard of living to rise, workers need to work more hours rather than fewer: if productivity per worker falls, standard of living must also fall. Opinions differ as to whether short-time is viable. Can more persons using existing equipment overcome the added expenses that stem from pay reductions that are less percentagewise than work-hour reductions, as in the example given above? Could the goal of expanding employment through this means succeed? Could it succeed if pay were reduced to correspond to the actual numbers of hours reduced?

Job Retraining

Job retraining has been a favored approach in the United States as far back as Johnson's Great Society programs. Retraining has been proposed as the antidote for a series of unemployment problems, from persons ousted from jobs because of imports to persons affected by downsizing in the course of corporate restructuring. Policy-makers' major objection to job retraining is that it is impossible to know for precisely which jobs trainees should be prepared. Experience has also shown that retraining for lesser paying jobs is unlikely to be successful. In addition, an internal Labor Department report on retraining, financed by the Trade Adjustment Assistance Act, which was published in the October 15, 1993, *New York Times*, concluded that the program has been largely ineffectual and has been used mainly as a source of income by the unemployed (until some job unrelated to the training is located). This finding is in line with experiences under the earlier Manpower Training and Development Programs of the Johnson Great Society era. Much of the problem with retraining done under the the sponsorship of unemployment programs is that it tends to be too poorly financed to add substantially to the skills of participants. For the interested reader, reports of the MDTA (Manpower Development and Training Act) and CETA (Concentrated Employment and Training Administration) programs, as well as those of the still functioning JTPA (Joint Training Partnership Act) programs, which emphasize cooperative planning between government and the private sector, will shed additional light on this subject.

Advance Warning

Advance warning is an approach that is written into law and designed primarily to ameliorate the lot of displaced workers by requiring the employer, under certain circumstances, to give advance notice of impending job loss (Worker Adjustment and Retraining Notification Act, 1988). The objective is to permit early job search as a means of shortening the *duration of unemployment*. In fact, the law does not seem to have increased the extent to which advance warning is given (Addison and Blackburn 1994). It is believed that at best the law is helping some displaced workers to some degree, but probably not the persons most likely to suffer from prolonged unemployment following displacement. Written notice two months prior to displacement (a provision of the law) appears to decrease joblessness only a very small amount (Addison and Portugal 1992; Addison and Blackburn 1994; Burgess and Low 1992; Ruhm 1992 and 1994). Studies have found long and detailed written notices associated with higher earnings in replacement employment (Addison and Fox 1993) and less subsequent job turnover (Nord and Ting 1991; Ruhm 1994), but the notices are not necessarily the primary reason for such differences.

NOTES

1. An additional 4.4 million workers with less than three-years job tenure also lost their jobs during this period, bringing the total to 8 million workers, but these latter workers do not meet the criteria for displaced workers.

2. The studies they cite are mainly those quoted later in this chapter.

3. Swinnerton and Wial and the Diebold group argued over methodology in print with Diebold and colleagues clinging to their conclusion that the assertion that job stability is falling substantially remains entirely unproven. Meanwhile, Swinnerton and Wial countered that they did not claim that the *entire* 1979–91 period was one of declining job stability, but stood by their conviction that, overall, the prospects for job security are lessening. They agreed that more work over longer periods is required (Diebold, Neumark, and Polsky 1996b; Swinnerton and Wial, 1996).

4. Actual losses are difficult to calculate because relevant data is rarely available and because establishment of a credible control group is difficult to achieve. A control group, in this case, would be a group of persons with similar characteristics to the persons in the group under study who did not lose their jobs and whose past and current employment and earnings experiences could be compared to those of the displaced workers under study.

5. Referring to the Displaced Persons Surveys, the major source of data for study of job insecurity, Munnell says that measurement difficulties are partly to blame for divergences in the conclusions of various scholars, but also notes that even the pessimists have found reductions in layoffs among some groups. Munnell hypothesizes that public anxiety regarding job stability may stem from the high levels of publicity that accompany corporate layoffs and the inclusion of persons not formerly subject to staff reductions: older persons, the white-collared, and the more educated.

REFERENCES

Addison, John T., and McKinley Blackburn. 1994. The Worker Adjustment and Retraining Notification Act: effects on notice provision. *Industrial and Labor Relations Review* 47, no. 4: 650–62.

———, and Douglas Fox. 1993. Job changing after displacement: a contribution to the advance notice debate. *Southern Economic Journal* 60, no. 1 (July): 184–200.

———, and Pedro Portugal. 1989. Job displacement, relative wage changes, and duration of unemployment. *Journal of Labor Economics* 7, no. 3: 281–302.

———. 1992. Advance notice and unemployment: new evidence from the 1988 Displaced Worker Survey. *Industrial and Labor Relations Review* 45, no. 4: 645–64.

Babcock, Linda, Mary Ellen Benedict, and John Engberg. 1994. Structural change and labor market outcomes: how are the gains and losses distributed? Unpublished paper, Carnegie Mellon University.

Bednarzik, Robert. 1983. Layoffs and permanent job losses: workers' traits and cyclical patterns. *Monthly Labor Review* 106 (September): 3–12.

Browne, Lynne. 1985. Structural change and dislocated workers. *New England Economic Review*. Federal Reserve Board of Boston. (January/February): 15–30.

Burgess, Paul, and Stuart Low. 1992. Pre-unemployment job search and advance job loss notice. *Journal of Labor Economics* 10, no. 3: 258–87.

Carrington, William. 1993a. Specific Human Capital and Worker Displacement. Dissertation, University of Chicago.

———. 1993b. Wage losses for displaced workers: Is it really the firm that matters? *Journal of Human Resources* 28, no. 3 (Summer): 435–62.

———, and Asad Zaman. 1994. Inter-industry variation in the costs of job displacement. *Journal of Labor Economics* 12, no. 2: 243–76.

Devens, Richard M., Jr. 1986. Displaced workers one year later. *Monthly Labor Review* 109, no.7 (July): 40–43.

Diebold, Francis X., David Neumark, and Daniel Polsky. 1996a. Job Stability in the United States. NBER Working Paper No. 4859.

———. 1996b. Comment on Kenneth A. Swinnerton and Howard Wial, Is job stability declining in the U.S. economy? *Industrial and Labor Relations Review* 49 (January): 348–51.

Fallick, Bruce. 1993. The industrial mobility of displaced workers. *Journal of Labor Economics* 11, no. 2: 302–23.

———. 1996. A review of the recent empirical literature on displaced workers. *Industrial and Labor Relations Review* 50, no. 5 (October): 5–16.

Farber, Henry.1993. The incidence and costs of job loss, 1982–93. *Brookings Papers, Micro Economics*: 73–132.

———. 1994. Are lifetime jobs disappearing? Job duration in the United States, 1973–93. Mimeograph. Princeton University.

Flaim, Paul, and Ellen Sehgal. 1985. Displaced workers of 1979–83: how well have they fared? *Monthly Labor Review* 108, no. 6: 3–16.

Galbraith, James. 1997. Time to ditch the NAIRU. *Journal of Economics Perspectives* 11, no. 1 (Winter): 93–108.

Gardner, Jennifer. 1993. Recession swells count of displaced workers. *Monthly Labor Review* 116, no. 6: 14–23.

Hamermesh, Daniel. 1989. What do we know about worker displacement in the United States? *Industrial Relations* 28, no. 1: 51–59.

Herz, Diane. 1990. Worker displacement in a period of rapid job expansion, 1983–87. *Monthly Labor Review* 113, no. 5: 21–33.

———. 1991. Worker displacement still common in the late 1980s. In U.S. Department of Labor, Bureau of Labor Statistics, *Displaced Workers*, Bulletin 2382 (June).

Horvath, Francis. 1987. The pulse of economic change: displaced workers of 1981–85. *Monthly Labor Review* 110, no. 6: 3–12.

Howland, Marie, and George Peterson. 1988. Labor market conditions and the reemployment of displaced workers. *Industrial and Labor Relations Review* 42 (October): 109–22.

Jacobson, Louis, Robert LaLonde, and Daniel Sullivan. 1993. Earnings losses of displaced workers. *American Economic Review* 83, no. 4: 685–709.

Kletzer, Lori G. 1989. Returns to seniority after permanent job loss. *American Economic Review* 79, no. 3 (June) : 536–43.

———. 1991. Earnings after job displacement: job tenure, industry, and occupation, 107–35. In John T. Addison, ed. *Job displacement: consequences and implications for policy.* Detroit: Wayne State University Press.

———. 1992. Industrial mobility following job displacement: evidence from the displaced worker surveys. *Industrial Relations Research Association 44th Annual Proceedings:* 621–29.

———. 1995. The role of sector-specific skills in post-displacement earnings. Unpublished paper, University of California, Santa Cruz.

Krugman, Paul. 1994. *Peddling prosperity: economic sense and nonsense in the age of diminished expectations.* New York: W.W. Norton & Company.

Kuttner, Robert. 1996. There's nothing "natural" about 5% unemployment. *Business Week,* November 14, 28.

———. 1997. *Everything for Sale:* the Virtues and Limits of Markets. A Twentieth Century Fund Book. New York: Alfred A. Knopf.

Medoff, James, and Andrew Harless. 1996. *The indebted society:anatomy of an oncoming disaster.* Boston: Little, Brown and Company.

Miller, S. M. 1999. Who counts at Census? Letter to Editor. *American Prospect,* no.42 (January/February):15.

Munnell, Alice. 1996. Remarks at a Conference, "Labor market structure and employment growth," 1, 2 May, 6–7. At the Jerome Levy Institute of Bard College; *Report of the Jerome Levy Institute of Bard College* (June).

Nardone, Thomas, Jonathan Veum, and Julie Yates. 1997. Measuring job security. *Monthly Labor Review,* 120, no.6 (June): 26–33.

Neal, Derek. 1995. Industry-specific human capital: evidence from displaced workers. *Journal of Labor Economics* 13, no. 3: 653–77.

Nord, Stephen, and Yuan Ting. 1991. The impact of advance notice of plant closings on earnings and the probability of unemployment. *Industrial and Labor Relations Review* 44, no.4: 681–91.

Ong, Paul, and Don Mar. 1992. Post lay-off earnings among semiconductor workers. *Industrial and Labor Relations Review* 45, no. 2: 366–79.

——— , and Janette Lawrence. 1993. The unemployment crisis in aerospace. Unpublished paper, University of California, Los Angeles.

Osterman Paul. 1992. Internal labor markets in a changing environments: models and evidence, 273–308. In Levin, David, Olivia Mitchell, and Peter Sherer, eds., *Research Frontiers in Industrial Relations and Human Resources.* Madison Wisconsin: Industrial Relations Research Association.

Papadimitrious, Dimitri, L. Randall Wray, and Matthew Forstater. 1998. Toward full employment without inflation: the job opportunity program. *Report.* The Jerome Levy Economics Institute of Bard College, (August): 5–8.

Ruhm, Christopher. 1991. Are workers permanently scarred by job displacements? *American Economic Review* 81, no. 1: 31–24.

———. 1992. Advance notice and post-displacement joblessness. *Journal of Labor Economics* 10, no. 1: 1–32.

———.1994. Advance notice, job search, and post-displacement earnings. *Journal of Labor Economics* 12, no. 1: 1–28.

Swinnerton, Kenneth A., and Howard Wial. 1995. Is job stability declining in the U.S. economy? *Industrial and Labor Relations Review* 48 (January): 293–304.

———. 1996. Is job stability declining in the U.S. economy? Reply to Diebold, Neumark, and Polsky. *Industrial and Labor Relations Review* 49, no. 2 (January): 348–51.

Topel, Robert. 1990. Specific capital and unemployment: measuring the costs and consequences of job loss. *Carnegie-Rochester Conference Series on Public Policy,* 33: 181–224.

U.S. Department of Labor. Bureau of Labor Statistics. *Worker Displacement, 1995–97.* Technical information: Released August 19, 1998. USDL 98-347.

Part VIII

The American Income Transfer System

The impact of the U.S. income-transfer system on employment has always been controversial, especially in regard to programs specifically directed towards the poor. What is known about the effects of the major Social Security programs, including health programs (Medicare and Medicaid) upon employment and employment-associated matters are reviewed in the final chapters of this work. For basic information, this discussion depends upon the most authoritative source, the publications of the Social Security Administration (Office of Research, Evaluation, and Statistics).

The U.S. income-transfer system has grown and developed by fits and jolts from sets of ideas, attitudes, and practices imported from the England of colonial days and utilized by local governments and states, and was molded into its present form during the early days of FDR's New Deal presidency. The various programs cannot be said to constitute a logically developed, coherent system but rather a jerrybuilt structure that arose from whatever social-welfare planners could extract at any given point in time from the representatives of a generally conservative public.

Only the shocks inflicted by the Great Depression, commencing in the early 1930s, and the subsequent sufferings of the population (25% unemployment among adult males, usually the only family breadwinners) created the change in public opinion that permitted enactment of the enabling legislation by the first Roosevelt Administration. The major pieces of this legislation were enacted during the first two years of Roosevelt's tenure, constituting the backbone of his *New Deal* program. They include the basic entitlement programs that, together, we refer to as "Social Security programs"—Old Age Insurance (OAS), Unemployment Insurance (UI), often referred to as "unemployment comp," and Worker's

Compensation (WC) . Enacted at the same time (at the insistence of Mrs. Roosevelt) was a "welfare-type" program for mothers with dependent children, entitled Aid to Families with Dependent Children (AFDC), which has been recently replaced by the Temporary Assistance to Needy Families Act of 1996 (TANF). The major health programs, Medicare, a social insurance program, and Medicaid, a "welfare"-type program for the elderly poor and some others, came into being in 1965. A listing of the major income-transfer programs is presented in Table 20.1. The major social-insurance support programs are shown in the left-hand column. Programs directed towards the poor appear on the right. The social insurances are *entitlement programs*, while the programs directed specifically towards the poor, often referred to as *welfare*, require that participants establish their eligibility through demonstration of the required level of financial destination, that is, through *means-testing*, a process that many feel degrading and humiliating, some declining to apply for this reason.

Chapter 20 describes major Social Security programs, with the exception of those focusing on health care. Chapter 21 discusses welfare programs. Finally, chapter 22 briefly describes and differentiates between Medicare and Medicaid, the principal income-transfer programs that focus on health care.

Table 20.1

THE U.S. INCOME TRANSFER SYSTEM

Social Insurances "Social Security"	Income Support "Welfare"

Old-Age, Survivors and
  Disability Insurance
Unemployment Insurance
Workers' Compensation
Railroad Retirement Act
Public Employees Program
Veterans' Benefits
	Temporary Assistance for Needy
	  Families
	Supplemental Security Income
	Food Stamps
	School Lunches
	Supplemental Food Program
	  for Women, Infants, and
	  Children
	Low Income Home Energy
	  Assistance
	General Assistance
	Earned Income Tax Credit
	Subsidized Housing

Health Care	
Medicare	Medicaid

The U.S. Social Insurances

The two major social-insurance programs that most directly affect employment are Unemployment Insurance (UI) and Worker's Compensation (WC). The role of Old Age, Survivors, and Disability Insurance (OASDI), commonly referred to as "Social Security," is less clear, but will also be discussed. In addition, the information that is available on the employment effects of smaller programs is reported here.

UNEMPLOYMENT INSURANCE

Employers and students of the Unemployment Insurance (UI) program tend to focus their attention on two issues: how UI affects the behavior of employers and how it affects the behavior of workers. Aside from employers' concern about the funding mechanism, their attention and subsequent reactions tend to focus on the duration and intensity of laid-off employees' job searches; the circumstances under which the insured unemployed choose to accept employment, including the extent to which the insured individual adheres to reservation-wage goals; and U.I. regulations that adversely affect job-search activity. Worker concerns have not been studied as such, but are inferred to be related to the availability and duration of benefits. Some researchers have speculated on affects of the UI program on workers' well-being in a larger sense.

Effects of UI on Worker Behavior

It is widely believed that many laid-off workers tend to maintain their unemployed status as long as their UI payments keep coming, but take any available employment when payments cease, especially when jobs with similar wage levels are sparse. It is also believed that some unemployed persons tend to "take a vacation" at employer expense, and postpone their job search. Some recent studies of worker behavior in regard to UI have found the actual situation to be more complex. One study concluded that workers who had the opportunity to return to work in the same industry do so relatively quickly despite the availability of UI; but when they are faced with the need to shift to another industry, they tend to keep job-hunting as long as they can collect UI (Fallick 1991). In the same vein, another study found that workers who initially expected to be recalled had longer spells of unemployment. than those who actually were taken back (Katz and Meyer 1990). A third study found that the job searchers who held out the longest before accepting employment tended to be those rehired by their previous employer, which was interpreted to mean that these workers were "waiting it out," rather than engaging in active job search. Another study of a group of unemployed Wisconsin factory workers revealed that under certain circumstances, a quick return to work is more important to some workers than holding out for their reservation wage (Heywood and White 1990).

Basic Facts About UI

Function: Federal-state, income-stability maintenance program for families whose earner is temporarily out of work.

Eligibility: Applicant status as unemployed involuntarily at the time of application, preceded by full-time employment during four of five preceding quarters, while reaching a specified level of earnings (differing by state) and expressing readiness to resume full-time employment, demonstrated by registration at the local state-employment service. Independent job-seeking is demanded by many states.

Covered employment: Most full-time jobs.

Financing: Employer-funded, supplemented by some Federal money for administrative expenses. Employer pays equivalent of 6.2 percent of the first $7,000 annually of worker's covered wages, minus savings due to experience ratings. (Exceptions: a few states also tax employees; for example, Pennsylvanians pay a UI tax of 1.45% of payroll.)

Benefits: Vary by state; usually limited to twenty-six weeks unless high unemployment elicits an extension by Congress.

Maximum weekly payment by state (1995): $133–362, excluding allowances for dependents, provided by thirteen states.

Tax status of benefits: Taxable. (Social Security Administration)

Intensity of Job Search and Duration of Unemployment. Rare attempts, via controlled experiments, have been made to ascertain the effect of the availability of UI on the intensity of job search and the duration of unemployment spells. However, those undertaken suggest that the imposition of stronger eligibility requirements and the enforcement of them can shorten the duration of unemployment. In one experiment, a $500 bonus given to UI-recipients who found work within eleven weeks and held it for at least four months shortened the average period of UI payments by one week (Woodbury and Spiegelman 1987). Another experiment, involving the imposition of different eligibility requirements on four similar groups of workers, found that pressure could induce workers to search more energetically and find and accept work sooner, albeit at a lower wage, than others searching longer, and that the groups ended the year with the same level of earnings (Johnson and Klepinger 1994). In other words, these researchers concluded that the enforcement of eligibility requirements could induce workers to increase the intensity of their job search, which would cause the duration of job search to fall without expense to the workers' reservation wage.

Encouragement of Strikes. In states where regulations permit strikers to collect benefits under certain circumstances, UI may actually encourage strikes. One investigation found that each 1 percent increase in the amount of the benefit appears to generate a 0.5 percent increase in the amount of strike activity (Hutchens, Lipsky, and Stern 1992). Also, the relative size and availability of the UI grant was found to affect worker behavior, as demonstrated by the widening gap between unemployment in the United States. and Canada. About the same during the 1950s, the gap has widened as Canada has liberalized eligibility requirements, permitting job-leavers as well as job-losers to collect benefits (Moorthy 1989/1990). In other words, workers may feel more free to strike or leave a job if they know that benefits will be available.

Shifts Between Industries. The availability of UI appears to have the effect of shifting employment from low-paying industries to high-paying ones. One analyst calculated that a 10 percent increase in UI benefits increases the proportion of employment in construction about 1.7 percent and decreases the proportion in the services by about 1 percent. This shift tends to raise wage levels in the communities involved (Deere 1991); leading to the conclusion that UI may have a beneficial effect on workers that transcends immediate payment. Yet another study suggests that Federal regulations impeding immigration of unemployed workers between states may be harming unemployed job-seekers and employers, as well, by raising costs of the program. Relocation in the course of job search is generally considered a constructive approach, not one to be inhibited (Goss and Paul 1990).

Effects of UI on Employers

Effect of Experience Ratings. The matter of greatest concern to employers are the UI provisions for *experience ratings* as the basis for employer contributions. The enabling legislation of the Great Depression era provides for establishing the amount of each employer's payroll-tax contribution to its state's Unemployment Trust Fund pool on the basis of the firm's turnover rates, the objective of which is to discourage staff reductions and encourage employment stability. Employers who hire and fire frequently pay punitively high rates, while those who maintain stable employment enjoy low rates.

However well-intentioned, this funding mechanism is widely believed to have a significant negative impact on the well-being of both employers and workers, exactly the opposite intended. One problem is that employers are penalized for layoffs during periods of cyclical down-turn, a circumstance over which they have no control. As a consequence, since employers are unsure as to how quickly the economy will rebound during an ensuing period of up-turn, they tend to refrain from calling back old staff or making new hires—instead, they put their remaining workers on overtime. This practice allows them to avoid incurring heavy UI tax penalties if they must lay off again. Also, the experience-ratings scheme causes employers to be hesitant to employ members of high-risk groups that we should be encouraging for social reasons.[1] It has also been claimed that low-layoff employers end up subsidizing high-layoff ones because of "incomplete" experience ratings that are held to artificially low levels by job-hungry states (Feldstein 1976 and 1978; Brechling 1981).

A number of investigators have concluded that some states "cap" their experience ratings and use loans from the Federal government to supplement low revenues, which offers employers an incentive to engage in layoffs they would not otherwise issue, because they are not penalized for doing so (Benham 1983). In situations where the experience rating assigned to an employer does not reflect actual layoff activity, the extent of layoffs has been found to be higher than average. When a more accurate experience rating prevails, fewer episodes of short duration unemployment occur. This means that high-turnover employers who underpay their workers have an advantage over those who make an effort to maintain stable employment. It has also been observed that UI, as one of the major payroll-tax schemes that places direct costs on employers, encourages them to engage in the hiring of temporary workers, since these individuals are not covered by the program.

In terms of adherence to purpose, the most serious criticism of UI is that it has ceased to be either a universal or counter cyclical program, as intended: the proportion of unemployed workers receiving UI has shrunk since the 1970s. In 1992, for example, only 37 percent of unemployed workers nationwide actually received benefits, which implies that UI has lost a good part of its function as an economic stabilizer for both families and the business community. While some experts state flatly that they do not know why only a minority of the unemployed now receive UI, a series of explanations have been offered (Aguilar and Testa 1995).

One explanation points to the changing characteristics of employment. With more women and youths working, the resultant part-time workforce is often ineligible, based on low number of hours worked or low level of earnings, or laid-off workers are often unable to meet the condition of being ready to work full-time. Low earners may also believe that they are ineligible and not think it worthwhile to apply. A series of investigators include belief on the part of the laid-off that they are ineligible and fall in union representation as major explanations of the reduction in use of UI, which was meant to be a "universal" program (Pearce 1986; Vroman 1991; Blank and Card 1991).

The movement of jobs to less unionized parts of the country has been identified as a major cause of the decline in UI usage, as unions have traditionally informed and encouraged members to apply (Vroman 1991; Blank and Card 1991). But why this is so is unclear. While more union members file than non-members, a survey of non applicants found that fewer than 3 percent professed ignorance of the program, so lack of knowledge is not the issue. [2] Also, the tendency of secondary labor market firms, major employers of women and youths, to contest claims at much higher rates than large primary labor force employers may also discourage people who are often part-time and rarely protected by unions from filing claims even when they are eligible. It has also been found that applications rise with the duration of unemployment (Vroman 1991), which suggests that unemployed somehow either gain more information or overcome their inhibitions against filing, which suggests that more study of the falling use of this important social insurance program is urgently called for. Another possibility for failure to file is that taxation of benefits may make UI less attractive than formerly.

Participation may also be falling because methods of counting the insured unemployed have changed. As a result, it has become more difficult for the "triggering device"—percentage unemployed in a state for a number of weeks—that brings extended benefits to the long-term unemployed during periods of high unemployment to take effect (Burtless 1991). Actions on the state level that modify laws and impose more stringent regulations in the belief that high UI taxes are bad for business, according to two well known researchers, explain the drop in participation in the UI program. In short, they concluded that eligibility has become harder to establish (Vroman 1991; Burtless 1991), but another respected set of researchers (Blank and Card 1991) found no such evidence.

Congressional Reform Efforts

In 1994 Congress acted to force change in the UI system, choosing to concentrate on shortening the job search period. To be eligible for Federal funding (a very minor share given to cover administrative expenses), states must establish worker profiling and reemployment services, which aim to facilitate job-search among that portion of the unemployed UI population most likely to benefit from service (Wandner 1994).

Congress's decision to take this route was motivated by findings that many UI recipients fail to find replacement employment during their twenty-six weeks of eligibility—for example, 34 percent during the first quarter of 1996 (Eberts and O'Leary 1996); and that some demonstration projects showed that the job replacement process could be expedited by offering job-search assistance, which in turn would lead to a reduction of benefits in the range of half a week to two weeks (Johnson and Klepinger, 1994). The pivotal factors in successful acceleration of job-finding appear to be the timing of the intervention (how soon help was offered, the intensity of service, and how much the staff actually monitored the recipients' job search. Unemployment Insurance, often dubbed "the welfare program for the middle class," has been roundly criticized because of its relaxed administration. Whether the new, institutionalized intervention effort will serve to tighten up the program and produce more adherence to program requirements remains to be seen.

Major Proposals. Considering the unanimity of opinion that the UI program requires revision, remarkably little effort has been expended toward this end, except for the relatively modest reemployment program noted above. The major recent proposals to reform the UI system are the following:

1. Raise the income ceiling on payroll taxes for the states, but lower the tax rate to protect small employers, a suggestion made in 1991 by Rep. R. Downy (N.J.), which was never seriously considered.
2. Lower costs through better internal administration by employers, that is, by encouraging employers to pay more attention to the causes of turnover; to make more frequent and stronger challenges of claims by ineligible workers fired for just cause; and to better document problem separations (Thompson 1989).

3. Build human capital investment programs into the state's UI system, something that already exists in a few states. This is controversial: critics claim that it confuses functions since UI is designed to be a temporary income transfer program, not an educational or job training organization (Schubert 1989).
4. Pay benefits in situations where employers reduce all workers' hours of employment to "spread the pain," which is already incorporated into the programs of a few states (Burdett and Wright 1989).
5. "Cash out" benefits for a lump sum (up to $4,000) for the purpose of enabling the unemployed recipient to go into business or some other type of self-employment, a proposal not supported by the business community because of doubts concerning the possibility of success (Reynolds 1988).
6. Require UI beneficiaries to register with the Public Employment Service (Director and Englander 1988).
7. Encourage unemployed workers to accept employment at a quicker rate than now prevails, by offering bonuses for locating and accepting a job within a prescribed period of time. (According to a review of outcomes of reemployment bonus efforts in several states by O'Leary [1998], savings have been incurred in situations where a low bonus amount combined with a long qualification period targeted to the 50 percent most likely to exhaust UI benefits is the best policy option.)
8. Change the basis for the "automatic trigger" for Federal involvement in extension-of-benefits from an arbitrary figure to some designated average length of unemployment in each state. This measure would be more indicative of the need for Federal intervention than any particular unemployment figure by itself (Medoff and Harless 1996). Whether this proposal would ameliorate the present situation is unclear: automatic triggering of eligibility for extended benefits makes things worse, according to observers; eligible states tend not to take advantage of the opportunity because they would have to share in the costs of the additional twenty-six weeks.

Obviously, none of the above suggestions deals with the aforementioned experience ratings, which all critics for the last thirty or more years have pointed to as a major problem with the system. The recommendations also fail to deal with the criticisms that UI no longer serves as a counter cyclical program, since only a minority of the unemployed now participate (Aguilar and Testa 1995:1–3). Those who do participate may have an experience similar to the following hypothetical case.

Insurance executive Dave Connors, 46, was laid off recently due to contractions in his branch of the industry. Reluctantly, Dave went to apply for Unemployment Insurance at his local State Employment Security Office. He found he was expected to register for available, appropriate, full-time employment at the local State Employment Service, to supply proof in form of a statement from his employer that he was involuntarily unemployed, and to engage in an active job search. He was to report back to the UI office periodically. Benefits would be paid up to a maximum of up twenty-six weeks. He was told to expect a delay in payment of benefits for one week.

Dave was unable to locate a job in his field by the end of the twenty-six weeks, so he hoped that Federal benefits would become available for an additional number of weeks. But this possibility depended on how bad the regional economy was. If an emergency were declared, Dave's benefits could possibly be extended.

WORKERS' COMPENSATION

Every state has a Workers' Compensation (WC) program that provides medical care, income, and rehabilitation to workers who are injured as the result of workplace accidents, and provides benefits to the survivors of workers who die as a result of workplace accidents. Originating in 1908, Workers' Compensation programs are the oldest of all Social Security system insurances. However varied, these mainly state programs are all designed to be "no-fault" in nature, aimed at making medical and maintenance help quickly available to injured workers and their families during the period of need. According to WC legislation, the worker does not have to litigate to prove employer-negligence. In fact, the injured worker gives up the right to sue the employer in return for speedy financial aid for medical care and weekly maintenance. The employer, in turn, pays insurance on a regular basis and is protected against the uncertain outcome of lawsuits when workplace accidents or deaths occur. Unhappily, in practice, payments are no longer always automatic and prompt, and a great deal of litigation is taking place.

Under the law, workers on the job who suffer accidents that leave them fully or partially disabled may file for benefits. The concept of workplace injury has been greatly expanded in recent years to include incidence of occupational diseases and even problems associated with stress. The ability to obtain redress for occupational diseases is often limited by the fact that the disease may not become apparent during the time limitations on the right to file a claim, often more than one to three years following last exposure to the conditions causing the occupational disease. About 87 percent of employed wage and salary workers in the United States are covered by the fifty-five different state and Federal plans. The most common, although not universal, exceptions are domestic, agricultural, and casual workers. Two other important exclusions, seamen in the U. S. merchant marines and interstate railroad employees, are covered by special Federal legislation.

Basic Facts About Workers' Compensation

Function: Provides immediate medical care, prompt periodic payments of replacement income, and vocational rehabilitation to workers suffering work place injuries.

Eligibility: Includes employees suffering from industrial accidents; sometimes, victims of occupational diseases.

Covered employment: Varies by state.

Financing: Employer-funded, with small worker contributions in a few states. Administrative costs are funded by the state or privately.

Benefits: Periodic cash payments for living expenses and for medical expenses during the period of disablement; death and funeral benefits to survivors. Usually calculated as a percentage of weekly earnings at the time of accident or death. Provision of physical and vocational rehabilitation for the injured worker. Extra benefits for injured minors, illegally employed.

Earnings limitations: Earnings above a specified amount render a worker ineligible for the program.

Tax status of benefits: Not taxable. (Social Security Administration)

Injured workers receive weekly payments in lieu of wages, plus payments for medical care. Sometimes lump-sum settlements are made. Should vocational rehabilitation services be required, these are usually offered by a state agency. Some states offer a maintenance allowance during the rehabilitation effort. Should a death occur, survivors receive death and funeral benefits.

Provision is made for the partially permanently injured as well as the fully permanently injured who are totally unable to work. Sometimes especially generous payments are provided for injured under-age workers who were illegally employed, the intent being to discourage their employment. The amount of the benefit tends to be about two-thirds of the worker's weekly earnings

Employers throughout the country are feeling the sting of the skyrocketing costs of WC programs, which stem, in broadest terms, from increased utilization, longer duration, higher benefits levels, and ever-rising medical costs. Overall costs in 1992 were ten times those of 1972. Some states and regional economies suffer, along with employers, because they have implemented broader or more generous programs, in general, than others. In some cases the costs are so severe as to impel companies to leave the area. (Moscovitch 1990). WC costs are so problematic in Pennsylvania, for example, that over half of a representative group of employers polled in 1996 by the Pennsylvania Chamber of Commerce and Industry stated that they would leave the state if they could, identifying "out of control" WC costs as their biggest problem (September 17, 1996, *Philadelphia Inquirer*). Pennsylvania employers who wish to leave, according to this report, often move to a neighboring state with a more favorable rate, but sometimes they are compelled to relocate completely out of the area.

The escalating costs of WC have been held responsible for plant closings, to which small firms are especially vulnerable because, unlike many large employers, they cannot afford to self-insure. Conversely, rising WC rates often cause employers to be reluctant to add additional employees, which causes the postponement or abandonment of expansion plans, widespread restructuring of jobs from full-time to part-time, increased use of temporary workers, and plant relocations from high-cost to low-cost WC states. Reportedly, the fear of future obligations is also the basis for employers' increasing refusal to rehire their own injured workers upon recovery or applicants with workplace injuries in their histories. Companies have been motivated to develop stratagems that would permit their withdrawal from the WC system, which lessens employee security. Finally, the heightened costs have the effect of lowering wages and salaries as the wage bill is eaten up by larger WC obligations.

The negative developments listed above are not due solely to WC costs, but WC is considered to constitute a major factor in employer decision-making with reference to them. Everyone suffers: employers are altering their business practices, fleeing high-cost states, and sometimes going out of business; insurers are fleeing problem states; workers are being deprived of desirable jobs and earnings; and communities are deprived of tax revenues while they are saddled with more rather than less responsibility for their residents.

Newspaper and business journal reports cite the following factors as contributing to the crisis in WC:

1. Declining economies that stimulate claims-filing by workers fearing layoff, especially those who are older and/or unwell (Calise 1992).
2. Increases in fraud in the system, on the part of employees, employers, and professionals. According to *Business Week,* October 19, 1992, physicians and lawyers are prominent among the professionals involved.
3. Increases in the level of benefits.
4. Increases in medical and legal costs.
5. Counterproductive practices by states in setting WC rates.
6. A series of management "neglects"—failure to ensure worker safety, to respond quickly to worker injuries as they occur, to produce medical and rehabilitative help; and failure to adequately analyze and challenge questionable WC claims.
7. The influence of the drug epidemic (Dauer 1992).
8. Demographic factors. According to the BLS, quoted in the August 4, 1991, *Philadelphia Inquirer,* there is a disproportionate number of youths and young adults on WC; that is, they make up the group responsible for about half of all workplace accidents.
9. Worker dissatisfactions.

Strategies for WC Cost Containment

Two approaches are commonly suggested for reducing or containing WC costs: management and prevention. A management strategy involves, for example, securing the trust of workers so that they will be willing to use and accept company doctors' verdicts concerning their injuries; and changing regulations to permit referrals of injured workers to health-maintenance organizations (HMOs), in order to avoid "doctor-shopping." (Such suggestions are employer-oriented. Employee-oriented cost-containment advocates would be unlikely to push for reliance on company doctors' opinions in this regard.) Preventive strategies tend to offer such remedial measures as beefing-up employers' industrial-engineering departments to create safer work environments, and reducing costs through both prevention and better disability management. One technique, suggested by a four-year study of cost-reduction efforts by 220 Michigan establishments, would be to offer an incentive to managers by forcing their departments to make WC payments for injuries sustained by workers in their departments. The same study also suggested offering transitional employment to recovering workers as a means of reducing payment periods (*Fortune*, June 29, 1992).

Litigation and occupational disease have attracted considerable employer attention as target areas for cost reduction. As noted in the August 16, 1992, *New York Times,* states are taking measures to both reduce or eliminate litigation as a means of determining eligibility, and achieving significant savings in the process. Despite the existence of the Occupational Safety and Health Act of 1970 (OSHA), large numbers of workers still are injured on the job each year and many die as as a result of such injuries each year. But the seemingly obvious good that comes from prevention is not always acceptable; the adoption of preventative measures may be costly and lead to the elimination of jobs, so preventive measures may be resisted by workers. Some workers would rather die slowly than have their plants shut down (Halle 1984). Aggressive action against fraud by employers, not always encouraged by insurance companies, also has brought significant savings.[3]

Prompt payment of claims, called for by WC legislation, has been dishonored in recent years. In some experiments, in which states adhered to original principles, litigation has been reduced. For example, the use of a state agency that determines how much workers should get and insures prompt payment has resulted in savings in Wisconsin. The systematic and aggressive challenging of unjustified claims by both employers and insurance carriers has also brought appreciable savings in states undertaking this effort (Thompson 1989; Roberts 1992).

States could also improve their situations by ceasing to engage in their currently counterproductive efforts to retain employment. A common practice is to place an artificially low "cap" on the WC tax, despite a big deficit in the state's trust fund, which results in the placement of a large proportion of the state's labor force into its uncovered workers' assigned risk pool, a residual market for employers, especially those in high-risk industries, who cannot buy insurance. Under such circumstances insurers often withdraw from the state; the state fund becomes exhausted; and the state places a surcharge on remaining employers, which prompts even more of them to leave the state.

Meanwhile, employers and employees alike continue to suffer from situations such as the following:

Building-supply manufacturer and distributor H.Q.H., a $30-million-annual business with 150 employees, is reeling from WC expenses involving just one employee. High costs of W.C. (and other programs) in Pennsylvania are pushing the firm to locate its new plant in Delaware where the tax structure is more favorable. Harry Hex, a 340-pound, 6'6" warehouse foreman injured his back defending himself against an attack by another employee. A physician chosen by Harry determined that he was entitled to both medical and salary indemnity (lost wages plus customary overtime). Harry so informed the firm, whereupon it forwarded the claim to its insurer. Medical expenses and wages were paid.

Three months after the injury occurred, Harry was unwilling to return to work, so the firm filed a Writ of Supersidious with the state Workers' Compensation Bureau, stating that Harry had been examined by six physicians, who opined that he could return to work. Harry's refusal to do so caused the case to go to arbitration. The W.C. office gave the case to an administrative law court judge, a lawyer hired by W.C. to hear the case, in January, 1992. The company was given to understand that a ruling would be made by April 1993. Harry continues to collect his salary. Should the company receive a favorable ruling, the insurer will try for reimbursement from the Supersidious Fund of the W.C., but the fund is "broke." When and if the insurer recovers, the company will be reimbursed. Meanwhile the company's experience rating rose from 0.8 to 2.4, boosting its annual WC payroll tax from $120,000 to $180,000. The company expects this one episode to cost it between $250,000 to $300,000 over a three year period. (Verbal communication, a Philadelphia area executive, April 1993)

The broadest proposal for WC reform comes from two analysts (Young and Polakoff 1992) who diagnose the WC problem as requiring "basic structural change." Their recommendations include: (1) the right to necessary medical-care income maintenance, and vocational rehabilitation for all workers injured on the job, irrespective of cause; (2) life insurance benefits to all dependents of workers fatally injured on the job, also irrespective of cause, plus help with job training; (3) full compensation for losses sustained when a worker is fatally injured or permanently disabled; and (4) promotion of worker health as a key to cost control.

While this constitutes a large agenda, much of it restates the original goals of the WC program and blends in the safety consciousness that prompted the passage of OSHA. Such a program would probably reduce litigation, but greatly increase coverage costs.

OLD AGE and SURVIVORS' INSURANCE: "SOCIAL SECURITY"

"Social Security," as Old Age and Survivors' Insurance (OAI) is popularly called, is the country's primary social-insurance program for income maintenance of elderly, retired persons. As such, it is of greatest interest to the public. In regard to the focus of this book, the extent to which Social Security affects employment and wages is not so clear. At this point in time, the overwhelming majority of the U.S. workforce is covered. Those who are excluded are covered by some earlier program such as the Railroad Retirement Act, are employees of state and local governments, or are household workers or farm workers whose earnings do not meet minimum requirements. The very small, remaining groups include some clergy and those in a family business. Also uncovered are those in the burgeoning illegal economy. Payments are loosely based on worker's earnings; retired spouse receives one-half of worker's benefits at age 65 (or own benefits, if larger.) Surviving spouse and minor children of a deceased worker also receive allowances, with automatic adjustments for inflation. The surviving spouse's benefit equals the diseased worker' benefit.

Basic Facts About Old Age and Survivors' Insurance (Social Security)

Function: Provides replacement income to retired workers and their survivors.

Eligibility: Persons age sixty-five (age 62, for lesser benefits), who have worked at least forty quarters in insured employment, and their survivors, spouses and children eighteen or under (nineteen if still in high school).

Covered employment: About 95 percent of all jobs in the official economy.

Financing: Paid for by a payroll tax of 6.2% on both employer and employee, up to a top limit of $68,400 (1998).

Benefits: Payments are loosely based on worker's earnings; retired spouse receives one-half of worker's benefits at age 65 (or own benefits, if larger). Upon death, surviving spouse receives the full amount of the worker's benefits. Payments are automatically linked to inflation. Minor children of a deceased worker also receive benefit payments.

Earnings limitations: Deductions in benefits for persons under age seventy who earn more than specified amounts (Ex: in 1998, one-third of earnings over $14,500 for persons age 65–69).

Tax status of benefits: 85 percent taxable, for families with adjusted incomes exceeding $44,000, and $34,000 for singles (as of 1996). (Social Security Administration).

Social Security, as OAI will be referred to here, is basically an income replacement program for former earnings, but is generally thought to be insufficient to meet the total income needs of retirees. For example, as of 1998 the maximum payment for a worker retiring at age sixty-five was $1,342 per month; the average monthly payment $765; the average retired couple's benefit, $1,288. The lower the lifetime earnings, the more important the Social Security pay tends to be to beneficiaries. In 1997 the payment replaced 25.4 percent of the annual earnings of the highest earners ($62,700), but 61 percent of the earnings of the lowest level earners ($11,118). When the allowances for spouses are included, the replacement income represented 38.1 percent and 91.4 percent of former earnings, respectively (Social Security Administration 1997). Maximum payments for year 2000: $1,433 for individuals.

Survivor's Insurance is a benefit to families of insured workers who die prior to retirement, that is, to spouses and minor children, offering continuity of income until children complete high school. This program was of greater importance in earlier days when women could not obtain employment; today it helps supplement low female wages. In December 1996 the average monthly benefit for a widow (or widower) was $515; the average for children, $487. Maximum year 2000 allowances: $1,373 for a widow or widower; $736 for the dependent children.

Many people express concern about Social Security in terms of what it will mean to them during retirement, which, again, may be summarized as "Will it be there when I need it?" When will outflow scrape the bottom of the till? Fortunately this great debate over the future of the Social Security system is beyond the focus of this discussion, but a few observations can be made.

First, there is nothing unique about the U.S. system's problems. All advanced nations are reeling from the pressures of increasing aging populations with ever-rising expectations. All advanced nations must reappraise society's ability to fund present programs. Better management, always welcome, is hardly the answer. Birth rates are falling, while greater proportions of each generation are being included in social insurance programs. The U.S. Social Security Administration, as noted by the *New York Times,* November 27, 1998, reports that there were 5.1 workers to every retiree in 1960; 3.3 in 1990; and that the proportion of payers to recipients is projected to fall to 1.9 by 2035. Although people think of themselves as benefiting from "their" payments, Social Security payments represent intergenerational transfers between old and young. In an attempt to establish confidence in Social Security solvency, Congress established the Old Age and Survivors Trust Fund and the Disability Trust Fund to emphasize the segregation of funds. But the funds are loaned to other governmental agencies and exist largely as bookkeeping items.

Investment in the Private Sector. Second, the suggestion that Social Security might be saved by investing a portion of the funds in the private sector is the subject of continuing controversy. The logic is that returns from the stock market would be higher than those from low-paying government bonds and could help save the system from bankruptcy. As of this writing, the proposal is being argued. Other prominent suggestions include proposals for encouraging older people to work more years by increasing the earnings limit on their benefits and for reducing the size of the automatic annual cost-of-living adjustment (widely regarded as overstated); and use the 1998 U.S. budget surplus to replenish the fund.

Punitive Earnings Tax as a Disincentive to a Longer Work Life. Third, discussion of the relevance of Social Security to the employment of retirement-age persons has traditionally decried the fact that earned income is taxed while unearned income from stocks, bonds, and other investments of more affluent retirees is disregarded. Put another way, earnings of persons ages sixty-five to six-ty-nine have been "taxed" at a much higher rate ($1 for every $3 earned income above $13,500, as of 1997) than has income from stocks and bonds. In response to these criticisms, the 1996 Congress agreed to raise the earnings limit of re-tirees in this age group in annual steps to $30,000 annually by 2002. After 2002 amounts are to be indexed to increases in average wages.

The punitive earnings tax had its origins in public policy objectives during the period of the Great Depression of the 1930s when the Social Security Act was written. The intent was to push the elderly out of the labor market, eliminating them from competition for available employment, by making work unprofitable. Today public policy leans toward encouraging a longer work life, yet paradoxi-cally, the trend is toward early retirement. In 1920, 55.6 percent of the work force was employed at age 65; in 1990, 16.4 percent. By December 1997 workers 65 and over totaled only 12.3 percent of their age group in the civilian labor force.

Whether the decision to work can be altered by manipulations of the Social Security system's "tax" on work   and other incentives and disincentives is questionable. The issue is whether Social Security benefits levels and disincen-tives to work, as expressed through the punitive earnings "tax," exert primary influence on the decision to withdraw from paid employment or whether other factors, such as the availability and size of private-sector pensions are more im-portant in influencing behavior. Many analysts believe that the latter represent the determining factors. Certain other factors that are unlikely to change also af-fect retirement decisions. For one, psychological issues play a part. Professionals with gratifying work are more likely to postpone retirement than blue-collar workers who find little satisfaction in their jobs and cherish their leisure more. One effect of the earnings tax has been to push those choosing to work from full-time to part-time status.

DISABILITY INSURANCE

The last of the major social insurances is Disability Insurance (DI). Estab-lished in 1956, the program benefits workers whose severe disabilities make em-ployment impossible. According to the specifications of the law, the individual must be unable to perform any work available throughout the United States, ir-respective of whether the person would be able to obtain the available work. However, as Congress has gradually added new groups of eligibles to the pro-gram, namely, disabled children of insured diseased and retired workers, disa-bled widows and widowers of insured workers at age 50, to cite some examples, the tie to employment has been diluted and little remains of the program's original intent. Still, to curb the potential for abuse, the DI law has a series of provisions designed to encourage recipients to return to work. Special considera-tion is given to the blind who have to meet much less stringent conditions of eligibility than other persons who seek disabled status. In December 1996 the average monthly payment to a disabled worker was $704, with additional pay-ments for dependent spouses and children (Social Security Administration 1997).

Remarkably little public attention has been directed toward DI. Clearly, it helps remove many marginally capable workers from the employment rolls.

With the criteria for eligibility ever broadening, its efficiency in drawing the line between employability and non-employability is unknown. The program may be said to contribute to maintenance of employment in the sense that DI payments expand the consumer power of its beneficiaries. Whether this is a socially desirable means of doing so is a matter of opinion. At present DI covers a huge population of persons certified as non employable who have never held a job. The program also includes disabled children with employed parents.

The following hypothetical case illustrates how DI is intended to work.

Harry Black, 31, an assembly worker, was injured in an automobile accident and is probably permanently disabled. Harry was covered for the full necessary 20 quarters (out of 40 quarters prior to his accident). Upon establishing himself as medically eligible (fully disabled), Harry could receive disability benefits. His wife and children are also eligible: his wife until the youngest child is 16; the children until they turn 18 (or 19, if in school). Harry will be expected to undergo a review every three years to establish that he continues to be genuinely unable to work. If Harry tries to work, he can earn up to $300 a month without being considered ineligible.

Basic Facts About Disability Insurance

Function: Provides replacement income for disabled workers and their dependents, with special consideration for the blind.

Eligibility: For workers with a strong prior work history and their disabled dependents, including some children disabled prior to age twenty-two, with a work record of at least half of the past ten years (20 quarters), less for younger workers; prior to age thirty-one, with employment for at least half of all quarters after age twenty-one (minimum of six quarters). Age, education, and work experience augment medical evidence, with less required of blind workers fifty-five and over.

Covered employment: About 95 percent of all jobs in the official economy (the same as all other OASDI programs).

Financing: Paid for by a payroll tax of 6.2 percent on both employer and employee, up to a top limit of $68,400 (1998); paid for as part of the OASDI deduction from paychecks.

Benefits: Similar to Old Age Insurance.

Earnings limitations: Earnings of less than $300 monthly are acceptable (in line with severe impairment), while earnings of $500 or more are taken to indicate capability for substantial gainful employment (SGA) and loss of eligibility.

Tax Status of Benefits: Not taxable.(Social Security Administration).

OTHER SOCIAL INSURANCES

Temporary Disability Insurance

One less familiar set of employer-based social insurance programs that need to be mentioned are the *temporary* disability insurance or cash sickness insurance programs offered by five states, Puerto Rico, and the railroad industry, to workers who have lost their wages due to some temporary, non-work-related disability (an inability to perform regular or customary work because of a physical or mental condition, including intervals of unemployment due to maternity). Such benefits, paid for solely by employers, are not available to persons receiving Workers' Compensation; some are a part of collective-bargaining agreements.

Railroad Retirement Act; Veterans' Benefits; State and Local Programs

Several additional Federal and state social insurance programs exist for special groups. They are the Railroad Retirement Act, Veterans' Benefits, and public-employee programs offered by on the local, state, and Federal government level. Some basic material on them is offered in *Social Security Programs in the U.S.* July 1997, published by the Social Security Administration.

Readers who are interested in a history of the development of the U.S. income transfer system and its philosophical underpinnings might refer to Andrew Achenbaum's *Social Security: Vision and Revisions* (1986) and Edward Berkowitz's (1992) *America's Welfare State*. Saul Blaustein's, Wilbur Cohen's, and William Haber's (1993) *Unemployment Insurance in the United States: The First Half Century* offers the fullest history of the development of UI. A good source of recommendations concerning Unemployment Insurance (often referred to as Unemployment Compensation) is the annual report of the Advisory Council on Unemployment Compensation, especially Aguilar and Testa, 1995.

NOTES

1. Many employers do not wish to incur or cannot afford the likely increase in experience ratings increases associated with persons who often must be fired or laid off, either because of behavior or low skill levels which make them eligible for employment which tends to be sporadic in nature.

2. Both union and non-union members reported that they failed to file because they thought themselves to be ineligible, an example of what is believed to be a widely held belief (Blank and Card 1991).

3. Examples of such actions are hiring investigators to determine whether supposedly disabled WC recipients are holding unreported jobs or engaging in vigorous sports.

REFERENCES

Achenbaum, W. Andrew. 1986. *Social security: visions and revisions*. Cambridge: Cambridge University Press.

Aguilar, Linda, and William Testa. 1995. Advisory Council on Unemployment Compensation in the United States, *Report and recommendations*. Transmitted to the President and Congress. (February) Washington, D.C., 1–3.

Benham, Harry. 1983. Unemployment insurance incentives and unemployment duration distributions. *The Review of Economics and Statistics* 65 (February): 139–52.

Berkowitz, Edward. 1991. *America's welfare state: from Roosevelt to Reagan*. Baltimore: Johns Hopkins University Press.

Blaustein, Saul, with Wilbur J. Cohen and William Haber. 1993. *Unemployment insurance in the United States: the first half century*. Kalamazoo, Mich.: W. E. Upjohn Institute for Employment Research

Blank, Rebecca, and David Card. 1991. Recent trends in insured and uninsured unemployment: is there an explanation? *Quarterly Journal of Economics* 106 (November):1157–89.

Brechling, Frank. 1981. Layoffs and unemployment insurance, 187–202. In Sherwin Rosen, ed., *Studies in labor markets*. Chicago: University of Chicago Press.

Burdett, Kenneth, and Randall Wright. 1989. Unemployment insurance and short-time compensation: the effects on layoffs, hours per workers, and wages. *Journal of Political Economy* 97, no. 6: 1479–96.

Burtless, Gary. 1991. The tattered safety net: jobless pay in the United States. *Brookings Review* 9 (Spring): 3–91.

Calise, Angela. 1992. Employers W.C. rates rises amid work force cuts. *National Underwriter* 96, no. 33 (17 August) 1991: 8.

Dauer, Christopher. 1992. Florida launches program to cut WC rate. *National Underwriter* 96 (5 January): 23, 43.

Deere, Donald. 1991. Unemployment Insurance and employment. *Journal of Labor Economics* 9 (October): 307–24.

Director, Steven, and Frederick Englander. 1988 Requiring unemployment insurance beneficiaries to register with the state employment service. *Journal of Risk and Insurance* 55, no. 2 (June): 245–54.

Eberts, Randall, and Christopher O'Leary. 1996. Profiling unemployment insurance beneficiaries. *Upjohn Institute Employment Research* (Fall): 1–4.

Fallick, Bruce. 1991. Unemployment insurance and the rate of reemployment of displaced workers. *Review of Economics and Statistics* 73 (May): 228–35.

Feldstein, Martin. 1976. Temporary layoffs in a theory of unemployment. *Journal of Political Economy* 84 (October): 937–57.

———. 1978. The effect of unemployment insurance on temporary lay-off unemployment. *American Economic Review* 68 (December): 834–47.

Goss, Ernie, and Chris Paul. 1990. The impact of unemployment insurance on the probability of migration of the unemployed. *Journal of Regional Science* 30, no. 3 (August): 349–58.

Halle, David. 1984. *America's working man: work, home, and politics among blue-collar property owners*. Chicago: University of Chicago Press.

Heywood, John, and S. White. 1990. Reservation wages and unemployment in manufacturing: a case study. *Applied Economics* (UK) 22, no. 3: 403–14.

Hutchens, Robert, David Lipsky, and Robert Stern. 1992. Unemployment insurance and strikes. *Journal of Labor Research* 13 (Fall): 337–54.

Johnson, Terry R., and Daniel Klepinger. 1994. Experimental evidence on unemployment insurance work-search policies. *Journal of Human Resources* 29 (Summer): 695–717.

Jones, Thomas. 1996. Social security: invaluable, irreplaceable, and fixable. *The Participant* (February): 1, 4.

Katz, Lawrence, and Bruce Meyer. 1990. Unemployment insurance, recall expectations, and unemployment outcomes. *Quarterly Journal of Economics* 105 (November): 973–1000.

Medoff, James, and Andrew Harless. 1996. *The indebted society*. Boston: Little, Brown, and Company.

Moorthy, Vivek. 1989/1990. Unemployment in Canada and the United States: the role of unemployment insurance benefits. *Federal Reserve Bank of New York Quarterly Review* 14 (Winter): 48–61.

Moscovitch, Edward. 1990. The downturn in the New England economy. What lies behind it? *New England Economic Review* 105, no. 4 (November): 973–1002.

O'Leary, Christopher. 1998. Profiling for reemployment bonus offers. *Employment Research* (Spring): 1–4.

Pearce, Diana. 1986. Unemployment compensation and women: toil and trouble, 141–61. In Barbara Gelpi and colleagues, eds., *Women and poverty*. Chicago: University of Chicago Press.

Reynolds, Larry. 1988. Can "blue collar" capitalism work? *Management Review* (September): 20–21.

Roberts, Karen. 1992. Predicting disputes in workers' compensation. *Journal of Risk and Insurance* 59 (June): 252–61.

Schubert, Walt. 1989. Unemployment Insurance costs: issues and dilemmas. *International Journal of Sociology and Economics* (UK) 16, no. 8: 60–67.

Social Security Administration. Office of Research, Evaluation and Statistics. 1997 *Social security programs in the United States.* SSA Publication No. 13-11758, July. Washington, D.C.: Government Printing Office.

Thompson, Roger. 1989. Unemployment: cutting the cost. *Nation's Business* 77 (November): 71, 73.

Vroman, Wayne. 1991. Why the decline in unemployment insurance claims? *Challenge* 34 (September-October): 55–58.

Wandner, Stephen. 1994. The worker profiling and reemployment services system: legislation, implementation, process, and research findings. U.S. Department of Labor, Unemployment Insurance Service, Occasional paper 94–4 (August).

Woodbury, Stephen and Robert Spiegelman. 1987. Bonuses to workers and employers to reduce unemployment. Randomized trials in Illinois. *American Economic Review* 77, no. 4: 513–30.

Young, Casey L., and Philip Polakoff. 1992. Beyond workers' compensation: a new vision. *Benefits Quarterly* 8, no. 3: 56–65.

21

The U.S. Welfare System

How the U.S. welfare system, a hodgepodge of programs, affects employment is rarely addressed except in terms of the highly visible, unpopular, recently abolished Aid to Families with Dependent Children (AFDC). This chapter briefly describes major welfare programs in the United States and reports what is known of their association with employment. Welfare programs are to be distinguished from the social insurances in that they are *means-tested*, that is, they offer benefits only after individuals prove their eligibility by going through a process of financial disclosure which is often considered demeaning. The immensity of the problem can be seen in the fact that, after public assistance rolls peaked in 1995, about 8.6 percent of all U.S. households were receiving some type of means-tested cash assistance: of the 69.6 million U.S. family households, 3.6 million families (5.2%) received some type of cash public assistance and another 2.4 million family households (3.4%) received Supplemental Security Income (SSI, a means-tested supplement to inadequate Social Security payments to very low-level wage earners).[1] Basic facts concerning income security programs described within this chapter depend heavily on Social Security Administration publications and periodic announcements through early 1999, especially *Social Security Programs in the United States* 1997.

TEMPORARY ASSISTANCE TO NEEDY FAMILIES

The program whose recipients have attracted the most attention and the most passion is now known as Temporary Assistance to Needy Families (TANF), the 1996 replacement for AFDC, which had become synonymous with the term "welfare program." Between 1935 and 1996 families were offered AFDC, which provided a low level of support to families consisting mainly of mothers and their children under eighteen years of age, although in later years some states permitted fathers with work histories to be included in the grant. Long-standing dissatisfaction with the program led to its abolition and the passage of the work-oriented TANF.

The basic objective of TANF is to move all adult welfare recipients into jobs within two years of their first receipt of financial assistance, and to limit dependency to five years throughout a recipient's lifetime. More power to declare the terms of eligibility and to implement them now resides in the states, which Congress believed to be a more parsimonious bunch than the Feds when it passed TANF. The states are mandated to move at least 25 percent of the present caseload into work within two years and 50 percent by 2002. However, up to 20 percent (the least employables) may be kept on beyond the five-year limit, a sop to liberals in Congress who were skeptical that many on the rolls are capable of meeting minimum employer requirements. Single parents were required to work a minimum of twenty hours weekly in fiscal 1996; thirty hours by 2000. States have the discretion to permit parents with children under age six to work twenty hours weekly and two-parent families, thirty-five hours (until 2000). For those who fail to obtain private-sector jobs, "work-fare" may be provided as a step toward permanent employment.The employment objective is emphasized, and Federal funding is tied to a given state's success in moving recipients off the rolls.

As of 1995, as noted above, 5.2 percent of U.S. family households were participating in the Aid to Families with Dependent Children (AFDC) program, which was, as of 1996, replaced by TANF. Though the Roosevelt Administration, originators of the program, thought welfare programs (of which AFDC was the largest) would shrink to inconsequential proportions as Social Security insurance programs developed, this has not been the case. The AFDC program grew slowly, rising from less than 1 percent of the U.S. population in 1940 to above 5 percent during a portion of the 1970s; falling to between 4 and 5 percent from about 1978 to 1988 and then peaking at about 5.5 percent in 1993, when it fell slightly to about 5.2 percent in 1995 (O'Neill and O'Neill 1997, 8–9).

Basic Facts About the Personal Responsibility and Work Opportunity Reconciliation Act of 1996

Name of Program: Temporary Aid to Needy Families (TANF)
Nature of Program: Discretionary, on part of each state; no mandates exist.
Target population: Destitute families with children.
Funding: By states, supplemented by Federal block grants.
Standards for state eligibility: Submission of a plan by the state which contains provisions for reductions in numbers of adults on state welfare rolls by 25 percent in two years, through employment or otherwise, including removal without any other provision.
Standards for states regarding family eligibility: None, except for work requirements and duration of life-time eligibility limited to five years.
Standards for states regarding amounts of family grants: None. (Jeffrey Katz. *Congressional Quarterly Weekly Report*, August 3, 1996: 2192–94)

At this point, the outcomes of TANF "work or else" and "five years is the limit" mandates cannot be predicted. The question most frequently raised about the potential for success is whether sufficient numbers of low skill jobs exist that could absorb the current welfare population, most particularly, those recipients in the old urban areas, deserted by industry, where a large proportion of the caseload lives. Suggestions for transporting people to suburban locations where jobs exist have occasionally been made, but they have been met mostly with silence in view of the failure of efforts in the 1960s. A series of newspaper articles have reported falling caseloads, but how many actually have jobs and how many of these are push-outs is unknown. It has also been reported that some recipients and their children have been forced to leave educational programs, college and skill-oriented training, as TANF legislation specifies that immediate job entry—or efforts involving large blocks of time to obtain such—is required to maintain eligibility for benefits.What will happen to persons dumped from the rolls when their eligibility ends after five years and what will become of their children has not been widely discussed in the press.

Job Availability

Discussion of welfare reform is limited here to the matter of job availability. No one has yet published an analysis of the labor markets of the fifty states, constituting thousands of local job markets, in regard to their capacities to absorb millions of welfare recipients who are now expected to find employment. Most labor economists believe, however, that, in the expansionary economy of the mid and late 1990s, that large numbers of low-skill, low-wage, entry-level job opportunities, particularly for women, to be available (Blank 1995; Burtless 1995). A large number of the welfare population could, under the circumstances existing during the 1990s, probably be phased into the job market without an increase in joblessness. As Burtless (1995) points out, while the U.S. labor force grew by 50.4 million between 1964 and 1989, about 2 million yearly, the number of jobs grew by 47.7 million, that is, about 95 percent of new job seekers were successful in locating employment. During the same period, the unemployment rate barely rose, moving from 5 percent to 5.2 percent.

One explanation of the ability of the labor force to absorb so many new workers, according to Burtless, lies in the fact that in the long term, employers tend to adjust their production methods to take into account the availability of labor. In the current situation, on behalf of the large-scale supply of low-skilled workers, employers may very well redesign jobs previously held by more skilled, higher paid workers. For example, during the 1970s, when faced with a huge supply of eager youth entrants, restaurant owners hired high-school dropouts to prepare and serve meals, work that was previously performed by experienced help.

Since the educational and skills levels of most welfare recipients are low—more than half, eighteen years and over, had less than four years high-school education in 1993—their prospects of earning an adequate family wage are poor, even if the work they locate is full-time and year-round. Over 70 percent achieved scores on the Armed Forces Qualification Test that put them in the bottom quarter of all test-takers for their age-group. Poor education alone, however, cannot account for the employment histories of these young women, according to Maynard (1995), who points out that young men of the same age with the same limited education are employed at double the rate of the female school dropouts discussed above, suggesting that cultural factors and alternatives to employment may also play a role in the poor work experiences and earnings of young female school dropouts.

Despite the sentiments expressed by some, that jobs are obtainable, most observers question the outcome of the movement into paid employment. Although large numbers of welfare recipients might locate jobs, no reason exists to assume that the entry-level jobs that they are likely to obtain would lead to family betterment in terms of higher wages or benefits such as health care. The poor prospects of most welfare recipients is largely due to their lack of educational attainment. According to an analysis by Burtless (1995), about half of the women most dependent on AFDC ("welfare") who were in their mid-20s had not finished high school and less than one-eighth had any education beyond high school.[2] With earnings associated strongly with education, the employment prospects of welfare mothers are not only poor, but worsening. Earnings have been falling for poorly educated women since the late 1970s. For example, according to Burtless, between 1979 and 1989, full-time earnings for female school dropouts aged twenty to twenty-four fell almost one-fifth and, since 1989, have continued to fall (in real dollars).

Job Instability. The chronic instability of the types of jobs usually obtained by the working poor makes the possibility of permanent financial independence unlikely for the subgroup eligible for welfare help. Many welfare recipients have long work histories of sporadic movements in and out of the job market. Estimates drawn from a particularly successful "welfare-to-work" program indicate that about 40 percent of welfare mothers are so-called cyclers: they collect checks for about twenty-four of the first sixty months after entering the rolls, then leave for employment but return for various reasons such as lack of child or health care, lack of social skills, and family problems that include resistance from men friends. Almost all lose their first job and less than one-fifth (18%) stay on the rolls for long periods of time (Pavetti 1993). The July 31, 1996, *New York Times*, quoted a spokesman for the U.S. Department of Health and Human Services who stated that about 70 percent of the recipients leave within two years, but about half return, on the average, and they spend about six years on the rolls.

The conclusion may be drawn that the outlook is distinctly unfavorable for the welfare population because of the nature of the jobs that are most available to them (low wages, income instability, and absence of benefits plus inability to pay for necessary support services, especially child care). As Burtless puts it, the problem is not too many *bad jobs*, but too few. Contrary to popular perceptions, if there were more low-skill jobs available, wages would rise—the competition for jobs would slow down; presumably scarcity would set in; and employers would have to coax job-seekers with higher wage offers—but this does not appear to be in the offing. Employers are increasingly taking the low-wage approach, with "welfare" mothers seeming to be just another group competing for a shrinking share of the nation's low-skill jobs. But movement out of poverty and income stability are not the objectives of the 1996 TANF legislation; saving money is. How much the unprecedented low unemployment levels of the late 1990s have specifically affected the welfare population is unknown. It is known that caseloads fell drastically during the late 1990s, but just what happened to the women involved is unknown. Even with unemployment rates at historical lows, can employers absorb the least employable women in our population, many of them illiterate (and, additionally, with heavy home responsibilities)? Whether the "strong boat which lifts all" can help the persons remaining on welfare at the turn of the century is unclear.

Policy Proposals

Some policy proposals aimed at improving the supply and demand equation concerning employment possibilities for adult welfare recipients have been made by Laurie Bassie (1995), an economist specializing in the welfare-to-work issue. Bassi's basic suggestions are as follows:

1. The use of reemployment bonuses.
2. Wage subsidies.
3. Self-employment subsidies.
4. Education and training for unemployed workers.

The purpose of the reemployment bonus would be to motivate the job-seeker to accept reemployment. Wage subsidies are suggested as a means of shortening periods of unemployment and reducing the unemployment rate. Subsidy of self-employment might be feasible through the use of Unemployment Insurance benefits. While the contribution of education to employment is generally accepted, how to make education work for the *disadvantaged* population is another matter. Experience since the 1960s has not been encouraging. Gains from government-sponsored training programs for   unemployed or disadvantaged workers have been practically nil, although slightly more encouraging for women than men (Barnow 1987; Bloom, Orr, Cave, Bell, and Doolittle, 1994). However, persons securing *employer-provided* education and training have been found to experience meaningful earnings increases, with the greater gain coming from on-the-job training as opposed to classroom education (Lynch 1992).

Stimulating Demand. In regard to stimulating demand for labor, Bassi suggests four measures:

1. Employment tax credits.
2. Training tax credits or grants.
3. Economic development initiatives.
4. Short-time compensation programs.

Bassi's first proposal is designed to give employers a financial inducement to hire the unemployed. The suggestion to subsidize employers' education and training programs is motivated by findings concerning the superiority of employer-based education and training programs over those offered publicly. By the late 1980s, forty-six states were subsidizing at least one training program through tax credits or outright grants to employers. States have tried to maximize benefits by limiting help to small and distressed firms and to those offering basic job skill training, as opposed to work-specific skills. Little is known about the effectiveness of these programs, but, according to Bassi, early reports are promising.

The suggestion that government engage in economic development initiatives on behalf of the welfare population is a large-scale strategy that involves harnessing various agencies of government to persuade employers to relocate into a community. This highly popular strategy has been heavily criticized in recent years as being a "zero-sum game," with communities giving enormous tax breaks to employers who would have settled somewhere else if not for the high bid of the "winner." Some see this as shortsighted strategy, resulting in gross overpayments for jobs promised (see Milward and Newman, 1989, for a review of research on this job-bidding war). In the same league are suggestions for establishment of enterprise zones, a tactic often pushed by mayors of old cities as a means of encouraging economic development; little solid evidence exists about the ability of this strategy to create additional jobs.

Use of short-time has been used extensively in Europe, especially Germany, and, to a lessor extent, in seventeen states of the United States. Better matching of supply with demand, the last of Bassi's suggestions, calls for providing (1) better access to labor-market information, and (2) help with relocation. The first involves beefing up the U.S. Employment Service (ES), long thought of as a problem performer although there is some evidence that contacts with ES result in job entry sooner than otherwise would have occurred (Jacobson 1994; Kulick 1994). The second, relocation, is also a problematic suggestion in that, while the young tend to move toward opportunities, persons with family obligations are hesitant to do so.

Early Developments

The *New York Times* has documented several developments since the passage of the 1996 welfare legislation. First, most states are choosing to continue their present programs (September 10, 1996; October 15 1996), not opting out, as feared by many welfare advocates. Second, New York City has given the country a foretaste of just how states and their localities may attempt to meet the mandate to have 20 percent of their caseloads working within two years. As of April 1998 the mayor had injected 34,100 welfare recipients into the city's Work Experience Program throughout city departments, a low-paid workforce that effectively replaced 20,000 regular city job slots, about 10 percent of the city payroll, including many unionized jobs (April 13, 1998).

Third, an unwelcome development to program administrators and state-level politicians alike is the reported interest expressed in unionization on the part of work-fare participants; some of these workers have reportedly asked why they should not be paid "real wages" for "real work." Fourth, big businesses such as Lockheed and Electronic Data Systems are apparently turning to welfare administration as a new growth area, proposing its privatization (September 15, 1996).

Finally, in 1997 the Department of Health and Human Services reported that welfare rolls have been falling throughout the United States since 1994 and continue to do so (February 1, 1997). No data exists, however, as to how many of the persons involved actually have jobs. Whether this shrinkage reflects the needs of a booming economy, increased motivation to work, or merely better push-out tactics on the part of state agencies is unknown. Also unknown is how many of the disengaged families have a current wage-earner in the household, but it is widely believed that many do not. Some early affirmation of this impression was furnished by a 1998 study by the New York State Office of Temporary and Disability Assistance, which found that only 29 percent of those leaving the rolls in New York City between July 1996 and March 1997 appeared to be employed (i.e., earning $100 or more per month), as indicated by employer wage reports a few months after they left assistance programs, TANF, or Home Assistance (*New York Times* March 23, 1998).

Basic Facts About AFDC (The Major Welfare Program for Families with Dependent Children Prior to Passage of TANF, 1996)

Maximum monthly cash assistance payment: $120 to $703, depending upon state, for a family of three.
Median state decline in value of grant since 1970: 51%.
Anticipated average stay on welfare of current population: 65% of families, 8 years or more.
Average length of stay of a family, including repeat spells: 13 years. (House Ways and Means Committee 1996)

The remaining portion of this chapter is devoted to brief descriptions of other important income transfer programs.

EARNED INCOME TAX CREDIT

Another income transfer program of increasing importance is the Earned Income Tax Credit (EITC). Of quite a different nature than TANF, the EITC is a relatively new program designed to encourage work as opposed to welfare dependency by offering a reward in the form of an income supplement given in a non-stigmatizing manner. Initially, the credit represented an effort to meet the criticism that Social Security taxes are regressive, that is, that they tax low-wage earners at a higher rate than the well-to-do. Under the Tax Reform Act of 1986, low-wage earners are effectively exempted from Federal income taxes through the device of raising personal deductions. In addition, the EITC was increased so that families earning under a certain amount (to be adjusted annually for inflation) would not only receive a refund of their deductions, but be given the difference between the amount they earned and the total credit to which they are entitled. For the lowest earners, the Federal treasury makes a contribution to the family. In the years following the passage of the legislation, the amounts of the credit were increased according to family size, to the point where payments to working poor families exceeded the value of their income tax and Social Security deductions.

Conceptually, the EITC is a preferred means of income redistribution to both conservatives and liberals because it rewards work over welfare, even when rewards are minimal, and because it is relatively inexpensive to administer. In 1993 Congress expanded coverage and raised benefits as part of the Clinton Administration's antipoverty effort. The long-term objectives of the enabling legislation remain and can be identified as payroll-tax relief for low-wage earners, recognized by policy-makers to be too high, and the encouragement of potential welfare applicants to seek employment over dependency. In other words, the goals are dual: to lessen the burden of payroll deductions for the *working poor* and to encourage the most marginally employable to enter the labor force.

Usage of the EITC is rapidly expanding. Initiated in 1975 as a modest program serving 6.2 million families, it was projected to serve 18.7 million by 1996 and cost almost as much as the Federal and state governments spent on AFDC, the major welfare program at the time. Average annual benefits have risen from $201 per family to $1,341 (projected) over the same time span. The *Philadelphia Inquirer* reported on March 13, 1995, that the EITC reached more people than did welfare, 18.3 million families as opposed to 5 million. And *Business Week,* September 28, 1998, noted that EITC benefited more than million working families at a cost of $28 billion.

EITC effectively raises the income of a two-child family earning $8,425 by 40 percent and a one-child family earning $6,000 by 34 percent. A single mother with two children who earned the 1995 minimum wage ($4.25) and who filed for the credit would have had her actual income raised to $5.87 per hour. In 1995 about 70 percent of benefits went to single-parent households, with the average check being $1,088. Unlike many programs designed for the poor, a large majority of eligible families (about 80%) are believed to be receiving benefits. One group as yet not reached are those among the working poor who are employed but have such low earning power that they do not file tax reports, fail to apply for the credit, or are ignorant of the program. The June 7, 1995, *New York Times* noted that, contrary to intent, the EITC program has become popular among the more affluent, as many middle-class families are using the program to help them get through difficult periods in their lives, such as severe loss of income due to a lay-off or prolonged illness of the wage earner. Also, a substantial number of ineligible families are attempting to get on the rolls (1994).

A concurring study by Jeffrey Liebman (1998) of Harvard University agreed that the near poor are helped more than those under the poverty level. Despite this limitation, however, Liebman found the tax credit to be effective in reducing the increasing income disparity experienced by the lowest fifth of households of families with children over the past twenty years. It has replaced about one-third of the 14 percent reduction in income share and is believed to have influenced the increase in employment of single mothers (about 10 percent since 1984). This suggests that the EITC may be achieving one of its prime objectives. As for charges of fraud, Liebman found irregularities to be no worse than for the income tax system as a whole. As the TANF program progresses and many welfare recipients lose their eligibility, the EITC may play an important role in enabling such persons to enter the labor force, since minimum wage jobs could be supplemented through this program.

Can the EITC achieve its ultimate goal—that of raising families with working members out of poverty? According to one expert, projections indicated that in 1996, the supplement, together with Food Stamps, should have been sufficient to realize this goal (Blank 1995). A contrary view was taken by another analyst, based on the interfacing of EITC with public assistance programs that then included AFDC, Food Stamps, and Medicaid, namely, that the EITC could not achieve its ultimate goal unless it was substantially modified (Levin-Waldman 1994). Several reasons back up this position. First, most EITC recipients are thought not to have a grasp of how the EITC operates. Instead of giving the benefits on a weekly or periodic basis, as was the intent of program planners, benefits are mainly received as once-a-year lump sums and used for special needs, not basic daily expenses. As such, the connection with employment and the role that EITC is supposed to serve as a work incentive tends to be lost. Second, as has been noted previously, many eligibles fail to apply and they lack incentive to get off welfare because of the benefits associated with it (Food Stamps, home heating relief, and medical care). Liebman's study, however, concluded that fears about the costs of disengagement from the welfare program and the possibility that EITC might discourage people's willingness to work are not, in fact, matters for concern, perhaps because the persons involved do not understand how the EITC scheme works. In short, the availability of EITC does not appear to discourage people from improving their situations to the point where they are no longer eligible for the credit.

An increase in the official minimum wage is one possible, if only partial, remedy to the criticism that the EITC does not, in practice, offer much work incentive. An information campaign, including help with tax reports, might alleviate the problem of lack of involvement among the very poorest families. If the program became truly effectual, might it encourage some underground workers to enter the legal economy? More experience is needed before the program's effectiveness may be thoroughly appraised.

For a good review of EITC issues, see John Scholz' article in the *National Tax Journal*, 47, March 1997.

FOOD STAMPS

The Food Stamps program, begun in its current form in 1964, aims to improve nutrition and alleviate hunger in low-income households. It has some relevance to employment issues in that about one-fifth of the heads of families receiving Food Stamps are employed, about 7 percent full time. Its relative popularity with the public, despite the fact that it is a welfare program, may stem from its availability to many working poor families who are otherwise ineligible for welfare. Also, the elderly status of another 7 percent is acceptable to the public. In fiscal year 1996 more than 25 million persons participated in the program. Administered nationally by the Food and Nutrition Service of the Department of Agriculture and locally by state welfare offices, local food markets, and banks, the Food Stamp program is paid for by the Federal government, with the states sharing in its administration costs.

Food Stamp usage appears to parallel rises in unemployment, indicating that working families are able to use the program in time of need. As of 1995, more than twice the number of families used the Food Stamps program as relied on AFDC, 8.4 million families as opposed to 3.6 million receiving AFDC (*Statistical Abstract of the United States*, Tables 581 and 583 respectively). It is also a subsidy of sorts for low-wage employers, since the existence of the program lessens pressure for wage increases for those at the bottom. Prior to passage of the 1996 welfare legislation, welfare recipients and employed persons with income up to 130 percent of the poverty level could qualify for Food Stamps. Currently, year-round access to the program for employable recipients is conditional upon their working at least twenty hours per week through the entire year.

Public criticism of the Food Stamp program tends to be muted, possibly because of the interest of the agricultural sector in continuation of the program and the large number of working and middle-class people benefiting, at one time or another, from the program. It has been pointed out that the addition of Food Stamps to a basic welfare grant (plus possible Energy Assistance, rent supplementation, and Medicaid) may give a welfare recipient a higher income than the take-home pay of a member of the working poor, thus posing a disincentive to work. This matter has not been exploited by those ordinarily interested in cutting welfare, however.

Not a great deal is known about the impact of Food Stamps on employment. A rare study (Hagstrom 1996, using data from the 1984 Survey of Income and Program Participation) explored whether the amount of Food Stamp benefits affected married couples' decisions to participate in the program and the subsequent work-leisure choices that they made, which affected eligibility and grant amounts. Findings were that the level of benefits influenced the decision to participate, but had little effect on the decision to work full-time, part-time, or not at all. The researchers projected that if the maximum grants were to be reduced by 25 percent, the proportion of husbands in poor households who would choose to work full-time would be about 1 percent; if limited to poor households who accept Food Stamps, about 3.4 percent. In the case of wives, it was estimated that a 25 percent decrease in benefits would impel about 12 percent of all wives in families receiving Food Stamps to work full-time.

Hagstom's findings are meaningful because, as of 1991, about a quarter of all poor U.S. families with children consisted of married couples with children living together as intact families. About 40 percent of all poor children in the United States lived in these families, according to a 1993 U.S. Census Bureau report cited by Hagstrom. The findings are interpreted as indicating that few couples modify their circumstances of employment in order to maintain Food Stamp eligibility or to secure higher benefits. These findings concur with those of an earlier study of single mothers' work-leisure responses to Food Stamps (Fraker and Moffit 1988).

Usage of Food Stamps fell drastically after 1996, about 21 percent between 1996 and December, 1998, for reasons not fully understood as of this writing (U.S. Department of Agriculture, reported by *New York Times*, February 24, 1999).

GENERAL ASSISTANCE

General Assistance (GA) is a purely state-based series of programs for destitute persons who are not covered by the Federal-state programs already described. Programs vary greatly from state to state, with GA being the last and least viable safety net for those without income, prior to turning to private charity (Salvation Army soup kitchens and the like). Depending on the state involved, GA may offer a small amount of regular or emergency help to some very poor persons who are ineligible for help under the Federal-state programs, for example, adults who have no dependent children who are ineligible for TANF. This may include persons physically unable to work who do not qualify for Disability

Insurance. GA is generally seen as a transitional program, helping unemployed people very minimally for a short period between jobs. The amounts given are extremely low by any standard.

Little is known about the influence of GA on employment behavior, but in the past some states altered their programs in the belief that youths, especially, were using the program as an alternative to work.

SUPPLEMENTAL SECURITY INCOME (SSI)

Supplemental Security Income (SSI) is a less well-known welfare program that offers financial help to several populations who are not otherwise covered by any social insurance program, or whose social insurance payment is below the poverty level: the needy aged (65+), and the visually or otherwise disabled, basically unemployables. Undertaken in 1972, SSI represented the first part of an effort to gradually phase out welfare programs, which were seen as demeaning and poorly funded because of lack of popular support. It is not an employment-associated program, but it attracts little public resistance, possibly because public hostility toward welfare mothers does not extend to the SSI population, who are not thought responsible for their plight. Originally undertaken with the aged in mind, the disabled, including many children, quickly became the major beneficiaries of SSI. Maximum SSI payments for the year 2000: $512 for individuals, $769 for couples.

For historical material referred to above, see Berkowitz's *America's Welfare State: From Roosevelt to Reagan* (Baltimore: Johns Hopkins University Press, 1991). For an outstanding discussion of the welfare-to-work issue, see Nightingale and Haveman's *The Work Alternative* (Washington, D.C.: Urban Institute, 1995). Perhaps the best description of actual welfare-to-work programs is contained in Grubb's *Learning to Work: the Case for Reintegrating Job Training and Education* (New York: Russell Sage Foundation, 1996).

NOTES

1. Percentage calculations are derived from Table 581, p. 374, the *Statistical Abstract of the U.S. 1997.*

2. Burtless used both Current Population Survey of the Census Bureau and data over a ten- to fifteen-year period from the National Longitudinal Survey of Youth (NLSY), a representative sample of young people studied over a period of years. NLSY data offers detailed information on the same individuals over a period of years.

REFERENCES

Barnow, Bert. 1987. The impact of CETA programs on earnings. *Journal of Human Resources* 22, no. 2:158–93.

Bassi, Laurie. 1995. Stimulating employment and increasing opportunity for the current work force, 37–156. In Nightingale, Demetra, and Robert Haveman, eds., *The work alternative*. Washington, D.C.: Urban Institute.

Berkowitz, Edward. 1991. *America's welfare state: from Roosevelt to Reagan*. Baltimore: Johns Hopkins University Press.

Blank, Rebecca. 1995. Outlook for the U.S. labor market and prospects for low-wage entry jobs, 33–70. In Nightingale, Demetra, and Robert Haveman, eds., *The work alternative*. Washington, D.C.: Urban Institute.

Bloom, Howard S., Larry Orr, George Cave, Stephen Bell, and Fred Doolittle. 1994. Title II AA impacts on earnings and employment at 18 months. In the Abt Associates' National JTPA Study.

Burtless, Gary. 1995. Employment prospects of welfare recipients, 71–106. In Nightingale, Demetra, and Robert Haveman, eds., *The work alternative*. Washington, D.C.: Urban Institute.

Fraker, Thomas, and Robert Moffitt. 1988. The effectiveness of food stamps on labor supply. *Journal of Public Economics* 35, no. 1 (February): 25–56.

Grubb,W. Norton. 1996. *Learning to work: The case for reintegrating job training and education*. New York: Russell Sage Foundation.

Hagstrom, Paul A. 1996. The Food stamp participation and labor supply of married couples: an empirical analysis of joint decisions. *Journal of Human Resources* 31, no.2: 383–402.

Jacobson, Louis. 1994. The effectiveness of the U.S. employment service. Report prepared for the Advisory Commission on Unemployment Compensation. Washington, D.C.: U.S. Department of Labor.

Katz, Jeffrey. 1996. Provisions of welfare bill. *Congressional Quarterly Weekly Report* (August 3): 2192–94.

Kulick, Jane. 1994. The evolution of the U.S. employment service and a review of evidence concerning its operations and effectiveness. Report prepared for the Advisory Council on Unemployment Compensation. Washington, D.C.: U.S. Department of Labor.

Levin-Waldman, Oren. 1994. The earned income tax credit and the need to synchronize public assistance. Jerome Levy Economics Institute Working Paper No. 131 (December).

Liebman, Jeffrey. 1997. *Lessons about tax benefit integration from the U.S. earned income tax credit experience*. Layerthrope, Mass. YPS for the Joseph Rowntree Foundation, Publisher.

Lynch, Lisa. 1992. Private sector training and the earnings of young workers. *American Economic Review* 82, no.1: 299–312.

Maynard, Rebecca. 1995. Subsidized employment and non-labor market alternatives for welfare recipients, 109–36. In Nightingale, Demetra, and Robert Haveman, eds. *The Work Alternative*. Washington, D.C.: The Urban Institute.

Milward, H. Brinton, and H. Newman. 1989. State incentive packages and the industrial location decision. *Economic Development Quarterly* 3, no. 3: 203–22.

Nightingale, Demetra, and Robert Haveman, eds. 1995. *The work alternative: welfare reform and the realities of the job market*. Washington, D.C.: Urban Institute Press.

O'Neill, David M., and June Ellenoff O'Neill. 1997. *Lesson for welfare reform: An analysis of the AFDC caseload and past welfare-to-work programs*. Kalamazoo, Mich.: W. E. Upjohn Institute for Employment Research: 8–9.

Pavetti, LaDonna A. 1993. The dynamics of welfare and work: exploring the process by which young high school graduates and high school dropouts work their way off welfare. Harvard University: Malcolm Wiener Center for Social Policy, Working Paper H-933 (July).

Scholz, John C. 1994. The earned income tax credit: participation, compliance, and anti-poverty effectiveness. *National Tax Journal* 47 (March): 51–81.

———. 1997. *Social Security programs in the United States*. Government Printing Office: Washington, D.C., July.

U.S. Congress. Committee on Ways and Means. 1992. Dynamics of economic well-being: program participation, 1992. Washington, D.C.: Government Printing Office.

———. 1996. *Green Book*. (November). Washington, D.C.: Government Printing Office: 11.

U.S. Department of Commerce. Census Bureau. 1996. Current population reports: household economics studies. Washington, D.C.: Government Printing Office.

———. *1997 Statistical Abstract of the United States*. Washington, D.C.: Government Printing Office: Table 581, 374.

22

Health Care Programs:
Medicare and Medicaid

This chapter reports on what is known about the impact of the two most important, national health care programs on employment. The two programs are Medicare, for the insured elderly and disabled, and, less well known, Medicaid, a medical welfare program for very poor people who are without any health-insurance coverage. As will be seen, although it is widely believed that employer-provided health insurance is a greatly prized work benefit, not a great deal of hard evidence exists as to how the presence or lack of availability of such insurance actually affects the behavior of those already on the job and those seeking employment.

MEDICARE

Medicare, the HI in OASDHI (the complete acronym for the total social-security system, Old Age Security, Disability, and Health Insurance) was instituted in 1965 to improve health care for the elderly, but now also includes disabled persons of all ages, a fact not widely known. Contrary to general impressions, Medicare does not cover all health costs of the eligible; the basic program (Part A) is limited to hospital insurance. Medical insurance to help pay for physicians or other health-care providers' fees, Medicare B, must be purchased. As a result, a portion of the eligible elderly are not covered for medical expenses due to inability to pay the premium ($45.50 monthly in 2000), which is supplemented from general revenues. Further, Medicare does not cover important costs such as long-term chronic nursing care and medical prescriptions, dental care, eyeglasses, hearing aides, and routine physical examinations. Funding of Medicare and just what expenses the program should cover—medicine, in particular—is expected to attract broad popular and legislative attention in coming years. The premium for Medicare-Part B is expected to double by 2007, lending urgency to the debate.

Since 1991 the states have been required to pay the costs of Medicare for certain very low-income uninsured elderly and disabled persons, as part of an effort to gradually include a larger part of the population in the program. Funding for Medicare comes from a payroll tax of 1.45 percent of annual earnings up to $125,000, paid by both employer and employee during the working years. Payments to providers are made by the Federal Hospital Insurance Trust Fund on a reimbursement basis (U.S. Department of Health and Human Services, Health Care Financing Administration 1997).

Toward the end of 1998, Medicare offered a new choice, Medicare C (sometimes called Medicare Plus Choice). In addition to the traditional fee-for-service arrangement or HMO enrollment (discussed below), Medicare enrollees have alternative choices. According to the brochure mailed to Medicare beneficiaries, Medicare options include:

(1) the original Medicare plan (fee-per visit; also referred to as fee-for-service);
(2) the original Medicare plan, with a supplementary policy purchased by the Medicare beneficiary through a private source;
(3) a Medicare managed care plan, several variations being (a) a health maintenance organization (HMO); (b) a provider sponsored organization (PSO); (c) a preferred provider organization (PPO); or (d) a point of service option (POS);
(4) private fee-for-service plans (PFFS) private insurance plans which may receive Medicare premiums for Medicare-covered services, all of which are included. Recipients are likely to be billed an additional amount above the standard Medicare premium; and
(5) a Medicare medical savings account (MSA.)

With the exception of the second item, purchase of a Medigap policy, the above-listed options represent additional choices. Brief descriptions of each option appear in the Medicare bulletin HCFA-02119, August 1998.[1] Enrollments in the new plans are specified to begin in late 1999, with selections to be effective January 1, 2000 (U.S. Department of Health and Human Services, Health Care Financing Administration 1998).

As of September 30, 1996, almost 38 million persons were enrolled in Medicare; 88 percent of them were aged persons; the remainder were disabled individuals. Part B coverage must be purchased: the annual premium for 1998 was $43.80, which was deducted from the retiree's or disabled person's monthly benefits check. The charge has been made that many of the retired working poor cannot participate in Medicare-Part B because of inability to pay the fee. As of 1995, while over 37 million persons participated in Medicare-Part A, 36 million were enrolled in Medicare-Part B (Social Security Administration 1997), suggesting that most eligibles find some way of paying the premiums. Remarkably little clarification of this issue has been forthcoming.

HMO Usage

For several years the Federal government has attempted to contain Medicare costs by offering inducements to the elderly to move to health maintenance organizations. These for-profit health care providers operate on the basis that they can reduce costs by requiring members to go though one physician (or "medical provider," sometimes a nurse) before gaining access to specialists. In the process doctors and hospitals are subjected to price squeezes to reduce costs.

Basic Facts About Medicare

Function: Provides health care for the insured elderly and disabled persons of all ages.
Administration: The Federal Hospital Insurance Trust Fund pays providers.
Eligibility: For Medicare-Part A, insured elderly and disabled persons of all ages, receiving Social Security benefits or at least two years.
Covered employment: Includes all persons who paid Social Security taxes and are eligible for Old Age Insurance (Social Security) payments.
Financing: For Medicare-Part A, a payroll tax of 1.45 percent on both employer and employee during earning years. For Medicare-Part B (optional), a premium paid by the Social Security recipient from the monthly Social Security benefit during retirement years.
Benefits: Medicare-Part A covers the first sixty days of each spell of hospitalization, after the first day; care in skilled nursing facilities, home health care services, and hospice care. Medicare-Part B covers physicians' fees, clinical lab tests, durable medical equipment, flu shots, and some other medically associated services. Medicare-Part C offers new options for securing services outside an HMO network, selections effective January 1, 2000.
Earnings limitations: None. (Social Security Administration)

Although some of the elderly reportedly liked the advantages offered by HMO involvement, such as the inclusion of medications and eyeglasses that must be self-paid under standard Medicare, a great deal of resistance built up over the need to obtain permissions to use specialists, over delays, and over problems in obtaining prior approval for emergency-room use, the same resistance observed among the general public. Such dissatisfactions have helped fuel a move to PPOs, preferred provider organizations. Less tightly managed, a PPO is a network of physicians who charge a monthly fee plus five to fifteen dollars a visit. Payments are often employer-subsidized, as in the case of HMOs. The attractive feature of the PPOs to HMO discontents is that, for an additional fee, about 20 percent of cost after a yearly deductible of several hundred dollars, members can go outside the network. As of late 1998, for the population as a whole, total membership in PPOs passed HMO membership, 105 million to 75 million, according to an American Association of Health Plans spokesperson (no breakdown for the elderly and disabled versus the under-65 insured population was given). Both types of plans are increasing in membership, but PPOs at a faster rate than the HMOs. At the heart of the employer shift to PPOs is growing disillusionment with the *gatekeeper* concept, the idea that money is saved when a generalist is used to make decisions as to the necessity of specialized care. According to the *New York Times,* September 29, 1998, consumers are fueling the shift by reason of their desire for more choice.

During late 1998 newspaper reports told of HMOs which, upon finding that costs eliminated their profit motive, were dropping Medicare services, leaving their Medicare enrollees without supplemental insurance (dubbed "Medigap"). Newspaper stories, among them an October 19 *New York Times* report, pictured frantic people without information concerning alternatives, without funds to pay for Medigap policies, and desperate as to how they would pay for expensive medications and other necessities not covered by Medicare-Part A. The distressed tone of the stories, however justified, neglected to indicate that these persons are not among the medically neediest persons, as the latter have not been enrolled in the Medicare HMOs because of inability to pay the Medicare B premium.

MEDICAID

In 1965 Congress established Medicaid, a means-tested welfare-type, federal-state health care program that pays for health care for very low income earners without health insurance. While the states must meet certain conditions to obtain funding, they have a great deal of discretion in specifying eligibility and how much help will be given. It should not be inferred that this was the first Federal intervention to help the medically needy, as the federal government has been sharing costs with the states since passage of the 1935 Social Security Act. In general, the eligibility requirements are such that many low-paid working persons, not covered by their employers but earning too much to qualify for Medicaid, effectively go without health care except in the case of emergencies, when they turn to hospital emergency rooms. For several years, to contain rapidly escalating costs, many states have been moving the medically indigent eligible for Medicaid into managed care plans, specially designed HMOs. The aim is to provide care that is better and less costly than that offered through hospital emergency rooms.

Mandatory Medicaid coverage extends to certain groups in the poverty population targeted by the U.S. Department of Health and Human Services or by the states themselves. Programs vary greatly from state to state. The groups included are "welfare" and Supplemental Social Insurance (SSI) recipients; all children now under age six, plus all children and youths up to age nineteen who were born after September 30, 1983, in poverty-level families; some elderly Medicare beneficiaries (those who cannot afford Medicare-Part B); very poor pregnant women; and some other groups. The provisions concerning children aim to assure that all poor children under age nineteen will have medical coverage by 2002. The right of legal immigrants as well as "illegals," to Medicare was withdrawn by the Personal and Family Responsibility and Reconciliation Act of 1996 except for cases in which the person has already worked ten years. The matter is periodically reopened by interested parties

In 1995 more than 36 million persons were receiving Medicaid at an annual cost of $159.5 billion, with expenditures expected to continue their history of steep annual increase (Social Security Administration 1997). The reasons for the upward movements in cost are similar to those cited earlier for Medicare, in addition to the fact that the Medicaid population has been expanding. In 1985 Congress included new groups, largely because many children of working parents were being left without health care due to employer retrenchments in dependents' coverage. Despite the burgeoning costs, fees for individual treatment are so low that, even with taxes imposed on the bills of insured patients, formally or informally, many physicians and hospitals decline to treat Medicaid patients. Thus, medical care may be inaccessible, even though theoretically available. Also, state regulations and eligibility procedures are frequently designed to make Medicaid difficult to obtain, especially when allocated funds are inadequate.At the same time, Medicaid has become a favored resource of the well-to-do who often hide assets or transfer them to children in order to become eligible for reimbursement for expensive services, such as nursing-home care, especially long-term chronic care, a development Congress has attempted to address through the Kennedy-Kassebaum Act of 1997. While the new prohibitions may make for more equity, no one expects them to have much impact on the overall rise of Medicaid costs, $165 billion dollars yearly, as of 1997, and expected to rise 10 percent annually. As reported by the New York Times, February 18, 1997, Medicaid is helping to pay for two-thirds of the costs of the 1.6 million persons in nursing homes. These costs, reported by Business Week, September 30, 1996, average $38,000 per year, sometimes running as high as $100,000.

Basic Facts About Medicaid

Function: Pays for medical care for certain groups of medically indigent persons.
Administration: Federal-state program, with funds dispensed by the states to vendors of services.
Eligibility: Most individuals receiving federally mandated income maintenance payments and some other groups not receiving cash payments.
Financing: Annual Federal contribution to each state, based on the average income of state's residents relative to U.S. average; 50 percent to 83 percent of costs of service, plus half costs of administration.
Benefits: Range of medical and dental services; hospital services (in-patient and
Earnings limitations: At state discretion . (Social Security Administration)

Effects of Medicare and Medicaid on Employment

Medicare and Medicaid eligibility requirements have important impacts on employment. For one, the requirements affect the re-employment of disabled persons as recipients tend to fear losing their health care benefits if they accept employment, most accessible jobs offering either unaffordable health care benefits or none at all. According to Robert Pear of the *New York Times* (November 18, 1999), only about 1 percent of the eight million disabled persons of working age who receive over $50 billion in cash benefits from Social Security and Supplemental Security Income each year are employed. A serious attempt to remedy this situation (HR Bill 1180, the Work Incentives Improvement Act, regarded as the most important effort to help disabled persons since passage of the Americans with Disabilities Act of 1990) passed the House overwhelmingly in late 1999, but was lost in the last-minute legislative crush in the Senate. Similar legislation is likely to be introduced in subsequent legislative sessions.

Perhaps the broadest and most immediately observable effect of Medicare and Medicaid on the work force and the business community concerns the cost of doing business and employer reactions to this pressure. The inadequacies of Medicare and Medicaid reimbursements cause cost-shifting on the part of health-care providers (mainly physicians, hospitals and other health-associated institutions).The cost-shifting results in paying patients being levied higher rates to make up for revenues lost to providers because of low Medicare and Medicaid payment levels. Employers of insured workers end up bearing the brunt as they are "taxed" by the health-care providers to supplement the revenue shortfalls, that is, the difference between the dollars the providers receive and what they customarily obtain from the more affluent. Additionally, rates are exaggerated to cover unreimbursed costs of caring for the uncovered poor. This cost-shifting has at least two employment-related outcomes: first, for individuals, wages and salaries are lower than they would be if the costs of health care were less; and second, many employers are reducing their health-care benefits for their employees or ceasing to offer them altogether. In addition, the differences in state-determined costs of Medicare and Medicaid have helped persuade some employers to move from a more generous to a less generous state. The high cost of benefits, in general, and health care, in particular, also tends to lower the *quality* of employment, inducing employers to reduce the number of full time jobs and substitute part-time, temporary, and independent contractor-type positions for the purpose of avoiding discretionary benefits payments altogether.

As business internationalizes more health care associated job migration may occur from the United States to other countries: foreign competitors often are unburdened by such costs, since their national systems bear the expense of health care. (This point was emphasized by Alan Greenspan in testimony before a bipartisan committee studying ways to prevent Medicare from going bankrupt, reported in the April 21, 1998, *New York Times.*) The high costs of health care, in general, are affecting work-leisure choices in that more members of families are induced to take either full-time or part-time jobs, the latter often a second job to make up for the loss of benefits in primary employment.

Medicaid, as a program for the very poorest, largely excludes the *working poor*. They are not poor enough to qualify, according to most states' stringent standards, but they lack employer-paid benefits and earn too little to purchase insurance on their own. With health-care needs largely uncovered except for sporadic care received in hospital emergency rooms, the working poor are rendered less efficient and reliable as employees. According to the United Hospital Fund, quoted in the *New York Times*, February 12, 1998, as of 1996, 17.6 percent of people under 65 were uninsured, up 1.7 percent since 1991. Most are believed to be employed.

A recent Dun & Bradstreet survey of small businesses throughout the United States suggests that much of the acute elimination or decrease of health insurance may be due to the problems of small businesses in meeting escalating costs. Coverage dropped 7 percent between 1994 and 1996, from 16.1 percent to 15.6 percent. This is considered significant because small business accounts for almost half of nonpublic employment, a statistic reported in *Business Week*, October 12, 1998. Even when employers do offer health-insurance coverage, employees are increasingly required to help pay for it (BLS 1998). The proportion making a contribution rose from about a quarter in 1980 to almost half by 1995, but many react by failing to participate in their employers' plan because of inability to pay their contribution (Cooper and Schone 1997). The 1995 Employee Benefits survey of medium and large private establishments found that where the employer offered health coverage, the average employee contribution was almost $34 for single persons and $118 for family persons per month. Inability to obtain Medicaid benefits are also believed to have negatively affected some women who would like to work but have refrained from doing so since it would mean losing health care for themselves and their children. In the recent past so-called welfare mothers, for example, lost such rights to Medicaid after one year of leaving welfare rolls to accept employment. How states, operating independently with minimal Federal guidelines under the Personal and Family Responsibility Act of 1996, will deal with the health needs of very poor employed women and their children remains to be seen.

NOTE

1. Information concerning new options may be secured through a Medicare information number (1-800-318-2596 or 1-877-486-2048) or by writing U.S. Department of Health and Human Services, 7500 Security Boulevard, Baltimore, Maryland 21244-1850.

REFERENCES

Cooper, Philip and Barbara Schone. 1997. Trends: more offers, fewer takers for employer-based health insurance: 1987–1996. *Health Affairs* 16, no. 6 (Nov./Dec.): 142–49.

U.S. Department of Health and Human Services. Social Security Administration. Office of Policy. Office of Research and Statistics. 1997. *Social Security programs in the United States.* SSA Publication No. 11758, (July). Washington, D.C.: Government Printing Office.

U.S. Department of Health and Human Services. Health Care Financing Administration, Baltimore, Md. 1997. *Your 1998 Medicare Handbook:* Publication No. HCFA 10050. Washington, D.C.: Government Printing Office.

———. 1998. *Medicare & You.* Publication No. HCFA-02119 (August). Washington, D.C.: Government Printing Office.

U.S. Department of Labor. Bureau of Labor Statistics. 1998. *Employee Benefits in Medium and Large Private Establishments, 1995.* Bulletin 2496 (April). Washington, D.C.: Government Printing Office.

———. 1998. Employee medical care contributions on the rise. *Issues in labor statistics,* Summary 98-3 (April). Washington, D.C.: Government Printing Office.

Bibliography

AARP Bulletin. 1996. "Dropouts" may help explain decline in midlife jobless rate. October.

Abbott, Andrew. 1988. *The system of professions: an essay on the division of expert labor.* Chicago: University of Chicago Press.

Abraham, Katharine G., and Susan N. Houseman. 1993. *Job security in America: lessons from Germany.* Washington, D.C.: Brookings Foundation.

Achenbaum, W. Andrew. 1986. *Social security: visions and revisions.* Cambridge: Cambridge University Press.

Acker, Joan. 1989. *Doing comparable worth.* Philadelphia: Temple University Press.

Acs, Gregory, and Sheldon Danziger. 1993. Educational attainment, industrial structure, and male earnings through the 1980s. *Journal of Human Resources* 28, no. 3: 618–48.

Addison, John T., and McKinley Blackburn. 1994. The Worker Adjustment and Retraining Notification Act: effects on notice provision. *Industrial and Labor Relations Review* 47, no. 4: 650–62.

———, and Douglas Fox. 1993. Job changing after displacement: a contribution to the advance notice debate. *Southern Economic Journal* 60, no.1 (July): 184–200.

———, and Pedro Portugal. 1989. Job displacement, relative wage changes, and duration of unemployment. *Journal of Labor Economics* 7, no. 3: 281–302.

———. 1992. Advance notice and unemployment: new evidence from the 1988 Displaced Worker Survey. *Industrial and Labor Relations Review* 45, no. 4: 645–64.

Aguilar, Linda, and William Testa. 1995. Advisory Council on Unemployment Compensation in the United States, *Report and recommendations.* Transmitted to the President and Congress. (February) Washington, D.C., 1–3.

Aigner, Dennis, and Glen Cain. 1977. Statistical theories of discrimination in the labor market. *Industrial and Labor Relations Review* 30 (January): 175–87.

Aldrich, Mark, and Robert Buchele. 1989. Where to look for comparable worth: the implications of efficiency wages. In Anne Hill and Mark Killingsworth, eds. 1989. *Comparable worth: analysis and evidence.* Ithaca, N.Y.: ILR Press.

Allen, Steven G. 1995. Updated notes on the inter-industry wage structure, 1890–1990. *Industrial and Labor Relations Review* 48 (January) 305–21.

American Management Association. 1986. *Hiring costs and strategies: the AMA report.* New York: AMA.

Amirault, Thomas. 1997. Characteristics of multiple jobholders, 1995. *Monthly Labor Review* 120 (March): 9–14.

Anderson, Elijah. 1990. *Streetwise: race, class, and change in an urban community.* Chicago: University of Chicago Press.

———. 1996. Foreword to W.E.B. DuBois, *The Philadelphia Negro.* Philadelphia: University of Pennsylvania Press (Original edition, 1899).

Anderson, Lowell D. 1992. Relationship of technology education to tech-prep. Paper presented at the Mississippi Industrial Teachers Educational Annual Conference, Chicago, Ill., November.

Appelbaum, Eileen, and Rosemary Batt. 1994. *The new American workplace : transforming work systems in the United States.* Ithaca, N.Y.: ILR Press.

Arbona, Consuelo. 1990. Career counseling research: Hispanics: a review of the literature. *The Counseling Psychologist* 18 (April): 300–323.

Arce, Carlos, Edward Murguia, and W. Parker Frisbie. 1987. Phenotype and life chances among Chicanos. *Hispanic Journal of Behavioral Studies* 9, no. 1: 19–33.

Arouca, D. A. 1984. Railroad collective bargaining–anatomy or pathology. *Proceedings of the Thirty-Seventh Annual Meeting,* Industrial Relations Research Association, December : 429–30.

Arrow, Kenneth. 1972. Models of job discrimination and some models of race in the labor market. In Pascal, Anthony, ed., *Discrimination in economic life.* Lexington, Mass.: D. C. Heath and Co.

———. 1973. The theory of discrimination. In Ashenfelter, Orley, and Albert Rees, eds. *Discrimination in labor markets.* Princeton: Princeton University Press, 3–33.

———. 1998. What has economics to say about racial discrimination? *The Journal of Economic Perspectives* (Spring): 91–100.

Babcock, Linda, Mary Ellen Benedict, and John Engberg. 1994. Structural change and labor market outcomes: how are the gains and losses distributed? Unpublished paper, Carnegie Mellon University.

Baker, Elizabeth F. 1969. *Protective labor legislation: with special reference to women in the State of New York.* Studies in History, Economics, and Public Law, Columbia University. New York: AMS Press (originally published 1925).

Baker, Michael. 1992. Unemployment duration: compositional effects and cyclical variability. *American Economic Review* 82, no. 1 (March): 313–21.

Balfour, Alan. 1987. *Union-management relations in a changing economy.* Englewood Cliffs, N.J.: Prentice-Hall.

Bandura, A. 1986. *Social foundations of thought and action: a social cognitive theory.* Englewood Cliffs, N.J.: Prentice-Hall.

Baran, Barbara, and Carl Parsons. 1986. Technology and skill: a literature review. Prepared for the Carnegie Forum on Education and the Economy, January.

Barber, Allison, Christina Giannantonio, and Jean Phillips. 1994. Job search activities: an examination of changes over time. *Personnel Psychology* 47 (Winter): 739–64.

Baron, John, Dan Black, and Mark Lowenstein. 1987. Employer size: the implications for search, training, capital investment, starting wages, and wage growth. *Journal of Labor Economics* 5: 76–89.

Bartel, Ann. 1991. Productivity gains from the implementation of employee training programs. NBER Working Paper 3026.

Bates, Timothy. 1985. An analysis of minority entrepreneurship: utilizing the census of public use samples. Fourth progress report. Burlington, Vermont.

———, and Daniel R. Fusfeld. 1984. *The political economy of the urban ghetto.* Carbondale: Southern Illinois University.

Batstone, Eric, Anthony Ferner, and Mike Terry. 1983. *Unions on the board: employee relations.* Oxford: Blackwell.

Becker, Gary. 1957. *The economics of discrimination.* Chicago: University of Chicago Press.

———. 1965. A theory on the allocation of time. *Economic Journal* 75 (September): 494–517.

———. 1975. *Human capital.* 2nd edition. New York: National Bureau of Economic Research.

———. 1981. *A treatise on the family.* Cambridge: Harvard University Press.

———. 1995. It's simple: hike the minimum wage, and you put people out of work. *Business Week* 6 (March): 22.

Bednarzik, Robert. 1983. Layoffs and permanent job losses: workers' traits and cyclical patterns. *Monthly Labor Review* 106 (September): 3–12.

Begun, James W., and Ronald Lippincott. 1987. The origins and resolution of inter-occupational conflict. *Work and Occupation* 14 (August): 368–86.

Bell, Linda. 1995. Union wage concessions in the 1980s: the importance of firm-specific factors. *Industrial and Labor Relations Review* 48 (January): 208–75.

Bellante, Don. 1979. The North-South differential and the migration of heterogeneous labor. *American Economic Review* 69 (March): 166–75.

———. 1992. An empirical analysis of employed and unemployed job search behavior. *Industrial and Labor Relations Review* 45 (July): 738–52.

———, and Mark Jackson. 1983. *Labor economics: choices in labor markets.* New York: McGraw-Hill.

———, and Philip Robins. 1990. Job search outcomes for the employed and unemployed. *Journal of Political Economy* 98, no. 3: 637–55.

Bendick, Marc Jr., Charles Jackson, and Victor Reinoso. 1997. Measuring employment discrimination through controlled experiments. In James B. Stewart, ed., *African-Americans and post-industrial labor markets.* New Brunswick, N.J.: Transaction Publishers, 77–100.

Bendix, Reinhard, and Seymour Lipset. 1959. *Social mobility in industrial society.* Berkeley: University of California Press.

Benham, Harry. 1983. Unemployment insurance incentives and unemployment duration distributions. *The Review of Economics and Statistics* 65 (February): 139–52.

Benson, George. 1996. How much do employers spend on training? *Training and Development* (October): 56–58.

Berg, Ivan. 1971. *Education and jobs: the great training robbery.* Boston: Beacon Press.

Bergmann, Barbara. 1971. The effect of white incomes on discrimination in employment. *Journal of Political Economy* 79 (March/April): 294–313.

———. 1974. Occupational segregation, wages, and profits when employers discriminate by race or sex. *Eastern Economic Journal* 1 (April/July): 103–10.

———. 1991. Does the market for women's labor need fixing? In Reynolds, Lloyd, Stanley Masters, and Colletta Moser. 1991. *Readings in labor economics and labor relations.* 5th edition. Englewood Cliffs, N.J.: Prentice Hall: 247–61.

Berkowitz, Edward. 1991. *America's welfare state: from Roosevelt to Reagan.* Baltimore: Johns Hopkins University Press.

Betz, N. E. 1991. Twenty years of vocational research: looking back and ahead. *Journal of Vocational Behavior* 37 (November): 305–10.

Bielby, William, and James Baron. 1986. Men and women at work: sex segregation and statistical discrimination. *American Journal of Sociology* 91, no. 4 (January): 759–99.

Bipartisan Committee on Agricultural Workers. 1992. Report cited in *New York Times*, 22 October.

Birch, David. 1987. *Job creation in America: how our smallest companies put the most people to work.* New York: Free Press.

Bishop, John. 1994. Formal training and its impact on productivity, wages, and innovation. In L. Lynch, ed. Training and the private sector: internationa comparisons. Chicago: University of Chicago Press.

Blair, Margaret. 1994. CEO pay: why such a contentious issue? *Brookings Review* 12 (Winter): 22–27.

Blackburn, McKinley, David Bloom, and Richard Freeman. 1990. The declining economic position of less-skilled American men: 31–76. In Gary Burtless, ed. *A future of lousy jobs: the changing job structure of U.S. wages.* Washington, D.C.: The Brookings Institution.

Blanchard, Oliver J., and Lawrence F. Katz. 1992. Regional evolutions. *Brookings Papers on Economic Activity.* Washington, D.C.: Brookings Institution (1): 1–75.

Blank, Rebecca, and David Card. 1991. Recent trends in insured and uninsured unemployment: is there an explanation? *Quarterly Journal of Economics* 106 (November):1157–89.

Blasi, Joseph, and Douglas Kruse. 1991. *The new owners.* New York: Harper Business, HarperCollins, paperback edition, 1992.

Blau, Francine, and Lawrence Kahn. 1997. Swimming upstream: trends in the gender wage differential in the 1980s. *Journal of Labor Economics* (January): 1–42.

Blau, Francine, M. Ferber, and A. Winkler. 1998. *The economics of women, men, and work.* 3rd ed. Upper Saddle River, N.J.: Prentice Hall.

Blau, Peter, and Otis Dudley Duncan. 1960. *The American occupational structure.* New York: John Wiley & Sons.

Blaug, Marc. 1973. *Education, work, and employment: a summary review.* Report of the Education Research and Advisory Group, a project of the International Development Research Centre, Ottawa, Canada.

Blaustein, Saul, with Wilbur J. Cohen and William Haber. 1993. *Unemployment insurance in the United States: the first half century.* Kalamazoo, Mich.: W. E. Upjohn Institute for Employment Research

Bloom, David, and Richard Freeman. 1992. The fall in private pension coverage in the U.S. *American Economic Association Papers and Proceedings* 82 (May): 539–45.

Bluestone, Barry, and Bennett Harrison. 1982. *The deindustrialization of America.* New York: Free Press.

Bluestone, Barry, and Teresa Ghilarducci. 1996. Making work pay: wage insurance for the working poor. Public Policy Brief No. 28. Annandale-on-Hudson, New York: Jerome Levy Institute of Bard College.

———. 1992. Training, wage growth, and job performance: evidence from a company database. NBER Working Paper 4027.

Blume, Lawrence. 1997. Population games. In Arthur, W. B., S. Durlauf, and D. Lane, eds. *The economy as an evolving complex system.* Menlo Park, Cal.: Addison Wesley Longmans.

Borjas, George. 1994. Long-run convergence of ethnic skill differentials: the children and grandchildren of the great migration. *Industrial and Labor Relations Review* 47 (July): 553–73.

———. 1995. Know the flow: economics of immigration. *National Review* 47, no. 7: 44–52.

———, and Richard Freeman, and Lawrence Katz. 1996. Searching for the effect of immigration on the labor market. *American Economic Review* 86, no. 2 (May): 246–51.

———, and Valerie Ramey. 1993. Foreign competition, market power, and wage inequality: theory and evidence. Manuscript (May). Quoted in David Howell, 1994. The collapse of low-skill male earnings in the 1980s: skill mismatch or shifting wage norms? Working Paper No. 105 (March). Annandale-on-Hudson, N.Y.: Jerome Levy Economics Institute, Bard College.

Boston, Thomas. 1990. Segmented labor markets: new evidence from a study of four race-gender groups. *Industrial and Labor Relations Review* 44 (October): 99–115.

Boudreau, John, and Sara L. Rynes. 1985. Role of recruitment in staffing utility analysis. *Journal of Applied Psychology* 70 (May): 354–6.

Bound, John, and George Johnson. 1992. Changes in the structure of wages in the 1980s: an evaluation of alternative explanations. *American Economic Review* 82 (June): 371–92.

Bragg, Debra. 1994. Emerging tech prep models: promising approaches to educational reform. *Centerfocus* 5.

Brechling, Frank. 1981. Layoffs and unemployment insurance, 187–202. In Sherwin Rosen, ed., *Studies in labor markets*. Chicago: University of Chicago Press.

Bronfenbrenner, Kate. 1996. Plant closings and labor rights: final report. Ithaca, N.Y.: Cornell University School of Industrial Relations. Submitted September 30 to Labor Secretariat of the Commission for Labor Cooperation. Included in Labor Commission's June 10, 1997 report, The effects of plant closings or threat of plant closings on the rights of workers to organize. Dallas, Texas, 75201-4240.

Brown, Charles, and James Medoff. 1989. Employer size and the payment of factors. *Journal of Political Economy* 97: 1027–59.

Brown, Duane, and Linda Brooks. 1991. Ethnicity and race in career counseling. In *Career counseling techniques*. Boston: Allyn and Bacon, 149–83.

———, and Associates. 1990. *Career choice and development: applying contemporary theories to practice*. 2nd edition. San Francisco: Jossey-Bass Publishers.

Brown, Michael T., et al. 1996. Annual review, 1990–1996: social class, work, and retirement behavior. *Journal of Vocational Behavior* 42 (October): 159–89.

Browne, Lynne. 1985. Structural change and dislocated workers. *New England Economic Review*: Federal Reserve Board of Boston. January/February: 15–30.

Bunning, R. L. 1992. Models for skill-based pay plans. *HR Magazine* 37 (February): 62–66.

Burdett, Kenneth, and Randall Wright. 1989. Unemployment insurance and short-time compensation: the effects on layoffs, hours per workers, and wages. *Journal of Political Economy* 97, no. 6: 1479–96.

Burgess, Paul, and Stuart Low. 1992. Pre-unemployment job search and advance job loss notice. *Journal of Labor Economics* 10, no. 3: 258–87.

Burtless, Gary. 1991. The tattered safety net: jobless pay in the United States. *Brookings Review* 9 (Spring): 3–91.

Business Week. 1995. Bonus pay: buzzword or bonanza? 14 November.

Butler, Elizabeth B. 1984. *Women and the Trades: Pittsburgh, 1907–1908.* Pittsburgh, Pa.: University of Pittsburgh Press (originally published 1909).

Byars, Lloyd, and Leslie Rue. 1984. *Human resources and personnel management.* Homewood, Ill.: Richard Irwin.

Byrne, John. 1995. Why executive compensation continues to increase. In *Compensation: present practices and future concerns, a conference report.* New York: The Conference Board, Inc.

Cain, Glenn. 1986. The economic analysis of labor market discrimination: a survey. In Ashenfelter, Orley, and Layard, P. R. *Handbook of labor economics.* Amsterdam: New Holland, 693–785.

Cairnes, John Elliott. 1967. *Some leading principles of political economy newly expounded.* New York: A. Kelley (Reprint; original publication London, 1864).

Calise, Angela. 1992. Employers W.C. rates rises amid work force cuts. *National Underwriter* 96, no. 33 (17 August) 1991: 8.

Caplow, Theodore. 1954. *The sociology of work.* New York: McGraw-Hill Book Co.

Card, David, and Alan B. Krueger. 1994. Minimum wages and employment: case study of the fast-food industry in New Jersey and Pennsylvania. *American Economic Review* 84 (4): 77–93.

———. 1995. *Myth and measurement: the new economics of the minimum wage.* Princeton: Princeton University Press.

———. 1998. A reanalysis of the effect of the New Jersey minimum wage increase on the fast food industry with representative payroll data. Working Paper No. 6386. Washington, D.C.: National Bureau of Economic Research.

Carnevale, Anthony, and Janet Johnson. 1989. *Job-related learning: private strategies and public policies.* Washington, D.C.: Government Printing Offic

Carnevale, Anthony, and colleagues, eds. 1990. *New developments in worker training: a legacy for the 1990s.* Madison, Wisc.: Industrial Relations Research Association.

Carrington, William. 1993a. Specific Human Capital and Worker Displacement. Dissertation, University of Chicago.

———. 1993b. Wage losses for displaced workers: Is it really the firm that matters? *Journal of Human Resources* 28, no. 3 (Summer): 435–62.

———, and Asad Zaman. 1994. Inter-industry variation in the costs of job displacement. *Journal of Labor Economics* 12, no. 2: 243–76.

Cathcart, James A., and Gil Graff. 1978. Occupational licensing: factoring it out. *Pacific Law Review* 9 (January): 147–63.

Cattan, Peter. 1987. Under-utilization in the U.S. manufacturing sector, 1960 to 1970. *International Journal of Sociology and Social Policy* 7, no. 4: 99–115.

Cheatham, H. E. 1990. Africentricity and career development of African Americans. *Career Development Quarterly* 3: 333–56.

Chiswick, Barry. 1988. *Illegal aliens: their employment and employers.* Kalamazoo, Mich.: W. .E. Upjohn Institute for Employment Research.

Coate, Stephen, and Glenn Loury. 1993. Anti-discrimination enforcement and the problem of patronization. *American Economic Review Papers and Proceedings* 83, no. 2: 92–98.

Cohany, Sharon. 1996. Workers in alternative employment arrangements. *Monthly Labor Review* 119 (October): 31–45.

Cohen, Elchanon. 1979. *The economics of education.* Revised edition. Cambridge, Mass.: Ballinger Publishing Company (Harper & Row): 13–26.

Cohen, Sanford. 1979. *Labor in the United States.* 5th edition. Columbus: Charles E. Merrill Publishing Co.

Collins, Michael, and Ronald Carvero. 1992. Part two: should adult and continuing education strive for professionalization? *New Directions for Adult and Continuing Education* 54 (Summer): 35–50.

Commission on the Future of Worker-Management Relations. 1994. Report and recommendations. Washington, D.C.: U.S. Departments of Labor and Commerce.

———. 1996. The status of tech prep in the United States. Paper presented at the Am- erican Vocational Association Convention, Cincinnati, Ohio. 6 December.

Commission on the Skills of the American Work Force. 1990. *America's choice: high skills or low wages*. Rochester, N.Y.: National Center on Education and the Economy.

Congressional Quarterly Almanac. 1990. Vocational education act provisions, 620–23.

———. 1994a. National education goals set: 397–99.

———. 1994b. Clinton signs School-to-Work Act: 400.

Cross, Theodore. 1969. *Black capitalism*. New York: Athenaeum.

Currie, Janet, and Bruce Fallick. 1996. The minimum wage and the employment of youth: evidence from the NLSY. *Journal of Human Resources* 31, no. 2: 404–28.

Cutler, David, and Edward Glaeser. 1997. Are ghettos good or bad? *Quarterly Journal of Economics* 112, no. 3: 827–73.

Darity, William A., Jr. 1982. The human capital approach to black-white earnings inequality: some unsettled questions. *Journal of Human Resources* 17, no. 1: 72–93.

———. 1989. What's left of the economic theory of discrimination? 333–74. In Shulman, Steven, and William Darity, Jr., eds. *Question of discrimination: racial inequality in the U.S. labor market*. Middletown, Ohio: Wesleyan University Press.

———, and Rhonda Williams. 1985. Peddlers forever? Culture, competition, and discrimination. *American Economic Review* 75 (May): 256–91.

———, David Guilkey, and William Winfrey. 1996. Explaining differences in economic performance among racial and ethnic groups in the USA: the data examined. *American Journal of Economics and Sociology* 55 (October): 411–26.

———, and Patrick Mason. 1998. Evidence of discrimination in employment: codes of color, codes of gender. *Journal of Economic Perspectives* 12 (Spring): 63–90.

Dauer, Christopher. 1992. Florida launches program to cut WC rate. *National Underwriter* 96 (5 January): 23, 43.

Davie, Maurice. 1949. *Negroes in American society*. New York: Whittlesey House, McGraw-Hill Book Company.

Davis, George, and Gregg Watson. 1985. *Black life in corporate America: swimming in the mainstream*. Garden City, N.J.: Anchor Press.

Daymont, Thomas, and Paul Andrisani. 1984. Job preferences, college major, and the gender gap in earnings. *Journal of Human Resources* 19 (Summer): 409–28.

Deere, Donald. 1991. Unemployment Insurance and employment. *Journal of Labor Economics* 9 (October): 307–24.

Dejardin, Conrad, and Nancy Kothernbeutel. 1992. The comprehensive community college: who took "comprehensive" and "community" away? *Community Services Catalyst* 22 (Summer): 19–21.

Delaney, John T., Paul Jarley, and Jack Fiorito. 1996. Planning for change: determinants of innovation in U.S. national unions. *Industrial and Labor Relations Review* 49 (July): 597–614.

DeLuca, Matthew J. 1993. *Handbook of compensation management*. Englewood Cliffs, N.J.: Prentice Hall.

Devens, Richard M. Jr. 1986. Displaced workers one year later. *Monthly Labor Review* 109, no.7 (July): 40–43.

Dickens, William, and Jonathan Leonard. 1985. Accounting for the decline in the union movement, 1950–1980. *Industrial and Labor Relations Review*, 38: 323–34.

Diebold, Francis X., David Neumark, and Daniel Polsky. 1996a. Job Stability in the United States. NBER Working Paper no. 4859.

———. 1996b. Comment on Kenneth A. Swinnerton and Howard Wial, Is job stability declining in the U.S. economy? *Industrial and Labor Relations Review* 49 (January): 348–51.

Dill, Bonnie T., Lynn Weber, and Reeve Vanneman. 1987. Race and gender in occupational segregation. In *Pay equity: an issue of race, ethnicity, and sex.* Washington,. D.C.: National Committee on Pay Equity.

DiNardo, John, John Fortin, and Thomas Lemieux. 1994. Labor market institutions and the distribution of wages, 1973–9: a semi-parametric approach. Unpublished manuscript, University of California-Irvine.

Director, Steven, and Frederick Englander. 1988 Requiring unemployment insurance beneficiaries to register with the state employment service. *Journal of Risk and Insurance* 55, no. 2 (June): 245–54.

Doeringer, Peter and Michael Piore. 1971. *Internal labor markets and manpower analysis.* Lexington, Mass.: D.C. Heath.

Dorsey, S. 1980. The occupational licensing queue. *Journal of Human Resources* 15 (Summer): 424–34.

Doucouliagos, Chris. 1995. Worker participation and productivity in labor-managed and participatory capitalist firms: a meta-analysis. *Industrial and Labor Relations Review* 49 (October): 58–75.

Douty, H. M. 1968. Regional wage differentials: forces and counter forces. *Monthly Labor Review* 91 (March): 74–81.

Doyle, R. J. 1983. *Gain-sharing and productivity: a guide to planning, implementation and development.* New York: AMACOM.

Drake, St. Clair, and Horace Cayton. 1945. *Black metropolis: a study of life in a Northern city.* New York: Harcourt, Brace & Company.

Driscoll, James W. 1979. Working creatively with a union: lessons from the Scanlon plan. *Organizational Dynamics* 8 (Summer): 61–80.

DuBois, W.E.B. 1899. *The Negro in business.* New York: AMS Press, 1971 (Reprint).

———. 1899. *The Philadelphia Negro.* Philadelphia: University of Pennsylvania Press, 1996 (Reprint).

Duncan, Otis Dudley. 1961. A socioeconomic index for all occupations: 115–24. In Reiss, A. J. Jr., and colleagues, eds. *Occupations and social status.* Stratford, N.H: Ayer, 1977 (Reprint).

Dunlop, John. 1989. *The management of labor unions.* Lexington, Mass: D.C. Heath & Company.

Durlauf, Stephen. 1997. The membership theory of inequality: ideas and implications. Working Paper, Department of Economics, University of Wisconsin.

Eberts, Randall, and Christopher O'Leary. 1996. Profiling unemployment insurance beneficiaries. *Upjohn Institute Employment Research* (Fall): 1–4.

Edwards, Alba. 1943. *Population: comparative occupational statistics for the United States, 1870 to 1940.* Washington, D.C.: Government Printing Office.

Ehrenberg, Ronald, and Robert Smith. 1994. Investments in human capital: education and training: 279–325. In *Modern Labor Economics.* 5th edition. New York: HarperCollins College Publishers.

Eininger, Max U. 1964. *The process and product of T & I in high school level vocational education in the United States.* Pittsburgh, Pa.: American Institution for Research.

Eisner, Robert. 1995. Our NAIRU limits: the governing myth of economic policy. *The American Prospect.* 22 (Spring): 58–64.

Elmslie, Bruce, and Stanley Sedo. 1996. Discrimination, social psychology, and hysteresis in labor markets. *Journal of Economic Psychology* 17 (August): 465–78.

Enslow, Beth. 1991. Up, up, and away. *Across the Board* 28 (July/August): 18–25.

Estey, Marten. 1981. *The unions: structure, development, and management.* 3rd ed. New York: Harcourt Brace Jovanovich.

Etzioni, Amitai. 1969. *The semi-professions and their organization.* New York: The Free Press.

Eurich, Neil. 1991. *The learning industry.* Report of the Carnegie Foundation. New York: Carnegie Foundation.

Evans, David, and Linda Sleighton. 1988. Why do smaller firms pay less? *Journal of Human Resources* 24, no. 2: 301–19.

Evans, K. M., and E. L. Herr. 1994. The influence of racial identity and the perception of discrimination on the career aspirations of African American men and women. *Journal of Vocational Behavior* 40 (April): 173–84.

Fallick, Bruce. 1991. Unemployment Insurance and the rate of reemployment of displaced workers. *Review of Economics and Statistics* 73 (May): 228–35.

———.1993. The industrial mobility of displaced workers. *Journal of Labor Economics* 11, no. 2: 302–23.

———. 1996. A review of the recent empirical literature on displaced workers. *Industrial and Labor Relations Review.* 50, no. 5, October: 5–16.

Farber, Henry.1993. The incidence and costs of job loss, 1982–93. *Brookings Papers, Micro Economics*: 73–132.

———.1994. Are lifetime jobs disappearing? Job duration in the United States, 1973–93. Mimeograph. Princeton University.

Farley, Reynolds. 1984. *Blacks and whites: narrowing the gap?* Cambridge, Mass.: Harvard University Press.

Feige, Edgar, ed. 1989. *Underground economies: tax evasion and information distortion.* New York: Cambridge University Pres

Fein, Mitchell. 1991. IMPROSHARE: a technique for sharing productivity gains with employees. In Rock, M. L., and L. A. Berger, eds., *The compensation handbook.* 3rd ed. New York: McGraw-Hill.

Feldberg, Roslyn. 1986. Comparable worth: toward theory and practice in the United States: 163-80. In Gelpi, Barbara, N. Hartsock, C. Novak, and M. Strober, eds. *Women and poverty.* Chicago: University of Chicago Press.

Feldstein, Martin. 1976. Temporary layoffs in a theory of unemployment. *Journal of Political Economy* 84 (October): 937–57.

———. 1978. The effect of Unemployment Insurance on temporary lay-off unemployment. *American Economic Review* 68 (December): 834–47.

Ferber, Marianne, and Jane Waldfogel. 1998. The long-term consequences of nontraditional employment. *Monthly Labor Review* 121 (May): 3–12.

Ferguson Ronald. 1995. Shifting challenges: fifty years of economic change toward black-white earnings equality. *Daedalus* 124 (Winter): 37–76.

Ferman, Louis, et al. 1990. *New developments in worker training: a legacy for the 1990s.* Madison, Wisc.: Industrial Relations and Research Association.

Fernandez, John. 1987. *Survival in the corporate fish bowl: making it into upper and middle management.* Lexington, Mass.: D.C. Heath and Company.

Filer, Randall K., Daniel Hamermesh, and Albert Rees. 1996. *The economics of work and pay.* 6th edition. New York: HarperCollins College Publishers.

Fix, Michael, George Galster, and Raymond Struyk. 1993. An overview of auditing for discrimination: 1–68. In Michael Fix and Raymond Struyk, eds. *Clear and convincing evidence: measurement of discrimination in America*. Washington, D.C.: Urban Institute Press.

Flaim, Paul, and Ellen Sehgal. 1985. Displaced workers of 1979–83: how well have they fared? *Monthly Labor Review* 108, no. 6: 3–16.

Flanagan, R. J. 1984. *Wage concessions and long term union wage flexibility*. Washington, D.C.: Brookings Papers on Economic Activity.

Flexner, Abraham. 1910. *Medical education in the United States and Canada*. New York: Carnegie Foundation, Bulletin No. 4.

Foley, Eugene. 1968. *The achieving ghetto*. Washington, D.C.: National Press.

Fraker, Thomas, and Robert Moffitt. 1988. The effectiveness of food stamps on labor supply. *Journal of Public Economics* 35, no. 1 (February): 25–56.

Franklin, J. 1997. Industry output and employment projections to 2006. *Monthly Labor Review* 120 (November): 39–57.

Frazier, E. Franklin. 1949. *The Negro in the United States*. New York: Macmillan.

Frazis, Harley, Diane Herz, and Michael Horrigan. 1995. Employer-provided training: results from a new survey. *Monthly Labor Review* 118 (May): 3–17.

———. and M. Gittleman, M. Horrigan, and M. Joyce. 1998. Results from the 1995 survey of employer-provided training. *Monthly Labor Review* 121 (June): 3–13.

Freedman, Audrey. 1989. Unions' future is bleak. *Personnel Administrator* 34 (December): 98–100.

Freeman, Richard. 1971. The economic theory of occupational choice. Chapter 1. *The market for college-trained manpower: a study in the economics of career choice*. Cambridge: Harvard University Press.

———. 1976. *The overeducated American*. New York: Academic Press.

———. 1977. Economic rewards to college education. *The Review of Economics and Statistics* 59 (February): 18–29.

———, and James Medoff. 1984. *What do unions do?* New York: Basic Books.

Friedman, Marcia. 1976. *Labor markets: segments and shelters*. Montclair, N.J.: Allanheld, Osmun, and Co.

Fullerton, Jr., Howard N. 1997. Labor force 2006: slowing down and changing composition. *Monthly Labor Review* 120 (November): 23–38.

Galbraith, James. 1997. Time to ditch the NAIRU. *Journal of Economic Perspectives* 11, no. 1 (Winter): 93–108.

Galle, Omer R., Candace Wiswell, and Jeffrey Burr. 1988. Racial mix and industrial productivity. *American Sociological Review* 50 (February): 20–23.

Gardner, Jennifer. 1993. Recession swells count of displaced workers. *Monthly Labor Review* 116, no. 6: 14–23.

Gellhorn, Walter. 1976. The abuse of occupational licensing. *University of Chicago Law Review* (Fall): 6–27.

Gelman, David, and colleagues. 1988. Black and white America. *Newsweek* (7 March).

Genovese, Eugene. 1961. *The political economy of slavery: studies in the economy and society of the slave South*. New York: Vintage Books.

Gim, R. H. C. 1992. Cross cultural comparison of factors that influence career choice. Paper presented at the Association for Asian American Studies Conference, San Jose, Cal.

Gittleman, Maury. 1994. Earnings in the 1980s: an occupational perspective. *Monthly Labor Review*. (July) 17, no. 7:16–27.

Glenn, Evelyn, and Charles M. Tolbert II. 1987. Technology and emerging patterns of stratification for women of color: race and gender segregation in computers: 319–31. In Wright, Barbara, and colleague, eds. *Women, work, and technology transformations*. Ann Arbor: University of Michigan Press.

Goldfield, Michael. 1987. *The decline of organized labor in the United States.* Chicago: University Press.

Goldin, Claudia. 1990. *Understanding the gender gap: an economic history of American women.* New York: Oxford UniversityPress.

————, and Cecilia Rouse. 1997. Orchestrating impartiality: the impact of "blind" auditions on female musicians. Unpublished manuscript. Harvard University, June.

Goss, Ernie, and Chris Paul. 1990. The impact of unemployment insurance on the probability of migration of the unemployed. *Journal of Regional Science.* 30, no. 3 (August): 349–58.

Gottschalk, Peter. 1997. Inequality, income growth, and mobility: the basic facts. *Journal of Economic Perspectives* 11 (Spring): 21–40.

Graham-Moore, Brian, and Timothy Ross. 1990. *Gain-sharing plans for improving performance.* Washington, D.C.: Bureau of National Affairs.

Granovetter, Mark. 1974. *Getting a job: a study of contacts and careers.* Cambridge, Mass.: Harvard University Press.

————. 1988. Economic action and social structure. In Wellman, Barry, and S. D. Berkowitz, eds. 1988. *Social structures: a network approach.* Cambridge, U.K., and New York: Cambridge University Press.

Grasso, John, and John Shea. 1979. *Vocational education and training: impact on youth.* Berkeley, Cal.: Carnegie Council on Policy Studies of Higher Education.

Green, Shelley, and Paul Pryde. 1990. *Black entrepreneurship in America.* New Brunswick, N.J.: Transaction.

Greenfield, Harry. 1993. *Invisible, outlawed, and untaxed: America's underground economy.* Westport, Conn.: Praeger.

Groshen, Erica L. 1991. The structure of the male-female wage differential. *Journal of Human Resources* 26, no. 3 (Summer): 457–72.

Grubb, W. Norton. 1996. *Learning to work: the case for reintegrating job training and education.* New York: Russell Sage Foundation.

Gustman, Alan L., and Thomas Steinmeirer. 1982. The relation between vocational training in high school and economic outcomes. *Industrial and Labor Relations Review* 36 (October): 73–82.

Hacker, Andrew. 1992. *Two nations: black and white, separate, hostile, unequal.* New York: Charles Scribners Sons.

Hagstrom, Paul A. 1996. The Food Stamp participation and labor supply of married couples: an empirical analysis of joint decisions. *Journal of Human Resources* 31, no.2: 383–402.

Halle, David. 1984. *America's working man: work, home, and politics among blue-collar property owners.* Chicago: University of Chicago Press.

Hamermesh, Daniel. 1989. What do we know about worker displacement in the United States? *Industrial Relations* 28, no. 1: 51–59.

Hammer, Tove, Steven Currall, and Robert Stern. 1991. Worker representation on boards of directors: a study of competing roles. *Industrial and Labor Relations Review* 44 (July): 661–80.

Hansen, J. C. 1987. Cross-cultural research on vocational interests. *Measurements and Evaluations in Counseling and Development* 18: 163–76.

Harmon, Lenore. 1989. Longitudinal changes in women's career aspirations: developmental or historical? *Journal of Vocational Behavior* 35: 46–63.

Harrington, T. F., and A.J. O'Shea. 1980. Applicability of the Holland model (1973) of vocational development with Spanish-speaking clients. *Journal of Counseling Psychology* 27: 246–51.

Hecker, Daniel. 1992. Reconciling conflicting data on jobs for college students. *Monthly Labor Review* 115 (July): 3–12.

———. Earnings of college graduates, 1995. *Monthly Labor Review* 118, no. 9, (September): 3–17.

Heckman, James. 1998. Detecting discrimination. *Journal of Economic Perspectives* 12 (Spring): 101–16.

Heckscher, Charles. 1988. *The new unionism.* New York: Basic Books.

Hendricks, Wallace, and Lawrence Kahn. 1983. Cost-of-living clauses in union contracts: determinants and effects. *Industrial and Labor Relations Review* 36 (April): 447–60.

Hershberg, Theodore. 1971. Free blacks in antebellum Philadelphia: a study of ex-slaves, freeborn, and socioeconomic decline. *Journal of Social History* 5 (Winter): 183–209.

Herz, Diane. 1990. Worker displacement in a period of rapid job expansion, 1983–87. *Monthly Labor Review* 113, no. 5: 21–33.

———. 1991. Worker displacement still common in the late 1980s. In U.S. Department of Labor, Bureau of Labor Statistics, *Displaced Workers,* Bulletin 2382 (June).

Herzenberg, Stephen. 1996. Review of Ottoson, Gary, and Douglas Thompson, *Reducing unemployment: a case for government deregulation* (Westport, Conn.: Praeger Publishers). In *Monthly Labor Review* 119 (September):47.

Heywood, John S. 1986. Labor quality and concentration earnings hypothesis. *Review of Economics and Statistics* 68 (May): 342–46.

———, and S. White. 1990. Reservation wages and unemployment in manufacturing: a case study. *Applied Economics* (UK) 22, no. 3: 403–14.

Higginbottom, Elizabeth. 1987. Employment for professional black women in the twentieth century: 73–91. In Bose, Christine, and Glenna Spitze, editors, *Ingredients for women's employment policy.* Albany: SUNY Press.

Hipple, Steven, and Jay Stewart. 1996a. Earnings and benefits of contingent and noncontingent workers. *Monthly Labor Review* 119 (October): 22–30.

———. 1996b. Earnings and benefits of workers in alternative work arrangements. *Monthly Labor Review* 119 (October): 46–54.

Holland, John. 1959. A theory of vocational choice. *Journal of Vocational Counseling,* no. 6: 35–45.

———. 1985. *Making vocational choices: a theory of careers.* 2nd ed. Englewood Cliffs, N.J.: Prentice Hall.

Hollenbeck, Kevin. 1996. An evaluation of the manufacturing technology partnership (MTP) program. Upjohn Institute Technical Report #96–007.

———. 1996. In their own words: student perspectives on school-to-work programs. Washington, D.C.: National Institute for Work and Learning.

———. 1997. School-to-work: promise and effectiveness. *Employment Research* (Fall): 5–7.

Holzer, Harry J. 1987. Hiring procedures in the firm: their economic determinants and outcomes: 243–74. In Morris Kleiner, Richard Block, Myron Roomkin, and Sidney Salsburg, eds., *Human resources and the performance of the firm.* Madison, Wisc.: Industrial Relations Research Association.

———. 1997. *What employers want: job prospects for less-educated workers.* New York: Russell Sage.

Horvath, Francis. 1987. The pulse of economic change: displaced workers of 1981–85. *Monthly Labor Review* 110, no. 6: 3–12.

Houseman, Susan. 1997. New Institute survey on flexible staffing arrangements. *Upjohn Institute Employment Research* 4 (Spring): 1–3.

Howell, David. 1996. The collapse of low-skill male earnings in the 1980s. Working

Paper No. 178. Annandale-on-Hudson, N.Y.: Jerome Levy Economics Institute of Bard College.

Howland, Marie, and George Peterson. 1988. Labor market conditions and the reemployment of displaced workers. *Industrial and Labor Relations Review* 42 (October): 109–22.

Hughes, M., and D. Demo. 1989. Self-perceptions of black Americans: self-esteem and personal efficacy. *American Journal of Sociology* 95, no. 1: 132–57.

Hutchens, Robert, David Lipsky, and Robert Stern. 1992. Unemployment Insurance and strikes. *Journal of Labor Research* 13 (Fall): 337–54.

Imel, Susan. 1996. Tech prep: trends and issues alerts. ERIC Clearing House on Adult Career and Vocational Education, Columbus Ohio.

Ippolito, R. 1990. Toward explaining earlier retirement after 1970. *Industrial and Labor Relations Review* 43 (July): 556–69.

Irons, Edward D. 1971. Black banking problems and prospects. *The Journal of Finance* 26, no.1 (March): 407–26.

————, and Gilbert Moore. 1985. *Black managers: the case of the banking industry.* New York: Praeger.

Jacobson, Louis, Robert LaLonde, and Daniel Sullivan. 1993. Earnings losses of displaced workers. *American Economic Review* 83, no. 4: 685–709.

————. 1994. The effectiveness of the U.S. Employment Service. Report prepared for the Advisory Commission on Unemployment Compensation. Washington, D.C.: U.S. Department of Labor.

Jamal, Muhammad. 1986. Moonlighting: personal, social, and organizational consequences. *Human Relations* 39 (November): 977–87.

Johnson, James H., Jr., Elisa Bienenstock, and Jennifer Stoloff. 1995. An empirical test of the culture capital hypothesis. *The Review of Black Political Economy* 23 (Spring): 7–27.

Johnson, Terry R., and Daniel Klepinger. 1994. Experimental evidence on Unemployment Insurance work-search policies. *Journal of Human Resources* 29 (Summer): 695–717.

————, and Walter Farrell, Jr. 1995. Race still matters. *The Chronicle of Higher Education* 42 (July 7): 48–56.

Johnston, Paul. 1994. *Success while others fail: social movement unionism and the public workplace.* Ithaca, N. Y.: ILR Press.

Jones, Derek C., Takao Kato, and Jeffrey Pliskin. 1994. *Profit-sharing and gain-sharing: a review of theory, incidence, and effects.* Annandale-on-Hudson, N.Y.: Jerome Levy Economics Institute of Bard College, Working Paper 125 (September).

Jones, Thomas. 1996. Social Security: invaluable, irreplaceable, and fixable. *The Participant,* February: 1, 4.

Kahn, Shulamit, and Lang, Kevin. 1991. The effect of hours constraints on labor supply estimates. *Review of Economics and Statistics* 73 (November): 605–11.

Kane, Thomas, and Cecilia Rouse. 1993. Labor market returns to two and four-year colleges: is a credit a credit and do degrees matter? Mimeograph, Harvard University.

Katz, Fred, and Harry W. Martin. 1962. Career choice processes. *Social Forces* 41 (December): 149–54.

Katz, Harry, and Thomas Kochan. 1992. *An introduction to industrial relations.* New York: McGraw-Hill.

Katz, Jeffrey. Provisions of welfare bill. *Congressional Quarterly Weekly Report.* August 3, 1996: 2192–94.

Katz, Lawrence, and Bruce Meyer. 1990. Unemployment insurance, recall expectations, and unemployment outcomes. *Quarterly Journal of Economics* 105 (November): 973–1000.

Kerckhoff, A. 1976. The status attainment process: socialization or allocation? *Social Forces* 55, no. 2: 368–81.

Keynes, John M. 1936. *General theory of employment, interest, and money.* London: Macmillan.

Killingsworth, Mark, 1990. *The economics of comparable worth.* Kalamazoo, Mich.: W. E. Upjohn Institute.

Kleiner, Morris, and Mitchell Gordon. 1996. The growth of occupational licensing: are we protecting consumers? *CURA Reporter* (December): 8–12.

———, and Robert Kudrie. 1998. Giving dentists a check-up. *Business Week* (12 January).

Kletzer, Lori G. 1989. Returns to seniority after permanent job loss. *American Economic Review,* 79, no. 3 (June) : 536–43.

———. 1991. Earnings after job displacement: job tenure, industry, and occupation, 107–35. In John T. Addison, ed. *Job displacement: consequences and implications for policy.* Detroit: Wayne State University Press.

———. 1992. Industrial mobility following job displacement: evidence from the displaced worker surveys. *Industrial Relations Research Association. 44th Annual Proceedings:* 621–29.

———. 1995. The role of sector-specific skills in post-displacement earnings. Unpublished paper, University of California, Santa Cruz.

Kochan, Thomas. A. 1980. *Collective Bargaining and Industrial Relations.* Homewood, Ill.: Richard D. Irwin.

———, Harry Katz, and Robert McKersie. 1994. *The transformation of American industrial relations.* Ithaca, N.Y.: ILR Press.

Kohn, Alfie. 1993 *Punished by rewards: the trouble with gold stars, incentive plans, and praise and other bribes.* Boston: Houghton Mifflin.

Koretz, Gene. 1998. The widening health care gap. *Business Week* (October 12): 28.

Kornweibel, Jr., Theodore. 1976. An economic profile of black life in the twenties. *Journal of Black Studies* 6 (June): 307–20.

Krause, Elliott A. 1971. *Sociology of occupations.* Boston: Little, Brown.

Krueger, Anne. 1963. The economics of discrimination. *Journal of Political Economy* 79 (March/April) no. 2: 481–86.

Krugman, Paul. 1994. *Peddling prosperity: economic sense and nonsense in the age diminished expectations.* New York: W.W. Norton.

Kruse, Douglas. 1991. Profit-sharing and employment variability: micro economic evidence on the Weitzman theory. *Industrial and Labor Relations Review* 44 (April): 437–52.

Kulick, Jane. 1994. The evolution of the U.S. Employment Service and a review of evidence concerning its operations and effectiveness. Report prepared for the Advisory Council on Unemployment Compensation. Washington, D.C.: U.S. Department of Labor.

Kumazawa, Makoto and colleagues. 1996. *Portraits of the Japanese workplace (social change in global perspective).* Boulder: Westview Press.

Kume, Ikio. 1998. *Disparaged success: labour politics in postwar Japan.* Cornell Studies in Political Economy. Ithaca, N.Y.: Cornell University Press.

Kuttner, Robert. 1996. There's nothing "natural" about 5% unemployment. *Business Week,* November 14, 28.

———. 1997. *Everything for Sale: the Virtues and Limits of Markets.* A Twentieth Century Fund Book. New York: Alfred A. Knopf.

Kuvlesky, W., and V. Patella. 1971. Degree of ethnicity and aspirations for upward social mobility among Mexican American youth. *Journal of Vocational Behavior* 17, no. 1: 231–44.

Landry, Bart. 1987. *The new black middle class*. Berkeley and Los Angelos: University of California Press.

Lawler III, Edward. 1981. *Pay and organization development*. Reading, Mass.: Addison-Wesley.

———. 1986. What's wrong with point-factor job evaluation. *Compensation and Benefits Review* 18, no. 2: 20–28.

———. 1986. Union growth and decline: the impact of employer and union tactics. *Journal of Occupational Psychology* 59, no. 1: 217–30.

———. 1990. *Strategic pay: aligning organizational strategies and pay systems*. San Francisco: Jossey-Bass.

———, and G. Ledford. 1985. Skill-based pay. *Personnel* 62, no. 9: 30–37.

———, and S. Cohen. 1992. Designing a pay system for teams. *American Compensation Association Journal* 1, no. 1: 6–19.

Ledford, Gerald, W. Tyler, and W. Dickey. 1991. Skill-based pay; case number 3: Honeywell ammunition assembly plant. *Compensation and Benefits Review* 23 no. 2 (March/April): 57–77.

Ledford, Gerald, Edward Lawler III, and Susan Mohrman. 1995. Reward innovation in Fortune 1000 companies. *Compensation and Benefits Review* 27 (July-August): 76–81.

Lee, Roy F. 1973. *The setting for black business development*. Ithaca, N.Y.: Cornell University Press.

Lewis, Robert. 1997. Looking for work in all the right places: cyberspace offers job opportunities. *AARP Bulletin*.

Leonard, Jonathan S. 1992. Unions and employment growth. *Industrial Relations* 31 (Winter): 80–94.

———. 1994. Use of enforcement techniques in eliminating glass ceilings barriers. Prepared for the Glass Ceiling Commission, U.S. Department of Labor. Washington, D.C.: U.S. Dept. of Labor, Glass Ceiling Commission (April).

Leong, Frederick, and F. Serafica. 1995. Career development of Asian Americans: a research area in need of a good theory: 67–102. In Frederick Leong, ed., *Career development and vocational behavior of racial and ethnic minorities*. Mahwah, N.J.: L. Erlbaum.

Leong, Frederick, and E. Chou. 1994. The role of ethnic identity and acculturation in the vocational behavior of Asian Americans: an integrative review. *Journal of Vocational Behavior* 40: 173–84.

Leong, Frederick, and R. Gim. 1995. Career assessment and intervention for Asian-Americans, 193–226. In F rederick Leong, ed., *Career development and vocational behavior of racial and ethnic minorities*. Mahwah, N.J.: Lawrence Erlbaum.

Levin-Waldman, Oren. 1994. The Earned Income Tax Credit and the need to synchronize Public Assistance. Jerome Levy Economics Institute Working paper No.131 (December).

———, and George McCarthy. 1998. Small business and the minimum wage. *Policy Notes*, no. 3. Annandale-on-Hudson, N.Y.: Jerome Levy Economics Institute, Bard College.

Lewis, H. 1963. *Unionism and relative wages in the United States*. Chicago: University of Chicago Press.

Lewis, Robert. 1997. Looking for work in all the right places: cyberspace offers job opportunities. *AARP Bulletin* 38 (May): 1, 11.

Lewis, W. Arthur. 1979. The dual economy revisited. *The Manchester School* 47, no. 3: 211–29.

Liebman, Jeffrey. 1997. *Lessons about Tax Benefit Integration from the U.S. Earned Income Tax Credit Experience*. Layerthrope, Mass.:YPS for the Joseph Rowntree Foundation, Publisher.

Lilard, Lee, and Hong W. Tan. 1986. Private sector training: who gets it and what are its effects? Santa Monica, Cal.: RAND Corporation. March.

Livernash, Robert. 1957. The internal wage structure. In Taylor, George, and F. Pierson, eds., *New concepts in wage determination*. New York: McGraw Hill.

Long, James, and Albert Link. 1983. The impact of market structure on wages, fringe benefits, and turnover. *Industrial and Labor Relations Review* 36 (January): 239–50.

Loury, Glenn C. 1998. Discrimination in the post-civil rights era: beyond market interactions. *Journal of Economic Perspectives* 12 (Spring): 117–26.

Lynch, Lisa M. 1991a. Private sector training and skill formation in the United States, 117–45. In G. Libecap, ed., *Advances in the study of entrepreneurship, innovation, and economic growth*.

———. 1991b. The role of off-the-job vs on-the-job training for the mobility of women workers. *American Economic Review* (May): 151–56.

Lynch, Lisa. 1992. Private sector training and the earnings of young workers. *American Economic Review* 82, no. 1: 299–312.

———. 1992. Different effects of post-school training on early career mobility. NBER Working Paper No. 4034.

———. 1994a. Payoffs to alternative training strategies at work. In Richard. Freeman, ed., *Working under different rules*. Washington, D.C.: National Bureau of Economic Research.

———, ed. 1994b. *Training and the private sector: international comparison*. Chicago: University of Chicago Press.

———, and Sandra Black. 1998. Beyond the incidence of employer-provided training. *Industrial and Labor Relations Review* 52 (October): 64–79.

Madden, Janice. 1975. Discrimination: a manifestation of male market power. In Cynthia Lloyd, ed. *Sex, discrimination, and the division of labor*. New York: Columbia University Press.

———. 1985. The persistence of pay differentials: the economics of sex discrimination. *Women and Work: An Annual Review* : 76–114.

Malcolm, Shirley. 1989. Increasing the participation of black women in science and technology. *Sage: A Scholarly Journal on Black Women* 6 (Fall): 15–17.

Mangum, Garth, and Stephen Mangum. 1987. The loss of competitive shelters: another insight into union decline. *Journal of Labor Studies* 12 (Fall): 4–19.

Marshall, Alfred. 1923. *Principles of economics*. Chapter 6. London: Macmillan.

Marshall, Ray, and Marc Tucker. 1992. *Thinking for a living*. New York: Basic Books.

Marston, Stephen. 1985. Two views of the geographic distribution of unemployment. *Quarterly Journal of Economics* 100, no. 2: 57–80.

Masters, Marick. 1997. *Unions at the crossroads: strategic membership, financial, and political perspectives*. Westport, Conn.: Quorum Books.

Mattera, Philip. 1985. *Off the books: the rise of the underground economy*. New York: St. Martin's Press.

Maurezi, Alex. 1981. Occupational licensing and the public interest. *Journal of Poltical Economy* (March/April): 399–413.

Maynard, Rebecca. 1995. Subsidized employment and non-labor market alternatives for welfare recipients: 109–36. In Nightingale, Demetra, and Robert Haveman, eds. *The work alternative*. Washington, D.C.: The Urban Institute.

Mazen, A., and Jeanne Lemkau. 1990. Personality profiles of women in traditional and nontraditional occupations. *Journal of Vocational Behavior* 36: 4–59.

Medoff, James, Charles Brown, and James Hamilton. 1990. *Employers, large and small*. Cambridge, Mass.: Harvard University Press.

Medoff, James, and Andrew Harless. 1996 *The indebted society*. Boston: Little, Brown and Company.

Meissenheimer II, J. 1998. The services industry in the "good" jobs versus "bad" jobs debate: a deeper look reveals a range of quality jobs in the industry. *Monthly Labor Review* 121 (February): 22–47.

Mellor, Karl F. 1986. Shift work and flextime: how prevalent are they? *Monthly Labor Review* 109 (November): 14–26.

Menanteau-Horta, Dario. 1995. Hispanic students: adjusting dreams to reality. *CURA Reporter* 25, no 1: 7–10.

Milkovich, George, and Alexandra Wigdor, eds. 1991. *Pay for performance: evaluating performance appraisal and merit pay*. Washington, D.C.: National Academy Press.

Milkovich, George, and Jerry Newman. 1996. Compensation. 5th edition. Chicago: Irwin.

Miller, L. A., and colleagues. 1992. Perceived barriers to careers involving math and science: the perspectives of medical admissions officials. *Teaching and Learning in Medicine* 4: 9–14.

Miller, S. M. Who counts at Census? Letter to Editor. American Prospect, 42 (January/February) 1999:15.

Milward, H. Brinton, and H. Newman. 1989. State incentive packages and the industrial location decision. *Economic Development Quarterly* 3, no. 3: 203–22.

Mincer, Jacob. 1962. Labor force participation of married women: a study of labor supply. In H. Gregg Lewis, ed., *Aspects of labor economics*. Princeton, N.J.: Princeton University Press.

Minow, Sol. 1992. Is there runaway executive compensation? In Brothers, Theresa, ed., *Rethinking corporate compensation plans*. New York: Conference Board.

Mishel, Lawrence and Jared Bernstein. 1993. The jobless recovery: deteriorating wages and job quality in the 1990s, Briefing Paper. Washington, D.C.: Economic Policy Institute. August.

Montemayer, E. 1994. Realigning pay systems with market systems. *ACA Journal* (Winter): 44–53.

Montoya, H., and R. DeBlassie. 1985. Strong-Campbell interest inventory comparsons between Hispanic and Anglo college students: a research note. *Hispanic Journal of Behavioral Science* 3: 285–89.

Moorthy, Vivek. 1989/1990. Unemployment in Canada and the United States: the role of Unemployment Insurance benefits. *Federal Reserve Bank of New York Quarterly Review* 14 (Winter): 48–61.

Moscovitch, Edward. 1990. The downturn in the New England economy. What lies behind it? *New England Economic Review*. 105 (4) November: 973–1002.

Munnell, Alice. 1996. Remarks at a Conference, Labor market structure and employment growth, May 1–2, at the Jerome Levy Institute of Bard College; *Report of the Jerome Levy Institute of Bard College* (June): 6–7.

Murphy, Kevin, and Robert Topel. 1990. Efficiency wages reconsidered: a review of theory and evidence: 204–44. In Weiss, Yoram, and Gideon Fishelman, eds. 1990. *Advances in theory and measurement of unemployment*. London: Macmillan,

Murrel, A., I. Frieze, and L. Frost. 1991. Aspiring to careers in male and female-dominated professions: a study of black and white college women. *Psychology of Women Quarterly* 15: 103–26.

Myrdal, Gunnar. 1944. *An American dilemma: the negro problem and modern democracy.* New York: Harper & Row Publishers (Anniversary Edition. 1962. New York: Random House).

Nardone, Thomas. 1986. Part-time workers: who are they? *Monthly Labor Review* 109 (February): 13–19.

———, Jonathan Veum, and Julie Yates. 1997. Measuring job security. *Monthly Labor Review* 120, no.6 (June): 26–33.

Neal, Derek. 1995. Industry-specific human capital: evidence from displaced workers. *Journal of Labor Economics* 13, no. 3: 653–77.

———, and William R. Johnson. 1996. The role of pre-market factors in black-white wage differences in urban labor markets. *Journal of Political Economy* 104, no. 5: 869–95.

Neumark, David, and Michael Wachter. 1995. Union effects on nonunion wages: evidence from panel data on industries and cities. *Industrial and Labor Relations Review* 49 (October): 20–36.

Nightingale, Demetra, and Robert Haveman, eds. 1995. *The work alternative: welfare reform and the realities of the the job market.* Washington, D.C.: Urban Institute Press.

Nord, Stephen, and Yuan Ting. 1991. The impact of advance notice of plant closings on earnings and the probability of unemployment. *Industrial and Labor Relations Review* 44, no. 4: 681–91.

Norwood, Janet. 1993. The statistics corner: interpreting the unemployment statistics, *Business Economics* 28, no. 1 (January): 56–60.

Oak, Frederick. 1994. Compensation survey. *Compensation and Benefits Review* (September/October): 19–22.

O'Leary, Christopher. 1998. Profiling for reemployment bonus offers. *Employment Research*, Spring: 1–4.

O'Neill, David M., and June Ellenoff O'Neill. 1997. *Lessons for welfare reform: analysis of the AFDC caseload and past welfare-to-work programs.* Kalamazoo, Michigan: W. E. Upjohn Institute for Employment Research: 8–9.

O'Neill, June. 1990. The role of human capital in earnings differences between black and white men. *The Journal of Economic Perspectives*, no.4 (Fall): 25–45.

Ong, Paul, and Don Mar. 1992. Post lay-off earnings among semiconductor workers. *Industrial and Labor Relations Review* 45, no. 2: 366–79.

———, and Janette Lawrence. 1993. The unemployment crisis in aerospace. Unpublished paper, University of California, Los Angeles.

Oppenheimer, Valerie. 1970. *The female labor force in the United States: demographic and economic factors governing its growth and changing composition.* Westport, Conn.: Greenwood Press.

Osipow, Samuel. 1983. *Theories of career development.* 3rd ed. Englewood Cliffs, N.J.: Prentice Hall.

———, and Louise Fitzgerald. 1995. *Theories of career development.* Needham Heights, Mass.: Allyn and Bacon.

Osterman, Paul. 1987. Choice of employment systems in internal labor markets. *Industrial Relations* 26 (Winter): 46–67.

———. 1990. Elements of a national training policy: 257–82. In Louis Ferman, and colleagues. *New developments in worker training: a legacy for the 1990s.* Madison, Wisc.: Industrial Relations Research Association.

———. 1992. Internal labor markets in a changing environments: models and evidence: 273–308. In Levin, David, Olivia Mitchell, and Peter Sherer, eds., *Research Frontiers in Industrial Relations and Human Resources.* Madison, Wisconsin: Industrial Relations Research Association.

Papadimitrious, Dimitri, L. Randall Wray, and Matthew Forstater. 1998. Toward full employment without inflation: the job opportunity program. *Report*. The Jerome Levy Economics Institute of Bard College, (August): 5–8.

Parsons, Donald. 1991. The job search behavior of employed youth. *The Review of Economics and Statistics* 73, no. 1: 597–603.

Patrick, Stewart. 1992. Developments and trends in executive compensation. In *Rethinking corporate compensation plans*. New York: Conference Board.

Pavalko, Ronald. 1971. Occupational choice. Chapter 3. *Sociology of occupations and professions*. Itasdo, Ill.: Peacock Publishers, Inc.

Pavetti, LaDonna A. 1993. The dynamics of welfare and work: exploring the process by which young high school graduates and high school dropouts work their way off welfare. Harvard University: Malcolm Wiener Center for Social Policy, Working Paper H-933 (July).

Pearce, Diana. 1986. Unemployment compensation and women: toil and trouble: 141–61. In Barbara Gelpi et al., eds., *Women and Poverty*. Chicago: University of Chicago Press.

Pearce, Sandra. 1992. Survival of continuing higher education: deans' perceptions of external threats. *Journal of Continuing Higher Education* 40 (Spring): 2–7.

Peck, Charles. 1995. *Pay and performance: the interaction of compensation and performance appraisal*: 8–9. In Hall, Thomas, ed. *Compensation: present practices and future concerns: a conference report*. New York: The Conference Board, Inc.

Phelps, Edmund. 1972. The statistical theory of racism and sexism. *American Economic Review* 62 (September): 659–61.

Phillips, A. W. 1958. The relationship between unemployment and the rate of change of money wage rates in the United Kingdom, 1861–1957. *Economica* 25, no. 97 (February): 285–99.

Piore, Michael. 1982. American labor and industrial crisis. *Challenge* (March-April): 5-11.

Portes, Alejandro, Manuel Castells, and Laura Benton. 1989. *The informal economy: studies in advanced and less developed countries*. Baltimore: Johns Hopkins Press.

Rayack, Elton. 1976. *An economic analysis of occupational licensure*. A report prepared for the U.S. Department of Labor.

Rees, Albert. 1989. *The economics of trade unions*. Chicago: University of Chicago Press.

Rees, Albert, and George Schultz. 1970. *Workers and wages in an urban labor market*. Chicago: University of Chicago Press.

Reiss, Albert J. 1955. Occupational mobility of professional workers. *American Sociological Review* 2 (December): 693–701.

Reskin, Barbara, and Heidi Hartmann. 1986. *Women's work, men's work: job segregation on the job*. Washington, D.C.: National Academy Press.

Reynolds, Larry. 1988. Can "blue collar" capitalism work? *Management Review* September: 20–21.

Richardson, Alan. 1987. Professionalization and intraprofessional competition in the Canadian accounting profession. *Work and Occupations* 14 (November): 591–615.

Rima, Ingrid. 1981. *Labor markets, wages, and employment*. Chapters 6 and 7. New York: W.W. Norton & Company.

Roberts, Karen. 1992. Predicting disputes in Workers' Compensation. *Journal of Risk and Insurance* 59 (June): 252–61.

Rogers, Joel, and Wolfgang Streeck. 1994. Workplace representation overseas: the works council story, 97–156. In Freeman, Richard, ed. *Working under different rules*. A National Bureau of Economic Research Project Report. New York: Russell Sage Foundation.

Rones, Philip, Randy Ilg, and Jennifer Gardner. 1997. Trends in hours of work since the mid-1970s. *Monthly Labor Review* 120 (April): 3–14.

Rose, Joseph B., and Gary Chaison. 1996. Linking union density and union effectiveness: the North American experience. *Industrial Relations* 35 (January): 78–105.

Rosenfeld, C. 1975. Job-seeking methods used by American workers. *Monthly Labor Review* 98 (August): 39–42.

Rossides, D. W. 1990. *Social stratification: the American class system in comparative perspective.* Englewood Cliffs, N.J.: Prentice Hall.

Rothstein, Donna S. 1996. Entry into and consequences of nonstandard work arrangements. *Monthly Labor Review* 119 (October): 75–82.

Rothstein, Richard. 1993. The myth of public school failure. *American Prospect* 3 (Spring): 20–34.

Ruhm, Christopher. 1991. Are workers permanently scarred by job displacements? *American Economic Review* 81, no. 1: 31–24.

———. 1992. Advance notice and post-displacement joblessness. *Journal of Labor Economics* 10, no. 1: 1–32.

———. 1994. Advance notice, job search, and post-displacement earnings. *Journal of Labor Economics* 12, no. 1: 1–28.

Runner, Diana. Unemployment insurance legislation enacted in 1998. *Monthly Labor Review.* 122, no. 1 (January): 20–28.

Rydzewski, L. G., William Deming, and Philip Rones. 1993. Seasonal employment falls over past three decades. *Monthly Labor Review* 116, no. 7 (July): 3–5.

Rynes, Sara, Robert Bretz, Jr., and Barry Gerhard. 1991. The importance of recruitment in job choice: a different way of looking. *Personnel Psychology* 44, no. 3: 487–518.

Scholz, John C. 1994. The Earned Income Tax Credit: participation, compliance, and anti-poverty effectiveness. *National Tax Journal* 47 (March): 51–81.

———. *Social security programs in the United States.* 1997. Governmnt Printing Office: Washington D.C., July.

Schramm, Carl J. 1982. Economic perspectives on the nursing shortage: 42–56. In Aiken, Linda, ed., *Nursing in the 1980s: crisis, opportunities, challenges.* Philadelphia: J. Lippincott.

Schultz, T. W. 1961. Investment in human capital. *American Economic Review* 51, no. 4: 1–17.

Schuster, J. R., and P. K. Zingheim. 1992. *The new pay.* New York: Macmillan.

Schwab, Laurent. 1986. Professional relationships and crisis in Japan. *Futures* 18 (April): 230–41.

Schubert, Walt. 1989. Unemployment Insurance costs: issues and dilemmas. *International Journal of Sociology and Economics* (UK) 16, no. 8: 60–67.

Shackett, Joyce R., and John Trapani. 1987. Earnings differentials and market structure. *Journal of Human Resources* 22 (Fall): 518–31.

Shank, Susan. 1986. Preferred hours of work and corresponding earnings. *Monthly Labor Review* 109 (November): 40–44.

Shimberg, Benjamin, Barbara Esser, and Daniel Kruger. 1982. *Occupational licensing: practices and policies.* Washington, D.C.: Public Affairs Press.

Shuler, Marjorie. 1923. Industrial women confer. *Woman Citizen,* 27 (January).

Silverberg, Marsha. 1996. Building school-to-work systems on a tech-prep foundation: the status of school-to-work features in tech prep initiatives. Mathematica Policy Research, Princeton, N.J.

————., and Alan M. Hershey. 1995. The emergence of tech-prep at the state and local levels. Mathematica Policy Research, Princeton, N.J.

Silvestri, G. 1997. Occupational employment projections to 2006. *Monthly Labor Review* 120 (November): 58–82.

Simpson, George, and J. Milton Yinger. 1985. *Racial and cultural minorities: an analysis of prejudice and discrimination.* 5th ed. New York: Plenum.

Simpson, Gwyned. 1990. Black women in the legal professions. Unpublished manuscript, New York.

Sleemi, Femida. Collective bargaining outlook for 1995. *Monthly Labor Review* 118, no. 1 (January): 3–22.

Sloane, Arthur, and Fred Witney. 1988. *Labor relations.* 6th edition. Englewood Cliffs, N.J.: Prentice Hall.

Smith, James, and Finis Welch. 1987. Race and poverty: a forty year record. *AEA Papers and Proceedings* 77, no. 2 (May).

Smith, Robert S. 1988. Comparable worth: limited coverage and the exacerbation of inequality. *Industrial and Labor Relations Review* 41, no. 2 (January): 227–39.

Smith, Shirley. 1986. The growing diversity of work schedules. *Monthly Labor Review* 109, no. 11 (November): 7–13.

Social Security Administration. Office of Research, Evaluation, and Statistics. 1997 *Social Security programs in the United States.* SAA Publication No. 13-11758, July. Washington, D.C.: Government Printing Office.

Sokoloff, Natalie. 1992. *Black women and white women in the professions: occupational segregation by race and gender, 1960–1980.* New York: Routledge.

Sorensen, Elaine. 1989. The wage effects of occupational sex segregation: review and new findings. In Hill, Anne, and Mark Killingsworth, eds. Colloquium on Comparable Worth. Cornell University. *Comparable worth: analysis and evidence.* Ithaca, N.Y.: ILR Press.

————. 1994. *Comparable worth: Is it a worthy policy?* Princeton, N.J.: Princeton University Press.

Squires, Gregory. 1979. *Education and jobs: the imbalancing of the social machinery.* New Brunswick, N.J.: Transaction Books.

Stern, David, and colleagues. 1994. *Research on school-to-work transition programs in the United States.* Berkeley: National Center for Research in Vocational Education.

Stinson, John F. 1986. Moonlighting by women jumped to record highs. *Monthly Labor Review* 109, no. 11 (November): 22–25.

————. 1997. New data on multiple job holding available from the CPS. *Monthly Labor Review* 120 (March): 3–8.

Strauss, George. 1984. Industrial relations: time of change. *Industrial Relations* 23 (Winter): 1–15.

Summers, Lawrence. 1990. *Understanding unemployment.* Cambridge: MIT Press.

Super, Donald. 1957. *The psychology of careers.* New York: Harper & Row.

————, and P. I. Overstreet. 1960. *The vocational maturity of ninth grade boys.* New York: Bureau of Publications, Teachers College, Columbia University.

Swinnerton, Kenneth A., and Howard Wial. 1995. Is job stability declining in the U.S. economy? *Industrial and Labor Relations Review* 48 (January): 293–304.

————. Is Job stability declining in the U.S.economy? Reply to Diebold, Neumark, and Polsky. *Industrial and Labor Relations Review* 49, no. 2 (January) 1996: 348–51.

Thernstrom, Stephen, and Abigail Thernstrom. 1997. *America in black and white: one nation, indivisible.* New York: Simon and Schuster.

Thompson, Roger. 1989. Unemployment: cutting the cost. *Nation's Business* 77 (November): 71, 73.

Thurow, Lester. 1969. *Poverty and discrimination.* Washington, D.C.: Brooking Institution.

Tilly, Christopher. 1992. Short hours, short shrift: the causes and consequences of part-time employment: 15–44. In du Rivage, Virginia L., ed. *New policies for the part-time and contingent work force.* Armonk, N. Y.: M. E. Sharpe.

Tomaskovic-Devey, Donald. 1993. *Gender and racial inequality at work: the sources and consequences of job segregation.* Ithaca, N.Y.: ILR Press.

Topel, Robert. 1984. Equilibrium earnings, turnover, and unemployment: new evidence. *Journal of Labor Economics* 2 (October): 500–522.

———. 1990. Specific capital and unemployment: measuring the costs and consequences of job loss. Carnegie-Rochester Conference Series on Public Policy, 33: 181–224.

———. 1993. Wage inequality and regional labor market performance in the United States. Paper presented at NBER Labor Studies Meeting, Cambridge, Mass., November.

Tyler, John, Richard Murnane, and Frank Levy. 1995. Are more college graduates really taking "high school" jobs? *Monthly Labor Review* 118, no. 12 (December) 18–27.

U.S. Congress. Committee on Ways and Means, 1996. *Green Book.* November 11 Washington, D.C.: Government Printing Office.

U.S. Department of Commerce. U.S. Bureau of the Census. 1992. School enrollment: social and economic characteristics of students. *Current Population Reports* (October) Washington, D.C.: Government Printing Office.

———. 1992. Dynamics of economic well-being: program participation. Washington, D.C.: Government Printing Office.

———. 1995. *1992 Black economic census.* Washington, D.C.: Government Printing Office.

———. 1995. *Characteristics of the black population.* Washington, D.C.: Government Printing Office.

———. *1995 Statistical abstract of the United. States.* 114th ed. Washington, D.C.: Government, Printing Office.

———. 1996. Current Population Reports. Household Economics Studies. Washington, D.C.: Government Printing Office.

———. *1997 Statistical abstract of the United States,* 117th edition. Washington, D.C.: Government Printing Office.

U.S. Department of Education. Office of Educational Reform and Improvement. National Center for Education Statistics. 1993. *Digest of education statistics.* Washington, D.C.: Government Printing Office.

———. 1996. *Digest of education statistics.* Washington, D.C.: Government Printing Office.

———. 1996. *The condition of education.* Washington, D.C.: Government Printing Office.

———. 1997. *Digest of education statistics.* Washington, D.C: Government Printing Office.

U.S. Department of Health and Human Services. Health Care Financing Administration. 1997. *Your medicare handbook.*: Publication No. HCFA 10050. Washington, D.C.: Government Printing Office.

———. 1998. *Medicare & you.* Publication No. HCFA-02119 (August). Washington, D.C.: Government Printing Office.

———. Social Security Administration. Office of Research, Evaluation and Statistics. 1997. *Social security programs in the United States.* SSA Publication No. 13-11758, (July). Washington, D.C.: Government Printing Office.

U.S. Department of Labor. Bureau of Employment Security. Manpower Administration. 1965. *Dictionary of occupational titles.* 3rd ed. Washington, D.C.: Government Printing Office.

U.S. Department of Labor. Bureau of Labor Statistics. 1980 *Handbook of labor statistics.* Table 165.

———. 1983. *Employment and Earnings* 30 (1) Washington, D.C.: Government Printing Office.

———. 1984. *Employment and Earnings* 31 (1) Washington, D.C.: Government Printing Office.

———. 1986. *Employment and Earning* 33 (1) Washington, D.C.: Government Printing Office.

———. 1988. *Employment and Earnings* 35 (1) Washington, D.C.: Government Printing Office.

———. 1991. *Employment and Earning* 38 (1) Washington, D.C.: Government Printing Office.

———. 1992. *BLS Handbook of Methods.* Bulletin 2414. Washington, D.C.: Government Printing Office.

———. 1992. *Employment and Earnings.* 39 (1) Washington, D.C.: Government Printing Office.

———. 1993. *Employment and earnings* 40 (1) Washington, D.C.: Government Printing Office.

———. 1996. Employment and Earnings 43 (1) Washington, D.C.: Government Printing Office.

———. 1996. *Monthly Labor Review* . Current labor statistics. 119, no. 10 (October) Washington, D.C.: Government Printing Office.

———. 1997. *Employee benefits in small private establishments, 1994.* Bulletin 2475. Washington, D.C.: Government Printing Office. Table 1 and Chapter 9. Washington, D.C.: Government Printing Office: 146–7.

———. 1998. Employee medical care contributions on the rise. *Issues in labor statistics,* Summary 98-3 (April). Released August 19, 1998. USDL 98–347.

———. 1998. *Employment and Earnings.* 45 (1) Washington, D.C.: Government Printing Office.

———. 1998. *Monthly Labor Review.* Current labor statistics. 121, no. 9: 66-109.

———. 1998. *Worker Displacement, 1995–97.* Technical information: Released August 19, 1998. USDL 98-347.

———. 1998. *Employment Situations News Release.* Publication available from any BLS office or on the Internet (BLS Internet address: stats.BLS.gov). Washington, D.C.: Government Printing Office.

U.S. Department of Labor. Collective Bargaining Forum. 1991. Concluding statement, labor-management meeting.

Vroman, Wayne. 1991. Why the decline in Unemployment Insurance claims? *Challenge* 34 (September-October): 55–58.

Wagel, W. H. 1989. Sola ophthalmics. *Personnel* 66 (March): 20–24.

Waldfogel, Jane. 1998. Understanding the "family gap" in pay for women with children. *Journal of Economic Perspectives* 13 (Winter): 137–56.

Waldinger, Roger. 1996. *Still the promised city: African Americans and new immigrants in post industrial New York.* Cambridge: Harvard University Press.

Wandner, Stephen. 1994. The worker profiling and reemployment services system: legislation, implementation process, and research findings. U.S. Department of Labor, Unemployment Insurance Service, Occasional paper (August).

Washington, Booker T. 1907. *The Negro in business*. Chicago: Afro-American Press, (1969 reprint).

Weitzman, Martin. 1984 *The share economy*. Cambridge, Mass.: Harvard University Press.

White, Harrison. 1995. Social networks can resolve actor paradoxes in economics and in psychology. *Journal of Institutional and Theoretical Economics* 151, no. 1: 58–74.

White, William D. 1987. The introduction of professional regulation and labor market conditions: occupational licensure of registered nurses. *Policy Sciences* (April): 27–51.

Whittington, Glenn. Workers'compensation legislation enacted in 1998. *Monthly Labor Review* 122, no. 1 (January): 16–19.

Williams, Bruce. 1987. *Black workers in an industrial suburb*. New Brunswick, N.J.: Rutgers University Press.

Williamson, Lisa. 1995. Union mergers: 1985–94 update. *Monthly Labor Review* 119, no. 2 (February): 18–24.

Wilson, William Julius. 1987. *The truly disadvantaged: the inner city, the underclass, and public policy*. Chicago: University of Chicago Press.

———. 1996a. *When work disappears: the world of the new urban poor*. New York: Alfred A. Knopf.

———. 1996b. The Levy Report interview. In *The Report*, Jerome Levy Economics Institute of Bard College, February: 6–11.

Wilson Center for Public Research. 1993. *Organizing focus*. AFL-CIO Industrial Union Department Executive Board Meeting, 19 March.

Woodbury, Stephen, and Robert Spiegelman. 1987. Bonuses to workers and employers to reduce unemployment. Randomized trials in Illinois. *American Economic Review* 77, no. 4: 513–30.

Wyly, Elvin. 1996. Women, work, and the city. *CURA Reporter* 26 (December): 12–18.

Young, Casey L., and Philip Polakoff. 1992. Beyond Workers' Compensation: a new vision. *Benefits Quarterly* 8, no. 3: 56-65.

Young, S. David. 1986. Accounting, licensure, quality, and the "Cadillac effect." *Journal of Accounting and Public Policy* 5 (Spring): 5–19.

———. 1987. *The role of experts: occupational licensing in America.*. Washington, D.C.: Cato Institute.

Zajac, Edward, and James Westphal. 1995. Accounting for explanations of CEO compensation: substance and symbolism. *Administrative Science Quarterly* 40 (June): 283–308.

Index

('i' indicates an illustration; 't' indicates a table)

About the Author

RUTH W. PRYWES is a former Adjunct Professor at Drexel University School of Business and Administration in the Management Department.

ISBN 1-56720-266-7

90000>

9 781567 202663

HARDCOVER BAR CODE